THE WHISKY KING

Also by Trevor Cole

Norman Bray in the Performance of His Life
The Fearsome Particles
Practical Jean
Hope Makes Love

THE
WHISKY
KING

THE REMARKABLE TRUE STORY OF
CANADA'S MOST INFAMOUS BOOTLEGGER AND
THE UNDERCOVER MOUNTIE ON HIS TRAIL

TREVOR COLE

HARPER
PERENNIAL

The Whisky King
Copyright © 2017 by Trevor Cole.
All rights reserved.

Published by Harper Perennial, an imprint of HarperCollins Publishers Ltd

First published by HarperCollins Publishers in a hardcover edition: 2017
This Harper Perennial trade paperback edition: 2018

HarperCollins books may be purchased for educational, business,
or sales promotional use through our Special Markets Department.

HarperCollins Publishers Ltd
2 Bloor Street East, 20th Floor
Toronto, Ontario, Canada
M4W 1A8

www.harpercollins.ca

Library and Archives Canada Cataloguing in Publication
information is available upon request.

ISBN 978-1-44344-224-4

Printed and bound in the United States

LSC/H 9 8 7 6 5 4 3 2 1

For Mary

CONTENTS

PART 3

PART 4

PART 5

LIST OF MAJOR CHARACTERS

THE PERRI GANG

ROCCO'S PARTNERS
Bessie Starkman (prostitution, gambling, bootlegging, narcotics)
Jim Sullivan (bootlegging)
Anne Newman (bootlegging)
John Taglierino (gambling)

TOP LIEUTENANTS
Mike Romeo (cousin)
Frank Romeo (cousin)
Tony Roma

Frank Ross (Sylvester/Sylvestro)
Tony Ross (Sylvester/Sylvestro)

IMPORTANT GANG MEMBERS
Bruno Attilio
Mike Bernardo
Charlie Bordonaro
Sam Calubro
Rosario Carboni
Andrea Catanzariti (cousin)
Frank Corde
Louis Corruzzo (cousin)
Frank (Shorty) Di Pietro
Giovanni (John) Durso
Ned Italiano
Anthony Marando

Alberto Naticchio
Tony Papalia
Mike Perri (brother)
Joseph Restivo
Matthew Restivo
Joe Romeo (cousin)
Jimmy Romeo (cousin)
Mike Serge (cousin)
Joe Serge (cousin)
Jules Speranza
Louis Wernick

ALLIES

HAMILTON
John Ben Kerr

TORONTO
Harry Goldstein
Donald (Mickey) McDonald
Max Wortzman

ST. CATHARINES
Domenico D'Agostino (cousin)
Antonio Deconza
Sidney Gogo
John Gogo

THOROLD/MERRITTON
Domenic Arilotta
Tony Calabrase
James D'Agostino (cousin)
John Trott (born Trotta)

WELLAND
Frank Longo
Domenico Longo
Sam Marabito and brothers
Frank Poles (cousin)
Jimmy Sorbara

GUELPH
Leo Addario
Fred Fazzario
Domenico Ferraro
Sam and Mike Sorbara

PORT CREDIT
Joe Burke

BUFFALO
Joe Penna
Nino Sacco

NIAGARA FALLS, NY
James Sacco
Joseph Serianni and brothers
Don Simone
Joseph Henry Sottile
Joseph Spallino

NEW YORK CITY/NEW JERSEY
Frank Costello
Charles (Lucky) Luciano
Rocco Pizzimenti
Arnold Rothstein

CHICAGO
Jack (Legs) Diamond
Domenic Sacco

Stefano Speranza

SUPPLIERS

DISTILLERIES
Corby's (Belleville)
Gooderham & Worts (Toronto)
Seagram (Waterloo)

BREWERIES
Grant's Spring Brewery (Hamilton)
Kuntz Brewery (Waterloo)
Taylor and Bate (St. Catharines)

LAWYERS

Michael J. O'Reilly, KC (Hamilton)
Charles W. Bell (Hamilton)
William R. Morrison, KC (Hamilton)

A. G. Slaght (Toronto)
Paul Martin (Windsor)
Joseph M. Bullen, KC (Windsor)

RIVALS

HAMILTON
Jimmy Celona
John Ben Kerr

TORONTO
Galliardo brothers

GUELPH/BRANTFORD
Domenic Sciarrone (Joseph Verona)
Joe Sciarrone

BUFFALO
Stefano Magaddino
The Good Killers

POLICE

HAMILTON
Magistrate George Frederick Jelfs
Police Chief William Whatley
Deputy Chief David Coulter
Constable/Detective Joseph Crocker

OPP
Inspector John Miller
Inspector William Stringer

RCMP

THE WHISKY KING

PART 1

1

TRAGICO
Tragedy

I T WAS 1923. PROHIBITION HAD SHUT DOWN THE LEGAL trade in liquor across most of Canada and the United States. But the whisky still flowed, and the pipeline was made of boats.

Rocco Perri, at thirty-five years old the most powerful bootlegger in Ontario, had built up a makeshift fleet of as many as fifty vessels—schooners, cabin boats and pleasure craft—that plied Lake Ontario and Lake Erie. Most of the men in these boats weren't criminals. As a rule, Rocco employed men without records, and he insisted they carry no weapons. It meant less trouble, and less scrutiny from police. Many of the skippers were simply fishermen trying to scrape up some extra money, especially during the cold months of fall and winter. The risks were small—few men would dare hijack a Perri boat and undermanned police forces rarely caught any rum-runner in the act—and they seemed insignificant against the chance of making hundreds of dollars or more on every run.

That was probably the calculation a Port Dalhousie kid named John Gogo made when he convinced his cruise-boat operator father, Sidney Gogo, to use his thirty-three-foot gasoline schooner, the

Hattie C, for a year or two of hauling liquor. Twenty-four years old and solid muscle, John Gogo could easily handle loading and unloading a cargo of thirty or fifty cases of whisky by himself, although he usually brought along a Toronto friend of his, a bookkeeper named Fred VanWinkle, to lend a hand and act as galley cook for thirty-five dollars a week. Over the summer of 1923 they'd made about fifteen trips together for the Perri outfit, mostly ferrying loads of Corby's whisky from the government dock near Belleville, Ontario, across the lake to the American side. But in late September Rocco Perri's common-law wife, Bessie Starkman, who handled the financial end of the business, ordered a big shipment for Toronto, and John Gogo got the call to head across the lake, pick up 210 cases of whisky from the Corby distillery, and bring it in the dead of night to the shores of Ashbridges Bay, in the city's east end. For a cargo that size he needed more help.

THE weather had been unsettled over the previous few days but Sunday, September 30 broke cool and clear. That morning John set off from Port Dalhousie with his forty-nine-year-old father, Sidney. They headed first to Toronto to pick up VanWinkle and Sidney's brother, James Gogo, who lived with his wife in the city's Parkdale neighbourhood. A carpenter by trade and twenty years younger than Sidney, James hadn't had much to do with his brother over the years, but he'd been pulled into this scheme because there hadn't been much work lately and his nephew John said there was money in it for him. James told his wife that he was going to spend the week helping his brother fix up his boat. There was no point in worrying her.

From Toronto the *Hattie C* made its way east along the lake's northern shore toward Prince Edward County. In the hold below, the four men had food for a week, at least two cases of empty bottles and, between the bunks, a heap of more than a hundred strong burlap bags. Bags were lighter and less bulky than wooden crates, allowing rum-runners to haul larger cargoes. Each bag would hold twenty-four bottles of whisky. And in a pinch, the men could dump the load over the gunwale and it would disappear.

On Monday, October 1, the humble schooner chugged around the headland of Prince Edward County and into the zigzagging waterway of the Bay of Quinte. A little while later, John Gogo pulled the craft up to the concrete government dock, where a boxcar of whisky sat waiting for them. And here is where the tricky work of rum-running began.

Liquor laws in the Prohibition era shifted like the pieces on a game board. Since 1916, Ontario's lawmakers had constantly had to adapt regulations to adjust to the political and societal forces pushing for and against the buying and drinking of alcohol. By 1923, the year that John Gogo was running liquor for the Perri organization, it was against the law to buy or transport alcohol within the province, but it was perfectly legal for Ontario distilleries to export their product to another country (even if, as in the case of the United States, that country had imposed Prohibition). Government officials, known as "outside customs inspectors," were stationed at docks and warehouses to ensure that the product from Ontario's breweries and distilleries being loaded aboard boats and trucks was indeed headed out of the province. And they required proof, specifically a B-13 shipping form, filled out with the details of the boat, its cargo, and that cargo's buyer and destination.

But those customs men could be bought off. If the cargo was bound for a destination within Ontario, all the boat skipper had to do was fill out the B-13 with a false name and a false destination and hand it back with a ten-dollar bill, and the inspector would sign it. So that Monday, Sidney Gogo filled out two B-13 forms with two different names for the boat master—Jones and Johns—and two different New York State destinations for the same purchaser. Documentation complete, the men transferred the cargo onto the boat, with strapping young John doing far more than his fair share of the heavy work.

With 2,520 bottles of whisky in its hold, the *Hattie C* sat low in the water as she headed back out into Lake Ontario and west along the north shore. Somewhere along the way the men transferred the bottles out of their wooden crates and into the burlap sacks, then dumped the empty crates where they wouldn't be seen. It was also John's bright idea to take the empty bottles they'd brought along, fill them with lake water coloured with a bit of caramel syrup, and add them to the Perri cargo, taking care to reapply the seals in a way that could fool almost anyone. That would allow him to reserve a sack full of Corby's whisky that he could sell on the side later. It was the sort of stunt only an arrogant kid would pull, and if his father thought it unwise, he may have let the math convince him. Sold for eight dollars a bottle, two cases of whisky meant an easy $192. And once the bogus bottles were distributed with the rest of the Perri cargo, nobody would be able to trace them back to this trip. It was a cheat, sure, but at least it wasn't going to kill anyone, not like a lot of the poison being passed off as whisky south of the border.

They weren't due in Toronto until Friday night, when the moon would be a sliver, so on Tuesday they pulled up to a dock near Newcastle and spent two nights there. Since they couldn't leave the boat—not with a twenty-thousand-dollar cargo in the hold—they stayed and did their best to pass the time, sewing up the burlap bags and entertaining themselves, perhaps with card games, a bit of fishing and dreams of what they were going to do with their wages. It got a little chilly at night, with a hint of frost on the gunwales, but Fred VanWinkle's simple meals helped keep them warm. The days were more comfortable, with moderate winds and a sky that was mostly clear.

Before they left Newcastle, Sidney got off the boat and boarded a train to Toronto. He needed to meet with Rocco Perri's representative, Frank (Shorty) Di Pietro, and establish the delivery details. It was a finely timed operation. The boat had to pull into shore in a secluded part of Ashbridges Bay, at the foot of Leslie Street. It had to happen at night, when Perri's REO Speed Wagon trucks were there, ready and waiting. Any delay would increase the chances of being discovered. That said, no one was too worried. This sort of delivery had been done plenty of times, and so far Toronto police had never come close to catching a rum-running boat.

Thursday morning, John started up the *Hattie C*'s engine and they pushed another twenty-seven miles west. The crew spent the night in Frenchman's Bay near Pickering, while Sidney slept at Fred VanWinkle's place at 89 Roseheath Avenue in Toronto.

On the buyer's end, everything was equally in control. At some point on Friday, Frank Di Pietro drove in from Hamilton to meet Sidney Gogo. He double-checked on the size of the cargo—105 sacks—and figured he was going to need two trucks to haul that load and maybe a car on top of that. It wasn't a problem; Rocco and Bessie had plenty of vehicles at their disposal. One of Rocco's men, Mike Romeo, drove a Marmon sedan that had the suspension to handle a load of whisky and the engine to outrun anything on the road. All Frank had to do was make the call. He opened a map and gave Sidney Gogo clear instructions on exactly where to pull the boat in, and assured him they would get their money when the cargo had been transferred. Then Sidney rejoined the *Hattie C* at a spot near the Woodbine Racetrack, east of downtown Toronto, gave John the details, and together the four men waited out the rest of the day while Lake Ontario gently lapped the sides of the boat.

That night, a convoy of Hamilton vehicles—Mike Romeo's Marmon and two trucks, one driven by Frank and the other by Mike's cousin Jimmy Romeo—arrived in Toronto and waited on York Street. At around 11 p.m., Rocco arrived at the wheel of his new Cadillac.

An observer on the street corner that evening might not have realized he was looking at the boss of this gang. Rocco Perri stood only about five feet, four inches tall. But he had an outsized person-ality—always smiling, quick with a joke—and the easy charisma of a wealthy tycoon. He dressed the part too, at least for public display, with sharp pinstripe suits, tan spats, bright straw boaters and colour-ful ties. And his fingernails were always manicured and polished to a shine. Tonight, however, Rocco was dressed in the dark overcoat and fedora of the racketeer at work. And he was all business.

He led the procession east, and as he turned right off of Queen Street, down Leslie Street, he must have been pleased. It was a perfect night for this kind of delivery: a layer of cloud obscured the narrow moon, so the darkness by the water was almost complete. That was good because this operation was going to take more than a few minutes. Besides the Romeo cousins, Frank had lined up two other men for the job, Louis Coronus and Frank Bucco. They all knew how to work fast, but it was no quick task to unload more than a hundred burlap bags of whisky, each weighing more than seventy-five pounds, haul them over marshy ground onto the bank and then load them carefully into trucks.

At the foot of Leslie they steered their cars off the road and into a secluded area among the bushes. Frank backed his truck as close to the water as the muddy ground allowed and Rocco ordered the men to turn off their lights. It was just before midnight.

By the dark edge of the lake near the Woodbine Racetrack, with not a soul on the water, John Gogo tried to start up the *Hattie C*. It took a bit of time; the big engine had become argumentative lately. But eventually they were chugging their way around the tip of Fisherman's Island and up Ashbridges Bay to the jagged shoreline. It was all soft ground there, filled in with sand and soil dredged up in the recent reclamation of the bay. According to the instructions passed on by his father, John had to steer the *Hattie C* into a small inlet and push the boat up the cut through shallow waters onto a mucky shore strewn with old tires.

A little after midnight, when the *Hattie C* arrived, they tossed a rope to waiting hands that pulled the boat snug to the shore, and everybody got to work.

DESK Sergeant George B. Hoag of the Toronto Police Service was on duty at the Pape Avenue station when, at half past midnight, the telephone rang. Hoag answered and listened with growing interest as a caller told him that right now, at that moment, there was a boat in the cut at the bottom of Leslie Street. Not only that, there were two auto trucks and two automobiles down there too, and the whole thing looked suspicious. For months there'd been talk in the neighbourhood of bootleggers unloading their cargo at this spot late at night, and the caller was certain that the men down there in the darkness were doing something wrong.

It was exactly the sort of tipoff the Toronto force had been waiting for. Finally they had a chance to catch major rum-runners in the act. The foot of Leslie Street was not half a mile away; they could be there in minutes. Hoag hung up the phone and immediately put out a call, dispatching Patrol Sergeant William Kerr with constables William Henry Mitchell and James Anthony Rooney.

Driving in the divisional car, plainclothesman George Fraser heard the call and turned toward Leslie Street. Each of the four men was equipped with a flashlight and a gun.

Down by the water, things were going smoothly. On board the *Hattie C*, Fred and James fed the bags from the hold to John, who passed them down to Rocco's men. With fifty-six sacks already loaded onto one of the trucks they were more than halfway through. Within another twenty minutes they'd be done.

And then everything went to hell.

Two police cars roared down from the end of Leslie Street, their lights blazing. As they lurched to a stop, Sergeant Kerr and constables Fraser, Mitchell and Rooney jumped out. One of them fired his gun in the air, and there was a moment of chaos as Rocco began shouting in Italian: "*Polizia! State attenti!*"—Police! Be careful!—and the men on land dove in every direction into the bushes.

They didn't stay hidden long. As the police spread out, Mitchell and Rooney stumbled on Di Pietro and the Romeo cousins and began putting them into handcuffs. They grabbed Rocco too and, with his boss arrested, Frank Bucco came out of hiding and gave himself up to the sergeant, who handed him off to Constable Fraser. Rocco and his men, all of them unarmed, knew better than to resist. In the eyes of the law, bootlegging and rum-running were "summary offences." They would have to pay a fine, or spend a few months in jail, but no one could get into serious trouble in a situation like this unless somebody did something stupid.

Not everyone, however, was so well schooled. At the first shot, James Gogo quipped to his brother, "That doesn't seem very healthful." The men ran for cover, James to the back of the boat, Fred, John and his father into the cabin. Through the windows they could see police with flashlights swarming the banks. John tried desperately to reverse the engine and pull the boat out of the tires and muck. Who knows what they imagined would befall them if they were caught, but clearly John could only think about getting away, getting the boat out into open water.

On land, Rocco was doing his best to establish the story he'd later try to sell to the police court judge. To the officer handcuffing him he gave the name Francisco Serge and kept insisting he was an innocent bystander—he'd merely been giving this man Di Pietro directions. But there was something pulling the attention of the officers away. Walking in the moonless dark toward the water, Fraser heard the chugging of an engine and alerted Sergeant Kerr, who could just make out the shape of a boat from the spill of the police car lights. He lifted his flashlight to get a better look and saw the *Hattie C* backing away from shore, toward the bay.

Kerr let out a sharp whistle and shouted, "Stop your engine! We have you cornered!" But the boat kept backing away, moving hard astern now across the inlet. He tried again. "Shut off the engine or I will sink your boat!" He took out his revolver and fired a warning shot. All he could see was the boat's faint outline, but it kept moving.

On the bank, helpless in handcuffs, Rocco could sense the growing danger. He shouted at the boat, "Stop! Turn off the engine!" The rest of his men joined him, shouting to the crew not to make trouble, in both Italian and English. About 120 feet away, on the north bend of the bank, Mitchell called out to Fraser, "What do we do, try and sink her?" To Fraser, who practised shooting with his revolver once a year, that sounded right. "Shoot low and sink her!" he yelled.

With .32-calibre bullets in their revolvers, the police had no hope of sinking a boat with a hull as thick as the *Hattie C*'s. And in a darkness barely alleviated by their wavering flashlights, they could hardly see where to aim—they were a hundred feet up the bank. How low was low enough? But Sergeant Kerr never hesitated. Without even knowing what he had caught these men doing, he lowered his gun and pulled the trigger. As he opened fire, so did the three constables behind him, Fraser, Mitchell and Rooney.

"Don't shoot!" shouted Rocco. "There are people on that boat! You could kill them!"

Sidney Gogo, crouching low by the wheel of the *Hattie C*, heard bullets splinter the cabin around him. Somewhere between fifteen and thirty shots came at them. At least eight bullets pierced the boat's hull and cabin. One bullet glanced off the engine and burned Sidney's neck. Another tore his coat. Another ripped through James Gogo's jaw as he huddled at the stern. Yet one more hit young John in the chest. He slumped forward over the engine, hitting the magneto, which shut the engine off. The boat began drifting, its momentum carrying it backward to the other side of the inlet, and the police stopped shooting.

On shore, Constable Mitchell shouted, "Get to the other side!" and Sergeant Kerr dashed across the marshy ground to the opposite bank, flashlight bobbing erratically in his hand. Mitchell was the first to board the *Hattie C* as it nudged the shore. Climbing up over the frost-covered stern, he heard groaning and saw James Gogo lying in a corner, hand to his bleeding jaw. "For God's sake, get a doctor!" called James. Then Mitchell approached the cabin and pointed his gun and flashlight through the open window. Inside, Sidney Gogo and Fred VanWinkle were trying to support John, his head lolling, his knees buckling beneath him.

A stricken Sidney looked up at Mitchell. "You have killed my son."

"There's a man wounded!" the constable shouted to the officers on shore. "Call for an ambulance." He went to confer with Kerr. "I think he's done for," Mitchell said.

Sergeant Kerr entered the cabin, his flashlight showing the way, and saw blood on the floor. Then his light found Fred and Sidney on the port side, with John in his father's arms. VanWinkle had been trying to feel for John's pulse and asked Kerr to see if he was alive. The sergeant took hold of the young man's wrist. "I think so," he said, but he knew Mitchell was right.

Constable Mitchell ordered Sidney and Fred to carry John off the boat as Kerr walked to the stern and demanded James Gogo's name. "Smith," said James, holding his jaw. He watched as Sidney and Fred carried John past and his eyes went wide. "He isn't dead, is he?" They lowered his nephew's heavy, muscular body over the side and he said it again, and again. "He isn't dead, is he?"

Kerr took out his notebook. "What is your right name?" he asked.

Dazed, James shook his head. "We don't give our right names in a thing like this."

By his father's estimate, John Gogo died fifteen minutes after being shot, and they waited more than an hour for an ambulance to arrive. An autopsy would later show the bullet had pierced John's heart and the base of his left lung. When Rocco and his men, and the crew of the *Hattie C*, were searched at the Pape Avenue station, police found a total of fifteen hundred dollars in cash—most of which would have gone to the Gogos for a job well done—but no weapons of any kind.

NEWS of the capture made immediate headlines in Toronto and Hamilton. The early stories focused on the drama of a liquor-boat raid that had left one man wounded and another dead. The size of the liquor seizure impressed the writers too; it was one of the most valuable in the province's history. The *Toronto Daily Star* dispatched reporters to interview the wives of the *Hattie C*'s crew. At

96 Macdonell Avenue, the "pretty" and "loyal little wife" of James Gogo had returned from spending the morning at St. Michael's Hospital, where her husband was undergoing surgery. "The little brown-eyed woman" had a puzzled look, said the *Star*. "I simply can't understand it," she said with tears in her eyes. "I am at a loss to account for his being with the other Gogo boys at all." Over at 89 Roseheath, Fred VanWinkle's wife—"a young, slightly built woman with fair bobbed hair"—had been so busy caring for their four-year-old son she hadn't even heard about her husband's arrest. "We have only moved in here last Saturday," she said. "I don't know what we will do now. We have no other relatives in the city. Can he get bail?"

That morning, a group of seven men appeared in police court in front of Magistrate James E. Jones to plead not guilty to the charge of illegal transport of liquor on the waters of Toronto Harbour. Rocco Perri was not among them, apparently having convinced police, at least initially, that he was Francisco Serge, an unlucky good Samaritan who'd stumbled inadvertently on a crime scene, a story that would have been backed up by his men. His cars were impounded, however, and since both of them were licensed in his name, the story didn't hold for long. Bail was set at three thousand dollars each and all were held in jail, except for Sidney Gogo. He stood before the bench, stunned with grief, as the lawyer for the Gogo family, W. B. Horkins, begged for Sidney to be released so that he might mourn with his wife and daughter.

"I shall allow him to go," said Magistrate Jones, accepting the Italian's impounded boat as security. "Gogo, you may go to St. Catharines. See to it that you return here by Monday next."

Detective John Miller of the Ontario Provincial Police, who was a veteran at investigating crimes involving immigrant men, happened to be in court that morning, and he cast a world-weary eye over the scene. As Sidney Gogo thanked the bench in heavily accented English and made his way out of court, Miller shook his head. "Take a good look at him," he muttered to a friend. "That is the last you will see of him."

Miller had it wrong. After his son's funeral, Sidney Gogo appeared in court whenever he was required. But even as Rocco's men and the *Hattie C*'s crew were being processed and tried on liquor charges, questions grew about why the arresting police that night had used their guns at all. "What right has a constable to shoot while enforcing the Ontario Temperance Act?" the *Toronto Daily Star* wanted to know. Over the weekend, Chief Coroner George W. Graham and the Crown's chief attorney, Eric Armour, KC, toured the scene of the shooting. Armour had pictures taken and diagrams made of the boat and the bullet holes. He was ready when the coroner's inquest into John Gogo's death began the night of Thursday, October 11, 1923.

"You were using firearms against defenceless men," Armour said to Sergeant Kerr on the stand. He showed the diagrams that revealed five bullet holes roughly two feet above the water line, and three more above the deck. "How do you explain the fact that some bullets went through the front doors on the starboard side at one foot five inches and two feet four inches above deck?" he asked Kerr. "How do you account for shooting *into* the boat to sink her?" When Kerr hesitated, Armour pressed him. "*Can* you account for it?"

"No," said Kerr. Later he admitted that if the men they'd discovered had been making their getaway in a truck, he and his constables would not have used their weapons. It was something about the boat that prompted them to shoot. As the police, one by one, gave their version of events, an unidentified young woman sat at the back of the court with tears running down her cheeks. Occasionally she broke into sobs as more of the details became known.

When the inquest resumed for four hours on October 17, more of the story emerged from those on the receiving end of the bullets. Sidney Gogo tried to walk the fine line of being true to the details of his son's death while selling the authorities on a fabrication—that they'd been transporting their liquor legally to a buyer in New York State and that storm damage and mechanical trouble had forced them to unload their cargo in Toronto in the dead of night. It was rocky going for Sidney. But when Horkins asked who fired the fatal shot, Sidney said he thought it was the man on the bank, near the side of the boat. Sergeant Kerr, in other words, or possibly Mitchell.

Then Rocco took the stand as a witness. He identified himself this time as Rocco Perri, a traveller for the Superior Macaroni Company, and reiterated the story he'd given police. Frank Di Pietro was a friend he'd known for three years, and that night, after the two had met by chance at the corner of York and Richmond streets, he had asked Rocco to show him the way to the foot of Leslie Street.

"When I seen that they were going to unload whisky I wanted to go home," said Rocco. Unluckily for him, that was when the police showed up.

The Crown asked if he knew a "Mr. Gogo."

"No," said Rocco. "Never heard of him."

H. Hartley Dewart, KC, the lawyer for the police, took a slightly different approach. "You drive trucks in your business?" asked Dewart.

"Yes," said Rocco.

"Do you ever carry anything other than macaroni?"

Rocco grinned.

"A little liquor?" suggested Dewart.

"Can you prove it?" said Rocco. The spectators in court laughed.

"No, I am expecting you to admit it."

The coroner commanded Rocco to answer the question.

"No," Rocco assured him. "I don't."

The coroner later described this testimony from Rocco as "weird and wonderful" and informed the jury that "I don't for a moment believe Perri is telling the truth."

On October 19, Rocco appeared in Toronto Police Court to answer the same charge of transporting liquor that had been laid on his men. Bessie came and bailed him out and the others were similarly released, pending sentencing. No one believed the story of the *Hattie C*'s crew, regarding their attempt to deliver their cargo to a mythical U.S. buyer. Ultimately, Magistrate Jones fined both Sidney Gogo and Frank Di Pietro one thousand dollars and costs. In defence of Sidney, Horkins appealed for leniency. "The confiscation of the liquor and this fine has made my client completely down and out," he said.

"Such men as he deserve to be down and out," said Jones. "My sole regret is that I am unable to see my way clear to fine or imprison the others." Rocco and the rest of his men were released without charges despite being, in the magistrate's words, "very undesirable citizens."

But for the court and for fascinated observers, the real drama lay in how the system would judge the actions of the police. At a half-hour before midnight on October 25, after just one hour and ten minutes of deliberation, the coroner's jury delivered its verdict: John Gogo had died from a bullet fired by a Toronto police constable, and the police had used their weapons "without justification." Coroner Graham called the inquiry one of the most important in the history of Toronto.

Crown Attorney Eric Armour announced that he would take criminal proceedings against all four officers. On Monday,

October 29, he met with Attorney General William Folger Nickle, who then met with the press. "When police constables illegally use firearms," Nickle said, "they are in exactly the same position before the law as any other person."

A week later, in what the *Toronto Daily Star* called, "a spectacle unprecedented in the annals of criminal procedure," the four constables charged with manslaughter first appeared in court. The trial itself began later in the month and lasted four days. Defence Attorney Dewart based his case on the honour of dedicated, honest policemen versus lawbreakers trying to evade capture. Yes, the officers had made an error in judgment, but he implored the jury to acquit: "Don't give comfort to the rum-runners of this province by your verdict."

Dewart was only partly successful. After four hours of deliberation, the jury returned late Saturday, November 24, to announce it had failed to reach a verdict. Seven jurors had voted to acquit, five to convict. The following February, the four officers were tried again. This time the trial lasted five days, but the result was the same—a hung jury. After two trials and costs of at least ten thousand dollars, Attorney General Nickle announced that the matter would be dropped. "It is not the custom to turn prosecution into persecution," he said.

If anyone was justified in feeling persecuted by the Canadian legal system, it was Sidney Gogo. He'd lost his son, and with the loss of his boat he was hobbled financially, so much so that after the trial he travelled to Rocco's home in Hamilton to ask for help. Unfortunately Rocco wasn't in, and Bessie, who wasn't known for her generosity toward Perri gang members and associates, scornfully turned him away.

But Rocco had always looked out for employees in times of need. Without mentioning it to Bessie, he took care of the expenses for John Gogo's funeral. And he went further. He ordered an enormous gravestone from Massena, in New York State, had the name "Gogo" carved in relief, and delivered it to Sidney in Port Dalhousie. It was the closest thing to an apology any mob boss could give.

2

PAESE

Country

SIXTEEN-YEAR-OLD ROCCO PERRE STOOD ON A PIER IN the port of Naples, Italy, and stared up at a huge, four-masted White Star Line steamer. From its centre, one enormous, gleaming funnel rose against the blue Neapolitan sky. Millions before him had experienced a moment similar to this, but this was Rocco's moment. This was his beginning.

Everyone he knew, it seemed, wanted to leave Italy for America. Historian John E. Zucchi has said the word itself was synonymous with wealth—*a fare l'America* was to "make a fortune." Thousands went every year, both the sojourning men who brought back the money they'd earned and the emigrants who never returned. To leave was an act of protest—against an excess of taxation, and a paucity of hope. If you were an impoverished young Italian who wanted more from life, it was what you did. So that's what Rocco was doing.

On April 14, 1904, the SS *Republic* was practically new, its maiden voyage having come just a few months before. But as his fellow Calabrians, families and working men, pushed around him to get aboard, Rocco neither knew nor cared that he was looking at the flagship of White Star's Boston-European service, a forerunner to the *Titanic*. He neither knew nor cared that her luxurious first-class accommodations would go all but unused on this trip, that for the next two weeks only a wealthy few would spend their days lounging on rich upholstery, enjoying fine cuisine under the decorative dome of the dining saloon, while admiring some of the finest wood carving on any vessel afloat.

He didn't care because he wouldn't see any of that while packed into the bowels of steerage with the more than seventeen hundred people taking this voyage with him, people who would be fed from kettles, who would sleep holding on to their satchels for fear of being robbed, who during high seas would vomit into buckets until the buckets overflowed. He only knew that this ship was taking him away from the worst kind of life, toward something better.

At least, that's what he hoped. As he walked up the gangplank without his family, jostled by strangers, Rocco patted his pocket. Some young men carried switchblades or daggers to better their chances on the ships that took them to their future in *l'America*, but Rocco Perre probably had playing cards. He liked to gamble.

PERRE'S birthplace, Platì, was the sort of southern Italian village that was easy to leave. Situated at the narrowing of the Cirella River, in a valley in the Aspromonte—the "rugged mountains"—of Reggio Calabria, the region at the very tip of Italy's boot, it was a blighted kind of place. A few centuries before, the wetlands of this region had served as a penal colony. By the time Rocco Perre was born here on December 29, 1887, it was peopled by poor goat herders and bread makers. They suffered through the earthquakes that demolished their primitive houses for the reward of the floods and mudslides that smothered them.

Rocco was the first of five children born to a small but sturdy shepherd named Giuseppe and a tall, slender mother named Elisabetta Romeo, who raised her children with an eye to God. His home was an unlovely *casa* of two rooms, no plumbing, and a basement for cold storage. His limited schooling came in the nearby church, Santa Maria di Loreto, where he'd been baptized. At home, his *madre* prayed, made cheese and cared for the children. His *padre*, who had hard eyes and smiled in the pained way of men who aren't used to it, herded goats and tilled his miserable few acres. Giuseppe also tended to acacia and olive trees on his property, and to a spread of land owned by a local moneyed doctor.

It may have been that doctor who offered young Rocco his first glimpse of a different kind of life. To aspire to something outside one's own experience, one needs to know what that thing might look like. To Rocco, it might have looked like a larger home, with finer furnishings—and an absence of dirty toil because you paid someone else to do it. If Rocco had to choose between the life his father led and such a life of ease and comfort—well, it was hardly a choice at all.

But to get that life, as a child of sooty, meagre Platì, it wasn't enough to set out for one of Italy's glittering cities. In the hierarchy of the country's imagination, southern Italians were the least likely to succeed. In Rome or Milan, they became the dishwashers, the labourers, never the doctors. Scorned, hungry, riven by cholera and malaria, and abusively overtaxed by a government bent on expansion, the Calabrese were resentful and restless. They had, said Italian writer and politician Luigi Barzini, a "feeling of being the victims of historical injustice and the prey of other people's greed."

That sense of injustice helped fuel the rise of a secret criminal society—the 'Ndrangheta. More powerful and ruthless even than the Cosa Nostra, it would be the 'Ndrangheta, in 1973, who would kidnap the son of billionaire John Paul Getty Jr. and send his ear to a newspaper as proof. Today it controls much of the world's drug trade from its base in the small Calabrian villages where it began. San Luca, in the valley of the Bonamico River, remains one of the 'Ndrangheta's two main strongholds. The other, nine miles to the north, is Platì.

The burning will to take what wasn't being given began to coalesce into the first, early form of the 'Ndrangheta—variously called the Picciotteria or the Camorra (a term borrowed from the underworld society of Naples)—just around the time a boyish Rocco was running between the legs of his elders. A turn-of-the-century Italian poet, Giovanni De Nava, wrote poems about the violent, knife-wielding young men of these groups. In a verse from one, "Malavita" (Underworld), he wrote:

Listen to me, I am a camorrista,
And I am the most skillful evildoer;
Wherever I proceed
The earth trembles . . . even the earth trembles!

As a young teen, Rocco probably knew some of these strutting *picciotti* thugs in their signature wide pants, neckerchiefs and bowler hats who terrorized the dusty streets of Platì and the villages beyond. His cheek bore a small scar that could have come from a *sfregio*, or knife wound. But it's unlikely he was one of them. He didn't need violence, or the threat of a flashing blade, to get what he wanted. Like a Calabrian Tom Sawyer, Rocco charmed people with his smile. Rather than intimidate you, he preferred to befriend you. "A prince"– that's how one of his associates, Milton Goldhart, would one day describe him: "Roc was the finest person I met in my life."

And he was not a joiner. Like most Italian criminal societies, the Picciotteria put new members through a process of initiation. You achieved admission, and you worked up the ranks. It was, in its primitive and blood-stained way, a rather corporate approach to advancement. Rocco Perre was more the entrepreneurial sort. He wanted something of his own.

In April of 1904, Rocco packed his satchel and left his two brothers and two sisters, his father, and his distraught, weeping mother, and set out for *l'America*. He was very likely recruited by an emigration agent. Every province in Italy, particularly in the South, crawled with *padroni*, agents who recruited for the railways or other labour-hungry industries in North America. It was illegal in America for companies to promise jobs to immigrants, or to pay for their passage, but the *padroni* worked beyond the law's reach, luring men with the possibility of higher wages in the United States. A labourer who made two lira a day in Italy might make eight lira in New York or Toronto (about $1.50), enough to send money home to help his destitute family. And the *padrone* would lay a hand on his shoulder and paint a picture of ease. He would help with immigration, and with accommodations in the emigrant's new home. One's dreams could be made real.

In the years 1903 and 1904 alone, more than 420,000 Italians decided to seek a better life far from the one they knew. So as Rocco made his way to the train station in Reggio Calabria—seventeen hours by foot, a few less by wagon—he wasn't alone. Twelve other men from Platì eventually boarded the same ship. Most were in their twenties, thirties and forties. At sixteen, Rocco was the youngest.

At Reggio Calabria, he boarded a packed train and spent most of that day and night chugging north to Naples. There, in order to board the ship, he had to give officials a story they'd believe. There was always a chance he could be turned away, either here in a part of

Italy that was strange to him, or at the receiving port in the United States. Most important was to assure officials he had family waiting for him, so Rocco lied, telling them he was going to America to visit his father, Giuseppe. After a cursory medical exam, he walked up the gangplank of the SS *Republic*, and took his place among the poor.

⁣⁣⁣⁣⁣⁣⁣⁣⁣⁣⁣⁣⁣⁣⁣⁣⁣⁣⁣⁣

I T WAS A VERY DIFFERENT SORT OF LIFE IN GAMBOLÒ, Italy. Still a small-town life, to be sure, and one challenged by taxation and government incompetence. But this was the North; the air was clearer here, the pride more palpable. Gambolò, home to a boy who would one day become Rocco Perri's most dogged adversary, sat some eight hundred miles removed from Platì's pitiable struggles, high in the province of Pavia at the edge of Lombardy, the richest region in the country. As agricultural provinces went in Italy, Pavia was among the most productive. Literacy in the North far surpassed that in the southern regions. And Milan, the country's economic and industrial engine, a source of so much art, fashion and design, a seemingly bottomless well of opportunity, sat right next door. Gambolò itself may have offered little more than a few churches. But if a lad, a *giovanotto*, wanted a prime seat for a life within reach of Italy's advantages, he could hardly do much better.

And yet, little Franco Zanetti wanted to leave.

A December baby like Rocco, Franco had been born in 1890 to a cabinetmaker named Ambrogio and his wife, Christina. They had an older son named Alfredo and, after Franco came along, welcomed three daughters as well.

Typical of a man whose occupation demanded attention to fine detail, Ambrogio was serious, tidy and reserved, qualities that his young son would one day share. But as the new century approached, the most important male relationship in Franco's young life was the one he had with his brother, three and a half years older. So in 1899, when twelve-year-old Alfredo announced that, like so many of his countrymen, he was leaving for *l'America*, eight-year-old Franco decided to leave with him.

Did they go with a relative? No records have survived, but if the parents of these two boys let them cross the ocean all by themselves, they did so with the knowledge that the young adventurers would be welcomed and cared for in their new country. A large contingent from Gambolò had already established itself in Springfield, Massachusetts. After landing, probably in Boston, the Zanetti boys headed about ninety miles inland and arrived in that city, just a few years after a local phys. ed. teacher named James Naismith had begun throwing leather balls through peach baskets at the YMCA International Training School.

Alfredo and Franco probably never touched a basketball. As Italians they joined other recent immigrants in Springfield's crowded south end. Intrepid, self-reliant and willing to work, they somehow made a place for themselves. Little Franco watched the way his older brother navigated through an unfamiliar world, finding ways of fitting in, and did his best to emulate him. The next oldest Zanetti child, Rose, joined them some time later. And when their mother, Christina, decided in 1903 that she could not be without her three oldest children, she dragged her two youngest daughters over the ocean to Springfield to try to convince them to come back to Gambolò. Rose and the boys refused. They were in America, and most of their family was now with them. Why leave?

A year later the father, Ambrogio, came to the realization his family was never coming back. So he left his town and his cabinetry business, and joined his prodigal brood. Over the next few years the Zanettis fashioned a secure base in Springfield. They were a family that played by the rules, and they thrived. For several years they lived in the middle of Springfield's Italian South End. Then they began to move, first to another part of the Italian district, then to a tiny house next to the Chicopee River. Eventually they settled in a nicer brick home beyond the Italian section. Alfredo got a job and worked for several years. Soon he was able to open a cigar and tobacco shop. Ambrogio, who eventually gave in to American pronunciation and called himself Ambrose, found work as a carpenter and joined the Italian American Citizens Club and the local fire brigade. In one way, however, he never quite settled in. A proud man, he refused to speak in his limited English; he didn't want others to make fun of him.

Franco could not have been more different. He was a learner, and he embraced the New World. He read constantly, about many subjects, including the sport of wrestling, which he loved because he could succeed at it despite being shorter than most other boys. When he had to, he worked at his brother's store, and when he didn't, he turned the pages of books, steadily improving his English. He adopted the name Frank and fed his growing sense that there was another life waiting for him, somewhere else he was meant to be.

⁙⁙⁙⁙⁙⁙⁙⁙⁙⁙⁙⁙⁙⁙⁙⁙⁙⁙⁙⁙⁙⁙⁙⁙

O N APRIL 27, 1904, AFTER A "MODERATE" VOYAGE, THE SS *Republic* landed at Charlestown, home of the Boston Navy Yard, where ships had been built since the American Revolutionary War. In his turn, Rocco climbed out of the SS *Republic*'s cramped, fetid lower deck. He made his way past the rich men in straw boaters and the women carrying parasols, got a glimpse of the Navy Yard's new dry dock, and lined up with his fellow steerage mates to submit to the immigration official's inspection and questions. Only steerage passengers had to submit to this scrutiny, and like the others he dreaded the coloured chalk in official hands. If he'd happened to pick up an eye infection or a cough on the voyage, an immigration official could at any moment mark his back with an *X* and order him home.

With very little grasp of English, but coached by his *padrone*, Rocco pulled the cap off his dirty head and answered the questions as best he could. Was he able to read and write? Yes. Who had paid for his passage? He had. How much money did he have on him? Twenty dollars. How was his health? Good. Crippled or deformed at all? No. Had he ever been in prison? No. Was he a polygamist? No. An anarchist? No. What was his final destination? Massena, New York.

MANY of the thousands who fled Italy for North America to leave poverty and violence behind were dismayed to find both waiting for them when they arrived. It turned out that victimization was an exportable commodity, and it thrived in its new surroundings.

Besides hard work, this new strange land required a combination code of language, money and connections to unlock its bounty and opportunity, and the new arrivals were not well equipped. Most immigrant groups relied on those who'd come before to look out for them. The second wave of Irish immigrants, for example, could expect established Irish-born contractors or politicians to kick a few jobs their way. But southern Italians had no such advantages. Even if there were well-established Italians in America at the turn of the century, they were largely northerners who had no interest in helping the southern latecomers.

Trying to find comfort and safety in the familiar, they coalesced into communities that came to reflect the ones they'd left, that included the same loyalties and conflicts, the same antagonism toward authorities. Even the same criminals. Italy wanted rid of as many of the brigands that plagued it as possible; often as not, rather than police them, it facilitated their emigration. So among the tired, bedraggled families in cracked shoes who came searching for a future arrived these men with their weapons, which immigration officials had no authority to confiscate. In cities such as New York, Toronto, San Francisco and Chicago, and even Springfield, Massachusetts, the Little Italys that arose became cauldrons of fear and criminality.

Extortion was often the game of choice, practised sometimes by individuals but usually by gangs, which by the 1890s were common. In San Francisco, a group of Sicilian immigrants, who adopted the name "La Maffia," developed a blackmail system that targeted the most successful members of the Italian community. Bankers, store owners, contractors and others would be threatened with death or ruin unless they paid up.

The practice spread east, to Brooklyn, New York, and occasionally popped its head up high enough to be noticed by those outside the southern Italian community. In September of 1903, in what the *New York Times* described as "a queer tale of conspiracy and extortion," an Italian named Nicolo Cappiello received a letter demanding money. Cappiello was a well-to-do Brooklyn contractor, a partner in the dock-building firm Olsen & Cappiello, who lived in a three-storey house on Second Place, Brooklyn. The letter he received said, in part, "If you don't meet us at Seventy-second Street and Thirteenth Avenue, Brooklyn, tomorrow afternoon, your house will be dynamited and your family killed." The letter threatened the same if he went to the police, and it was marked with an elaborate drawing of three crosses and a skull and crossbones, and signed *Mano Nera*—"Black Hand."

The men threatening Cappiello included three of his own friends, as well as members of this new gang. They managed to get at least one thousand dollars out of him, and demanded more—another short note, written in Italian, told him, "I swear to you on my honour that during this month you will be killed. The Black Hand will follow all"—before he went to the Brooklyn police and pleaded for protection.

The police told him he'd probably get more letters and not to worry.

"I'm not worrying," said Cappiello, looking worried.

Once four of the men were arrested and the story spread, the Black Hand became infamous. In decades to come, "Mafia"—the name for Sicily's criminal underworld—would come to be the handy catch-all term for Italian organized crime. But for the police, politicians and newspapers of the early 1900s, "Black Hand" was the expression of choice.

Consequently, the Black Hand took on an aura that surpassed its reality. Assumed by the press and the public to be a vast and organized secret society, it was more factually a criminal methodology. Invoked with crude death symbols at the bottom of scribbled extortion letters, or the imprints of blackened hands on doors, it was used by ruthless—or desperate—Italians to exploit the weakness and isolation of their fellow immigrants, and it thrived because of Italians' unique understanding of, and acquiescence to, the way the *we threaten / you pay* system was supposed to work.

The practice spread to the smaller centres of New York State. Soon, well-to-do Italians in Buffalo began to receive Black Hand letters. So did the established immigrants of Syracuse. Sticks of dynamite placed on the doorsteps of people who wouldn't pay began to explode. You could almost chart the Black Hand's advance on a map, and by 1906 the next small city in its path was the place Rocco Perre called home.

3

INIZIO
Beginning

ROCCO SPENT FOUR YEARS IN MASSENA, WORKING AS A labourer and acclimatizing to the ways of North America. He had a lot to learn.

Slowly he figured out how to get along in English, even if he couldn't read the language or write it. He adapted to the winters, grudgingly. And to the food, although nothing tasted as good as the pastas and cheeses his mother had made in Platì. Mostly he learned about the people.

He observed Americans' bizarre patriotism, such as in June of 1906, when Massena bedecked its streets in bunting, streamers and flags to welcome veterans of the Grand Army of the Republic, who came in by train, coach and shiny motor buggy for a special Civil War reunion. He saw the decorous manner of the people, except when they were drunk, and observed the way Americans took their affluence and their rights as citizens for granted, and had no notion of true poverty. No idea what it felt like to be pressed under the heel of the powerful, with no recourse but crime.

He saw the economic boom occurring in Massena—it was hard

to miss. Once famous as a health spa, the town of four thousand was turning its attention to industry. Here and in the neighbouring towns, there were paper mills, power plants, mines and factories. Newspaper editors from other counties came to witness the transformation for themselves: "A few years ago, Massena was a nice little town at the end of a railroad," they wrote. "Today Massena is on the line to Montreal. It has a canal. It has its steamboat lines, and its ramifications of railroads all through its back yards." They saw new streets with new construction running in every direction, and more money than ever before. "The whole thing," the editors concluded, "is stupendous."

And here Rocco got his first taste of the way most of that affluence skipped over the people who made it possible. As in any place on the continent where industry flourished, Italians provided much of the labour, but far from being appreciated and rewarded for it, they were sneered at, taken advantage of. A group of Italian families living by the Grasse River upstream from Canton, New York, were seen as a "gang of Italians" that threatened the local drinking water. The same visiting editors who extolled the new wonders of Massena also marvelled at the "army of dagos" building up the place.

Rocco watched how citizens and figures of authority behaved toward each other in North America. Respectful, for the most part, but not always truthful. You could operate a saloon without a licence. You could run a gambling room, even though it was illegal. There were a number of these establishments a few miles away in Canton and more a little farther away, in Gouverneur. The men who ran those rooms were always getting caught. All they did was pay a fine.

Rocco had a chance to see all of this and also the violence that Americans associated with the influx of Italian men. In February 1905, an Italian who'd worked at the paper mill stabbed his foreman, the knife glancing off a rib. Later that year, one twenty-year-old shot another after a quarrel. In March 1906, local newspapers reported that two more men were shot dead in an unlicenced Italian saloon where "shooting and stabbing affrays are of frequent occurrence."

Did teenage Rocco play a part in this criminal activity? There are vague rumours, the stuff of family legend, that he briefly fell in with an extortion gang who tried threatening local store owners for money. He was also said—despite being barely five feet, four inches tall—to have bloodied the face of a northern Italian over the affections of a young woman. All anyone knows for sure is that after four years of soaking up all that Massena had to teach him, Rocco reached the age of twenty and decided to leave.

He had ambition. No matter how big Massena was getting, it wasn't nearly big enough. No matter how much opportunity it offered, he wanted more. By May 1908, something or someone had convinced him that Montreal was the place to try. It was the nearest big city, the likeliest place to find that thing, that image of success, that had pulled him across the ocean.

By the time he left, he was writing his last name as "Perri." A few months after he had arrived in America, Rocco had declared himself to immigration officials, the first step in becoming a naturalized citizen, and that's how they had written it down. But it hardly mattered; one other thing Rocco had learned by now was that North Americans were confused by Italian names. You could change them, become someone else, and they barely noticed. Identity was flexible here—that was a useful thing to know.

⁗⁗⁗⁗⁗⁗⁗⁗⁗⁗⁗⁗⁗⁗

ITALIANS HELD TOGETHER IN THEIR NEW LAND, FOR BETTER or worse, in part because it was how they had always lived. This was particularly true in southern Italy, where when someone spoke of his home country, his *paese,* he meant the village he'd grown up in. So his *paesano* was a member of a tight, intimate circle—and one of the few people he could trust.

And yet, Frank Zanetti was different. He was from the North, which could have been reason enough, but he also seemed driven to push away from the familiar, the sentimental, the things others held close. He had left home as a child, and before long his family had joined him. As a young man, he needed to push away again.

He found work on his own in Springfield, taking a job as a printer. Then he met a young woman named Grace Russell. She wasn't Italian, and perhaps, for someone who rejected the way his father clung to the old language, that was part of the attraction. In fact she had been born in Three Rivers, Massachusetts, to French-Canadian parents. Her father was George Russell, who owned a livery stable; her mother was Cordelia Basnier.

Frank spent as much time as he could with Grace and her parents, soaking up the French they spoke. Grace's father taught Frank how to handle horses. Then one chilly night in the autumn of 1909, while the two of them were alone, Frank and Grace behaved recklessly. Some weeks later, it horrified them to learn that Grace was pregnant.

They didn't marry immediately but, to the relief of Grace's parents, they did marry. In June of 1910, when Grace was about eight months pregnant, they escaped the judgmental eyes of Springfield and travelled twenty-seven miles south to Hartford, Connecticut. On a sunny Wednesday, June 15, they stood together in the office of Justice of the Peace Frank M. Mather in the Halls of Record. Grace was just nineteen years old, two months younger than Frank, so she needed a parent's permission to become Frank Zanetti's wife. Her mother, Cordelia, grateful that her daughter would not be forced to live in shame, was with her to sign where required.

Frank had no family standing with him, no one to bestow parental blessing, so he lied for the official record and said he was twenty-one. After a brief and utilitarian ceremony, Justice Mather declared Frank and Grace married and wished them well. Six weeks later, on July 30, Grace gave birth to their daughter, Rena May Zanetti.

The young family lived at 36 Loring Street in the southwestern section of Springfield, just around the corner from the home Grace's parents rented on Fremont Street, so close they might have walked from one house to the other in their slippers. The other advantage to this location, for Frank, is that it put the greatest possible distance between himself and his own Italian family. While he and Grace lived on Loring, Frank's parents lived at 374 Water, at the edge of the Chicopee River, clear on the other side of the city.

But even that wasn't far enough away for Frank. He kept looking for a way to put even more distance between them. And in 1911 he found it.

At the time, government officials in the Canadian prairies were doing everything they could to attract settlers. They put the word out in newspaper advertisements: Here was the largest continuous wheat field in the world, nine hundred miles long by four hundred miles wide, barely 8 percent of it under cultivation, and land could be had by anyone with a few dollars and enough will to break the acres and make them farmable. And those adventurous folks wouldn't be alone, no sir. Enough people settling together could make a town.

"Kerrobert" announced a newspaper ad that was typical. "One year ago, open prairie. Today, an incorporated town of 800 people . . . Kerrobert is strategically situated in as fine a wheat country as we have in all Western Canada." For uninformed readers, the ad took care to place Kerrobert; it might have been in the middle of nowhere, but it was just a few hundred miles from somewhere—125 miles west of Saskatoon, two hundred southeast of Edmonton, and so on. "It is therefore destined," readers were assured with a flourish of faulty logic, "to become a large railroad, industrial and distributing centre."

The railroads were equal players in this effort, with the Canadian Pacific Railway, the Grand Trunk Railway and others selling land in far-flung settlements that would, in turn, require the lifeline of a railroad. In Edson, Alberta, the Grand Trunk Pacific Development Company offered town lots for $150 each. It was a grab for profits, as far as some journalists were concerned. "The genius who thought out the townsite development scheme could hear a dollar rattle in a sack of flour a mile away," said a northern Ohio writer in July 1911. He called the Edson development "the scene of as fine a swindle as ever engaged the attention of a court," and tried to warn the "enthusiastic young man" who felt lured to any such prairie wilderness, be it in Alberta or Saskatchewan, to avoid the "argus eyed real estate leaches [sic]" and the "gauntlet of weasels selling 'Life's Opportunity' at from 17 cents to $1 per share."

Frank Zanetti was just such an enthusiastic young man, and his was exactly the sort of ambition these promotional efforts were meant to inflame. They'd worked on plenty of others—over the previous two decades, Saskatchewan's population had expanded elevenfold. So when he came across an ad in *Il Progresso Italo-Americano* newspaper, placed by a lawyer-turned-farmer named Albino Ernesto Cotti who hoped to lure fellow Italians to join his Saskatchewan settlement, Frank found himself staring hard at the words.

He had already been primed by his in-laws to think well of Canada (and he'd already begun to learn French, which would surely be of help). Now, in his detailed advertisement, Cotti was as persuasive as any lawyer could be, describing the rewarding life of a prairie farmer and painting a picture of limitless opportunity. In anyone with imagination the words would have conjured images of proud men on horseback (Frank knew about horses!), and rich harvests of grain from one's own soil (he didn't know how to harvest, but he could learn!). The settlement was growing, the time was now, and Cotti laid out the steps someone like Frank needed to take. The path to his future was clear.

Young Frank, who had a wife and a new baby, and an urge to move, thrilled to these words. Once he'd finished reading, and let the idea sink in, he told Grace they were no longer going to live in Springfield, and he was no longer going to be a printer.

Together, they were going to be homesteaders near a place called Moose Jaw.

~~~~~~~~~~~~~~~~~~~~~~~~~~~~~~

M ONTREAL DID NOT WELCOME ROCCO THE WAY HE'D thought it would. It was a large, challenging city and his timing was bad. Labour unrest rumbled constantly, and Rocco arrived in the midst of a crippling bricklayers' strike that threatened to turn violent. Soon after that ended, twenty-two hundred CPR mechanics in the city dropped their tools. When the railway brought strike breakers into the city, a mob of four hundred attacked them, breaking the leg of one man and splitting open the head of another.

At the same time, Montreal had a large Black Hand problem. Stabbings and extortion in the north end of the city made things harder for Italians just trying to get a job. In September of 1908, Antonio Granito, a twenty-five-year-old bricklayer with two children, was attacked with knives in the city's north end, his chest slashed and his throat cut before his body was dumped by the CPR tracks. It was around midnight when in the darkness he'd cried out

"Murder!" and "Help!" But no one had paid any heed because, as a newspaper explained, "such cries are common in the Italian colony."

Rocco saw no path here to the future he wanted. After six months, during which he may have worked briefly as a waiter, he put Montreal behind him and headed west into Ontario. Like many Italians he landed first in Toronto, where he managed to establish some kind of lodgings at 77 Elm Street, near the YMCA. After a few months or a year, he made contact with people who told him about a way to make some real money. But to take advantage of it, he had to go north.

A few years before, in 1903, the railway had been cutting through the tiny, nothing town of Cobalt when, quite by accident, they discovered silver. Now they were digging up a fortune there—millions of ounces of silver every year, some of it in chunks bigger than a man's fist. Mining companies were developing new techniques to pull the metal out of hard rock. Everybody was getting in on it. The year the discovery was made, Cobalt's population was barely a hundred. By the time Rocco arrived five or six years later, he was one of about ten thousand people looking to get rich.

God, it was a filthy place. Garbage and discarded building materials piled high in the dirt streets. Without proper sanitation systems, people were living in an open sewer and dying of typhoid. The mining companies, which owned all the land, poured their wastewater directly into the local streams. When anyone, Rocco included, wanted a drink of clean water he had to get it delivered in a milk can. But there were about thirty thriving mines in the area, and anyone who had two nickels owned stock.

Rocco could not get in on this bonanza, not directly. He was still learning the language, and he had no money. But he could work. Employment agencies in the region gave jobs to men like Rocco, sending them to far-off labour camps. He would later claim to have spent some time in this period working at a stone quarry in Parry Sound, but never mind; by the time he said that, what Rocco did and what he claimed he did usually had very little in common.

For the first while, life in Cobalt surely looked no better to Rocco than the grinding disease-ridden poverty of Platì. Bunkhouses were jammed with men and infested with bugs. Even so, workers still had to pay for room and board, and if they lacked the funds a company might advance them the money. After a season of work, a labourer could easily find himself in debt. Men stole from each other. There were fights. It was a hard, miserable life. You made friends where you could, but you trusted no one.

And there were hardly any women! In Cobalt, a bonnet was a rare sight among the dirty felt bowlers, and the few women who were brave enough to come had plenty of men vying for their attention. Men who could flash dollar bills and stock certificates, even a silver nugget you could dent with your teeth.

Still . . . if you look at a problem just the right way, it becomes an opportunity. There was more than one road to silver in a dirty mining town, and during these first few years in Ontario, hard as they were, Rocco found one of those other roads.

He was in his early twenties, the age when the fuzzy edges of what any man might become turn hard and clear, the age of so many entry-level criminals of the early Italian criminal societies, the soldiers of the Black Hand, or the Picciotteria. Rocco may not have been a soldier, but he came of age in the same culture, one that saw government authority as antagonistic and something to be subverted, one that viewed poverty as a vile condition to be escaped by any means, and one that existed on the fringes of its adopted economy, barred from the established doors to success.

And in Cobalt, a ruthless, frontier mentality prevailed. It was similar to the conditions found at the time in certain larger centres, like Chicago, where a rapacious energy, combined with unreliable policing, made the criminal option more viable, especially in the mind of a young man predisposed. More than fifty years later, sociologists studying the phenomenon of Italian emigration and crime would note that nothing like the Black Hand, or other money-oriented criminal practices, managed to take hold in Brazil or Argentina, despite the large number of Italian immigrants in those countries. In Latin America, where the populace wasn't so driven by the pursuit of wealth, it was anarchism—another form of authority subversion—that came to be attributed to Italian immigrants. But in North America, and in Cobalt, money was the common goal. Money was the only reason for Cobalt to exist.

Drawn by that money, and by the number of Italian immigrants working in Cobalt, the Black Hand was active there too. In 1909 the leader of the local gang was convicted of murdering a man in nearby Haileybury, and they were involved in other scenes of violence. Had Rocco fallen in with this gang? It's possible. A telling bit of evidence exists that indicates he was now, at the very least, connected to the underworld: On June 18, 1911, when Rocco was twenty-three and living in Cobalt, he wrote a letter to a man in Toronto named Frank Griro.

A few inches taller than Rocco, Griro was a bit of a dandy, a wide-jawed twenty-five-year-old who often stepped out wearing a tall Christys' hat, a blue serge suit and tan shoes. A barber by trade, sometimes going by the name of Rossaro, he had until recently run a restaurant and a lodging house at 172 York Street, in a section of shabby storefronts just south of the Ward, Toronto's immigrant slum. Renting beds out to newly arrived Italian men was an easy business, and there were ways to supplement that income. Griro was also said to be involved in what police and newspapers referred to as the "white slave trade," otherwise known as forced prostitution. French prostitutes were apparently his specialty. He was a cool character, not easily ruffled, and among his acquaintances were several members of the Camorra, including Joe Musolino, a sharp-featured, mustachioed crime boss who had come from Niagara Falls, New York, and set up his headquarters in a dark York Street restaurant.

Rocco had met Musolino too.

It was a Sunday in Cobalt when Rocco set himself to the task of writing his letter to Griro. He may have had help: the handwriting had a graceful flourish, very unlike the hard, crabbed hand of a young man with so little education, although it did contain mistakes in spelling and grammar, and used very little punctuation. At the time, "Italian" was more a collection of regional dialects than a universal language. Rocco knew his own Calabrian dialect, and for this letter he may have had the help of a public scribe or of a friend who was less familiar with it. Or perhaps a kind of code was being used. Either way there were some oddities that made translation difficult. But with a minimum of punctuation added, the letter read in part:

> *Dear Friend,*
>
> *I come to you with this letter of mine and with it I tell you that I am enjoying good health and I hope this present letter finds you this way as well.*
>
> *And now dear Franco I would like to ask a favour from you. That you find Musolino or else Sam the Sicilian, because they know which house I have placed my [fornitura] which I must pay for. I would like you to please go there and pay. That I will be coming in at the beginning of next month and I will pay you everything. If not, the owner of the house will then sell it all and I will lose it. Do not give him the load.*

Dear Franco, the number is 77 Elm Street under the base-
ment. I do not have more. Do let me know if my cousin Andrea
is in Toronto. I do not have more. Lina sends you her regards
and I, and I am your friend.

Rocco Perri
Cobalt, Box 586

Then, in a less neat, perhaps hasty addition, Rocco's letter closed with a cryptic warning: "If a letter comes that will say that you are sending the stuff don't send it because someone has stolen my letters and knows every address and he will run away."

What did it all mean? The cousin Rocco referred to was apparently Andrea Catanzariti, whose mother, Rosa, was the sister of Rocco's mother, Elisabetta. The salute from Lina suggests she may have been the one helping Rocco to write the letter, which would explain its feminine touch.

But what *fornitura* at 77 Elm Street did Rocco hope to save? The police who originally found this letter translated *fornitura* as "furniture." But *fornitura* can mean "supplies" or "goods." Perhaps it was silver; in mining towns like Cobalt, "high-grading"—the systematic thievery of small amounts of ore by miners—was a frequent problem. Griro had already been arrested at least once for dealing in stolen goods; it's possible that Rocco had become part of a silver-smuggling ring, and that Griro was his Toronto connection. Or maybe Rocco was storing a supply of something he planned to bring into Cobalt to sell.

Whatever prompted Rocco to send his letter, it stands as proof of his early connection to the underworld, and it might never have been found if not for a sensational event. Just weeks after Griro received this letter from Rocco, Toronto police discovered it as part of a search of Griro's lodgings and of several nearby York Street addresses. The police were there because on the afternoon of Sunday, July 30, 1911, at the corner of Church and Front streets, Frank Griro murdered a man.

For months Griro had been hounded by two expensively dressed York Street extortionists, brothers Frank and Salvatore Sciarrone, who were members of a Camorra gang run by Joe Musolino. They operated in the traditional way, demanding money from the Italians they threatened and, in the words of a *Globe* report, "keeping two-thirds of the Italian colony in the central part of the city in a state of terror."

First Salvatore, then Frank Sciarrone pressured Griro for regular payments—five or ten dollars at a time—until Griro chose not to be terrorized any longer. He bought a .38 calibre Iver Johnson revolver and, when the opportunity arose on that Sunday afternoon, fired two bullets into Frank Sciarrone at close range.

The details emerged in an elaborate, twenty-seven-page confession that Griro gave to Toronto police late on the night of August 10, as he sat illuminated by the electric lamps that had recently been installed in city hall. "I will tell you big story," he began. During Griro's subsequent trial for murder, the court found itself quite impressed by his tale, and his talk of underworld Italian societies right in Toronto's midst. Despite the Crown calling several Italian immigrants to the box to dispute the local presence of anything like the Black Hand, or the Mafia, the jury declared Griro not guilty. Before sending him on his way, the judge briefly admonished him. "Don't be imposed upon by people who tell you that they belong to 'Black Hand' societies," he said. "These people only talk of them to frighten you."

Griro knew better, of course. And, now that he was associating with the likes of Joe Musolino, so did the twenty-three-year-old Rocco.

4

PERSUASIONE

Persuasion

A TIDE OF HUMANITY FLOWED WEST. IT WAS A SPECTACLE so remarkable that reporters came to watch.

On one evening alone, the evening of March 15, 1911, nearly two thousand people arrived in Toronto by train, from eastern Canada and from the United States, on their way to Winnipeg and beyond. Representatives of the Salvation Army and other agencies were there to meet and advise them as best they could. The settlers learned, among other things, that it was too early in the season to begin homesteading, but that for the time being they could probably find jobs as farm hands and labourers. As they were growing in earnest, western cities were laying out for improvements. With about twenty thousand citizens, Moose Jaw may have been small compared to Regina or Saskatoon, but the previous year it had spent $1 million on new structures, including an impressive new Land Titles Building, and this year that number was set to more than double. On top of that, it had put down over a mile of creosoted wood pavement to smooth the passage of its incoming wagons and built almost twenty-five miles of sidewalks.

About two weeks after that throng of passengers descended on Toronto, Frank Zanetti and his little family began their own trek west, heading north from Springfield to Montreal, then passing through Toronto, riding the edge of the Canadian Shield over the crown of Lake Superior, and finally plying the wide ocean of prairie to Saskatchewan. In early April, they unloaded their belongings on the front step of a town that had been through a terrible winter. In January it had taken a wagon team three days to travel sixty-five miles through hard drifts to bring supplies to Moose Jaw, which had been cut off for more than two weeks. Along the way they came upon a man trying to transport the body of his dead wife, who had been at the thirty-two-mile journey from their homestead for five miserable days. Another man, whose horse could not make it through the snow, had carried a sack of flour six miles on foot.

Frank Zanetti put his father-in-law's horse-handling lessons to use immediately, getting a job as a ranch hand on the property of John Paulson. He spent whatever time he could spare looking for a suitable parcel of land, and by November, he thought he'd found it—a 160-acre square of rolling prairie about twenty miles south-west of Moose Jaw in the community of Hillsborough. It lay just north of what is now Old Wives Lake, the largest natural lake in southern Saskatchewan. Johnstone Lake it was called then, named for Sir Frederick Johnstone, a baronet who'd passed through on his way to the Rockies as a young big-game hunter fifty years before. It was salty, shallow and fed by rain and runoff. After Frank and Grace established a claim on their undulating acreage in November 1911, the lake lay like a promise on the southern horizon, growing and shrinking in size according to the season, sometimes shimmering blue, sometimes a mud flat that attracted shore birds.

With the help of other Italians lured west by Ernesto Cotti, Zanetti built a makeshift home on this land, from sod or logs, and he and Grace and little Rena stayed there through what must have been the most difficult winter of their lives. In the spring they planted a garden as they saw others doing. And on June 18, 1912, Zanetti arrived at the large red-brick-and-white-stone land titles office on Fairford Street, entered between the Doric columns that flanked its front door, and applied for a land grant. In the application he declared himself a citizen of the United States, a family man with a wife and a child.

As he would do with everything in his life, Zanetti went at the task of homesteading with great earnestness. That first summer he bought or borrowed the necessary equipment and horses, got help from a few of his neighbours, and broke ten acres of land, cutting into the grassy earth and turning it over in slabs. It was the hardest work he'd ever undertaken. That fall he used the money he'd earned ranching to buy a horse from a neighbouring rancher named Thomas Linton, along with the lumber needed to build an actual ten-by-twelve-foot house, a stable and a well. Thomas Linton must have been impressed with Zanetti's efforts because the following spring he hired Zanetti to work on his ranch.

The next summer Zanetti broke another fifteen acres and planted all twenty-five. Gradually he became comfortable with the climate and adept at the usual transactions of farming. He traded his horse to another Italian colonist, Marco Ferrard, for a brown gelding. Then he traded the gelding and an extra twenty-five dollars to another farmer for two smaller geldings. Soon after that, through a series of trades, he parlayed one of these horses and a saddle into a "green" horse (which he let roam on open pasture) and a two-year-old bay gelding, as well as a bridle and a pair of green chaps. Eventually, while he was working for rancher Thomas McRae, Zanetti sold the bay for $105.

To his fellow Italian colonists, and to the ranchers who were coming to know and like him, it looked as though Frank Zanetti was setting himself up for a good, productive life on the prairies. But it wasn't to be.

|||||||||||||||||||||||||||||||||||

ROCCO WAS WELL INTO IT NOW.

About fifty miles northeast of Cobalt sat the town of Elk Lake, straddling the long, thin body of water for which it was named. In the winter of 1911–1912, the town was caught up in the same silver fever that gripped Cobalt, and there was a large pulpwood depot there too—more than enough activity to keep six large hotels busy and to attract the interest of investors and others.

A Toronto man known as D. A. G. Glionna—the *D* stood for Donato—owned a house in Elk Lake. At the time, the Glionnas were the leading family of Toronto's Italian community. Over the previous summer, one young Glionna had been honoured as the first Italian in the province to become a doctor. As for Donato, he had been elected the first president of the Umberto Primo Benevolent Society, an organization dedicated to supporting and advancing the cause of the city's Italian immigrants. More than once, Donato had spoken out against Italians being refused work or about the loss of the only Italian-owned hotel licence in the Ward (that Italian owner being, in fact, another Glionna). Meanwhile Donato's father, Francesco, who had started as a carpenter, was not only one of the city's oldest Italian residents, he was also one of the wealthiest, owning a number of houses and lots across the city. Some of the houses were on Chestnut and Agnes streets, in the heart of the Ward. And a few could be found on Elm Street, just a few doors from where Rocco kept his *fornitura*. For all these reasons, the Glionnas were prime targets for extortion.

In January of 1912, Rocco was living about ninety miles south of Cobalt in North Bay, a town with a significant Italian population. By now, things were starting to click for him. He'd just turned twenty-four, and he'd been in North America nearly eight years. He was getting the hang of spoken English, although he couldn't yet write it. He had a bit of money and he liked to spend it—some of it on sharp clothes, including a brown pinstripe suit that he wore with a black peaked cap and leather boots, and some of it on his friends.

Rocco was comfortable around violent, dangerous men. He wasn't one of them, but he knew how to talk to them, and he wasn't against loaning them some cash when they needed it, or giving them a hand in other ways. He was coming to understand that the power imbalance those gestures created was useful to him.

He'd come to know a dangerous hood named Camillo Tuzoni, who used the alias Alfredo Cotellesso (which became "Fred Coteless" in Ontario police reports). That winter in North Bay, Tuzoni was out of work and living with Rocco. One night the two men were drinking. Rocco didn't drink much himself, preferring to keep a clear head, but Tuzoni was knocking them back. Rocco chose that moment to raise the subject of fifty dollars that Tuzoni owed him. In his current straits, Tuzoni had no way to pay the money back, which of course Rocco knew. But he told Tuzoni that he'd forgive the entire debt if Tuzoni would do him a small favour. He wanted Donato Glionna's Elk Lake house burned down.

It was an early example of something Rocco would do the rest of his career. He was beginning to think bigger than other young criminals, so if there was a crime to commit, he employed others to do it for him. From a legal sense, it was smart, putting a layer of separation between himself and the crime he wanted committed. From a business sense, it was more efficient. It expanded the possibilities of what could be done.

In this case, Rocco's Toronto associates were probably attempting to extort Glionna. When he resisted, he needed to be sent a message. Better to burn down a house in a remote town than in Toronto where there was a greater chance of getting caught. Rocco wasn't going to do it himself, so he enlisted Tuzoni. He told him that if wouldn't do this for him, this small favour, he would be turned out in the middle of a northern Ontario winter "with no funds and no friends to go to."

That was Tuzoni's version—threats weren't really Rocco's style—but either way, Tuzoni agreed. The two of them made it up to Elk Lake, where Rocco supplied Tuzoni with gasoline and candles. Rocco then returned to North Bay, ensuring that he was far from the scene when his man carried out the plan. When the time came, Tuzoni rigged the house, and it exploded into flames about two hours after he lit the match.

But in the wake of the fire, the local police managed to track Tuzoni down. On February 5, while he was locked up, he scribbled a few words in Italian on some scraps of paper and handed them to police, asking for a telegram to be sent to "Rocco Perro" in North Bay. Translated, it read in part: "I have been arrested. Tell me what to do."

One thing Rocco would have told him was not to use anything like his real name in a message sent from prison. Rocco had an alias—Giuseppe (Joe) Portolesi—for such occasions. When he got Tuzoni's telegram he lit out, and by the time the police came looking for him in North Bay he was long gone. Tuzoni did manage to stick to proper criminal procedure during the trial, keeping his mouth shut against his solicitor's earnest advice to tell everything he knew. So he took the fall. On February 16, 1912, he was sentenced to ten years in Kingston Penitentiary.

It wasn't until three months after the trial that Tuzoni decided he'd gotten a raw deal and confessed that the whole thing had been Rocco's idea. He spelled his name correctly too. The prison scribe who took down Tuzoni's words wrote: "If any information against said Rocco Perri, will facilitate matters in regards to a commutation of sentence or giving said Perri his just deserts, he is willing to do anything to further justice."

But it was too late. Amid the inquiries between police departments, which reached as high as the chief commissioner of police in Ottawa, someone thought it likely that Rocco had gone south to Toronto. But Toronto was a big city. There was no telling where he might be.

THE "Ward" was a contraction. Its original name was St. John's Ward, and it was largely the property of Thornton Blackburn, an escaped slave from Louisville, Kentucky, who had found work and made his fortune in Toronto in the 1830s and '40s. A 142-acre zone bordered by College and Queen streets to the north and south, and University Avenue and Yonge Street, west and east, the Ward became a landing place for waves of the dispossessed. It was here in the 1850s that Blackburn provided affordable shelter to other fugitive slaves. A few decades later, the residents were mostly Jews escaping the brutal pogroms in eastern Europe. Gradually they were joined by new arrivals from Italy, Poland, Germany and elsewhere, factory workers and shopkeepers who became easy marks for unscrupulous landlords who took advantage of their unfamiliarity with English or with local standards.

The more time passed, the denser the population in the Ward became, and the worse conditions got. Lodging houses without proper plumbing or sources of water packed in as many as thirty men, six or more to a dark, windowless room, and charged them each exorbitant rents of about a dollar a week. Alleys and laneways became heaped with rubbish. Human waste would be tossed by the bucket into reeking backyards. Daylight could be seen through roofs and plaster. Inside walls ran wet when it rained. Cellars grew dank and flooded. Flies swarmed markets and kitchens, and vermin prowled the edges. The worse conditions got, the more Edwardian Toronto averted its gaze. That attitude allowed crime bosses such as Joe Musolino and Totto Galliardo, a Sicilian, to exert extraordinary influence in and around the Ward.

In the early summer of 1911, around the time a certain letter sent from Cobalt arrived at an address on York Street, inspectors from Toronto's health department roamed through the entire district with clipboards and pencils, taking notes. When they brought their findings to the city's medical health officer, Dr. Charles Hastings, he was forced to make public some shocking news: Toronto's immigrant slum was as bad as any in North America. In July he declared 108 houses in the Ward to be unfit for human habitation. And he implored the good citizens of Toronto to turn away from the complacency of their well-appointed lives and bear witness to the "unpleasant details of the life and sorrows of the lower classes."

Hastings made it clear that much of the blame for the "disgusting hovels" in which too many lived belonged with any landlord who charged too much and provided too little, "simply because he is dealing with a foreigner who is not familiar with conditions and who is entirely at his mercy." And he quoted Chicago physician George Frank Lydston in declaring where all of this would lead: "It is not surprising that an endless stream of thieves, murderers, prostitutes, lunatics, epileptics and hospital patients issue from such recruiting stations as the city slums . . . Here is the very fountain head of the river of vice and crime."

One could hear, in the report and in the subsequent press coverage, the pinched nose of Protestant disapprobation at the practices of the "foreign element." The *Toronto Daily Star* sent a reporter to view the disaster for himself, and after just a block and a half he had seen enough. "House after house is kept in a deplorably dirty state," he wrote. "There is practically no personal tidiness among the inhabitants. The men and women are slovenly in the extreme. The children in summer wear practically no clothes at all." Occasionally, it was possible to come across a stylishly dressed or attractive girl, the reporter admitted, but they were the exceptions. "The majority of the young women take no pains to dress neatly."

And yet life and love unfolded within these blighted streets. During their fact-finding tour, which cost the city eight hundred dollars, Toronto's health inspectors visited the homes of 2,051 families. One would have been at 63 Chestnut Street, where Harry Toben and his young wife, Besha, lived with their two small daughters.

Like four-fifths of the residents in the Ward, they were Jews from eastern Europe. Harry, who delivered bread for a local bakery, had come from Russia. Besha, whose name became Bessie in Toronto, had arrived from the Polish region of Russia with her parents, Sam and Gello Starkman, and four siblings. The two young immigrants had met and fallen in love in the Ward. And on December 15, 1907, when Harry was twenty-three and Bessie was just eighteen, they'd been married by Rabbi M. H. Levy.

But theirs was a hard life in a miserable setting, and after a few years it seemed a life unlikely to realize the dreams of a bright-eyed, intelligent young woman who prized the sorts of stylish hats and dresses that might win even a newspaper reporter's approval. Harry's job handling the reins of a bakery wagon paid almost nothing, and he had no prospects for anything better. With two young daughters to care for—Gertie, born in August 1908, and Lily, born in January 1911—the Tobens needed every bit of extra money they could find, so they took in boarders, such as Samuel Menkin, who had a small barbershop next door.

And then one day in 1912, Rocco Perri, needing a place to lay low after his Elk Lake adventure, arrived in the Ward looking for work and a room to rent.

Perhaps Bessie walked by him one day on her way to a shop. It seems that shortly after arriving, Rocco found a temporary job among the teams of men laying streetcar tracks through the Ward. Perhaps he saw a pretty auburn-haired woman posting a notice about the room on Chestnut Street. When they met, there was something about Rocco that Bessie immediately liked. Of course he was young, like her, and not bad looking. But it was more than that. He was different somehow.

He wasn't a tall man, but he presented the confidence of one. He had a charming ease that separated him from the depressing surroundings—the dilapidated storefronts with their hand-painted signs in Hebrew, the horses clopping along muddy streets, the dirty children playing underfoot. When Bessie spoke, he looked directly into her eyes, with a gaze that was not dull and hard like that of so many men. And—this was such a refreshing change from her bread-wagon husband—he smiled.

Rocco smiled as if he liked the look of her, that much was clear. And as a mother of two and the wife of a man who took her for granted, Bessie must have enjoyed being seen that way. But there was more to this man's smile. It was if he knew something about her, that she was not defined by this hopeless place, that she was better than this small existence. It was a smile that told her life could be easy.

Bessie convinced her disappointing husband to rent Rocco a room. And after three months of watching this new boarder, and the way he moved through the world, of listening to him and getting close to him—and after three months of measuring the future he seemed destined for against the one her husband could give her—Bessie did the unthinkable. She left her husband and her two little children. She left the life she had known and the limitations that came with it. She gave herself to Rocco, and he took her gladly.

J ust as Frank Zanetti seemed to be getting the hang of being a prairie homesteader, two people entered his world who would, indirectly, change the course of his life. The first was an Irish immigrant named Patrick Henry Doyle, known to most as Paddy. The owner of a large ranch east of Zanetti's property, Doyle had once been a member of the North West Mounted Police. He'd left the force in 1895 after nine years but, in moments of leisure, he liked to reminisce. Zanetti listened intently as Doyle talked about his days in Regina wearing the red serge; about the time he was searching a CPR boxcar and found thirty-six bottles of illegal Irish whisky and forty gallons of ale hidden in barrels of sugar; about the day he stood guard as they put a rope around Louis Riel's neck.

The second person of influence was a man known to Frank as Doctor Feltas, who arrived in Moose Jaw in November of 1913. Immediately upon his appearance in the town, striking a handsome figure in a lumberman's red blanket coat, Feltas began giving classes in the sport of wrestling at the large YMCA gym. Of course, Frank Zanetti had loved wrestling from his days in Springfield. Since the season of farming work was over, there's every chance he took advantage of this opportunity, riding his favourite saddle horse the twenty cold miles into Moose Jaw to sweat it out on mats spread on the gym floor. He would have seen as well as anyone how admirable a fellow this Feltas was—tall, impressively shouldered and exceedingly friendly, to say nothing of his creditable skill in wrestling tights.

But Doctor Feltas was not the man he pretended to be. He was an undercover detective from Pinkerton's National Detective Agency, hired by city council to investigate the "rough element" in the city, as well as rumours of misbehaviour by the local police force. On the first day of January 1914, Zanetti learned the truth about the "Mysterious Dr. Feltas" and his "slick piece of detective work" the way almost everyone else did—from a story in the Moose Jaw *Evening News*.

The Pinkerton name was famous. Founded in Chicago by a bearded Scot named Allan Pinkerton, Pinkerton's—with its logo of an eye that never slept—had opened its first Canadian office in Montreal in 1899. It was known for its groundbreaking investigative techniques, such as identifying suspects through fingerprints and employing female undercover detectives. Crime writer Dashiell Hammett learned all about the methods of hard-nosed detectives by working as a Pinkerton's operative for seven years. The agency never revealed a detective's real name to a client, using only an "operative number" in reports, and by such careful practices it had built a sterling reputation for its work uncovering swindles in the banking industry. For all these reasons, Canadian officials frequently called in Pinkerton's to supplement the efforts of their undertrained local police forces.

When the Doctor Feltas story broke, readers of the *Evening News* learned that for the previous six weeks the detective—"a very gentlemanly and well-educated man"—had been investigating complaints against the police department, which included a failure to clamp down on various forms of immorality, from gambling and drinking to "houses of ill fame," the common term for brothels. He'd formed a special daily wrestling class for policemen in an attempt to win their trust and gain insight into their activities. And he'd managed to become drawn into the community. "His knowledge of the wrestling game led him to be chosen as the referee at a boxing bout and wrestling match," said the paper. And thanks to his skill at making friends he "was soon very popular."

Ultimately the local police magistrate who read the Pinkerton man's report described it as "made up entirely of hearsay" and therefore "worthless for any purpose." But still, something about the Feltas revelations resonated with Zanetti. For the last few years he himself had lived under a kind of assumed identity. Since coming to Canada, the people he met had never quite gotten his last name right. Maybe it had something to do with his signature—the way he crossed the *t*s on the way to dotting the *i* made a sort of *h* shape at the end of his name. People read Zanetti as Zaneth and called him so, replacing the man he had been with someone new, and he had never corrected them.

To learn now that a man he had known as "Doctor Feltas" was in fact someone entirely different, living a secret life was, for this Italian-turned-American-turned-Canadian homesteader, perhaps like pulling back the wizard's curtain to reveal something even more amazing. It made a profound impression on him, and he did not forget it.

The Feltas story stayed with him as he broke and planted fifteen more acres on his land—land that was proving to be miserable for farming—and applied to become a naturalized British subject (a status that was bestowed at the beginning of 1915). It stayed with him as he and his wife struggled to find happiness amid the inevitable hardships of the homesteader's existence, and as some of the men he knew (including Ernesto Cotti) went off to fight for Canada in the First World War and died.

It stayed with him for some three years in all, until Frank Zanetti arrived at a day when he could no longer face being a farmer. The day he decided that he needed a new direction in his life.

IIIIIIIIIIIIIIIIIIIIIIIIIIIII

IT's ROMANTIC TO IMAGINE THAT LOVE CAN ALTER A person's destiny, can cause a man, set on a certain path, to change his direction mid-stride. In the case of Rocco Perri, it might even have been true. For a while.

The first few years together were hard for Bessie and the short, charming Italian for whom she'd thrown everything away. They were hard, in part, because Rocco apparently tried to find legitimate work. In 1913 they put some distance between themselves and Toronto by travelling south to St. Catharines, Ontario. The Niagara region was booming with new industry, and Rocco hired onto the teams of largely immigrant labourers that were beginning to rebuild the Welland Canal.

There had been three previous versions of the Welland Canal, which created a narrow shipping path between lakes Erie and Ontario. It was the fourth version, cutting a deeper and more direct route, on which Rocco worked, for about twenty cents an hour. Maybe he saw it as part of the bargain, an attempt to bring respectability to an arrangement that reflected poorly on Bessie. Her own parents and siblings would have nothing to do with her. And the black-garbed Italian women she encountered were equally quick to shun her, as a woman who had abandoned her husband and children, and as a Jew.

But there was another factor that may have been even more

important, another reason Rocco may have wanted to try to make a legitimate life in Canada. In the fall of 1913, Bessie had become pregnant with their child.

Presented with something new and life-changing, a man leans on past experience. Rocco's own father, Giuseppe, had worked doggedly and honestly to provide for his large family. As quick as Rocco had been to reject that life, it was the only model he had of fatherhood. Whether or not it was Bessie's pregnancy that prompted Rocco's decision to leave Toronto and divert from the path he'd been on, it must have contributed to his willingness to submit, at least for a while, to a more law-abiding one.

The work in Welland was difficult and dangerous—on average, over the course of the twenty years spent building the fourth canal, one labourer was killed every two months—and its reward was poverty. People who knew Bessie and Rocco in those early days saw how difficult their lives were. They saw Rocco wearing pants and shoes until they were worn through. They saw Bessie dressed in tatters and going without food so that Rocco could eat enough to work. "That woman went through a lot for the man she loved," said a friend who knew Bessie then. The two were devoted to each other, but this was not the life either of them had hoped for.

They weren't alone in their deprivation. Many immigrants were shut out of the prosperity that seemed to flow readily to others in proximity to the Welland Canal. On the morning of May 15, 1914, a crowd of as many as two hundred unemployed workers marched to the city hall of what was then the joint municipality of Welland-Crowland. The group's leaders told the chief of police that without work they would starve. The *Welland Telegraph* decried the advertising in Europe that was luring workers to the region on the promise of plentiful canal jobs that either didn't exist or weren't being given to new immigrants. A reporter visited the "foreign section" of town and found that in one small house sixteen people "were living on biscuits and the little that neighbours had given them for two weeks. The men had not done a day's work since they came to Welland four months ago."

In the midst of this crisis, in May 1914, Bessie gave birth to a boy. No record of the child's birth exists, so it's possible she delivered him at home, with the help of the Italian women she'd come to know in St. Catharines. Rocco wanted him to have a name that reflected his heritage, a name that reached back into Italy's proud past, so they called him Anterico. Surrounded by shortage and uncertainty, living in poverty, Rocco and Bessie must in this moment have felt a mixture of joy and trepidation. Perhaps, at least briefly, they thought their sacrifices had been worthwhile.

With the beginning of war in Europe, the tension of unemployment and need in Welland only increased. Some plants expanded to take on the contracts to make shrapnel shells and the like, but during the war construction on the canal ceased. Jobs became scarcer than ever, so the "hordes of hungry foreigners" and "men wearing clothes hanging from them in shreds" remained a fixture. Rocco's own small family was surely among them.

Under the circumstances, it's hardly surprising that the whole Welland Canal and Niagara region—the strip of land suspended between the lakes, which included the towns of St. Catharines, Thorold, Welland, Merritton and Port Colborne, east to the Niagara River—became a hotbed of organized crime. One of its chief organizers was Filippo Mascato, the owner of a St. Catharines bakery, and it didn't take long for Rocco, proud young father in desperate need of money, to start working for him.

His job with Mascato didn't last long before Mascato, apparently sensing increasing police interest in his activities, left St. Catharines and returned to Italy. But while it did, Rocco made contacts that would prove useful in the years ahead. Among those he met was a southern Italian named Germo (Jimmy) Celona, a violent extortionist who lived near St. Catharines with his wife, father and two brothers. Rocco had a way of handling Celona's temper, and in those days Celona's wife may have been one of Bessie's few friends. Come the fall, she needed a friend. She and Rocco both did.

The first sign of trouble came on September 24, a Thursday. Anterico, now almost five months old, began fussing more than usual and didn't want food. The next day he was worse. He had diarrhea and seemed to be in pain, and when Bessie felt his head it was warm to the touch. She was getting worried. In the conditions that existed among the immigrant population of the Welland Canal region in 1914, infants were vulnerable to sickness, and they didn't always get better. Already that year in St. Catharines, at least forty-six children under the age of three had died.

Bessie and Rocco took Anterico to a doctor, and soon he was admitted to St Catharines General and Marine Hospital. It was a good hospital, the site of Canada's first nursing school forty years earlier. Their doctor was J. G. Harkness, who diagnosed the boy with gastroenteritis, an infection of the intestines. He told them he would do all he could.

But the child didn't improve. Over the next few days he turned pale. With his diarrhea and unwillingness to eat, he became dehydrated. At the time, the only procedure for introducing fluids into a dehydrated patient was a Murphy drip, which involved infusing fluids via the rectum, but this child's intestines were inflamed.

As he became more dehydrated, Anterico's eyes took on a sunken look. He was becoming less responsive. Dr. Harkness pressed a stethoscope to the boy's chest and heard his heart racing, his breathing becoming quick and shallow. He would have told Rocco and Bessie those were very bad signs. Finally, on Sunday,

October 4, after ten days of illness, little Anterico stopped breathing and died.

Perhaps it was about then that Rocco and Bessie knew for certain they weren't destined to have an ordinary kind of happiness. Perhaps it was then, or not long afterward, that they began to nurture other aspirations. Bessie was ambitious enough to decide that if she couldn't have a child with Rocco, she would try to have everything else. And twenty-six-year-old Rocco, who had ambitions of his own, now had the added incentive of making Bessie happy.

The path they chose out of their sorrow and impoverishment would lead to one of the great ironies of Rocco Perri's life. In the years to come, Rocco would become so wealthy that at one memorable moment he would hold a fistful of diamonds in his hand. The irony is that he would do it on the most sorrowful night of his life.

They couldn't know that at the time, of course. At the time, all they wanted was a place to begin.

5

MERCE
Commodity

HAMILTON, ONTARIO, WAS BUILT TO MAKE MONEY. Located at the southwestern end of Lake Ontario, it was never a strategic military or cultural outpost, which could have been said of the very British York (which became Toronto). It wasn't an expression of political or religious will, like many cities and towns in the United States. From the beginning, in the words of historian John C. Weaver, Hamilton was "an emphatically commercial centre."

Its existence was a land developer's idea. The townsite largely comprised property bought up by George Hamilton—a man of ample beard and elegant top hat—in an effort to restore his family's fortunes. His Scottish father, Robert, had acquired riches and more than a hundred thousand acres of land as a supplier to Loyalist settlements and troops in the late 1700s, and this wealth had passed to George upon Robert's death in 1809. But in 1814, as a result of one of the many battles in the Niagara region that persisted through the three years of the War of 1812, much of the Hamilton property went up in flames. Not one to be discouraged, clever George had a brainstorm.

He'd heard about plans in Upper Canada's legislative assembly to set up a judicial centre in the geographically unique region west of Burlington Bay. There were beautiful hills and ravines there, and the Niagara Escarpment, just to the south, did a rather effective job of gathering the streams of the region and directing them toward the bay. Beautiful land, rushing streams plus a shipping-friendly harbour—it seemed like a good place to set up a new official district. George Hamilton bought up the most promising parcel of land. Along with Nathaniel Hughson, who owned an adjacent parcel to the north, he worked to get a courthouse and a jail located in the middle of the region to create the "judicial centre" everyone wanted and thereby boost property values. Then he drew up a plan with blocks of fifty-foot lots facing a grid of streets and began selling them off. That made Hamilton, according to Weaver, "the first speculative townsite to evolve into a major Canadian city."

It was a rough and masculine city, with 20 percent more men than women, and its economy was craze-oriented. In the 1820s and '30s, it was the steamboat craze that drove Hamilton. Briefly it was real estate. By the middle of the century, railroads had become the rage. The city bought stock in the Great Western Railway, which linked Hamilton with Windsor and Sarnia to the west and Niagara Falls to the east. This rail network far surpassed anything in New York State, and as construction and city-building increased in the Great Lakes region, cities such as Rochester and Buffalo shipped their materials through Hamilton, which became a major centre for the boom (and for pickpockets, who liked to work the trains). By 1854 the city's population had reached some ten thousand but swelled further with immigrant labourers. Isabella Lucy Bird, a British travel writer who knew North America well, wrote, "It is, I think, the most bustling place in Canada . . . Every external feature seems to be acquiring fresh and rapid development. People hurry about as if their lives depended on their speed." She concluded that Hamilton was "a very Americanized place."

By the 1870s Hamilton had earned the label the "Ambitious City." It was a hive of industry. Much of what had been a robust local business in banking and insurance moved to Toronto— although the Bank of Hamilton still had a presence, with eighty offices west of Ontario—so Hamilton began to concentrate on making things. It was largely geography that pointed it toward iron and steel. Pennsylvania and West Virginia to the south provided metallurgical coal while the Lake Superior region offered iron ore. And Hamilton was surrounded, in Ontario and New York State, by growing cities that needed building supplies. As the city evolved, it became attractive to immigrants with metalworking skills. The city became renowned for its stove foundries. It adopted new steel-making processes, such as the open-hearth technique, which slowly melted iron and scrap metal together and made it possible to control quality like never before. It made sewing machines and farm implements, shipped off orders of ten thousand kegs of nails and screws. From 1905 to 1910, the number of people employed in manufacturing rose by 67 percent. International Harvester was responsible for a lot of this, choosing Hamilton for its rail connections, its steel companies, its access to cheap hydroelectricity from Cataract Power (less costly than the thermal electricity produced in Toronto) and its waterfront.

Hamilton's march toward its manufacturing destiny didn't come without trouble. With the rise of factories came the rise of unions. It was in Hamilton, in 1872, that James Ryan organized Canada's first regional labour federation and campaigned for a nine-hour workday. By the turn of the century, relations between workers and owners had become fractious. The most violent confrontations came in November 1906, during a three-and-a-half-week strike by tram operators for the Hamilton Street Railway Company, who wanted the same twenty-two cents an hour their counterparts in Toronto were making. After days of rock throwing and window smashing progressed to toppling streetcars and dynamiting tracks, the city's mayor asked the government to send troops. On Saturday, November 24, Hamilton's sheriff stood on the steps of city hall and officially read the two-sentence Riot Act, ordering the crowd of three thousand people "to disperse and peaceably to depart." When they didn't, maybe because they couldn't hear him, the chief of police unleashed the police and soldiers. Wave after wave, on foot and on horseback, came at the mob with nightsticks and rifle butts, until a hundred people, men and women, lay bleeding on the ground.

The hair of Hamilton's boom was hardly ruffled by this breeze. As a transportation conduit and a manufacturer of materials, Hamilton had tied its industrial expansion to the economic activity in other parts of North America. When these regions expanded, so did Hamilton. Between 1910 and 1913, over thirty new factories opened in the city. In 1914 the first electric streetlights were installed. The following spring, after a brief lull, the industry of war fuelled another boom. Carriage and automobile traffic increased between Hamilton and Toronto, prompting the construction of Canada's first concrete highway, one of the longest between two cities anywhere in the world. By the end of 1915, the number of men employed in foundries and machine shops had jumped nearly 50 percent, and jobs in the iron and steel trades had more than doubled. With the influx of people (Hamilton's population rose from seventy thousand in 1910 to one hundred thousand in 1914), the cost of renting a home increased significantly, but a greater percentage of people owned the homes in which they lived.

As usual, however, immigrants, particularly Italians, found this prosperity hard to grasp. By some estimates, the number of Italians in Hamilton tripled between 1911 and the start of the First World War, to about five thousand, giving them, considering the population, a far greater presence in Hamilton than in Toronto. But they were often shut out of the systems and institutions that British subjects took for granted. Many lived in crowded boarding houses in the northeastern section of the city, closer to the waterfront, where smoke spewed incessantly from factories. City directories that carefully recorded the names and addresses of English speakers often listed immigrants anonymously under the words "Foreigner" or "Italian." In 1913, it became a kind of game among the worst of men to ride the electric streetcars that intersected Hamilton and spit tobacco juice at the Italians digging the rail line trenches.

And the same pressures that produced crime within the Italian communities of other cities worked similar sorcery in Hamilton. For three years, beginning in 1906—in what may have been the first appearance of the Black Hand in Canada—a wealthy Italian fruit dealer named Salvatore Sanzone was hounded by a gang led by John Taglierino. Four gang members including Taglierino were arrested and, over the course of several months, tried for sending Sanzone letters extorting one thousand dollars. By the end of December, 1909, three of the gang had been sentenced to ten years in prison, but Taglierino had been acquitted and released.

Other sorts of crime also flourished. Being an industrial city with a rapidly expanding population, Hamilton was home to a large number of single men. Between 1910 and 1915, crimes of immorality spiked dramatically. Prostitution became an especially intractable problem as "disorderly houses" and "houses of ill fame" proliferated. In 1910 a female detective recently assigned to the city said, "There is more white slave trafficking in Hamilton than in any other city of its size in the whole of America—not Canada, but America."

It was to this city, rife with criminal opportunity and infrastructure, that Rocco and Bessie moved in 1915. They'd managed to scrape together a little money and wanted to buy a house. Recent innovations in banking had made it possible for some people to buy on installments, and perhaps they had just enough for a down payment. But it wasn't that simple.

By now economic and social status in Hamilton was clearly defined along geographical lines. The barristers and doctors and long-established merchants of the city bought in the southern and more westerly sections. Wealthy people were backing away as far as possible from the factories near the waterfront. The farther south one went, the closer one got to the steep, treed slopes of the escarpment—commonly called The Mountain—the grander the houses became.

People of Rocco and Bessie's low status had to make do with the more humble homes north of the east-west conduit of King Street, where the atmosphere was noisier, the air sootier, and the population density far greater. Still, it was a time when many immigrants found it hard or impossible to buy a house even here, even if they had the money. Anti-immigrant prejudice permeated the city. In at least one instance it was even made official; the rules regarding a planned community in the most westerly part of the city refused sales to "Negroes, Asiatics, Bulgarians, Austrians, Russians, Serbs, Rumanians, Turks, Armenians . . . or foreign-born Italians, Greeks or Jews."

Nevertheless, Rocco and Bessie managed to find a small wood-frame house at 157 Caroline Street North, on the west side of the street, between Mill and Harriet. That placed it just two blocks from the Hess Street Synagogue, which pleased Bessie, and about three blocks below the main railway station. They were able to buy the house by putting it in Bessie's name.

Rocco was finally done with hard manual labour. He was officially in the food business now, no doubt having learned the trade from baker Filippo Mascato in St. Catharines. In the first floor of the house he maintained a store, while he and Bessie lived in an apartment upstairs. It's said that near the house on Caroline he rented warehouse space for the foodstuffs he sold, including dried pasta and olive oil, and fresh produce, which he also sold at Hamilton's large farmers' market, just a few blocks away.

But of course, this was almost entirely for show. Rocco hadn't crossed the ocean to be a fruit peddler. Running a little store in a poor neighbourhood was never going to meet Bessie's requirements for happiness, nor did it take advantage of the opportunities Hamilton presented. The Perris, Rocco and Bessie, had other businesses in mind.

‖‖‖‖‖‖‖‖‖‖‖‖‖‖‖‖‖‖‖‖

SCRABBLING IN THE DIRT TO MAKE A PALTRY CROP grow, striving in primitive, makeshift surroundings for something more than bare, mean subsistence—the loneliness and hardship of a homesteader's life could shake the hope from anyone. It definitely took its toll on a naïve young couple from Springfield. In fact, it pushed Grace Russell Zanetti toward despair, until finally she faced the bleak certainty of her future on that plot of land outside Moose Jaw and rebelled. She bundled up four-year-old Rena and fled, leaving Frank to his horses and his few plowed acres. Mother and daughter returned to Springfield to live with the Russell family, and in early February of 1915, amid the endless drift of a Saskatchewan winter, Frank Zanetti sued for divorce from his wife on the grounds of desertion. It was granted by the decree of Judge William Hamilton of Springfield on February 17.

Frank didn't leave immediately. He'd waited a long time for the land he'd claimed to become officially his, and he was determined to wait even longer. It wasn't until a year later, on March 11, 1916, that he was finally granted the patent on his homestead. Two months later he signed for a three-hundred-dollar mortgage, at an annual interest rate of 10 percent, and officially acquired the title to the land on August 9.

But by then he was just going through the motions. Three months after acquiring the title to his land, Frank sold it. On November 10, 1916, he transferred the ownership of his 160 acres to a farmer named Richard Wilson, "in consideration of the sum of one dollar." As he was now a man of no address, he identified himself as a farmer of Valjean, which was the location of a nearby post office. And he swore to three things on the transfer document, the first two quite standard and typeset: (1) that he was the transferor named in the document; (2) that the value of the land and its buildings and improvements was $1,600 (a figure often used). The last, rather tragic oath was handwritten beneath the first two: (3) "That I have no wife."

On the day he declared himself alone, Frank signed the transfer document "Frank Zanetti," and returned, broke and somewhat broken, to his Italian family in Springfield. He spent most of the next year at 128 Easter Avenue, recovering his sense of self and considering his options. He was a failed farmer and a failed husband; he needed a way to redefine himself. As he brooded, he found himself unable to shake the feeling inspired in him by the stories old Paddy Doyle had told, and by the revelation of a man hired to live as someone else. The more he thought about that, and about the possibility of shaking off what he had become and starting a completely different kind of life, the more convinced he became of what he had to do.

So on September 28, 1917, twenty-six-year-old Frank Zanetti sat down with a piece of lined paper, picked up a fountain pen and composed a short letter to the Royal North West Mounted Police. "As I would like to be a member of the R.N.W.M.P. of Canada," he wrote, trying so very hard to sound like the Canadian men he'd gotten to know, "I whish you would be so kind to answer me, givin' full particulars." He signed it with a version of his name that he thought would sound—not Italian: Frank W. Zeneth.

About a week later, an application form arrived in the mail, along with instructions to go to a doctor and get a full physical assessment, which he did immediately. But he was worried. There was one particular stipulation in the form he was not sure he could meet: that he stand at a height of at least five feet, eight inches. Apparently only tall men could be Mounties. And in the doctor's office, try as he might, Frank could not force his body to reach higher than five feet, seven and a half inches in his socks.

He was crushed. "I felt very bad, and I was ready to give it up," he later admitted. But his doctor, who may already have nudged the measurement higher for Frank's benefit (a subsequent doctor put Zanetti's height at just five feet seven inches), talked him into applying anyway. So on October 17, when Zanetti wrote back to the force's Regina headquarters with the results, he declared his height to be his only fault, and then stretched the rest of himself to compensate. "I am Italian by birth, British subject, and I can speak three languages including some French," he wrote. "I have had five years experience in the ranch near Moose Jaw, Sask, I can ride very good, used of the climate, and well acquainted with the country." He then declared himself to be two years older than his actual age, as he had ever since the day of his marriage, and also that he was a single man. In addition, he said he'd "never had a drop of liquir in all my life, and I can furnish the best of refferences." He signed it "Frank. W. Zanetti," with that curious and confusing way of crossing the double *t*s.

When those references were asked—all of them ranchers Zanetti had worked for—they each wrote that "Frank W. Zaneth" was surely one of the brightest, most honest and reliable men they knew. Said Thomas Linton, "I consider him an exceptionally good man."

With that, the RNWMP command said never mind about the height. As it happened, the force had a place for a short, bright man who knew more than one language and didn't look like a Mountie. In fact, although they didn't tell him this, they had something in mind for the Italian from Moose Jaw that was very much along the lines of that Pinkerton's agent he so admired.

And so, "Frank Zaneth" was in.

⦙⦙⦙⦙⦙⦙⦙⦙⦙⦙⦙⦙⦙⦙⦙⦙⦙⦙⦙⦙⦙⦙⦙⦙⦙⦙

YOU COULD MAKE A LOT OF MONEY IN THE PROSTITUTION business. As early as 1908, a Chicago brothel run by an infamous Parisian couple, Alphonse and Eva Dufour, was generating income of about eight thousand dollars a month— $723 a month from one young woman alone. By 1916, when Rocco and Bessie were running a small brothel out of their store on Caroline Street, the monthly per-prostitute take could well have been up to a thousand dollars. Employing just two women, they could easily have been grossing twenty-four thousand dollars a year. Compared to the average wage for a Hamilton worker of roughly six hundred a year, Rocco and Bessie were setting themselves up for the big time.

That wasn't all; they were branching out into gambling too. It probably started as a simple numbers racket. The numbers game was an illegal early form of lottery betting. Started centuries ago in Italy, it was popular among the poor because its floor of entry was low—a player could bet as little as a nickel—and the payout was big, usually six hundred times the original bet. It was mostly a big-city game, and every city had its own version. In some American cities it was called the "policy" racket or game, for its ironic similarity to insurance (money paid now for possible future benefit), and newspapers in the late 1800s occasionally reported the arrest of a local "policy dealer." New York City's Giosue Gallucci, a short, mustachioed Neapolitan who was allied with the Camorra, had used his numbers racket and his political savvy to become the most powerful man in Italian Harlem, until he was gunned down in 1915 as part of the Mafia–Camorra War.

From running numbers it was a short step to taking bets on horses. In the early part of the century, the region around Hamilton and Toronto was notorious for its betting action. In 1923, a young reporter named Ernest Hemingway investigated the local gambling underworld for the *Star Weekly* and learned that ten thousand people in Toronto alone gambled on the races every day, laying bets totalling over one hundred thousand dollars, most of that money being routed through Montreal. "For years," Hemingway wrote, "Toronto has been known all over the world as the biggest betting town in North America." In Toronto, just about every office or factory employing a large number of men had its own book-making agent and, given its even greater concentration of factories, Hamilton was an equal player.

As he built his gambling business over the next several years, Rocco recruited agents in those factories, as well as in restaurants and cigar and candy shops, paying each of them a tiny percentage of every bet they took. As his racket grew he hired strongmen too, to protect his growing territory. In this, he probably had help from Black Hand leader John Taglierino. It is known that Perri and Taglierino later partnered in their gambling efforts, in Hamilton as well as Toronto, so it's likely their association began earlier. In fact, it may well have been the presence of Taglierino's gang in Hamilton that initially drew Rocco and Bessie to this city. In any endeavour, it's good to have help.

Before too long, according to OPP reports into Perri's gambling activities, Rocco controlled all the gambling that took place within a forty-mile swath around Hamilton. Besides the clientele found in restaurants, stores and factories, one of the most lucrative betting markets was among women. They particularly loved the action at the Woodbine Racetrack, and it was a market that went largely untapped. "Few Toronto bookmakers like to handle bets from women," wrote Hemingway. "None of the big commission men who handle bets for Montreal books will accept a bet from a woman." But Rocco did. Those old OPP reports included the revelation that one of the Perri agents specifically targeted women bettors.

This was surely Bessie's influence. She was, in many ways, the perfect partner for Rocco. Somebody had to handle the "book" for all of these bets, recording the names, keeping track of money in and money out, managing the levels of risk. There was no one Rocco trusted more than the woman he called his wife, and she had a gift for it. She was smart and focused. She kept the books for the prostitution business as well, and she handled the girls.

It was highly unusual for a woman to be so deeply involved in an Italian-run gang. In the Cosa Nostra, the 'Ndrangheta and the

Camorra, women were generally unwelcome in the inner circle. But Rocco wasn't beholden to the ways of any brotherhood. He was his own man, an entrepreneur, and for the kind of business he imagined building, he needed her. They had complementary strengths, and she wanted to be involved—it was her business as much as his.

For these first few years in Hamilton, Rocco and Bessie used an alias, going by the last name Suseno. At least, that's how it sounded. The names of immigrants were still being written down phonetically by officials, so the spelling depended on who was holding the pen. Rocco's first name sometimes showed up as Robert or Rock, while his alias was occasionally written "Susino" or "Sussino." For Bessie, who called herself Rose, the last name was recorded as Cyceno. We know this, because that's how her name was written on a Hamilton police court docket.

In early 1917, Bessie and Rocco's prostitution business was doing quite well. So well that Hamilton police had become aware of some odd goings-on at 157 Caroline Street North. A number of men were hanging around, coming and going at all hours. More than that, one client had reported to police that he had paid two dollars to be with a prostitute at that address and while he wasn't looking someone had stolen all the money in his wallet. After that complaint, police paid a visit to the house to question Bessie and Rocco, who calmly denied everything. Bessie even acted the part of an offended housewife. *Prostitutes? Here?* What a thing to suggest!

The police weren't fooled and for several weeks they watched the address. The night of March 5, 1917, as a sharp, cold wind rattled windows along the street, four policemen—constables Chamberlain, Wallace, Young and Joseph Crocker—decided the time was right. They approached the house, barged in and found eight Italian men, one from Toronto and the rest from north Hamilton, along with two women. They arrested them all.

The next day, Bessie appeared in court on the charge of "keeping a disorderly house." Working girl Mary Ashley was there too, charged as an "inmate" of the house. (Rocco, significantly, was not there. According to court records he was out of town on "macaroni" business.)

Though this was her first time in court, Bessie handled herself with remarkable calm, even humour. Her self-possession must have been one of the things that Rocco loved about her. She seemed to treat the whole thing as a game. She pled not guilty and insisted that Mary Ashley was nothing to her but a boarder. In fact, Bessie said, as soon as she'd discovered the young woman's shocking occupation, she'd ordered her to leave.

The deputy chief of police, David Coulter, who handled the questioning that day in court, wanted Bessie to identify her tenant for the record. He pointed at Mary in the dock and asked, "Is that her?"

"I don't know," replied Bessie, smiling. "But I'll see." She then raised titters among observers as she scampered over to Mary and seemed to examine her very closely. After a moment she returned to the witness box and announced, "Yes, that's her."

The levity extended to Coulter as well. When Bessie explained that the men who had been arrested were her friends, there from Toronto and Montreal for a visit, Coulter asked how long she had lived in Hamilton. She lied and said "about seven weeks."

"My," Coulter replied, "what a lot of friends you made in seven weeks."

Finding himself unconvinced by anyone's story in this affair, the judge fined Mary Ashley twenty dollars and each of the men five dollars. Bessie received a fine of fifty dollars or two months in jail. She was now officially a known underworld figure.

The fun had just begun.

6

EBBREZZA

Intoxication

PROSTITUTION HAS ALWAYS BEEN A VICE, BUT IN THE early part of the twentieth century liquor was the great evil. That sentiment had been building for decades or longer. The idea that inebriation was wicked, and that total abstinence offered the only defence, had been around almost as long as the "public house" in Britain. When colonists came to the New World on ships, they brought that puritan idea with them. Other ships brought the whisky and rum.

In the mid-1600s, Maryland punished drunks with fines of a hundred pounds of tobacco. Then they tried six hours in the stocks. In the 1730s, Georgia attempted to outlaw the liquor that was getting between the colonists and their work. German immigrants brought a powerful thirst for beer to America in the early 1800s, just as the first railroads gave breweries an easy way to transport those heavy barrels. As saloons proliferated in every town and city so did drunkenness, a flourishing matched only by the wave of religious revivalism that was spreading throughout the United States. While many Americans found God, others drank until they threw up on their shoes and defended their right to do so. The clash of these two forces led to the founding of the American Temperance Society in 1826. It wasn't long before politicians began voting in laws prohibiting alcohol in Maine (1851), Vermont (1852), Connecticut (1854) and eight more states from Massachusetts to Iowa (1855).

Naturally the temperance movement spread to Canada. In the early part of the nineteenth century, when an astonishing 147 distilleries and ninety-six breweries were providing drink for fewer than fifty thousand Upper Canadians, at least ten thousand people belonged to temperance societies. New Brunswick's legislature outlawed the importation of alcohol in 1853, and three years later passed a law to make drinking it illegal. The Dunkin Act of 1864 gave local communities in Upper and Lower Canada the power to hold votes on whether to prohibit the sale of alcohol, and fourteen years later the Scott Act, also known as the Canada Temperance Act, gave this power to provinces.

Women, tired or fearful of drunken husbands destroying their families, became a powerful force in the temperance movement. The Women's Christian Temperance Union, which started in Ohio in 1873 and in Ontario a year later, fought for a "sober and pure world" and soon expanded across the continent. Empowered by finding their voice in the fight against the ills of drink, women began to reach for wider influence. From the temperance movement flowed the turn-of-the-century suffrage movement. The Anti-Saloon League joined the fight in the United States and turned into a potent lobby, endorsing politicians who supported the cause.

As the North American mood turned ever more firmly against alcohol—while the number of drinkers grew—the "evils of drink" made for grand newspaper fodder. Editors dressed themselves in both science and faith, quoting doctors who condemned even moderate drinking as hazardous, and religious leaders who decried it as the path to moral ruin. And they took every opportunity to highlight the depravity of the alcoholic.

"Crazed by drink!" wrote the Toronto *Globe* in September 1912 in a story that detailed the downfall of a former soldier, a Hamiltonian who had shot his wife and blown away his own face, orphaning three children. "Drink was his undoing," concluded the *Globe*, as it railed against the legal distribution of liquor: "The traffic that destroys the nerve and inflames the blood and crazes the brain and unhinges the moral sense, changing the producer into a parasite, maddening the husband into a murderer—that traffic is not only an economic burden, it is a crime against the nation."

When Canada entered the First World War, the zeitgeist turned even more broadly against liquor. With the nation's brave boys getting maimed and killed overseas, with every effort and penny needed to support them, any revelry at home seemed unconscionable. So provincial governments used the impetus of the war to enact legislation that turned the idea of temperance into the laws of prohibition.

The Maritime provinces were largely dry with the exception of Halifax and part of New Brunswick, although the wave of prohibition skipped over Quebec. In December 1914, Manitoba's government asked its hotel bars to close at 7 p.m., and the following March, Saskatchewan announced it would abolish bars during wartime. In July, Alberta voted by large majority to go dry. It came down to Ontario, and despite the prominence of the alcohol industry there— after all, it was a brewer, Joseph Bloor, who had given his name to one of Toronto's main east-west streets—local prohibitionists were encouraged. "Personally," said Reverend Ben Spence, secretary of the Ontario branch of the temperance group Dominion Alliance, "I believe we have a better Premier in Ontario than in any of the other Provinces; why should we not have a better law?"

Ontario's premier was Conservative William Hearst. A devout Methodist and lawyer, Hearst had promoted reforestation, fire prevention and workers' compensation as premier. He saw prohibition as another good and set about to make it happen.

A clever politician, Hearst started slowly. There were demands from the Liberal opposition to do as Saskatchewan had done and close all bars for the duration of the war, and equally ardent demands from hotels and liquor interests to keep them open. Hearst ordered that as of November 1, 1915, all bars would close at 8 p.m. during the week, rather than 11 p.m. Saturday hours would remain unchanged. A *Toronto Daily Star* headline summed up the reaction—"Both Sides Are Dissatisfied"—which to Hearst probably seemed like a win.

By the spring of 1916, with nearly half of the forty-eight states south of the border having passed anti-saloon legislation, the Canadian Parliament had rejected the notion of Dominion-wide prohibition and left it to the provinces to decide. Hearst's government introduced a full-scale prohibition bill—Bill 100—which when passed would make Ontario officially dry for three years, from September 16, 1916, until a referendum in 1919.

Liquor interests described themselves as "crucified" and "heartbroken," but prohibitionists were delighted. The day the legislation was announced, Reverend Spence of the Dominion Alliance couldn't contain his jubilation. He shook hands with everyone who walked into his office. "This act!" he exclaimed. "Why, man, it will abolish the liquor traffic in Ontario!"

Well, not quite.

The rules of what would be called the Ontario Temperance Act (OTA) dictated that no intoxicating beverages could be sold in Ontario. And in case there was any doubt, "any liquor which contains more than 2½ per cent of proof spirits shall be conclusively deemed to be intoxicating." There was one chief exception: the sale of products with alcohol intended for medicinal or scientific purposes. Alcohol had always been the main "active ingredient" in various health tonics and potions; a product like Lydia E. Pinkham's Vegetable Compound, for "female complaints," offered a 40-proof wallop. But many people believed in the curative power of straight whisky, and you could get a prescription for that too. Doctors and druggists willing to play the game had patients lining up. In the two and a half years following the passage of Bill 100, more than one million quarts of liquor would be supplied to patients by doctors' orders. One physician wrote out 222 prescriptions for liquor in a single day.

There were other gaps in the legislation. The problem for the government was jobs and tax income—there were plenty of both at stake in Ontario's distilleries and breweries. So even though the OTA made it illegal to sell wine, liquor and beer within the province, the law had been written to allow manufacturers to keep *making* alcoholic products and to send them out of the province. And because importing and exporting were matters of federal jurisdiction, nothing in the Act prevented alcohol from coming into Ontario. Private citizens were free to import whatever they liked to drink, as long as it was for personal use in their own homes.

All in all, the Ontario Temperance Act was one of those problems that looked remarkably like opportunity. Instantly a new phenomenon was born: mail-order booze. An Ontario resident would send a purchase request, with cheque attached, to a company in Montreal. He wouldn't even have to give up his favourite Ontario-made brand. The Montreal firm would then place an order with the distillery or brewery, or dip into its own purchased stock held in a Toronto or Hamilton warehouse, and return an all-important out-of-province purchase receipt to the customer. The customer, now essentially acting as an agent for an out-of-province purchaser, would take the receipt to the local distillery or warehouse and pick up his "exported" liquor.

Labatt established its own mail-order office in Hull, Quebec, across the river from Ottawa, and advertised that any customers "desirous of obtaining the famous old Labatt products can do so without inconvenience or delay." Meanwhile two bartending brothers from Prince Edward County, Ontario—Harry and Herb Hatch, who'd bought a small package-liquor store on Yonge Street in Toronto and might have remained nobodies if not for Prohibition—immediately moved to Montreal. There they set up a mail-order business and launched themselves down a path that would lead them soon to prestige and fortune, and a close association with the Perri gang.

Rocco and Bessie, operating their Caroline Street North brothel, were equally quick to grasp the implications of the new rules. If it was possible for a man to order booze by mail and drink it at home, it was far more difficult to go out and drink among friends. After September 16, 1916, bars and taverns closed all across Ontario. In Hamilton, just over fifty hotels and liquor stores shut down. Many quickly reopened as "standard hotels" or "temperance bars," operating under OTA rules, but that meant no whisky, no rum, and beer that topped out at 2.5 percent alcohol. In Toronto, the legal hotels and bars were so empty they practically echoed. Anyone who wanted to go out for a decent drink knew that there had to be another option.

"Speakeasy" has come to be the accepted term for any Prohibition-era establishment serving illegal liquor, but at the time "blind pig" was much more commonly used, because there were far more of them. The speakeasy had pretensions of refinement, a place where you might dress up, drink cocktails and expect to be entertained—but that required investment on the part of the owner, and payoffs to local authorities, which took time and effort. The blind pig, on the other hand, was a dive for people with no greater expectation than a morning hangover. That took no time at all.

The expression had been around for a couple of decades. Even before provincial governments enacted widespread Prohibition, the "local option" provided by the Dunkin Act had allowed Canadian communities to vote themselves dry, and wherever they had, blind pigs had filled the need. They could be anywhere—in the back room of a store, in a home with the curtains drawn—and only if you knew someone could you get in. By 1907, the term was widely enough known to permit a satirical treatment in the *Globe*, in which the blind pig was portrayed as an elusive nocturnal animal:

> There seems a peculiar and seductive excitement in hunting or studying the blind pig . . . Its secluded lair is sought down the unlit and guarded side entrance, where the observer vainly peers and strains his eyes to discern the forms he meets or passes. The unsteady gait, suggestive of blind staggers, reveals the proximity of the *sus caecus*. Pushing through doors and hallways, guided by the sound, a dim light reveals the animal's hiding place . . . Heavy cushions and cloth are shuffled continuously to deaden the clinking, clattering sounds of the chase and to dull the whispered conversations. The chase of the blind pig is full of excitement.

Rocco had plenty of opportunity to learn about blind pigs when he lived in Cobalt. One "moderate estimate" in 1908 put the number of blind pigs in that dry mining town at thirty-five. By 1911 when Rocco was there, the total was over a hundred—nine in one building alone. In many of them, customers would use the stolen ore they had squirrelled into their pockets as currency. Indeed, it's entirely possible the *fornitura*, or "supply," Rocco was writing to Frank Griro about was booze. There had been blind pigs run by Italians in North Bay when Rocco was there too. In fact, before he met Bessie, it seems that wherever Rocco had been in Ontario, even in little Elk Lake, one could find a thriving economy in hideaways serving illegal liquor.

So as soon as Prohibition descended upon Ontario, Rocco and Bessie added booze to the pleasures offered at 157 Caroline Street North. Gambling, sex and now liquor—compared to extortion, it was practically virtuous. They were simply in the business of giving people what they wanted. Bessie did the ordering, sourcing their liquor by mail from Montreal the same as any private citizen (the Hatch brothers were one of their suppliers). And Rocco sold it in a back room, illegally, for fifty cents a glass.

For roughly the next year, with the exception of a couple of police interruptions and a court appearance, their prospects developed exactly as they might have hoped. Overseas the trenches in France were filling with blood and muck, German airships bombed London, the Americans joined the fray, and newspapers carried daily reports of the dead and wounded. But for Rocco and Bessie, life was good.

They began to order enough liquor to supply not just their own store, but others too. Any hotel or dive where you could put money down on the Perri numbers was a likely spot to serve Perri booze. One of the first was probably Joseph (Joe) Murphy's Athletic Hotel in Hamilton's Market Square. At the same time that Toronto hotels and bars were complaining about a lack of customers under the new "standard hotel" restrictions, Murphy was bragging that at his place, business was booming. Before long it was an obvious under-world hangout, and Murphy was a known Rocco Perri associate.

The money came in so steadily that before Rocco and Bessie had turned thirty they were able to begin living the life they'd long imagined. Rocco bought himself a fast car. They began to think about moving to a nicer home. In the warm summer months, they hosted swank parties aboard rented boats on Lake Ontario. Rocco dressed in sharp suits, smoked cigars and smiled as brightly as the jewellery Bessie wore. They hired bands to play music—one of the hit songs of 1917 was "All the World Will Be Jealous of Me."

The law was still a fluid thing. In the United States, about two dozen states had instituted Prohibition and politicians felt increasing pressure to impose it nationwide. On August 1, 1917, the U.S. senate passed a constitutional amendment banning the manufacture, sale and transportation of intoxicating liquors and set it on a course toward ratification. In Canada, Robert Borden's Conservative government could see as well as anyone that there was a steamroller coming and it could not get out of the way. In November it took a small step and announced that, given the situation in Europe and the vital importance of food stocks, none of the nation's grain could be used for the manufacture of distilled potable liquor. Prohibition activists, though pleased, noted that while distillers had used 88 million pounds of grain the previous year, brewers had used nearly 100 million. Why weren't they prohibited too? Reverend John Bailey of the Dominion Alliance took a rather accurate read of the situation. "It would almost seem as if the pressure of public opinion alone could move the Food Controller to act," he said. "So I suppose that the only thing for us to do is hammer away until the final step is taken."

The final step came the following month, when the federal government invoked the War Measures Act. Effective December 24, 1917 (and until a year after the war was over), it was illegal to import any beverage with more than 2.5 percent alcohol into Canada. The government also had to deal with the matter of the estimated 16 million gallons of spirits already in the country—much of it in Quebec, where that Christmas you could order a quart of Gooderham & Worts Ordinary Rye for ninety cents, or a case of Robertson's Choice Old Whisky (thirty-two years old) for thirty-four dollars. So as of the following April 1, it would be illegal to transport liquor into any part of Canada where liquor itself was illegal. That meant no shipments of Robertson's or anything else from Montreal.

As to the matter of whether *making* the stuff would become illegal in Canada, the government promised an answer soon. On the evening of February 26, 1918, a crowd packed Toronto's Massey Hall to hear the prime minister speak on this issue of national importance. Unfortunately, the PM was called away to Washington. So at the last minute the assignment fell to the immigration minister, James Calder, from of all places, Moose Jaw. "I am here by accident," Calder told the crowd through his bushy moustache. "I understood you wanted Sir Robert Borden." Calder had never spoken to an eastern audience before, and he seemed a little awestruck by the Toronto crowd. He hoped they would be "just as human" as audiences he'd addressed in the west. He told his Massey Hall listeners that leaders in the west had doubted whether there was support for Prohibition in the east, and the federal government had doubted it too. But then, when Saskatchewan and Manitoba and Alberta had gone dry, Ontario had joined them. And so the time for "political juggling" had gone by. "There is work to be done yet," said Calder. "The work is not completely rounded out." He suggested the government would put the "capstone" on its liquor legislation soon. Calder's sincerity earned him a rave review in the *Toronto Daily Star*, which called his speech "one of the clearest and most incisive addresses ever made to a large audience by a Crown Minister."

Less than two weeks later, the federal government announced that on April 1, the same day liquor transport was to be shut down, all manufacturing of intoxicating liquor (except for Quebec beer and Ontario wine until the end of the year) would be prohibited. "The Federal enactment has destroyed, for the present at least, the whole power of the liquor interests in the country," wrote the *Globe*. The law still allowed private citizens to keep a small amount of liquor in their homes for personal use; they just couldn't buy it in dry provinces like Ontario, and they couldn't bring it in from elsewhere. Of course, liquor for sacramental, industrial, artistic, mechanical, scientific and medicinal purposes remained legal, with special permission. In Woodstock, Ontario, a doctor tried giving out prescriptions for people to "bathe" in liquor. He didn't get away with it, but the pharmacy business still thrived.

Within the next few months, Rocco and Bessie relocated. They sold 157 Caroline and moved exactly one block west to 105 Hess Street North (even closer to Bessie's synagogue). Upstairs was an apartment for Rocco and Bessie, reached by an outside staircase. Downstairs at the front was a grocery store with space to serve more illegal liquor to more paying customers. In the back was another apartment with a kitchen, a fourteen-by-twelve-foot living room, and two bedrooms, which were put to use in the other money-making branch of the business.

With the demand for liquor greater than ever, now that even the mail-order loophole was closed, the issue for Rocco became the practical matter of how to ensure a steady supply, and how to get it past the police. He wasn't the only one trying to solve this problem. In the middle of April, just a couple of weeks after the nationwide clampdown on manufacturing and distribution, police patrolling Toronto's Union Station noticed a Russian man stepping off a train from Montreal. He had a bottle of beer in one of his coat pockets and a bottle of cherry brandy protruding from another. Although it was a rather paltry cargo, the officers decided it was all they needed to take the man by the arm and make the first official arrest of someone illegally importing liquor into Ontario.

Then they opened the man's large suitcase. Inside they found ten gallons of pure alcohol tightly packed in custom-made one-gallon tins.

The real game of Prohibition had begun.

PART 2

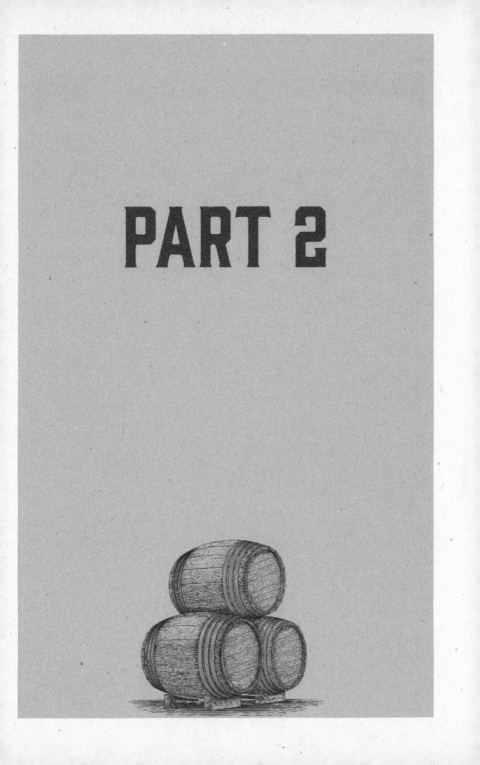

7

COMPLICAZIONE
Complication

THE IMMEDIATE FUTURE WAS CLEAR. FROM NOW UNTIL at least a year after the war, nearly the whole of Canada was going to be dry. No selling liquor, no importing it, no transporting it, no making it. Meanwhile, here were all these people who still wanted to drink it. For the brave, ambitious few, it was time to get creative.

In Yorkton, Saskatchewan, two immigrant brothers in the hotel and mail-order booze business, Harry and Sam Bronfman, got into drug wholesaling—long before their family name would become synonymous with wealth, intrigue and influence in Montreal. Within a few days of the new rules, Harry acquired a three-hundred-thousand-dollar line of bank credit, bought a drug licence and started the Canada Pure Drug Company. That allowed the Bronfmans to import bulk loads of liquor and sell it to corner drugstores, or to supply companies that made alcohol-infused tonics and cures. They secured their supply of alcohol when Harry also acquired the contract to sell Dewar's whisky, which the Hudson's Bay Company had been forced to give up because it had not been smart enough to think of the drug company angle.

In Hamilton Rocco used his contacts, and by now he had plenty. Equipped with a new car, he could convincingly pose as a travelling salesman for the Superior Macaroni Company and establish territory and connections as far afield as Buffalo and North Bay. It wasn't long before Rocco knew whom he could sell to and whom he could count on for help in Guelph, Brantford, St. Catharines, Thorold, Niagara Falls—essentially every town with a sizable Italian population within a day's drive.

Prohibition was coming in the United States, but it hadn't come yet, so the best and easiest source of alcohol lay about fifty miles due east, at the U.S. border through Niagara Falls. And, seeing as how Hamilton hugged the end of Lake Ontario, the easiest way to get large amounts of alcohol around that border was to use a boat. That's probably how Rocco first began working with John Ben Kerr.

Ben Kerr had a remarkable combination of skills. He made most of his income, about a thousand dollars a year, as a plumber. In his spare time he performed as a piano player. He had a moody charisma that women liked, going by the name "Bensley" and noodling around with songs like "Golliwog's Cakewalk" for extra cash.

Kerr's other area of skill was boats. He knew marine engines, and he owned a storage lot with fifty boat lockers on the Hamilton waterfront. Boat racing had been popular in Hamilton ever since the emergence of the gasoline engine, and inside one of Kerr's lockers sat his own souped-up twenty-eight-foot cruiser.

The boat-storage facility wasn't as full as Kerr would have liked—he had a lot of competition—and because he had a mortgage on it, he needed money. As it happened, one of the places Rocco visited on his liquor rounds in Hamilton was Jim Thompson's Boat

House, a busy speakeasy by the wharf. If Rocco didn't already know about Kerr, there must have been a cool, damp night, shortly after April 1, when he came in and saw Kerr's cardboard sign on the wall advertising ALL NIGHT SERVICE—FAST MOTOR BOAT FOR HIRE. It is certainly true that before long, a customer at Jim Thompson's could look through the crowd of faces and bottles and see Rocco and Kerr at a table, talking. Shortly after that, Rocco began moving beer and liquor by boat.

UNFORTUNATELY, not all of Rocco's interactions with his contacts went as smoothly. On the afternoon of April 16, 1918, he went to visit Germo (Jimmy) Celona at Celona's candy store at 72 York Street, in the heart of Hamilton. Within minutes, all hell broke loose.

In the four years since Rocco and Celona had known each other in St. Catharines—back when Rocco was developing his underworld skills alongside Filippo Mascato, and comforting Bessie through the death of their child—Celona had started working for the powerful Sciarrone gang, headquartered in Guelph. The gang's leader was Domenic Sciarrone (alias Joseph Verona), a Calabrian who was very likely related to Toronto's Frank and Salvatore Sciarrone, the brothers who had extorted Frank Griro. In fact, Domenic had lived for a time in Toronto, where he'd been naturalized in 1912, and as far as police could determine, he still maintained a base there at 17 Portland Street. No matter where he lived, though, he was a powerful and dangerous force who was pushing fingers into every city in the region.

Jimmy Celona was one of those fingers. At least six months prior to this particular April afternoon, he'd moved to Hamilton with his wife to establish an extortion operation and thereby extend Sciarrone's territory. Celona and his wife lived in a rooming house on West Cannon Street and spent a few months threatening Hamilton's Italians for money in an ad hoc way—making enough to dress himself and his wife in expensive clothes—before setting up his York Street store as a front. Suspicious neighbourhood store-keepers were certain it was being turned into a brothel; the candy in the window never changed, but there were always plenty of young women and men hanging around the place at night.

Violence, however, remained Celona's chief money-making venture. Rocco saw this first-hand. In March, Celona was one of several Italians at Rocco and Bessie's place—still very much a work-ing brothel—when Rocco heard an argument breaking out in his cellar. He went downstairs and saw a twenty-one-year-old named Tony Speranza, who apparently owed Celona money, kneeling on the cellar floor as Celona held a razor to his neck. Rocco calmly talked some momentary sense into Celona—"I take him nice and easy," he later said; "I take him good"—and pulled the razor from his hands.

On the April day when Rocco arrived at the store to chat, Celona was inside playing cards with one of his men. While they were talking, Celona looked out the window of his store and saw two young men. One of them was Domenic Paparone, a twenty-one-year-old tough whom Celona considered a cousin, and who had come to the city from Welland because Celona had offered to get him a job. The other young man, wearing a green cap and a grey suit, was Domenic Speranza, Tony's sixteen-year-old brother. He had recently been invited by Celona to a baptism, to which he'd been expected to bring a gift of money, and he had failed to show.

The next thing Rocco or anyone knew, Celona was marching out of the store toward the Domenics, ready to rumble. It's pos-sible he took a kitchen knife with him. Speranza later testified that

Celona rushed up and grabbed him by the throat. He may have slapped or punched him too. "I want fifty dollars because you didn't come to the baptism," Celona said. When Speranza said he didn't have it, Celona pulled out his knife and told him, "This is the last day you live."

Speranza may not have had money in his pocket, but he did have a revolver. Seconds later—after two shots and a cry of "Mama!"— smoke was coming from the barrel of Speranza's gun and Celona had fallen to the sidewalk. As Paparone tried to pull his friend away Speranza took a step to leave, then changed his mind. He stood over Celona's body, pointed his .38 and fired two more bullets.

When the police arrived, Rocco must have given quite an array of answers as to his identity, because when he appeared a few days later as a witness at the inquest he was identified in one paper as Rocco Paral of 105 Hess Street, and in another as Rocco Peri Susenno of 72 York Street. He also must have gotten on the phone quickly to Celona's family after the shooting, because while the inquest was under way, Celona's grief-stricken wife, father and two brothers all stayed with Rocco and Bessie at 105 Hess Street. It was handy they had the extra beds.

At the trial in November, Rocco spoke with calm assurance. Despite his connection to Celona's family, he didn't hesitate to suggest where blame for the altercation might have lain. Questioned by Speranza's lawyer, a tall red-headed barrister named Michael J. O'Reilly, KC, he described Speranza as "A good boy, not quarrelsome." And he made clear that Celona was quick-tempered and belligerent.

"I've seen him hit and kick Italians three or four times since he was in Hamilton," said Rocco. Asked if Celona typically beat people up to get money, he said, "I think so, because that is the way he lived . . . He didn't seem to be getting a living any other way."

Even if Rocco crafted that statement to protect his own interests, and even if it was politically wise to shift blame to the dead man rather than to the living, there was still something noteworthy about it. Those few words—"the way he lived"—marked the difference between Rocco and the typical Black Hander, or *mafioso*. While Celona used intimidation to achieve his ends and hewed to the historic lines of Italian hostility—Calabrian vs. Sicilian vs. Neapolitan—Rocco stood apart.

Domenic Speranza was ultimately convicted of manslaughter and sentenced to life in prison. But those regional alignments, transferred intact to the streets of Hamilton and other nearby cities, had their own justice system, which meant Celona's death would spark a series of retaliatory murders. In the context of this narrative, it would get bloody in southern Ontario. Rocco probably anticipated that, even as he testified on the stand, but he seemed unconcerned. Whether it was by design or personality, he aligned himself with no band or family or village. He was his own man, and so he had no obvious enemies.

During the inquest into Celona's death, Rocco was asked by Crown Attorney S. F. Washington if he and the accused murderer, Domenic Speranza, were friends. Rocco grinned, and his reply was simple: "All Italians are my friends."

It was one of the secrets of his success.

||||||||||||||||||||||||||||||||

F RANK ZANETH WAS THE FIRST OF HIS KIND. BY APRIL OF 1918, he was a fully trained constable in the Royal North West Mounted Police, making a paltry $1.25 a day like every other fresh recruit. But he entered service with the knowledge that he was unique. Commissioner Aylesworth Bowen Perry, a man distinguished by piercing eyes, a full white moustache, and a determination to modernize the force he led, told Zaneth that he was the first man recruited for the force's new "Secret Service," which Perry himself would be commanding.

In this still young country, police work, whether national or local, had mostly been shaped to a blunt and direct military model. Crime was simple, often violent, and the methods for dealing with it followed suit. But there were new, complex forces at work in the world—the Bolshevik Revolution in Russia, for example, which seemed to Canada's nervous leaders like a kind of political contagion—and they demanded a different approach. Impressed by the results of organizations such as Pinkerton's, the government was beginning to see the value in a subtler kind of law enforcement. Zaneth's job would entail going undercover to gather information wherever the government had concerns. And Zaneth was perfect for this job because he could manage in several languages, his character was unimpeachable, he had an earnest desire to please his superiors, and he looked even less like a Mountie than his application had suggested. Because, aside from being Italian, it turned out Zaneth was even shorter than he'd thought. According to the description in his official engagement files, he stood just five foot five and three-quarter inches. He was a man who might go anywhere without raising suspicion.

His first assignment, just six months after he'd posted his tentative letter in hopes of joining the force, took him to Quebec City, to the heart of the conscription riots that were rocking parts of the country. He spent two weeks amongst a group of draft evaders, alone and without guidance, and it went well enough that he managed to make some arrests. A couple of months later, still hard up for money after his Moose Jaw misadventure, he applied for the extra pay he had been promised for the period he spent undercover in Quebec. "I have the honour to request that I may be granted $1.00 per diem extra" he wrote, using the formal language of internal RNWMP communications. The request was forwarded up the line. It's not clear whether the money was granted.

Next came a group of union agitators in the coal mines of Drumheller, Alberta. This time Zaneth was given a cover identity. The miners were a mix of nationalities—some of the agitators were Italian, others English-speaking, while many of the workers they hoped to convince to go on strike were Austrians from a region north of Italy where the language was Galician. Apparently Zaneth spoke Galician well enough, so he became "Harry Blask," a paroled enemy alien originally from the Austrian Piedmont, and now a card-carrying member of the Industrial Workers of the World. His red IWW card had been taken off a prisoner.

Zaneth boarded a CPR train on September 12 and headed to Calgary, where a CNR train took him eighty-four miles northeast through the Alberta badlands to the Red Deer River Valley and the hoodoos of Drumheller. For roughly two months, he lived and worked as a coal miner, sleeping in the crowded bunkhouse with as many as fifty or sixty other men, washing out of a pail, and spending his days setting explosives, drilling holes for timbers, shovelling coal into cars and trying not to choke on the black dust. In addition to that dangerous work, he attended union meetings, made surreptitious notes when he could, and managed to win the trust of two strike leaders—R. L. Bradshaw, the secretary of the United Mine Workers local in Drumheller, and Tony Cacchioni, president of the local operating at the mine in nearby Wayne. Bradshaw taught him the secret IWW handshake. Cacchioni served him a dinner of macaroni. Zaneth stayed in Drumheller and worked as a miner until the middle of November, when he was ordered to travel to Rocky Mountain Park and check on the activities of a radical miners' union in Canmore.

For his back-breaking, lung-fouling work in the mines, "Harry Blask" was paid between $1.27 and $1.91 an hour, or about four times what Zaneth made as an RNWMP constable, if you counted his extra dollar a day for plainclothes work. But Zaneth couldn't keep that money. Whatever the difference between his police pay and the money he made as a miner, regulations demanded it be handed over to the Crown.

This was the unanticipated catch to being an undercover officer, and Zaneth—who likely needed to send money to Grace to help with the raising of Rena—found handing over that money almost as hard as the work itself. He quietly fumed about the inherent unfairness of it. But he did it, accepting his meagre $1.25 a day with the hope of a dollar more, because he was a man who followed the rules.

IN HAMILTON, THE PERRIS WERE GETTING WEALTHIER by the day. More and more customers were clamouring for alcohol, and Rocco was building a reputation as the bootlegger with the men and the connections to deliver it. By the middle of 1917, he and Bessie were at the beginning stages of an empire.

And yet, Rocco was missing something in his life. Since the death of Anterico, Bessie had shown no interest in trying for another child. She was content with the two children she already had, Gertie and Lily, and she was making a greater effort to see them during surreptitious visits to Toronto. Some days she drove into the city and waited for them outside McCaul Street Public School. As the girls emerged after classes, she would hide behind a lamppost or the corner of a building, then jump out to surprise them. Other times she would wait for them in the kitchen of a neighbour, someone who understood that she could not see them at home. The richer she became, the more gifts of toys and clothes and money she would bring. Bessie would not tempt fate trying for another child when she had two beautiful daughters on whom to lavish her love.

Maybe Rocco wasn't looking for a way to have a child of his own, not in so many words. But he had the ache in him of something unresolved, some need not quite fulfilled. Luckily for him, with Bessie managing the business end so magnificently at home, Rocco had an opportunity to roam in search of the thing he was missing. So, in his fine suits and his boater hat, with his money roll, his cigars, his winks and his smiles, that's what he did. And as he roamed around a city and a region that were increasingly his for the taking, as he scanned the horizon for some undefined opportunity or trouble, he ended up meeting a woman named Olive, who was both.

Sarah Olive Rutledge. Most of her life, she had been a pretty country girl, raised in Hastings County near the town of Bancroft, where she'd gone to high school. Her Methodist parents had a meagre farm in a sparsely populated area called Musclow, and for twenty years, Olive had lived with them in the hermetic shelter of their love and care. She had grown from girl to young woman with no real idea of how attractive she was, or how exciting the world could be for someone like her. And then in 1917, when Olive was twenty-one, she had broken free and travelled south to Hamilton, where she had found a job at the growing Chipman-Holton Knitting Company, the Dominion's largest manufacturer of seamless hosiery, makers of "Little Darling" and "Little Daisy" stockings for infants and children.

It would have been easy for Rocco to cross paths with her. She worked at Chipman-Holton's handsome brick building at the corner of Canon and Mary streets, a little east from Hess Street, but still in the north section of town. She lived three blocks away in a boarding house at 77 Wilson Street, in conditions far more crowded than she was used to. But every night she had a chance to go out, to meet new people in lively places filled with noise and laughter—and men.

One night, as Rocco was scanning the crowd in one of the speakeasies he supplied, his gaze fell on this slender beauty. She had her Irish father's blue eyes and thin, arching eyebrows, and she tied her dark hair with strings of beads. There was nothing Rocco liked more than a beautiful young woman, so he went over to her table and introduced himself, using the name Rocco Ross (when he needed an alias, Rocco often used the last name of one of his associates; there were two young brothers in the organization who used that last name, Frank and Tony Ross). No doubt he set a drink in front of her too.

Things developed quickly between them. Olive was young, impressionable and new to being wooed. For his part, Rocco immediately saw the advantages of being a "travelling salesman" whose business pulled him away for days or weeks at a time. Soon, Rocco was living two lives, one in which he and Olive Rutledge were practically inseparable, and the other in which he lived and worked with Bessie, the love of his life. He travelled between these worlds for months without one being aware of the other. It's possible that Bessie felt somewhat vulnerable when her man wasn't around, and maybe Rocco felt guilty. (Extramarital affairs were generally disdained within Italian crime circles.) So he bought a guard dog for the house. And if there were people in Rocco's world who straddled both lives—favoured customers, his men, the cousins who worked for him—they knew enough to keep their mouths shut.

For a few months, the letters Olive sent to her parents were filled with nothing but good news. Of course she told them about the wonderful, successful man she was seeing. A salesman, and so generous—he was always buying her beautiful things. She couldn't reveal where she'd actually met him, so she said they'd met while living in the same boarding house. And now she was sure he was going to propose marriage. Wasn't it amazing how quickly life could change? One day she was cooped up and lonely on a farm with her parents, and the next she was driving around a city in a fast car with a charming man whom she loved. Her life really was playing out like a storybook. Rocco and Olive Ross—they were perfect together, and they would be so happy.

And then one day, early in 1918, Olive learned she was pregnant. This was no longer just a love story; the situation had become serious. Olive knew her reputation—at the time a woman's most important asset—was at stake. She demanded that Rocco do what a man must do in such a circumstance. He had to marry her.

By now, Rocco had become used to dealing with dangerous situations, although admittedly this one was a little different. He had Bessie to think about, of course, and all that she meant to him, and to the business. But he did love this girl, and he very much wanted a child. So the thing to do, he decided, was to marry Olive—as Rocco Ross. It would give Olive what she wanted, which would make her happy and calm. And because marrying under an assumed name was surely non-binding—he may even have consulted his lawyers on this matter—it would give him an out, should he ever need it.

They married on March 4, 1918, at a parsonage in Hamilton. This was the story Olive told her parents—and she had a ring on her finger to prove it—when she returned to the farm to give birth. Rocco would have explained that it was impossible, with his business, to attend to her needs. Best to live with her mother and father where they could care for her properly. He would visit when he could.

IN the midst of all this, Rocco did a stupid thing. Late in April 1918, having just bought a flashy new roadster a week or two before, he went tooling through the Hamilton intersection of Jackson and Hughson streets. At that moment, perhaps distracted by thoughts of Olive and what might be to come, he slammed into the sedan of garage owner R. F. Chadwick, which was being driven by Chadwick's young chauffeur, Arthur Carscallen.

At once Carscallen climbed out of his employer's damaged vehicle and demanded the name of the short Italian who'd bashed into him. Rocco, who so far had managed to keep the last name of Perri out of Hamilton police records, refused to give it to him. So Carscallen took down his plate number. And because not giving one's name in an accident was a court-worthy offence, Rocco and Carscallen appeared on Saturday, May 18, in front of Police Magistrate George Frederick Jelfs.

Jelfs was a character. Born in Dorset, in southwest England, he was a deeply religious, sixty-five-year-old Hamilton institution who had a habit of saying and deciding whatever he damn well pleased, even at the expense of lawyers and police. Ultimately, when he stepped down after thirty-six years, Jelfs would be lauded for his "rugged honesty," but until then it was frequently vexing.

In 1914, when a defence counsel suggested there wasn't enough evidence to commit his client on a charge of cutting and wounding another man, Jelfs replied, "There is enough evidence there to hang him. There is so much evidence that in some of the states across the border he would never be allowed to reach the jail alive." Thirteen years earlier, a Hamilton Crown attorney had sued Jelfs for defamation because of comments Jelfs made in court regarding the lawyer and the then-popular card game "bridge whist." One can only imagine.

The simple traffic accident that had Rocco in court that day in May forced him to reveal his real name, but he fought the charge, represented by a barrister named Norman Kay. Rocco had liked what he'd seen watching Michael J. O'Reilly handle Domenic Speranza's murder trial and had gone to the same Hughson Street firm when he needed help. Norman Kay was O'Reilly's junior partner.

Kay argued his client's case vigorously. He proposed that the accident was Carscallen's fault, and that it was he who had left the scene without giving his name, not Rocco, even supplying a witness willing to testify to that effect, more or less. Unfortunately, it came out under cross-examination that the witness, Peter Florin, wasn't employed and not long before had been slapped with a fine for loafing.

"I have no faith in what such a man as you would say in the witness box," Jelfs informed him, and Rocco paid his twenty-dollar fine. And the next time he bought a car, a few months later, he put it in Bessie's name.

As the end of 1918 approached, Rocco and Bessie celebrated the success of their year. The Great War had just ended, and there were a lot of men coming home who would need a drink, which could only be good for their prospects. But there were challenges coming too. One by one, states south of the border were ratifying the Eighteenth Amendment. Rocco wasn't really one to read the papers, but Bessie was surely watching. She knew that soon America would reach the thirty-six states required to turn dry, which meant she and Rocco needed to develop new sources of supply.

But even with that prospect on their minds, there was still a lot to be happy about and every reason to throw a party. So on New Year's Eve, they got dressed up and filled the downstairs of 105 Hess Street with revellers. Between twenty and forty raucous Italians crowded inside, looking for the kind of hospitality you could only get from a bootlegger. Music filled the house. There was dancing and liquor. And in keeping with Rocco's style, the guests weren't exclusively from one region of Italy or another; his door was open to everyone. Some of them might have been customers, neighbours; others were Rocco's men. One was Tony Martino, a quiet twenty-seven-year-old who had come from Welland to work at the International Harvester factory and probably helped Rocco run numbers there. He was married, but his wife was still in Italy, so he lived in a boarding house on Murray Street West. It was just a few blocks from Hess, so for a little fun on New Year's Eve he'd decided to go over to Rocco's place. It was a bad decision, as it turned out.

For a few hours, the hostilities between regional factions stayed mostly below the surface, but as the intoxication levels rose so did the friction. Some time around two in the morning, while the music and dancing were still going strong, Martino became snarled in a fierce argument with Alberto Naticchio, a tall, lean man whose chiselled face bore a kind of mean arrogance. About the same age as Martino, Naticchio sometimes worked at the Dominion Steel Foundry. The rest of the time he worked for Rocco, and at that moment he had a .32 automatic loaded with steel-nosed bullets tucked in the pants of his dark grey suit. He seemed keen to use it too—a couple of hours earlier he'd fired about seventeen shots out of his boarding room window at midnight to celebrate the new year. He was now so drunk and argumentative that Rocco told him to go cool off outside. Amid the hubbub of the crowded kitchen,

Naticchio goaded Martino into coming out with him to settle things. They left through the back door into an alleyway.

A few minutes later, constables Robert Smith and Walter McLean were walking the snow-crusted streets of their separate beats nearby when they each heard three shots. Neither was overly concerned—firing guns into the cold night air on New Year's Eve was obviously the thing to do in this part of Hamilton. Nor did Constable Smith seem very bothered when he saw a man running across Hess Street, falling on the ice, then getting up and running off down Cannon Street. Still, when they heard loud music coming from a house on Hess, the constables each thought they should walk over and inquire. Smith arrived first and, strangely, when he walked into the party house and asked about the shots, no one had the slightest idea what he was talking about.

And then someone outside noticed a body splayed in the snow.

Martino was still alive, but he'd taken a bullet through the liver. Domenic Racco, who had known Martino since they were boys in Italy, leaned over his friend. "Who shoot you?" he asked. Martino didn't know the man's name. They carried him bleeding into the house and laid him on the kitchen table, and as McLean arrived Martino was mumbling something in Italian. When the constables asked what, someone offered that he was saying his address. He continued to mutter—"Leave me alone" and "Go easy"—as he was carted away in an ambulance. He died soon after.

The only clue to the murderer was a fedora someone had left behind in the snow. It was pinched in the front with its brim pulled downward, and when Hamilton detective Reg Shirley arrived and got a look at that hat, it struck him as familiar. He recalled seeing that very hat on someone who'd appeared in court before, someone who pinched his fedora and tugged down its brim in just that way: Alberto Naticchio.

A day or two later, as police combed the Italian section of Hamilton, they arrived at a boarding house at 104 Caroline Street North. There, on the wall of one of the rooms with several beds, they spotted a picture of Naticchio posing in an absurd cowboy outfit, complete with neckerchief and cowboy hat set at a rakish angle. Naticchio himself wasn't there, and no one at the boarding house would admit to knowing him. But there was a little girl standing at the edge of the room, the six- or seven-year-old daughter of the couple who ran the boarding house. She told the police that the man in the picture did live there, but he'd recently left.

Back at the Hess Street store, Rocco and Bessie had some strategizing to do. Rocco had made arrangements to help Naticchio flee to the United States—Alberto may have been a hothead, but Rocco looked out for his men. When police came by on Thursday, January 2, they tried to put them off with shrugs and denials: They didn't know anyone involved, killer or victim. Someone died out there? It had nothing to do with them.

But they saw that wasn't going to work. In a week they would have to give evidence at the inquest into Martino's murder and they needed to offer something plausible. Together on the Saturday, with Naticchio safely out of the country, Rocco and Bessie came forward to police and admitted yes, they'd thought hard about it, and actually they did remember an Alberto being at the party. And that was his hat. But a lot of people they didn't really know had come to that party; it was an open house. That seemed to set them up well for the story they planned to tell at the inquest.

Unfortunately, even if the police were temporarily assuaged on the shooting matter, all of the attention on the Hess Street store, all that talk of New Year's Eve revelry, had piqued their interest in another way. And so that night, a Sergeant May and two constables marched up to their front step and began banging on the door.

Rocco and Bessie were out at the time—"at an entertainment" they would later claim—but in their absence, the police charged in. And when they swarmed through the house they found eighteen quarts of whisky under a bed in one of the upstairs rooms, a gallon can of simple grain alcohol in the upstairs kitchen (the kind used to stretch one bottle of whisky into three or four), two dozen empty bottles in the bathroom, a hundred gallons of over-proof wine in the cellar, and a supply of whisky labels and seals from a Canadian distillery. Rocco and Bessie arrived home to find their door open, their store filled with police and their operation exposed.

Oh, the local press loved this—the first big story of the Prohibition era. It vied for space with the death of Teddy Roosevelt on the front page of the *Hamilton Herald*. Hess Street grocer Rocco Perri Sussino "must have bathed in booze," crowed the *Herald*, "washed his teeth with it, used it for shaving, gargled his throat with it, shampooed his raven locks with it and utilized it as a massage." Somewhere Olive Rutledge, sad to have had to spend New Year's Eve alone, read the newspaper and thanked the stars that *her* Rocco wasn't involved in anything like this.

In court on Monday, with Rocco in custody (it was his name on the business), Magistrate Jelfs surveyed the evidence and said, "It looks to me as if the prisoner has been trafficking in liquor to a large extent."

A key point was whether the upstairs apartment could be considered a private house, even though it was above a store; if so, it would mean the liquor found there could be deemed a legal private supply. The magistrate said no. Rocco's lawyer, Norman Kay, contended that because getting to the apartment required going outside first, it was indeed a private house. And he pointed out the magistrate himself had ruled exactly that in a case the previous summer.

"Well, I was wrong then," grumbled Jelfs. "I was misled by

somebody." There was no convincing him otherwise. Bessie had to write a thousand-dollar cheque—more than a year's salary for an average Hamiltonian—to pay the fines and get Rocco released.

Rocco wasn't happy with this outcome. He decided he was through dealing with the junior partner at O'Reilly & Kay, and hired the main man, the eloquent and genial forty-six-year-old Michael J. O'Reilly, a graduate of Osgoode Hall and a "staunch Liberal" in the words of the *Globe*. The senior partner went back to court with a liquor licence inspector willing to testify that Rocco's liquor supply was private "cellar stock." Rocco and Bessie not only got their money back, they got their liquor supply back too. The victory cost three hundred dollars in legal fees, but it was worth it.

And then came the Martino inquest. On the evening of Thursday, January 9, about fifty very interested Italians packed the gallery of the police court. Once it established the essential facts of Martino's death—including the lurid detail that the killing bullet had passed through his abdomen and come to rest on the other side in the lining of his vest—the court called Rocco to the stand.

Before the jury, Rocco admitted that he had known Tony Martino for "five or six months." And yes, the man had often come by the house to visit over that time. But he had not been at their New Year's Eve party. The Crown attorney asked him whether one of the guests, who was drunk, had been ordered out of the house that night. "I didn't put anybody out," said Rocco. "But I told a couple of friends of mine to go home because they were drunk." The Crown asked if he remembered their names. "No," said Rocco, "I know so many people."

When Bessie took the stand, her wide cheekbones, thick auburn hair and fashion sense made an impression—"pretty" and "stylish" the *Herald* called her. In her few moments of testimony she described herself as Rocco's wife and backed up his story.

A number of witnesses called that night wished they were any-where else. It was still rare for Italian immigrants in most North American cities to help police solve crimes within their community, so obfuscation during an inquest like this had to be expected. Even so, one or two of the witnesses betrayed a remarkable level of fear. One of Naticchio's fellow boarders at 104 Caroline Street North was called in after he had mentioned seeing Naticchio lying on his bed at ten o'clock New Year's Eve. When he took the stand he was visibly trembling, and when the Crown asked whether Naticchio had owned a hat like the one in evidence, he couldn't bring himself to speak.

"What's the matter with you?" said the Crown. "What are you shaking like that for? Nobody's trying to hurt you."

By the end, frustrated beyond tolerance, the coroner, Dr. Hopkins, said, "I never before heard so much equivocation and lying from the witness stand." He could have been more under-standing. Dr. Hopkins had seen for himself what came of angering the wrong people in Hamilton. Just eighteen months before, the body of a man "from Hamilton's foreign colony" had been found in the bay, wrapped in heavy chains, with a bullet hole in his head. It was not a place to talk freely.

Once all the witnesses were heard and the coroner had his say, it took the inquest jury sixteen minutes to make its decision: "We find that Tony Martino came to his death from a bullet fired from a revolver, and we believe that the man, Alberto Naticchio, men-tioned in the evidence, fired the fatal shot." This wasn't a binding decision. A coroner's inquest, then as now, was held to determine five things: who was the deceased; where and when did the death occur; what was the medical cause of death; and what was the means of that death—accident, suicide, homicide, and so on. The fact that the jury fingered Naticchio didn't, in itself, make him guilty, but it increased the pressure on police to find him so that he could be tried. They figured that by now he was south of the border, and they sent out a circular offering a hundred-dollar reward for information leading to his arrest.

It took two years, but eventually Naticchio was found in Pennsylvania, and he was tried in Hamilton. Remarkably, he got off. His defence, paid for by Rocco, was orchestrated by famed Hamilton lawyer Charles W. Bell. A veritable renaissance man, Bell was not only a defence lawyer for violent criminals, he was also a prolific Broadway playwright. His biggest success, the 1917 romantic romp *Parlor, Bedroom and Bath*, would eventually be remade as a Buster Keaton movie. Given all that, it was fitting that Naticchio's defence involved concocting a fictional character: a party guest by the name of Tony Latriano. It was Latriano who had been arguing with Martino in Rocco and Bessie's kitchen. It was Latriano who had shot Martino in a rage. It was Latriano who had convinced Naticchio to run off to the United States. Why? Because he had witnessed the murder. And to the court in Hamilton, this seemed at least plausible. Its Italian citizens were still so little documented, so misunderstood, that men could move in and out of its foundries and boarding houses, through its back doors and side streets, and leave no trace.

When Rocco took the stand at the preliminary hearing, he was asked if he knew this mysterious Tony Latriano. He gave the perfect answer. "I might know him," Rocco said, "but not by that name." At the trial a few months later, his name had become Lobriano, and the court was left so confused that Naticchio had to be released. Immediately, he fell back in with the Perri gang, which was busier than ever.

8

FIDUCIA
Confidence

BOOTLEGGING AND ORGANIZED CRIME IN SOUTHERN ONTARIO developed along specific regional and family fault lines. By 1919, thanks in part to the convenient elimination of Jimmy Celona, Rocco and Bessie controlled Hamilton and some of the surrounding territory, and had fingers into St. Catharines. Guelph, Brantford and Welland belonged to the powerful Sciarrone gang led by Calabrian brothers Joe and Domenic Sciarrone, who had connections in upper New York State. The Sicilian Galliardo brothers operated in Toronto's Ward district (taking over from Joe Musolino, deported in the wake of the Griro affair). Joseph Serianni ran a Calabrian gang with his brothers Samuel and Charles in Niagara Falls, New York, partnered with Joseph Henry Sottile. They contended for that territory with a Sicilian boss named Don Simone.

Aside from these large gangs, there were smaller players throughout the region. Frank Longo was a brutal Black Hander who sometimes worked with the Sciarrones in Welland when he wasn't causing injury to his wife; the D'Agostino brothers operated in St. Catharines, allied with the Perris; and Jim Sullivan (or Sullirano) ran booze from his base in Fort Erie.

Most of these gangs controlled their own territories and stayed out of each other's way, or worked together when it suited them, as the Sciarrone gang did with the Seriannis, and the Galliardos with Don Simone. But occasionally tremors erupted along the fault lines. More often than not, they emanated from Domenic Sciarrone.

In the early moments of Sunday January 12, 1919, for example, just three days after the inquest into Tony Martino's murder, twenty-one-year-old Fortunato Tedesco came home from a dance hall in Guelph. A lantern moon that night shone so brightly it cast shadows against the snow. As Fortunato approached the back door of the house where he lived with his parents, he heard something, turned and took a blast from a single-barrel shotgun to the chest and neck.

A married couple walking through the neighbourhood heard the bang. "I'll bet there's some of those foreigners being shot up," Harold Carrol said to his wife. "Now you watch and see if we don't see someone running." As Harold finished speaking, a man in a dark coat and felt hat came running from the direction of the sound. When he saw the couple, he slowed to a walk and covered his face as he passed. As that was happening, baker Joe Tedesco was in his backyard, kneeling in the blood-soaked snow, kissing the face of his murdered son.

The Ontario Provincial Police sent Inspector John Miller to investigate. At the time, Miller, fifty-one years old, was the OPP's best and most experienced detective, a relentless digger who offered blunt assessments of both criminals and police. During an investigation in Toronto two years before, he refused to work with a particular constable because he gave off "such a strong smell of liquor." Now he made it clear what he thought of how Guelph's constabulary had handled the crime scene. No search of the area was made, nobody looked for footprints; hell, it was the murdered man's friends who found the gun. "Nine hours passed before anything was done by the police," reported Miller. "In the meantime the chances for tracing anyone was gone."

Still, it didn't take Miller long to surmise that Domenic Sciarrone was behind Tedesco's murder, and likely many more besides. Sciarrone owned two bakeries; one in Guelph, and one in Thorold, near Welland. But Miller knew those were fronts. He had the Sciarrone family sized up: "This gang is so strong that they are able to levy amounts of money from those who are in fear of them, and are amassing wealth. They have Automobiles and Diamonds and live without working."

As he kept digging, Miller determined that for some time, and for various reasons, Sciarrone had been targeting Joe Tedesco. Joe's son—who had once told his father that one of them would be killed—had simply been collateral damage.

During the coroner's inquest after the murder, before any charges were laid, Sciarrone was forced to take the stand, testifying under the name Joseph Verona. His lawyers obtained a blanket objection to the testimony, meaning anything he said could not be used against him. Even so, he denied everything. And he radiated such contempt and menace as he sat in court that the Crown attorney paused during questioning to observe, "You are a bad man."

While Inspector Miller was out probing the Italian residents of Guelph for answers on the January 12 murder, and attempting to quell his irritation at the lack of co-operation he was getting, another man was killed. This time it was in Welland. At six-thirty the morning of January 29, Domenic Paparone, the friend of Domenic Speranza who had been there on the day of Jimmy Celona's murder but managed to avoid conviction, was walking to work. Without warning someone rushed up behind him and shot him in the back, piercing his heart. Again, the OPP put Inspector Miller on the case, and again he reported that Domenic Sciarrone was surely involved. Paparone, it was clear to Miller, had been killed to avenge the death of Jimmy Celona, who had worked for Sciarrone.

But Miller went even further: While Sciarrone may have been behind the killing, he was convinced Joseph Celona had done the shooting. "This man is a brother to the man who was murdered at Hamilton some time ago . . . And I am informed that at the time of the murder at Hamilton, Joe Cilona [*sic*] said that he would kill the man who killed his brother." Police issued an arrest warrant for Joe, describing him as a clean-shaven man wearing a fancy short overcoat, and a diamond ring on his left hand, typical for members of the Sciarrone gang. It also noted that he had last been seen in Toronto, in the company of Rocco Perri.

<hr />

A S THE CALENDAR TURNED TO 1919, THE CANADIAN government was getting worried about Bolsheviks in the increasingly militant unions of the western provinces. With several big labour events planned for Calgary in the early months of the year, Frank Zaneth was sent to infiltrate the International Association of Machinists. As "Harry Blask", he wound up winning the job of union secretary next to its leader, George Sangster, who also happened to be a member of the banned Socialist Party of Canada (SPC) and vice-president of the Calgary Trades and Labor Council. That meant Zaneth had access to Sangster's correspondence and to the leaders of Alberta's most radical unions.

In Calgary, Zaneth attended regular SPC meetings, distributed banned Socialist literature, and generally sold himself as one of the IWW's most active members. He also found time to send a memo to his commanding officer in Calgary, trying again for that extra one-dollar per diem, this time retroactively for his dangerous undercover work as a coal miner in Drumheller and Canmore. Inspector J. W. Spalding passed Zaneth's request up the line with a note of his own typed at the bottom: "This man appears capable but I am not as yet familiar with his work . . . Please advise if you will grant extra pay." A short while later the per diem was approved.

One day, working as secretary at the Calgary Trades and Labor Council, Zaneth was introduced to James Davis, who would later claim to have blown up a Chicago safe and delivered half a million dollars in jewellery to the IWW. While shaking his hand, Zaneth tried the secret IWW grip and Davis responded in kind. "I made it a point to cultivate this man Davis' acquaintance," he reported, "because I knew I could learn from him all that I desired."

Over the next few months, Zaneth's reports from Calgary fuelled fears in Ottawa of a coming Bolshevik revolution. He attended Thursday night "speakers" classes in which members were taught public speaking so they could better rouse fellow workers, and Sunday night economics classes that taught the writings of Karl Marx. He reported on the growing momentum among labour organizations toward forming a united group they called the One Big Union, and walked a picket line with his union boss, George Sangster. But by May, rumours had begun to circulate among union leaders that there was an impostor in the ranks.

On May 13, Superintendent A. B. Pennefather, commander of the southern Alberta district, was complaining to colleagues about being "up to my neck" in work. Right at the top of his pile of concerns sat Zaneth. He hammered out a memo and sent it up the chain to F. H. Routledge, the force's assistant commissioner in Regina. "Inspector Spalding reported to me that the Russian Jews of the Socialist Party of Canada in Calgary, were, he thought, getting wise to Zaneth," wrote Pennefather. "They have gone so far as to blame him for the arrest of Legere [Ben Legere, a party member] in Lethbridge."

Zaneth had played his part well enough that James Davis and the rest of the IWW members in Calgary were standing by him despite the suspicions. But when Zaneth was asked to show his IWW documents, he had none to offer. So he stalled, saying they were in a trunk in Estevan, Saskatchewan. That gave him a reason to get on a train and head to Regina headquarters for a meeting.

"I would suggest," wrote Pennefather, "that he be picked up in Regina by one of our men as an Alien Enemy." Once that was done they should give his arrest "the utmost publicity," said Pennefather, and tell the papers that Blask was a suspected IWW member.

Three days later, on May 16, Zaneth telegrammed Davis to let him know of his bad luck: "ARRESTED HERE TODAY. [SIGNED] HARRY BLASK." Reporting on his court appearance and fine, the Regina press referred to him as a "well-known agitator." That buffed Zaneth's image considerably among most of the union folks in Calgary, although two of them called the Regina police head-quarters repeatedly on Sunday to find out if Harry Blask really had been arrested, and a befuddled sergeant had not known what they were on about. Luckily when Zaneth returned, he was able to show his new alien registration papers. As for why he'd come back without his IWW documents, which had been the whole point of the trip, he could only shake his head and explain how the damned police had confiscated everything when he was arrested.

Zaneth's scramble for authenticity coincided with dramatic events in Winnipeg. Fighting for decent pay, an eight-hour work-day and the right to organize, the Winnipeg Trades and Labor Council had voted in favour of a general strike. On May 15, some twenty-four thousand workers, both union and non-union, had walked off the job, shutting down the city and sparking headlines all over North America. Zaneth's assignment was to stay in Calgary and report on the "Red element," which he did often from a picket line, just one of the workers striking in support of Winnipeg's effort.

It was a time in Canada when many people had little concept of what a trade union was, or what "collective bargaining" meant, and the Canadian government was crowded with politicians who feared revolution. On June 6, 1919, Parliament introduced—and passed in less than an hour—an amendment to the Immigration Act that would allow it to deport any immigrant seeking to violently overthrow the government. Then the arrests began.

First, in the wee hours of June 17, mounted police officers descended on Winnipeg strike leaders' homes and offices, rounding up everyone they viewed as a threat. Then, in an effort to decapitate the radical labour movement, the RNWMP issued orders to detachments in more than half a dozen western cities, calling for coordinated raids of the offices and homes of union leaders in search of evidence of seditious conspiracy. In Calgary, Harry Blask's boss was on the list, and shortly after midnight on July 1 George Sangster was one of those rousted out of bed by police.

Zaneth yet had work to do on this file. Harry Blask was still a useful active member of the Industrial Workers of the World, and the One Big Union remained a concern. He lived, as undercover agents typically do today, a strangely double life, attending meetings as Blask, maintaining his façade around union members, then finding private moments to type out reliable reports like a good RNWMP officer. When a miner who was broke needed to sleep at his place, he could not even let his guard down at home. He worked such long hours that at one point he needed a doctor's care for a week.

"Const. Zaneth has worked most faithfully," Inspector Spalding reported to his superiors. (He added that Zaneth was "also anxious to secure more pay.")

But despite all his precautions, some union members were becoming suspicious, and Zaneth began to worry again about his cover. As Harry Blask, he had been presenting himself as unemployed, but he sold subscriptions to *Searchlight*, a Calgary miners' union newspaper, without taking a commission. People were beginning to wonder where he was getting his money.

He gave different stories to different people, depending on the circumstance. Someone asked if the IWW in Chicago was sending him money. Zaneth thought it best to say yes. In another case, he said that his father in Springfield was supporting him. He also claimed at least once that he covered his room and board by playing poker (which throws light on how he must have passed his evenings in Moose Jaw after Grace left him). Even so, while never naming Zaneth, people began to mutter about the "stool pigeon" in their midst. At a gathering where Zaneth was present, one of them pulled out a knife and rammed its blade into the table, saying that whoever the stoolie was, "I'd just like to cut the heart out of the son of a bitch."

Zaneth could only agree—"I'm with you, Jack"—then report back to headquarters: "The way things are shaping at present, there is every possibility of me being uncovered."

His bosses considered sending him to Chicago to interact with the IWW there. It would get him out of immediate harm's way and help restore his standing among the "Red element" in Calgary. Superintendent Pennefather thought it a very good idea. "He has been a most excellent man in obtaining reliable information," he wrote, calling Zaneth "probably the best we have." Yes, yes, was the general view, all the way up to the assistant commissioner—send Zaneth to Chicago.

And yet nothing happened. Somehow a letter on the matter from the assistant commissioner to Pennefather had gone missing—"It is certainly very remarkable how this letter has disappeared," the assistant commissioner fumed in September; "It was placed in a small envelope and addressed to you 'personally.'" So for two months, Zaneth had to sweat it out in Calgary. Somehow, through sheer consistency and acting ability, he managed to go undiscovered. And then, on September 24, 1919, the biggest threat to his cover occurred, and it came from lawyers working for the government.

The Crown was preparing for its sedition trials against eight radical leaders, and it wanted to put Zaneth on the stand. Over the previous six months in Calgary, he had contributed significant intelligence to half a dozen major case files, and his evidence was vital to the outcome of the trials.

With memos and meetings, the RNWMP held off the lawyers as long as they could. Inspector Spalding had come to greatly admire Zaneth's work and was loath to see him go anywhere, let alone be revealed. Assistant Commissioner Routledge leaned against the idea as much as he could—Zaneth was a "valuable man," revealing him would be a "great pity" and using him after exposing him "would scarcely be safe."

Alfred J. Andrews, the deputy minister who was leading the prosecution, fully appreciated the sacrifice he was asking of the Mounties. Yes, he knew putting Zaneth on the stand would render him useless for further undercover work, at least among the western Socialists. But, he said, "Much as I value the opinion of the Officers who hesitate to produce this man, I really think on the whole it should be done."

At the beginning of November, the young constable was promoted to detective corporal—perhaps to increase the authority of his testimony, but also to reward him for a job well done. Five weeks later, he walked into a Winnipeg courtroom in full Mountie regalia.

‖‖‖‖‖‖‖‖‖‖‖‖‖‖‖‖‖‖‖‖‖‖‖

THE CHILD ROCCO HAD FATHERED WITH THE YOUNG Miss Rutledge was a girl. Being a romantic, Olive named her Autumn, probably for the season in which she was born, which Olive would have seen and smelled so vividly on the farm in Musclow.

Rocco visited as often as business allowed. It was common knowledge he loved children, and he was overjoyed to have one of his own. Once the winter of 1919 was over and Olive was fully recovered from giving birth, he took mother and daughter to live in St. Catharines. He couldn't have Olive showing off their daughter in Hamilton, so he ordered one of his men to find a place for her to live. The choice was a six-room brick house at 80 Geneva Street, rented for twenty-five dollars a month. Rocco filled the house with about two thousand dollars' worth of furniture and made his secret family comfortable, a safe distance from Hamilton.

Whenever Rocco "came home" to St. Catharines, he would drive up in his new blue-green Liberty touring car, sporting varnished wooden spokes and a clattering, state-of-the-art Continental "Red Seal" engine. He'd bought it after selling his previous, bruised auto a few months after his accident. It didn't do for the boss of a grow-ing racket to drive around in something less than "smart."

By now the difficulty of maintaining two completely separate lives must have forced a reckoning with truth, because it's clear that at some point Rocco told Olive his true identity and revealed the existence of Bessie. On census documents, Olive listed her last name as Perri, and occasionally in her letters home she would allude to another woman in her husband's life. Nevertheless, she appears to have believed that her relationship with Rocco was real and lasting: on those census documents she listed him as head of the family.

As for Rocco's other life, in the business of illegal liquor things were definitely breaking his way. The more the government clamped down on legitimate means of getting booze, the more people needed bootleggers. As far as Rocco was concerned, the more restrictions the better. So it was good news when an outbreak of influenza late in 1918 led doctors to prescribe the liquor cure more frequently. Rising exploitation of the loophole meant Ontario's ruling Conservatives would have to act.

Premier William Hearst couldn't help but feel the pressure. All of the major political parties in Ontario were officially pro-temperance. But one—the new United Farmers of Ontario—practically staked its existence on it. Prohibition was far more popular among rural voters than urban, and because rural voters were more numerous then, the UFO party was quickly gaining in popularity. In response to the UFO threat, Hearst introduced legislation in April 1919 to abolish the private sale of liquor altogether and make selling booze a government responsibility. This augured very well for bootleggers like Rocco, especially since that very month Quebec held a referendum on Prohibition and stayed convincingly "wet" on the matter, ensuring a source of supply.

But that Quebec vote added to a growing mood that, with the war over and soldiers returning, Ontario's populace deserved some say in whether Prohibition should continue. Premier Hearst himself admitted, "We had no mandate from the people to pass the Temperance Act" three years before. So at the same time that it spoke of closing loopholes in the OTA, the Hearst government submitted a bill calling for Ontario's own referendum on the issue.

No date for the referendum was set immediately, but sometime that fall seemed likely, while a probable provincial election loomed the following spring. And then politics again pushed its face through the door. When the opposition Liberals elected a new leader, Hartley Dewart, in the summer of 1919, Premier Hearst had a thought: Might it not be very clever to call a quick election, while the Liberals were in new-leader disarray? Yes, thought Hearst, it might.

He set the Prohibition referendum date for sometime in October, but declined to be more specific, and he delayed on naming a date for the election. Through the first week of September, and the second week, and the third, he waited. And then on September 23, feeling good about his political instincts, Hearst announced that the referendum and the election both would come on October 20. As it turned out, he hadn't quite thought this through.

Calling for the two votes on the same day ensured a one-issue election. And it was the issue on which other parties—one in particular—were now considerably stronger. Rocco and Bessie must have rubbed their hands together along with Prohibition's staunchest advocates. Bessie, ever practical, took the opportunity to adjust their bank accounts. The Bank of Toronto account in her name contained twenty-five thousand dollars—equivalent to nearly $325,000 today. If it got much larger it was sure to attract attention, and there was no doubt it would get larger. On October 11, she closed that account and quickly opened two others, in the Imperial Bank and the Standard Bank, under the name Bessie Starkman.

When the vote came, thousands of men and women in Toronto crowded around the newspaper bulletin screens on Bay, King and Richmond streets. Staring upward, they learned that Prohibition had won the referendum in a landslide. The vote was 406,676 to 246,683, with rural dry votes completely overwhelming the urban wet ballots. The same forces that brought in Prohibition also pushed

Hearst's government out of office, and even stripped Hearst of his own seat. The rural-based pro-Prohibition United Farmers of Ontario won in forty-five ridings, while the Liberals won twenty-nine. Hearst's Conservatives came third with twenty-five. The UFO, led by a Methodist Sunday School teacher named Ernest C. Drury, formed a coalition government with the Liberals, and Drury made Prohibition-believer William E. Raney attorney general.

The statutes of the OTA were locked into Ontario law, for the near future at least. Rocco and Bessie rejoiced.

\|\|\|\|\|\|\|\|\|\|\|\|\|\|\|\|\|\|\|\|\|\|\|\|\|\|\|\|\|\|\|\|\|\|

F RANK ZANETH WAS NATIONAL NEWS. THERE WERE plenty of undercover agents around the world in 1919. Turn-of-the-century Russia had some 6,500 secret political operatives. But Canada was a younger and more innocent place. In Canada, the concept of an undercover federal cop was so new and unfamiliar that to see one taking the witness stand in court was electrifying. "Secret Service Man Gives Sensational Evidence in Winnipeg Trial" proclaimed Toronto's *Globe*, above a Canadian Press story that ran December 6 in newspapers across the country.

To some, the idea of allowing a Mountie who pretended he was something else to testify in court just seemed *wrong*. Robert Cassidy was the lawyer defending Robert Russell, the Winnipeg General Strike leader accused in the first of the conspiracy trials, and Cassidy was beside himself listening to Frank Zaneth speak about his work as a sham Socialist. "This is an outrage upon the decency of the law," he exclaimed. "You could not hang a cat on such evidence!" Cassidy was driven to such a "high pitch of excitement," in one reporter's words, that at one point the judge was moved to ask him, "Is this trial getting on your nerves?"

For his part, Zaneth seemed quite relaxed on the stand. When he said that, in Calgary, "I got mixed up with Socialists," he smiled. He spoke easily and at length about the strike committees and Socialist meetings he attended, about his conversations with the radical leaders, about nearly freezing to death one night when he was ordered by a union leader to get a look at a load of rifles recently delivered to a nearby military armoury.

As detailed as his testimony was, the defence and others could not get over the idea of a Mountie who *lied*. Union members were furious, and some threatened to do Zaneth harm the next time he showed his face. "I'd like to shoot him," said one. "Don't you worry," said another, "someone will get the son of a bitch before very long."

But his testimony proved effective; Robert Russell was convicted and sentenced to two years for seditious conspiracy. That guaranteed Zaneth would appear as a witness at subsequent conspiracy trials. The following February, at the Winnipeg trial of seven strike leaders, Zaneth admitted to the defence counsel R. A. Bonnar that his job required him to dissemble frequently in the course of his work.

"You are a liar then?" asked Bonnar.

"Yes," said Zaneth, "I suppose I am."

Bonnar asked him if he was a "wolf in sheep's clothing" when he was posing as a member of the Socialist Party.

"You might call it that," said Zaneth.

Said Bonnar, "Isn't that on the order of being a sneak?"

Justice Metcalfe interceded. "I will not permit a question like that," he said. "This man we all know was acting under orders of the Mounted Police. I will not permit him to be called a sneak."

Playing slyly to the postwar sensitivities of the court, Bonnar pressed Zaneth on the Austrian nationality of his alias, Harry

Blask, and on his pronunciation of certain words, such as *Kamerad* for "comrade."

Again the judge spoke up. "You are accusing this man of being a German," he said. "There is no evidence to that effect. He says he is of Italian birth. I will not have the witness abused or untrue insinuations made."

Bonnar continued his questioning. "How do you pronounce your name in Italian?"

"Zanetti," said the corporal.

"Why did you change it?"

A courtroom was no place to delve into the unknowable, no place to try to articulate the mysterious psychological forces that made him who he was, and made him wish to be something other. So here, finally, in a small, private act of self-preservation, Frank Zaneth truly did lie. To the question of why he'd changed his name, he replied, "I didn't. My father did when I was a child."

||||||||||||||||||||||||||||||||

ROCCO AND BESSIE WERE ABOUT TO GET VERY RICH. ON January 1, 1920, the Dominion government repealed nearly all of the Orders-in-Council. Armistice may have been signed fourteen months before, but as long as armies had remained mobilized the constraints of the War Measures Act had stayed in effect. Now though, as far as Canada was concerned, peace had arrived, and it was time for life to get back to normal.

Booze, in other words, could once again flow—into bottles and over borders. Provincial legislation still applied; regular people couldn't buy or sell anything over 2.5 percent alcohol in Ontario without a doctor's prescription (which perhaps explained the persistence of the influenza outbreak). But you could—for now—buy it outside the province and bring it in for personal use. And distilleries and breweries could once again make their products, just as long as they shipped them out of the province. On the eve of the repeal, shipping companies were advised to staff up quickly in order to handle the orders of liquor that would be coming in from Quebec.

As early as January 2, newspapers were breathless with conflicting reports. Ontario was being flooded with booze from Montreal—"Ontario Getting 150,000 quarts of Liquor Daily" wrote the *Toronto Daily Star*. Ontario was not being flooded with booze from Montreal—"Anticipated Flood Has Not Materialized" wrote a *Globe* correspondent in the town of Belleville.

But there is no doubt whisky was moving. In Yorkton, Saskatchewan, the Canada Pure Drug Company of Harry and Sam Bronfman shipped in trainloads of whisky—thirty thousand cases in just a couple of weeks—for the purpose of exporting to the United States and the western provinces. It was so much liquor that the customs agent in Yorkton worried the Bronfmans' warehouse would collapse. By January 8, "the irrigation of the desert of Hamilton" was under way, as the *Hamilton Spectator* reported that "heavy cargoes of booze yesterday and to-day were being imported both from Montreal and Ontario distilleries."

It was no mistake that imports were coming to Ontario from Ontario. A reborn mail-order system meant that customers could once again buy booze from distilleries in Waterloo, Toronto, Windsor and Belleville by ordering through out-of-province outlets. In Saskatchewan alone, sixty mail-order firms opened to handle the western Canada business. Anyone of legal age could buy "imported" booze from a local distillery, with just one proviso: he had to go straight home with it. The minute he broke the seal of a bottle, or deviated from the direct route home, even to get milk or pick up his mail, he was breaking the law and subject to a fine of two hundred dollars.

For Rocco and Bessie, all of this was good news. They were perfectly positioned to direct some of the new flood of liquor to the hotels, roadhouses, blind pigs and speakeasies they served, and they had no qualms about deviating from any path.

Quickly, as they expected, the news got even better. At midnight on the night of January 16, just two weeks after Canada's repeal of the War Measures Act, the gears of U.S. Prohibition engaged. The Eighteenth Amendment, ratified exactly one year earlier, immediately took effect, simplifying what had become a messy tangle of anti-liquor legislation south of the border. Prosecuted according to the stipulations of the Prohibition Enforcement Act (a.k.a. the Volstead Act, for Judiciary Committee Chairman Andrew J. Volstead), Americans were prohibited from making, selling or transporting any beverage containing more than half a percentage point of alcohol. And lo, a huge market opened up for any Canadian with the enterprise and moral flexibility to exploit it.

In Montreal, according to legend, on learning about the Volstead Act becoming law, Harry Hatch told his brother they were going to be millionaires. When Herb asked how, Harry said, "Well, you know. We got it. They ain't got it."

In Hamilton, Bessie got on the phone to line up suppliers; Rocco organized his men and firmed up his clients, people like Joe Burke at Port Credit's Lakeview Inn, who kept his champagne and liquor in an ice room beneath a trap door. All of their allies— the Italian families in Guelph, St. Catharines, Niagara Falls and Buffalo, the suppliers in Waterloo and Montreal, the connections in Chicago and New York—now came into play as never before. And when American customs officers immediately began boarding trains from Toronto and Hamilton looking for booze being smuggled across the border, the boats of Ben Kerr and other hardened men willing to power through the icy waters of Lake Ontario, Lake Erie and the Detroit and Niagara rivers, became more important than ever.

THERE was one extra benefit of the repeal of the War Measures Act: betting on the horse races was, at least briefly, quite legal. There were rumours, however, that during its next session the Dominion Parliament would curb gambling with new legislation. So that January, according to one account, Rocco put on a thick coat, gathered a group of his men and went to the races. On a January Friday that was nineteen degrees colder than normal, he placed a huge bet on good-looking Toronto jockey Arthur Scholes in a ten-mile race that ran from Hamilton to Dundas and back. And he won big. To the cheers of the crowd, Scholes brought his horse home nearly two minutes in front of the favourite.

You can picture Rocco's men slapping him on the back as he lit a big cigar. Truly everything was going his way.

9

DELIRIO
Delusion

I T WAS THE ERA OF EVERYMAN RISK AND REWARD. THERE was illicit money to be made, and Prohibition unlocked the mechanism. Suddenly anyone with a boat or an automobile—or just a set of bloomers roomy enough to hide the bottles strapped to one's legs—could get a piece of the action.

Ordinary Canadian whisky, imported via Montreal, cost about six dollars a gallon in Ontario, or eighteen dollars for a case of twelve quarts. Those, at least, were the prices set by the Liquor Licence Board of Ontario. But if you were an American dependent on bootleg deliveries, you paid $120 a case in the Michigan border towns, or fifteen dollars for a single quart. Farther from the border, the risks got higher and so did the prices. A man in Iowa happily bought ten cases of Canadian whisky at $250 per. For a story he wrote for the *Star Weekly*, Ernest Hemingway—still a month from his twenty-first birthday—found a smuggler bound for Detroit who anticipated a $1,450 profit on the twenty cases he planned to take across the river, past the paltry border patrol.

The demand was there and every means of delivery. Mothers

in velour coats and cloche hats would cross the border pushing prams with bottles hidden under their infants. In winter, hardened Windsor men, their boots fitted with spikes, would push loaded dories equipped with metal runners across the frozen Detroit River. Others bought old junker autos for ten dollars or less to tow those boats and shrugged if they fell through the ice. With so little police presence along the border, almost anything worked. The real problem was a shortage of supply.

With the advent of the War Measures Act, Ontario distilleries had shut down. Now that they could open again, it took a while to get them up and running. Rye whisky was still the liquor of choice in Canada, and once whisky was distilled, the law demanded it be aged for two years before being sold. As a group, Ontario's distilleries were able to negotiate a nine-month relief from the aging requirement, but with Prohibition to the south they kept production small, failing to appreciate the enormity of the bootleg market. And one old-money distillery family, the Gooderhams, who owned Gooderham & Worts on the Toronto waterfront, found the whole notion of selling to bootleggers distasteful. Rather than associate with them, patriarch William Gooderham chose not to reopen his distillery, preferring to put the hulking Victorian-era buildings up for sale.

For the first two or three years of the new reality, many bootleggers had to make do with selling moonshine. Untold numbers of rough but effective stills were set up in attics, basements and sheds across Canada. The authorities managed to sniff out some of them—in the first ten months of 1919, police shut down eighty-five stills, more than three times the number of the previous year—but a great many more went undetected. They sent a stream of potent liquor to blind pigs and liquor dives north and south of the border.

Some of that liquor was toxic—moonshine whisky was sometimes doctored with poisonous fusel oil, for example, to give it the aroma and body of the real stuff. Too much and you could die, as six people did in Pana, Illinois, after drinking liquor laced with a large amount of fusel. But in the midst of a whisky shortage, that risk hardly seemed to matter. One August, an unidentified Toronto bootlegger worried aloud in the *Globe* that the rush on drink during the Canadian National Exhibition would exhaust his entire stock.

Major bootleggers like Rocco and Bessie Perri needed a larger and more reliable supply of product. So for the time being, they served their markets primarily with strong beer, which ran at 9 percent alcohol. It was more quickly made than distilled spirits, and in vast quantities, at twenty-two Ontario breweries. Three of those provided Rocco and Bessie with most of their supply: Grant's Spring Brewery in Hamilton, Taylor and Bate in St. Catharines and Waterloo's Kuntz Brewery. Much of the twenty-five thousand dollars Bessie pulled out of the bank the previous October may well have been spent setting up business accounts with these suppliers.

By now the Perris had such a large clientele that they couldn't keep all their liquid inventory at 105 Hess. So they established a small warehouse, as it were—a frame house at the end of Burlington Street, where they temporarily stored their stock, and where Rocco or a few of his men could stay for a few days whenever they needed to keep out of sight. The location near the Hamilton waterfront, barely a block from Ben Kerr's marine garage at the tip of Bay Street North, made for easy unloading in the dead of night. The police were aware of Rocco's use of this house, but they had no proof of what was going on inside, and with resources stretched thin they lacked the manpower to watch it.

By mid-1920, Rocco and Bessie were making enough money that Bessie insisted they move. It was time to get away from their half-house, half-grocery-store on Hess Street where prostitutes worked in the back rooms and a man had bled onto the kitchen table from a gunshot wound. It was time to buy a new home and live in a manner that reflected not just their aspirations but their means.

In Hamilton, moving up in the world meant moving south. It meant crossing the King Street divide that separated the immigrants and striving lower classes of the north from the Establishment nearer the escarpment. So for about six thousand dollars they bought a two-and-a-half-storey row house with eight rooms, a tall cellar and a side gable roof at 166 Bay Street South. On a street of leafy trees and Establishment neighbours, it was an address that said they'd arrived.

But while Rocco and Bessie wanted to live in style, they preferred, unlike some wealthy bootleggers, not to announce their presence. The house they chose was far from grand—"unpretentious" and "plain-looking" it would later be called. The centre of a three-unit row of dark-brick townhouses, it sported a large, brick-pillared porch with a second-floor balcony above, and bay windows looking out from the front parlour and master bedroom. But the house was larger than it appeared, extending toward the back of the property with two brick additions, one of them a kitchen, dating back to the 1890s. Inside, once Bessie was finished decorating, its floors were covered in expensive, hand-woven Persian rugs. Tapestries and fine art hung on the walls. The parlour featured a beautiful piano for Bessie to play. Rocco had a basement billiard room in which to smoke cigars and drink whisky with the local political and police officials his lawyers were helping him cultivate as allies. A gleaming white kitchen offered every modern convenience. There were enough bedrooms that they had room for house guests, sometimes Bessie's daughters when they were older, sometimes one or two men who acted as drivers or bodyguards for Rocco. Below the house, a hidden door opened to a secret cellar for liquor storage. Outside, a large, two-car garage housed a roadster and a sedan, and there was space behind for Rocco's men to park a truck when they were sleeping over. At first, there was no guard dog; the previous summer the city had fined Rocco fifty dollars and forced him to have the dog put down. But before long he acquired a ferocious German shepherd. There was valuable merchandise to protect, and there were times when he couldn't be there himself—or didn't want to be.

Rocco was still a young man, just thirty-two. But his prosperity with Bessie was establishing itself so firmly that, after nearly ten years together, their relationship was beginning to feel more like a business partnership than a marriage. Rocco was drawn to the other, sweeter, simpler pleasure in his life. During his business trips to St. Catharines, it was so easy to drive over to Geneva Street. He could spend time on the floor with Autumn, playing papa. He spent enough nights with Olive to give her reason to hope he would one day, finally, stay. And in the summer of 1920, on a night when Rocco probably made promises he didn't intend to keep, they conceived their second child.

Perhaps he thought this arrangement could go on indefinitely. Or maybe he thought that when it ended, it would end quietly, with a bit of money to soothe the wound. Either way, it would be another two years before he would find out he was wrong.

⁗⁗⁗⁗⁗⁗⁗⁗⁗⁗⁗⁗⁗

I n February 1920, The Royal North West Mounted Police changed its name to reflect its responsibilities across the reach of Canada. (Although, being a frugal organization, it still used its old internal stationery, crossing out "North West" and typing "Canadian" above.) By April, the RCMP was looking at the end of Frank Zaneth's three years of enlistment and the possibility that he might leave. A. J. Andrews, the deputy minister who had effect-ively ended Zaneth's work as an undercover Socialist by insisting he testify in the Winnipeg trials, was now one of Zaneth's biggest fans. There was, he wrote, "nothing I can now say which would be too flattering to this young chap. His evidence in this case was most clean cut and decisive and the opposing attorneys were not able to shake him on any material point." Andrews had heard that Zaneth's period of enlistment was due to expire and said, "I would be very sorry to see him retire."

But Zaneth had no intention of retiring. And when the RCMP thought to transfer him to its brand new Quebec division, headquartered in Montreal, he agreed and suggested that first they send him to Springfield. In the years since he'd left, the Massachusetts city had become a hotspot for Socialist extremism. Even his father, Ambrose, had become affiliated with the IWW. Zaneth told his superiors that he was sure he could use his contacts there to join one of the radical American organizations and establish credentials that would allow him to infiltrate related groups more easily in Montreal.

He likely had other, more personal reasons for orchestrating this trip. Zaneth had apparently managed to keep the existence of his child and ex-wife a secret from his superiors. Now Grace, who was living with her parents in the township of Ware, a suburb of Springfield, but still using the last name Zanetti for the sake of her daughter, had met a tradesman named Raymond Fountain and hoped to remarry (as soon as Fountain's current wife passed away). An extended stay would give Frank the opportunity to spend time with nine-year-old Rena before the circumstances of her life changed. And not to be forgotten, Frank had his own romantic needs as well; his prospects were better where there were people who knew him.

With his commanders' permission, he spent part of a month

in Springfield. He also travelled to Boston and New York City but wasn't able to get anything like the access to socialist organizations that he'd promised. The only success he had came from running into an old contact who helped him obtain blank membership cards for the Communist Party of America and the Left Wing Section of the Socialist Party of Greater New York. It was a meagre reward for the effort and expense, but Zaneth tried to sell it as something important. "It would appear," he reported to his superiors, "I have been a member of the two mentioned parties for a considerable length of time."

In the middle of May, Zaneth returned to Montreal and reported to the commander of the Quebec district, working under a new assumed identity: James LaPlante. In his office, Zaneth's new commanding officer, Superintendent Belcher, read the detective corporal's eight-page account of what he'd accomplished over the previous month and sat for a moment. Then he rolled a piece of paper into his typewriter and banged out a quick note to the commissioner: "This N.C.O. did not get the credentials he thought he would be able to get . . . I think he will have a hard time concealing his identity for any length of time in this part of the country."

Smart man, that Belcher. Over the summer in Montreal, Zaneth attended meetings and rallies for the Socialist Party of Canada, both English and French chapters, trying to gain the confidence of its leadership. He befriended the female owner of a tiny, left-wing bookstore on rue Ste-Catherine and soon began working there part time. As James LaPlante, he seemed to be getting along fine well into the fall—until the afternoon of Sunday, October 17. While he was in the bookstore, talking with the owner at the counter, a man entered the store. He was David Rees, a member of the United Mine Workers Union. Rees walked up to "LaPlante" and grinned. "Hello, Harry," he said. "What are you doing down here? Oh, no, your name's not Harry anymore." Then he proceeded to tell the bookstore owner all about "Harry Blask's" undercover exploits out west. Two days later, a story by Rees appeared in the newspaper published by the British Columbia Federation of Labour, exposing Zaneth and running his picture with the caption, "Here he is."

It was all over.

In his office, the Quebec district superintendent rolled Zaneth's succinct account of his cover being blown through his typewriter and pounded out a note at the bottom: "This is only what could be expected." He asked the commissioner that Zaneth be allowed to stay in Montreal and switch to straight detective work. "Another man is badly needed here and I am sure that he has the makings of a good detective for general investigations."

Despite some concern over the sergeant's safety if he stayed in Montreal, the higher command agreed. And so, for a time, Zaneth's undercover career was put on hold.

||||||||||||||||||||||||||||||||

T EMPERANCE ADVOCATES WERE FURIOUS. THEY HAD managed to elect a prohibitionist Ontario government and nothing had changed. In fact, the practice of delivering local Ontario beer and liquor to Ontario drinkers via orders through Montreal was more popular than ever, so popular it had acquired a nickname: "short-circuiting." Now temperance groups wanted to know what the government was going to do about it.

In November of 1920, a provincial committee of bearded and bespectacled men gathered to discuss the issue. Attorney General Raney pleaded patience. Police were stretched thin, he suggested. "There are thousands of people in a position to break the law who have to be watched."

They had liquor taxes and distillery jobs to protect too. But to be seen as doing *something*, the government devised a bill. They wanted to stop the movement of liquor, on the roads and waterways of Ontario, if that liquor was going to be drunk anywhere in the province. "It will deal an effective blow at the rum-running which has been the scandal of the Ontario boundary" voters were assured. And in a referendum held on April 18, 1921, Ontario voted in, by a margin of 166,385 votes, what became known as the Sandy Act, named for F. G. Sandy, the MPP who had introduced it. As of July 19, the law was clear: Ordering through Montreal? Over. Transporting liquor into Ontario? Finished. Stocking up your private cellar? Kaput. The government had turned off the mail-order business.

Exporting though—that was still perfectly fine. A truck or a boat could load up with booze as long as it was being sent out of the country. You just had to be able to prove it, which meant having the right paperwork. Did the Bill of Lading give the details of the shipment? Did the B-13 form show that the booze had been purchased by a buyer in a foreign destination? Did the customs man stamp that B-13 to clear the shipment for export? Well then, go right ahead.

Welcome to the next great loophole.

Almost immediately, breweries began selling thousands of kegs to bootleggers like Rocco. The distilleries still had not recovered, particularly Corby's, near Belleville, owned by Consolidated Distilleries of Montreal, where sales had fallen to five hundred gallons a month. But in 1921 the president of Consolidated Distilleries, Sir Mortimer Davis, had a clever idea: hire that Harry Hatch fellow, who had pounced so quickly on the Montreal angle, as sales manager. Hatch was happy to deal with bootleggers; all that big operators like Rocco and Bessie needed to open an account was twenty thousand in cash.

Within two years, the boat traffic to Belleville's government dock—a fleet that became known as Hatch's Navy—had pushed sales at Corby's to about fifty thousand gallons a month.

Manufacturers employed an elaborate subterfuge to get around the restrictions of the Sandy Act. The first step was to line up people willing to pose as foreign buyers. In the case of the Seagram distillery in Waterloo, that buyer was often Irwin S. Yarrow, who ostensibly purchased liquor for export to Mexico City. Bessie had to give him the money for that, so roughly every two weeks cheques for $3,800 or $4,200 or even $8,100, signed by Bessie, would be credited to Yarrow's account. At the distillery, Rocco's big slat-sided trucks would load up. The shipper would give Rocco's man the B-13 form, filled out with the shipment's true volume and monetary value, along with its fictitious buyer and foreign destination (a location in Michigan or New York State was fine, but a destination in Mexico or Cuba was safer because it was harder to check). In the case of Corby's, loads consigned to a New York State buyer named "J. Penna" would be hauled to the government dock, where one of Rocco's boats would be waiting. Besides the Gogos' *Hattie C* there were the *Atun*, the *Elmo*, the *Kitty*, *Miss Ontario* and many others. The skipper would sign the B-13 form with a false name, then his crew would load up the vessel while someone paid off the outside customs inspector who stamped the form to make it official. For enough money, some customs officers would stamp a batch of blank B-13s and let the bootleggers fill in the details. A lot of customs officers ended up driving around in very expensive cars.

From there, Rocco, his men and others like them would employ the bootlegger's version of short-circuiting: ferrying the loads to another spot miles down the shore, waiting until nightfall and then unloading them back into Ontario to supply hotels, dance halls, roadhouses and other customers. In January of 1921, Toronto's chief of police tried to refute the charge that the city's downtown was now "overrun with blind pigs."

Not all of the orders came back into Ontario, of course. Some shipments did get hauled across water to the United States. Bootleggers supplied by the Hiram Walker distillery had a short, easy trip from Walkerville to the other side of the Detroit River. At this stage of his career, Rocco usually sent his shipments into New York State across the Niagara River from Bridgeburg, Ontario, just about two miles north of where construction crews would start building the Peace Bridge in 1925. Shipments intended for Frank Costello, a Calabrian gangster quickly gaining authority in New York City, usually went first to the French islands of St. Pierre and Miquelon, tucked close to Newfoundland, which gave distillers proof their shipments had landed at a foreign destination and gave their effort to avoid paying excise extra legitimacy. From there it was an easy sail to "Rum Row" off the east coast of the United States, where ships from Scotland and elsewhere would anchor and unload into waiting boats. Many shipments meant for Ontario went the long way through those islands as well.

These were heady times. Of course, the more money that was at stake, the more there was to fight for. One of the first to learn that lesson was Thomas Mathews, a Stoney Creek farmer with connections to bootleggers. In September 1920, someone shoved a long knife into the left side of his chest, beneath his arm, and let him fall. The following June, someone plunged an equally long knife into the chest and abdomen of a twenty-seven-year-old Italian known in Hamilton as James Saunders. A known gangster who worked for Domenic Sciarrone, Saunders had stupidly stolen a cache of whisky from a house on East Jackson Street. When his body was found on June 18 and police looked at his driver's licence, they learned Saunders had recently lived at 166 Bay Street South. For a time, he had worked for Rocco Perri. It may have been Rocco's whisky he'd stolen.

If Rocco was troubled by the death of someone who had lived under his roof, or if he was implicated in the man's punishment, at least he had somewhere to get away from it all. That summer of 1921, after the murder of James Saunders, he visited the Rutledge family in Musclow.

The previous February, in a St. Catharines hospital, Olive had given birth to their second little girl. And in another gesture of doomed romanticism, she had named the child Catherine, after Rocco's recently deceased sister. Then, with a toddler and a newborn, she had returned to the family farm. Now, as the weather warmed, Rocco spent an entire month there.

It was a poor property, and Olive's mother was an invalid, so despite Olive's efforts the dilapidated house was increasingly ill kept. Rocco helped the family with money. And they, in turn, treated him like a son—a son still named Rocco Ross, as far as they knew, since Olive hadn't yet told them the truth. They had, admittedly, been a little confused in February when they arrived at the hospital and asked for Olive Ross, only to be told their daughter was registered as Olive Perri. But they were simple people, and Olive's husband was quite a forceful and certain individual, so they decided not to press the matter.

And anyway, he seemed to make their daughter happy.

||||||||||||||||||||||||||||||||||

FRANK ZANETH HAD FOUND LOVE, TOO. MARGHERITA Scevola—Frank called her Rita—had more in common with him than Grace Russell ever had. Like Frank, she was a northern Italian, born in Pavia just like him. She had sailed from

Italy on the S.S. *Cretic*, landing August 17, 1920, and arriving in Springfield soon after. Given how quickly their relationship progressed, it's possible she'd come at the urging of family who told her of the successful Mountie who was ready to take a new wife.

It seems that Frank had finally arrived at some kind of peace with his past, and his origins. Not only did he want to marry Rita, he wanted to marry her in Springfield, surrounded by his family. On March 4, 1921—the day after Grace Russell married Raymond Fountain—Frank asked his superiors for permission to marry and to live out of barracks with his new wife. A week later his request was approved. The ceremony took place on April 2 in the large and picturesque Our Lady of Mount Carmel, the main church of Springfield's Italian Catholic community, and three weeks later Rita joined Frank in Montreal.

Though he was no longer useful as a Socialist infiltrator, Zaneth had fans in the RCMP's Quebec district. "He is doing excellent work here, and is a keen intelligent man," Superintendent Belcher had told the commissioner. By the time he married Rita he'd been promoted to acting detective sergeant.

For the next several years, Zaneth worked as a control officer. It was mostly a desk job, handling the undercover operatives who were investigating Quebec's Communist movement. For someone with so little formal education and training, the job gave him an opportunity to learn the ways of the RCMP from the inside. Once or twice, though, he did manage to get out into the field, which allowed him to keep his skills sharp for the day he would need them, among criminals far more dangerous than Communists.

10

RISOLUZIONE
Resolution

A WET, MILD WIND BLEW THROUGH THE FIRST DAYS OF February 1922. In Toronto, someone caught a cabbage butterfly in his backyard. But to Olive Rutledge, mother of two little girls, the world must have seemed very cold.

She had been through an emotionally trying and confusing few months. All through the previous fall, she had been pressing Rocco to resolve their situation. She'd grown tired of living with her parents in their rundown hovel in Musclow, helping to care for her ailing mother as well as her own children. And the idea of returning to St. Catharines, where she had no family and few friends, was hardly more attractive. She wanted to be with Rocco, to raise their children together. At one point, in an effort to push the matter, she threatened to expose their relationship to Bessie. But Rocco wasn't a man to be intimidated, and by then Bessie likely already knew.

Earlier that winter, Olive had been so determined to force matters that she'd gone looking for a new house to live in with Rocco and the children, and she'd found one, close to the children's school and to her parents' home. She'd told him the down payment wasn't much—just $850—but it was up to Rocco to pay it, to make them a family and provide for their children's future. It was true he had never denied the children's needs, but it was time now for certainty and security. She was through living on hope. She wanted it done, and she wanted it in writing.

Then in December, during her family's celebrations of Christmas in Musclow, Olive had opened an envelope from Rocco. Inside was a gift of six hundred dollars, and a lovely letter, dated December 21, 1921, in which he'd seemed to grant her nearly everything she wanted. He told her she needed to stay with her mother just for another week, because he was getting a house in Hamilton for Olive and the girls to live in. "I know the children cannot stay in the woods," he wrote. "And I like to see them every day." Rocco signed this letter "R. Ross," apparently to keep up the fiction with her parents. But his words, at least, seemed genuine; people who read the letter later described it as "endearing." Olive's joy in this moment must have been hard to contain. No doubt she began to make plans, assuring people that her new life with the man she loved was going to begin very soon.

And then nothing. For weeks there was no further word, Rocco didn't appear, and people in the community began to whisper.

At least part of the reason for Rocco's silence was a sudden plateful of other concerns. Over those same weeks, Attorney General Raney was cranking up the pressure on bootleggers. Some of the hotels and roadhouses Rocco supplied were raided. Soon Raney sent a wave of OTA "spotters" into Hamilton—some of them officers, some of them paid informants—bent on finding liquor stashes. Several of Rocco's own trucks were nabbed; in one year he lost eighty thousand dollars in seizures and other expenses. For a short while, the best ally he had was Magistrate Jelfs who, by agreement or by sheer willfulness, dismissed many of the resulting arrests for lack of evidence. It was, said Jelfs, a matter of conscience.

Olive couldn't have known the degree to which Rocco's attention was preoccupied. All she knew was waiting. Already the anxiety, the strain of her situation, had added years to her face. She was twenty-five and looked a decade older. Now, with the extra worry, she stopped eating. She grew thin with torment, and still she had nothing to show for her faith. Nothing but Rocco's silence and the whispers that rose around her like a sour, caustic cloud.

Finally, in February, she couldn't take it anymore. Finally she had to act. She picked up the phone and asked the operator to connect her to the office of a Hamilton barrister, an ex-army man by the name of Colonel Frank Morison, KC. She made an appointment to see Morison and then hung up and began to pack. She packed two trunks as well as a suitcase and two additional club bags. Along with a great number of the expensive dresses Rocco had bought her, she piled in cooking utensils and household linens, as if she were preparing for the house he'd promised her. Then she bundled her daughters—three-year-old Autumn and eleven-month-old Catherine—in winter clothes and took them to the train station.

On Tuesday, February 7, Olive and her little girls arrived in Hamilton. A taxi took them and their belongings to the large, four-storey Hotel Stroud, at the corner of Merrick and MacNab streets. Olive checked in herself and her daughters under the name of "Mrs. Rutledge." After they were settled, Olive picked Catherine up, took Autumn by the hand and walked a few short blocks to the imposing Bank of Hamilton building at the corner of James and King streets. Just a few years before, a stuntman called the Human Fly had scaled the outside of this tall building, thrilling a huge crowd of onlookers. Now, inside, the elevator operator took Olive and her girls to the seventh floor, where Colonel Morison had his office. Morison welcomed them and called in his stenographer, Miss Velma Williamson. Some time later, when Olive emerged from Morison's office, she had secured a lawyer to help her negotiate with Rocco.

Days of anxious waiting followed. Harry Stroud, who managed the hotel owned by his brother, John, could not help but notice how fretful and restless Olive was. Nearly every twenty minutes she would ride the elevator down from her room, pace about waiting for the lobby phone to ring, then ride the elevator back up again to check on her children. Down and up, down and up. And at least nine or ten times a day, she would lift the receiver and call someone. "I am not here for my own part, but for the welfare of my children," she said into the phone. "I am merely asking for their protection."

At times, Olive sounded bitter as she spoke to Rocco. They had been together for four years, she said at one point, "And this is what I get for it." Sometimes, the conversation became heated. "What?" she yelled at one point, "You won't give me a goddamned cent? Well, you'll see what I can do about it!" On another occasion, she began to weep. "God will strike you dead for saying that!" she said, then hung up and seemed inconsolable.

It wasn't just Rocco on the other end of the line, it was Bessie too. Who knows how long she had known about Olive, but she was involved now. At least once, Bessie called the hotel herself and asked Stroud to get Olive on the phone. If it had been up to Rocco alone, he likely would have given Olive whatever she wanted. But where Rocco could be sentimental and generous with his money, Bessie was neither. It was Bessie, the wife who had given up her own children for Rocco, who wouldn't give Olive a goddamned cent, even if it was Rocco saying the words.

By February 10, Morison had drawn up the terms of a possible agreement: a lump sum of five hundred dollars, continuous monthly payments for the children after that and relocation of Olive's furniture in St. Catharines to wherever she wanted to live. He required Rocco and Olive to come to his office to sign the papers. In the lobby of the Hotel Stroud, Harry overheard Olive on the phone: "If you come in your car, I'll go with you."

Early that evening, a large stylish car of a sort not usually seen in Hamilton—probably Rocco's new Marmon, the marque he had come to favor—pulled up in front of the hotel. Harry Stroud watched a short, stout man in a dark hat and a brown coat waiting by the car for Olive, who came holding Catherine in her arms. It occurred to Stroud just then that Olive had left her three-year-old up in the room, so he ordered one of his employees, William Dixon, to run out into the street as the car was leaving to take down its licence plate number. Dixon came back with the number 56-659, one of three new licences Bessie had registered a month before.

It was a contentious meeting in Morison's office. At one point, Rocco and Olive took their argument outdoors into the cold. A lawyer in a nearby building saw the two of them at the corner of Main and James. Olive needed Rocco's signature on the document, and as she beseeched him Rocco appeared intensely irritated, wanting to leave. But eventually, later that night, the Marmon brought Olive and her baby back to the hotel. While they'd been gone, Stroud must have brought Autumn down to the lobby where he could look after her. As she ran to the door to greet her distraught mother, she noticed Rocco about to leave in his car.

"Good night, Papa," she called.

The next day, Olive took her children to visit Morison in his office. And later the Marmon came again for Olive. Something about the Hotel Stroud—perhaps its manager's nosiness—didn't sit well with Rocco. Or maybe he preferred to have Olive and his children stay in a hotel he controlled. Before long some men arrived in a wood-panelled truck, possibly the new REO Speed Wagon Bessie had recently registered, to take their things to the Hanrahan Hotel on Barton Street in the city's north section. When Olive registered this time, she gave a false home address—Cornwall.

If by this point Olive held out any hope that things would be resolved for the best, she lost that hope during the next thirty-six hours. In the cold early hours of Monday morning, driven to the breaking point of despair, she climbed out of the window of her second-floor room and shrieked into the darkness for help. Joseph Hanrahan, the owner of the hotel, clambered out after her and brought Olive back inside. She seemed calm for a while. But well before dawn she was so desperate to get outside without being seen that she climbed out of the window of the ladies' bathroom and used a rope to lower herself to the ground. Joseph Hanrahan, anxious not to have something befall Rocco Perri's mistress while under his protection, found her roaming Cannon Street in the darkness and brought her back again. She agreed to leave in the morning.

In the light of day, Olive was no better. She checked herself and her daughters out of the hotel, but seemed unable to leave. Three times she ordered a taxi to take her out of the city, and three times when the car arrived she refused to get in, even as people tried to persuade her. Eventually a car did take her south seven blocks to a third hotel, the Wentworth Arms. It seems that she was driven by Rocco's men; the desk man at the Wentworth Arms took note of two people he considered foreigners who came to stay with Olive. He didn't much care for them, but he liked Olive. To him she seemed a gentlewoman with fine manners and remarkably intelligent children.

That evening her troubles continued. Whether it was something she ate, or the culmination of a week of emotional turmoil, three-year-old Autumn became ill. When Olive spoke to the hotel clerk, James Allen, it seemed to him she was upset about something more than a sick child. The woman could not stay still. And when the hotel physician, Dr. Greenway, recommended she take Autumn to the hospital, Olive couldn't make up her mind. When she did finally agree, she left Autumn at the hospital and returned immediately to the hotel.

Sometime on Tuesday, Olive checked out of the Wentworth Arms. She carried her baby, Catherine, but left her luggage behind, and walked out into the snow-covered streets of Hamilton. It was well below freezing, but Olive wore a fur-collared jacket, a black hat, pale blue stockings and summer shoes on her feet. No one knows where she went, or whom she saw, over the next several hours. She may have gone to visit Autumn in the hospital; she may have wandered aimlessly through the downtown streets. Finally, at one o'clock in the morning on Wednesday, February 15, she walked up King Street East, not far from the office of her lawyer, Colonel Morison, and entered a humble restaurant named Noble's Lunch.

She was in an almost frenzied state. She set little Catherine on the cigar counter and approached two Italian men, asking one of them, Harry Basile, to watch over her baby while she made a phone call. Basile knew Rocco—as he would explain later, any Italian knew most every other Italian in the city—but he had no idea this was the man's child. He looked after the baby as Olive went to the public telephone with a document in her hand, the legal agreement that had yet to be signed. She asked the operator for Regent 8267W. That was Rocco's number.

When the telephone rang at 166 Bay Street South, Bessie picked up. There ensued a brief and loud conversation between the two women, until finally Olive said, "Tell him that I forgive him." Then her hands went limp, she dropped the phone and the sheet of paper and ran from the restaurant, leaving little Catherine in the care of two bewildered Italian men. When Harry Basile took the child to the police, he was stuck there until five in the morning answering questions.

Over the next few hours, Olive hardly stopped moving. A milkman in the midst of his early morning deliveries found her wandering the streets and gave her a ride in his milk wagon. As the horses pulled them along, breathing clouds of mist into the frigid air, Olive told the milkman she wanted to go up Hamilton Mountain, to the top of the escarpment, the highest spot for miles. Instead, he took her to the head of Wentworth Street, where she boarded a streetcar to King and James. There she got out, ran across the street and fell in front of an oncoming streetcar that nearly killed her.

A little later, two policemen, detectives Chamberlain and Thomson, found Olive with Autumn at Hamilton General Hospital. They took her to police headquarters where, along with Police Inspector Campbell and Detective Ernest Goodman, they questioned her about the abandonment of her child. Why leave her baby in the arms of strange men? She wanted to get away from it, she said. Pressed further, she told them the whole story. She told them about Rocco, and Colonel Morison and the agreement. Detective Goodman asked if she and Rocco were married and Olive admitted the truth. She'd thought once that they would get married, she said, but then she'd found out he already was. But, Olive said, Rocco had always cared for his daughters, and she knew he always would. "You can't drive him," she told Detective Chamberlain. "But leave him to me, and I will handle him."

To these faces of authority, she presented herself as rational, if a little overexcited. Inspector Campbell and one of the detectives walked her from the station to the corner of King William and James streets, where Campbell lifted an arm and pointed to

Colonel Morison's office near the top of the Bank of Hamilton. "That high building over there," he said.

After a ride up the elevator, Olive and the police met briefly with Morison, who mentioned that Rocco's lawyer in this matter, the man with whom he had been negotiating the support agreement, was Charles W. Bell. One of the detectives thought a chat with Mr. Bell was in order. His office was just one block away, in the Sun Life Building. And so the trio, Olive and two police, walked south to James and Main. Bell was at least somewhat prepared for this encounter. In the course of their conversations, Morison had already told him that, judging from her manner and the things she was saying, Olive Rutledge seemed quite deranged.

Somehow during this short walk, Olive decided that the thing to do now, the thing that would solve everything, was to get Mr. Bell to convince Rocco to marry her. It was true they'd gone through a ceremony once, in that little parsonage, to become Mr. and Mrs. Ross. But of course that had been a sham. This time, she decided, it would be for real. And sitting across from Bell in his richly appointed office, she said this to him. She wanted him to convince Rocco to marry her. But while Bell had a certain expertise in farcical romances, he knew that in this case there was no hope. Bessie was too formidable, too important to Rocco. He would never leave her. And Bell said as much to Olive. In the brief time they spoke, he made that fact, that there was no hope, very clear.

It was just after noon when the police left Olive to deal with her affairs. Her children were waiting for her at the General Hospital. But first, she wanted to go back to speak with her lawyer.

She walked north that one short block to the Bank of Hamilton building and took the elevator to the seventh floor. The door to Morison's office was locked—everyone had gone to lunch—so she simply stood there, waiting. Each time he passed the floor in the elevator, Tommy Armour, the elevator boy, noticed Olive standing at the head of the nearby stairs, looking down between the floors. "She appeared to be in good spirits," he said. He offered to show her to a place where she could sit down but she declined. "She seemed quite content to wait in the hall."

Finally Morison's stenographer, Velma Williamson, arrived back from lunch. When she found Olive at the door, she let her in. There was an outer office where Morison's clients could wait for him more comfortably. But as she showed Olive where to sit, Williamson had a sense that there was something not quite right about her. Something strange in her nervousness. At one point Olive went to the window and said, "It is a splendid view that you have from here."

Williamson decided she needed some assistance. As quickly and discreetly as she could, she nipped down the hall to the office of C. E. Bull and Co., where she knew she would find Owen Dunn, a tall and handsomely dressed young man. She asked him to come quickly to help watch over the woman in their office. "I'm afraid she might jump out of the window," she said.

Dunn thought this was a joke, but he went anyway. As he walked into Morison's office, he couldn't see anyone there. A frosted glass partition, which defined the waiting area, blocked his view. Then the two of them heard the sound of a window opening. Dunn raced around to see Olive climbing out onto the narrow stone ledge.

"Come here!" he shouted and lunged toward her. Reaching through the open window for Olive, his fingers barely touched the back of her hand. "Had my fingers been but one inch longer," he said later, "I could have caught hold of the woman."

She dropped silently, before the lunchtime crowd below had even become aware she was there. One man from the Brant Ice Cream Company happened to look up and saw her entire fall. Just before Olive hit the sidewalk, a woman screamed. It may have been a witness nearby, or it may have been Olive herself. The thud of impact could be heard a block away, but there was no blood, aside from a small trickle from her nose. During an autopsy later, the coroner found that she had died of massive internal injuries, including a broken rib that had pierced her heart.

THE sensational press coverage that followed made one thing clear: Sarah Olive Rutledge had jumped in despair over the future of her children. So the question that arose above all was, who was their father? The police knew, because Olive had told them. But even during the first phase of the coroner's inquest, they kept the name to themselves. They were briefly accused of a cover-up—someone suggested Rocco had gifted the police with turkeys over Christmas, and so they were protecting him. Magistrate Jelfs pronounced this unlikely, though he did offer to hear out any man willing to put his name to the charge.

If the police were indeed doing their best to track Rocco down in order to question him, he managed to disappear. He stayed out of sight, and possibly out of the country, even after the second phase of the inquest on February 27, when his name was officially entered into the record and then splashed across the front pages.

In his absence, attention turned briefly to the other father involved, Olive's father, George W. Rutledge, who came to the city "in his farmer's coat and Sunday clothes" and presented a tragic figure on the witness stand. He had learned of his daughter's death from the newspaper, and he had in his possession certain letters. One of these, in which Rocco had made promises, was signed R. Ross; the other was from Olive's invalid mother. In this letter she told the court her daughter had been wedded to Mr. Ross, but that he was now trying to repudiate this union on the grounds that they had married under a false name. Olive's father seemed mystified still as to the true identify of her husband, or whether there had ever been a ceremony; no record of it seemed to exist.

When his part in the inquest was over, George Rutledge hoped to take Olive's body back to Musclow, but the cemetery there was some miles from the train station, and a recent blizzard had rendered the route impassable. So she was buried privately in Hamilton Cemetery. Charles W. Bell paid the $158 in undertaker's fees out of his own pocket on the assumption Rocco would pay him back, and gave George Rutledge fifty dollars for his costs. As for his client paying to support the two children, who were to live with the Rutledges, Bell said that was unresolved. Olive's death had raised such a hullabaloo that any settlement negotiations had stopped.

When it came time for a verdict, the coroner's jury recommended that Rocco "be apprehended and made to provide for the children," and it regretted, for the record, that it could not punish him more severely. And when the little Calabrian who had worked so diligently to keep his identity out of the press and police records finally returned to the city a week or two later, he did so as a household name.

11

PERICOLO
Danger

TRAGIC EVENTS CAN HAVE A CLARIFYING EFFECT, EVEN for a gangster. If Rocco had entertained even a moment of indecision about the contours of his future, if he had ever imagined for a second that his life might one day include love and children with Olive Rutledge, all that confusing possibility was wiped away. Now Rocco had to reassess. He'd allowed himself to be distracted at a crucial time in his organization's development. He had humiliated Bessie, the person on whom he relied more than anyone. And he'd brought unwanted attention to his world. It was time to focus on what needed to be done.

One of the first steps, probably on the advice of his lawyers, was to become a naturalized Canadian citizen. It was a simple fact that the Canadian legal system was harder on foreigners. It gave them no benefit of the doubt. Italians in particular were seen as agents of chaos and violence, and events kept providing examples. The previous November, George Timpani had wanted out of a gang in Niagara Falls, and the gang had wished him well with four bullets to the head. Later the same month, someone had shot Vincenzo

Castiglione three times and burned his body black in Hamilton's east end. And most recently, at the very moment Olive was becoming unhinged on the streets of Hamilton, two Italian bootleggers in Welland—Pasquale (Patsy) Villella and Domenic Predote of Crowland—had gotten into an argument at the house of Sciarrone brothers associate Frank Longo. Predote had accused Villella of being an OTA spotter. They'd continued their argument at a nearby street corner and shot each other dead in the snow.

It was bad for business, and Rocco had to do something to separate himself. The more he engaged with the upper echelons of society and looked for co-operation from the legal authorities, the more he needed to be seen as one of them—or at least not so different. Becoming a naturalized citizen was just a good PR move. On March 13, his application brought him, impeccably dressed and neatly combed, before Judge C. G. Snider at the Hamilton General Sessions.

Snider was well aware of Rocco Perri; at the very least, he read the papers like anyone else. From the bench he asked if Rocco had ever been in any trouble, to which Rocco smiled and admitted to having been caught speeding now and then. Snider considered this, and made a handwritten note on the application form: "This man has the reputation of being in illegal liquor traffic quite extensively." Still, he had nothing solid to go on and couldn't think of a reason to deny the application—one wonders if a discreetly passed envelope aided this assessment—and so he judged him "qualified and fit to be Naturalized as a British subject."

There were a few upstanding and civically involved local citizens who kept tabs on who was being granted the great privilege of naturalization. One was Mrs. Thora D. McIlroy, governor of the citizenship committee of the Local Council of Women, who was still mortified by the dreadful Olive Rutledge affair. Another was Reverend H. F. Veals, a member of the Hamilton Temperance Federation. "It's a funny thing," the minister said, "that the authorities couldn't locate Perry [*sic*] a week or so ago in connection with that Rutledge inquest, and now he comes right out in the open and asks for naturalization papers." When letters of protest arrived in Ottawa, the undersecretary of state, Thomas Mulvey, wrote to Hamilton's police chief, William Whatley, and asked him to submit a report on the character of this Rocco Perri individual.

Whatley was a very tall man with a grandiloquent air and a silver-handled cane to match. As a Brit he had served in the Boer War, and as a Canadian he had fought the Hun, all the while behaving as a gentleman. "I never knew of a man possessed of more tact," Magistrate Jelfs would say of him. Whatley didn't need Mulvey to prompt his action on the Rocco Perri naturalization front. From the minute he heard about Rocco appearing in front of Judge Snider he'd realized something had to be done.

Already possessed of enough information to write a damning report on Rocco Perri, Whatley had felt the need of more hard evidence. Just two days after Rocco's citizenship appearance, police picked up one of Rocco's men, Bruno Attilio, for possession of cocaine and morphine. It was the first indication that Rocco and Bessie might have branched out into drug trafficking. Although they made sure Attilio had a good lawyer—the distinguished Michael J. O'Reilly represented him in court and demanded to see the search warrant—it didn't prevent Attilio's conviction.

Whatley couldn't stick Attilio's crime to Rocco, but he wasn't done yet. The day after Attilio's court appearance, while Rocco and Bessie were both out, five detectives arrived at 166 Bay Street South with a search warrant, looking for drugs, illegal liquor, anything. Two stationed themselves at the back door of the house and three broke in through the front. Inside, they found and arrested Perri's driver, Rosario Carboni, for possession of an automatic weapon. Carboni had stashed the gun in his suitcase—his "grip," in the parlance of the 1920s. They also found Louis Corruzzo, who a year before had lived, like Carboni, with the Perris for several months. When the police entered, Corruzzo ran out the back door and fell down the stairs, where the waiting detectives picked him up. They arrested him for possession of a revolver and shoved him into a police car. During the raid, Rocco walked into the house and raised his arms to be searched, but the police found nothing on him. Since he paid men like Carboni and Corruzzo for protection, he had no need to carry any himself.

Bessie covered the bail for both men, and again it was Michael J. O'Reilly for the defence. Rocco made sure the Perri gang always took care of its own; it's one of the reasons his men were so loyal, willing to take the rap for him if necessary. Magistrate Jelfs sentenced both men to three months in jail plus a hundred-dollar fine or an additional month. In the case of Carboni, who hadn't been carrying his weapon, O'Reilly asked Jelfs if he would "knock off" the extra month. Jelfs refused, and O'Reilly could only shake his head and mutter: "Three months and a hundred dollars for having a revolver in a grip." It was just another example of punishment being suited to the criminal, not the crime. (The sentence was later reduced on appeal to the fine only.)

On March 24, Chief Whatley submitted his report regarding Rocco Perri and the sorts of criminal activity to which he could positively be linked. Prostitution, a breach of the Temperance Act, men with guns, a vicious dog, a fine for failing to return to the scene of an accident—all these things and more were enough for Whatley to conclude that Perri was "not, in my opinion, a fit and proper person to be granted Canadian citizenship." On April 12, Rocco's application was denied.

But this was too important a matter for Rocco to simply give up. A few days later he and his lawyer, Charles W. Bell, met to craft an affidavit explaining away every legal issue. "In connection with these matters, I may speak upon my oath," it began, and went on for several pages. Nothing he'd been accused or convicted of was true. Young Mary Ashley wasn't a prostitute; she was a guest who'd been sleeping with her fiancé. "If my wife and I had known that there was anything improper going on between the young man and the young girl, we would not have allowed her in our house," he wrote. The liquor conviction? That had been overturned. "My wines and liquors were restored to me and I also got back $700.00, the balance of the $1,000.00 being, I thought, for my Attorney's fees." As for the men with guns, Rosario Carboni had been in the U.S. Army and thought he was allowed to carry a weapon. The other man (a man who had lived with the Perris and been included in their census report) was a friend of Carboni's and they didn't know him.

"Outside of one or two men who seemed to have been bent on worrying me because I am an Italian," finished Rocco's statement, "I have always had the best of treatment from the Police of Hamilton, and I think that they have relied on me and do still. If anyone objects to my becoming a Canadian Citizen, which I have tried hard to deserve, I cannot understand why it is."

Bell tried to galvanize support another way as well, by writing to Thomas J. Stewart, the Conservative MP for Hamilton West. In his letter, Bell made it clear that one of those men "bent on worrying" Rocco was Magistrate Jelfs. "Unhappily we know all too well the bent of Magistrate Jelfs' mind—the doubt is always given *against* the person charged. Jelfs cannot help that—it's the way he's built." As for the men with loaded weapons, well, "That surely might happen to any Italian who had another visiting him—if it were taken into account, there would be few Italians ever naturalized." Lastly, as a man who didn't hide his own political ambitions, Bell suggested with a nudge and a wink that if Stewart would be a friend to Rocco in this matter, Rocco would, *ahem*, be a friend to him: "I am sure we can count on him in times to come."

It didn't work. A few weeks later, Thomas Mulvey rejected Rocco's appeal. Societal acceptance was going to have to be won some other way.

ıllıllıllıllıllıllıllıllıllıllıllıll

I N MONTREAL, FRANK ZANETH WAS GETTING ALONG fine as a manager. Without knowing it, he was preparing himself for the day he would go after Rocco. The city of Montreal seethed with vice and crime. Working with Staff Sergeant Ernest Salt in the RCMP's Sherbrooke Street headquarters, Zaneth ran the narcotics squad, and he helped manage the various operatives investigating the rising phenomenon of bootlegging. Before long he'd be investigating counterfeiters too.

Here, as everywhere he worked, Zaneth was trusted and valued, and the people who worked with him every day wanted to see him get more recognition for his efforts. But as was so often the case, for reasons known only to them, the higher-ups resisted. On January 30, 1922, with Zaneth having been stuck at the provisional status of "acting sergeant" for two years, his Quebec division boss, Inspector C. E. Wilcox, sent a letter to the commissioner. Wilcox thought it was high time that Zaneth be confirmed to the rank of sergeant, and it was his honour to "recommend" this confirmation.

Two days later he received his reply: "No action is being taken in this matter for the present." Another eight months went by before the new commander of the Quebec district, Inspector J. W. Phillips, gave it another try, this time wording it as a "request."

Apparently, that did the trick. With a quick initial at the bottom of the memo, Zaneth's confirmation was approved.

〓〓〓〓〓〓〓〓〓〓〓〓〓〓

N O MATTER HOW MUCH ROCCO MAY HAVE WANTED TO be welcomed into Canadian society, his associates continued to complicate matters. On March 16, 1922, the very day police were searching Rocco and Bessie's house, there was more violence in Welland.

Once home to so many unemployed immigrant men, the region was now thick with Black Hand–style extortionists. When they weren't killing their victims, they were shooting one another. At the corner of Crowland and South Main streets, a short, heavy twenty-something named Salvatore Licato ambushed a barber named Mike Lobosco and shot him four times through the chest. OPP Inspector John Miller determined Lobosco had been killed in retaliation for shooting another Italian in Buffalo. And much to Miller's annoyance—"This man should not have got away"—it was to Buffalo that Licato escaped.

A week or two later, Maurizio Bocchimuzzo—a twenty-six-year-old Niagara Falls bootlegger who was part of a cross-border smuggling ring—was killed by a rival gang and dumped in a secluded spot by a river on the New York side. His body went undiscovered for at least a week until it was found on April 3, after someone had posted a helpful sign along the side of a nearby road: "Look here, look!"

Investigators couldn't say whether the murders were connected, but no one could deny that with the increasing competition to exploit Americans' thirst for liquor, the border territories were becoming much more dangerous. This violence wasn't happening in isolation, of course; it echoed an escalation that had been occurring in Chicago, Detroit, Pittsburgh and New York. But there may have been more to that similarity than mere coincidence. Much of the violence in the large northeastern cities appeared to be driven by an efficiently murderous group of Sicilians known as the Good Killers, who police had estimated were behind as many as 125 killings. The secretive head of that group, Stefano (The Undertaker) Magaddino, had been based in Brooklyn, but after an attempt on his life in the fall of 1921, he had chosen to relocate to Buffalo and take up bootlegging in upper New York State.

So far, the deaths had been confined to the lower ranks of the regional outfits. But five weeks after Bocchimuzzo's body was found, the violence reached upward, to Rocco's level. On May 10, 1922, Domenic Sciarrone (alias Joseph Verona), the diamond-wearing gang leader who had been implicated in so much of the violence in Guelph and Welland, the fractious forty-five-year-old Calabrian who operated by intimidation and retaliation according to the old village versus village traditions, met an appropriate fate.

He'd served the previous few months in prison for his involvement in a whisky still operation in Guelph. Now that he was out on parole, Sciarrone had left Guelph on Tuesday, May 9, intending to travel to Niagara Falls, New York. His wife, Mary, called it a "business meeting" and perhaps it was—Sciarrone had Calabrian connections and ambitions in the city—but it would be a meeting in the form of a mobster banquet at a saloon. First though, before he went to Niagara Falls, he drove to meet with Rocco Perri at Freelton, Ontario, roughly the midpoint between the Sciarrone and Perri territories. Perhaps this was merely a catching up after Sciarrone's months away. Or maybe it was something else—a warning.

Despite the ten-year difference in their ages, Rocco and Sciarrone went way back. Sciarrone had interests in a mine in Cobalt, so Rocco may have worked with him there. Or perhaps, since Sciarrone came from Reggio Calabria, their ties went as far back as Rocco's childhood. That shared history would have been at the back of Rocco's mind even as he considered a troubling possibility.

If Buffalo was fast becoming Magaddino's territory, Niagara Falls, New York, belonged to a gangster named Don Simone. Every bit as powerful and attention-shy as Magaddino, Simone was also a Sicilian, and it's possible that at least initially the two men were allied. Having been behind bars for a while, Domenic Sciarrone might not have been fully aware of that, or of Magaddino's growing influence. Now he was heading to a gathering of gangsters that was potentially less friendly than he realized.

What if Rocco knew something was about to happen? What if, despite the fact that Sciarrone was now a rival, and a difficult one, Rocco preferred dealing with the devil he knew. It's possible that he met with Domenic Sciarrone in Freelton that afternoon to tell his fellow Calabrian not to go to that gathering in Niagara Falls.

If so, Sciarrone ignored him. Later that night, when Sciarrone left (or was escorted from) the saloon of Louis Deviti, where the banquet was being held, four men went with him. A little after 11 p.m., as they drove along the Niagara escarpment on the Lewiston Highway, someone in the back seat took out a gun and put a bullet into the back of Sciarrone's head, one into his cheek and a third, as Sciarrone slumped forward, into his arm. A car door opened, and his body was dumped unceremoniously over the side of the hill with one hundred dollars in his pocket, a diamond stickpin in his lapel, and an impressive diamond ring still on his finger.

The press immediately linked Sciarrone's death to the murder of Jimmy Celona in Hamilton four years before and the retaliatory killing of Domenic Paparone a year later, describing it as the latest event in a Black Hand feud. Sciarrone's funeral came three days later, on a warm Saturday in Guelph, attended by his wife, Mary, and his nine children, along with seemingly every important Calabrian gangster in southern Ontario. The pallbearers gripping his casket were Frank Longo from Welland, Antonio Deconza and James and Domenico D'Agostino from St. Catharines, and Frank Romeo and Rocco Perri from Hamilton.

The murder of a mob boss demanded a response, of course. Immediately Joe Sciarrone, Domenic's equally violent brother, turned toward finding and punishing the killers. And just as before, Rocco Perri seemed to be right in the middle of it.

BEVERLY was a rural region of farmers' fields and lonely dirt roads that lay directly between Guelph and Hamilton, which made it familiar to many of the bootleggers employed by the Perri and Sciarrone gangs. Around suppertime on May 17, 1922, a number of folks in and around Beverly heard a shot in the distance. Some thought it was a tire blowing; to others it sounded like a rifle. The next day, a group of farmers transporting a load of hay happened on the body of Jimmy Loria, lying in a swamp. Loria had been shot with a .32 automatic in the back of the head, and at the time of his death he seemed to have been under the impression he was among friends, because he was killed while he was relieving himself at the side of the road (the police report made a point of noting that "his private was out of his trousers"). The bullet, which severed his spinal cord, was still lodged in the roof of his mouth.

Loria had lived a peripatetic gangster's existence in Hamilton, spending more money on his teeth and his clothes than his place of residence. He died with a lot of gold bridge work in his mouth while wearing a stylish blue suit and a soft grey velour hat. His pockets still held a gold, jewelled watch and sixty-two dollars in cash, which told police that robbery was not the motive. Tucked inside Loria's hat was a slip of paper with the totals of a liquor order written in pencil for various brands of Scotch and brandy. His pockets contained a notebook with two letters, one of which was a love letter. Apparently Jimmy was trying to convince some lovely young woman not to become a nun. "I desire to call you," he'd written in Italian, "and say the convent is not a place for you, and you will find yourself unhappy by hiding away your great beauty from the world."

The other letter, also written in Italian, was more mysterious, so strange in fact that police at the time looked at it and shrugged: "What were you doing at three o'clock in the morning outside the city in a small house . . . Have you a word of command. Zero . . . A robbery, a carbine, a dagger, two revolvers, a bottle of poison . . . Have you two brothers? Where are they? One in the hospital at Palermo, who is curing himself of a quarrel and the other one is gone in as a monk and you can find him in Alornela." The letter made repeated references to a quarrel, to brothers and a brotherhood. It included vaguely religious references and ended with a section written in a code of letters and numbers.

To the local detectives working the case, it seemed nonsensical. What they didn't realize was that the letter echoed writings by the 'Ndrangheta found in 1897 by Italian police in the small municipality of Seminara in the province of Reggio Calabria. The letter proved that Jimmy Loria was a Sicilian who was being threatened by the Calabrian mob.

On the morning of May 19, the superintendent of the OPP's criminal investigation branch in Toronto read the news report of Loria's murder. That instant he picked up the phone. He had no doubt which detective he wanted on the case.

Inspector William Stringer could have been created by Hollywood. Ruggedly handsome in his trilby hat and always happy to pose for a picture, he was a hell of an investigator. Years later he would be dubbed "Sherlock Stringer" by the *Toronto Daily Star* and go on to become OPP commissioner, the first non–ex-military man to hold the position. Famous for preferring to tackle a fleeing suspect rather than draw his gun, Stringer liked to say that crimes weren't solved by monumental intelligence, but by plodding perseverance. He'd been with the OPP since 1910, spending much of his time tromping through northern frontier settlements, but he'd been in the criminal investigation branch for just two years when the Loria assignment came to him. Unlike John Miller, he was relatively new to the world of Italian slayings, but over the course of several weeks he'd figured out a few things.

He drove down to Lockport, New York, to talk to Mike Lorenzo, who was behind bars for grand larceny. A friend of the recently murdered Domenic Sciarrone, Lorenzo told Stringer about the Calabrian and Sicilian gangs operating in Guelph, Hamilton and Niagara Falls. Stringer spent days nosing around Hamilton, staying in hotels and eating ninety-five-cent dinners. He located a Hamilton mobster named Angelo Salvatore and learned that Loria had stabbed and wounded him two years before. (Loria kept a grip in a Guelph train station in which photographs were found linking him to Salvatore as well as to one of the two hoods who'd gunned each other down in Crowland.) He also learned that Loria was a Sicilian, having travelled from Licata province, while the heads of the outfits in Guelph (Sciarrone), Hamilton (Perri) and Niagara Falls, New York (Joe Serianni), were all Calabrians. (A *Hamilton Herald* reporter also did some digging and discovered Loria's parents lived in Palermo, which offered another link to the brothers in the coded letter.) And he noted just how many Italians had recently been murdered in Guelph, Hamilton, Welland, Niagara Falls and St. Catharines. "I am convinced that these murders among the Italians especially the Sicilians are the results of vendettas carried out secretly by organizations of Calabrians and Sicilians," wrote Stringer in his May 31 report. He described the assassinations as "the most baffling crimes that the police have to deal with."

Even so, there were clues to the motive for Loria's death. Stringer had a suspicion that Loria had been one of the men who'd escorted Domenic Sciarrone out of the Deviti saloon before his fatal drive, and that his murder had come in retaliation. When he showed Louis Deviti a picture of Loria, Deviti wouldn't say whether he'd seen Loria walk Sciarrone out, but he admitted he recognized the face. And while Stringer was working the case, Hamilton Police Chief William Whatley sent him an anonymous letter he'd received, addressed to "Illustrious Mr. Magistrate." Referring to the murder of "Jimmy Lagoria," which Stringer understood to be Loria, the letter said that two days before his death, he'd taken a ride with four men. One of them was a man called Restivo.

Stringer didn't know it, but Rocco Perri had a Joseph Restivo on his payroll.

Ontario's deadly summer of 1922 was just getting warm.

At around 10:45 on the morning of June 4, a thirty-five-year-old gangster dressed in a dark blue suit with green pinstripes was found crawling along a lonely stretch of dirt road about a quarter mile outside Oakville. He had been shot twice in the head with a .38 revolver and died a few minutes after police arrived on the scene. In his wallet he had twenty dollars in real money, and forty dollars in crudely counterfeited U.S. bills—one-dollar bills "raised" to twenties by pasting *20* over the *1*, a technique that didn't bear close scrutiny but had occasionally worked when the bills were passed in certain Asian stores in Hamilton. In the man's pocket was a letter from his mother in Alcamo, Sicily, not far from Palermo, offering to send her son money if he found business bad in Canada and wanted to come home.

Again the OPP put Stringer on the case, and he was soon digging through some sordid business involving a liquor dive and a thirteen-year-old girl who'd been kidnapped from Montreal and forced into prostitution. After a few days John Miller was called in to help work the investigation, and after a lot of confusion about the name of the dead man, whom some knew as Frank Cicce or "Chi Chi," others as Antonio Bambini, he was finally identified as Antonio Lialle. A long-time Toronto rum-runner, linked to Jimmy Loria and the Sciarrone brothers, Lialle was said to be a close friend of a Rocco Perri associate named Frank Sylvestro, alias Frank Ross (the informant for this was Perri gang member Bruno Attilio, who described Ross as a man of "very bad character"). Before he was murdered, Lialle had spent time with the young Montreal girl— although not for sex, she said—and had served three months in jail for pointing a gun at a police officer during a liquor raid.

It seemed at first that Lialle might have turned "stool" on his gang and paid the maximum price, or perhaps he was killed in a quarrel over the girl. But Stringer couldn't help thinking that Lialle's death bore a lot of similarity to the other recent killings. Mentions of the Good Killers began to surface in the press in connection to the spate of murders, but Stringer wasn't ready to pin blame. "The murders are planned in their respective cities and in order to effectively conceal their identity the murderers take the victim to an isolated spot in the country in a friendly way and there slay him," he reported. "In all these recent cases the victims have been engaged in the illicit liquor traffic." There was also the fact that Lialle was Sicilian.

Along the way, Stringer's investigations took him to Merritton, a rural district snug against St. Catharines. He was looking for the car that belonged to a suspect in the murder, and there was some suspicion it had been hidden on a farm on St. David's Road, where an Italian named John Trott lived. When Stringer arrived at the farm on June 25, the car had been moved and Trott was gone. According to the neighbours, Trott was away "trying to locate and capture his wife who ran away with another Italian," which was a story that seemed to come up a lot when Italian men dropped out of sight for a while.

The case remained unsolved, and the Trott connection didn't lead anywhere immediately. But it was a name to remember, because again—although Stringer didn't know it at the time—John Trott worked for Rocco Perri.

AT least one more domino still had to fall in Ontario's summer of murder, and its name was Joe Sciarrone.

There were a lot of ways the Sciarrone brothers weren't like Rocco. They were hot-headed and vengeful—as far as Inspector John Miller was concerned, there hadn't been a murder of an Italian in the previous ten years in Ontario that wasn't in some way connected to the Sciarrones. They were dishonest even compared to most bootleggers—in at least one case delivering watered-down wine to a widow who'd paid for liquor, which did not sit well with the widow's sons. And they were terrible employers.

During his investigations, Miller discovered that before he was killed, Antonio Lialle had run liquor for the Sciarrones using the alias Frank Cicce. They had agreed to look after him if police nabbed him while he was working for them, covering his fine or compensating him for any time he spent in jail. This was common practice among the better class of bootlegging bosses—it was certainly Rocco's practice. But in this case, wrote Miller, when Lialle was arrested and sent to jail for four months, "the Sciarrones left him cold."

And unlike Rocco, they had no long-term vision, making every decision for immediate gain. Not only did they hew to the old ways of intimidation and extortion that set Italian against Italian, they cheated the people it was most dangerous to cheat. In one case a man who was being extorted came to them for help, agreeing to give the Sciarrones five hundred dollars with the understanding they would give three hundred to the gang of extortionists and keep the balance for making the gang go away. They kept the whole amount, which angered not only the victim of the extortion but also the gang extorting him. In another case, a robbery in Brant County netted $1,400 that was meant to be split among Joe Sciarrone, a taxi driver, and two men serving time in Kingston Penitentiary. Sciarrone kept the entire $1,400.

For all these reasons, rumours began to spread that Joe Sciarrone was a marked man. And nothing about his situation improved when Joe began boasting loudly, for anyone to hear, that he was going to get the men who'd killed his brother. So no one was surprised when, in August, someone in a passing Ford took a few warning shots at Joe and his brother-in-law Sam Sciarrone as they were walking with another man along a street in Brantford. And people were even less surprised when Joe ignored the warning and carried on making threats.

This wasn't going to end well.

Early on Sunday, September 3, Sciarrone and his brother-in-law took a radial train from Brantford, where Joe lived, to Hamilton, where they met Rocco and Bessie at 166 Bay Street South. The four had lunch there, during which they undoubtedly discussed Joe's continuing quest to find and punish his brother's killers, which Rocco had ostensibly been helping him to do. Perhaps, over one of the occasional glasses of wine that Rocco drank, he counselled calm and patience. Maybe he told Joe it was time for the vendetta to end. Or maybe he knew that talking sense to Joe Sciarrone would be futile and, instead, told him what he wanted to hear—that he would help him finish the job.

Either way, after the meeting, the four drove in Rocco's car, along with two men who worked for Rocco, to the house of Mary Sciarrone, Domenic's widow, on Alice Street in Guelph. From there they went as a group to Guelph Cemetery, to visit Domenic's grave. Afterward, Rocco and Bessie returned to Hamilton, leaving Joe and Sam to spend the night in Guelph. While he was in Guelph, John Miller would later learn, Joe tried to borrow a shotgun from Mary Sciarrone, to supplement the revolver he already packed, telling her yet again that he was going to get his brother's killers.

Sometime on Monday, September 4, Joe Sciarrone left Guelph. He had told his wife that after Guelph he intended to go to St. Catharines, Thorold and Welland, where he planned to see three men in particular: in St Catharines, Antonio Deconza, who had been one of his brother's pallbearers and who had made a moving speech at his funeral; in Thorold, John Trott; and in Welland, mob boss Don Simone, who lived in Niagara Falls, New York, but who would often come to Welland to meet with Sciarrone. It was Simone who Sciarrone suspected of having arranged his brother's murder.

The next day, Joe Sciarrone's corpse was found at the bottom of the Welland Canal, not far from a partially dug grave. Someone had taken a lot of trouble after beating his head in. He was stripped of money and anything that would identify him, including a fine gold watch. Sciarrone's head and upper body were covered with three sugar bags tied with a cord at his neck. Then his corpse was wrapped in two rugs from a car, tied up with twine and weighed down with blocks of cement.

Determining what had happened between Guelph and the canal—where and how and with whom Joe Sciarrone had travelled—became the focus of John Miller's investigations over the next few weeks. Ultimately a picture emerged.

After Guelph, Sciarrone had gone to Hamilton by train, where he was met at the station by Rocco Perri and a gangster named Charlie Bordonaro, in the same Ford that had been used in the shooting attempt the month before. Bordonaro was a close Perri associate who had recently switched from bootlegging to dealing narcotics. Together the three men drove to St. Catharines to pick up Antonio Deconza, and continued to a bakery in Merritton, where they met up with James D'Agostino, another of Domenic's pallbearers, and John Trott. Someone would later tell John Miller that the rugs in which Joe Sciarrone's body was found wrapped came from John Trott's car, though he could never find any evidence to prove it. There was very likely one other man in that group, Miller was told—a Sicilian who lived in Toronto named Joe Galliardo, part of the Galliardo crime family allied with Don Simone. From all he'd heard, Miller was certain it was Simone who'd wanted Sciarrone dead, and likely Galliardo who'd done the deed. The others, including Rocco, now the ranking Calabrian in Ontario, were there to make sure it went smoothly, and to sanction the event.

He could never find enough proof to make an arrest, but Miller had a theory. "We frequently get the opinion that the Sciarrone family are all doomed to be killed because of something they did years ago," he wrote. In keeping with that line of thinking, he noted that Sam Sciarrone was not planning to stick around. "He is at the present time closing up his affairs so as to get away from the country."

But the real answer was probably simpler: the Sciarrones were doomed by their approach, their way of doing business. If they had behaved differently, men like Simone and Rocco Perri could have worked with them—they'd tried to for years. Simone had made his forays into Welland, Rocco was collaborative by nature, and it made sense to combine forces bridging the border. But the Sciarrones weren't the collaborative kind, and so they became a problem. Joe Sciarrone "has been such a bad man himself," wrote John Miller, "that many [think] that what happened to him was [what] was coming to him, and there is very little sympathy for him."

Whether or not Rocco was directly involved in the murders of Domenic and Joe Sciarrone, whether he was helping to carry out Don Simone's wishes or pursuing his own interests, there's no doubt he benefited from their elimination. Removing the Sciarrones effectively added Guelph, Brantford and the Niagara peninsula to his existing territory and cleared a path to the U.S. market. Suddenly there was no bigger crime boss in Canada than the smiling little Italian.

12

GUAIO
Problem

B Y THE AUTUMN OF 1922, THE PERRI GANG WAS MOVING
up to a thousand cases of liquor a day. Rocco and Bessie's
gross revenues were easily one million dollars a month, their
profits before operating expenses nearly four hundred thousand.
With 114,000 people, Hamilton was now the fifth largest city in
Canada, and with the addition of the Sciarrone brothers' territory
and control of the Niagara border, everybody knew who was boss
in southern Ontario. With big business came big headaches, of
course. But Rocco could have been forgiven for thinking he had
everything under control.

Then came an unforeseen complication, and it came in the
unlikeliest place of all: Thorold, Ontario.

Bootlegging thrived in this town of about five thousand straddling the Welland Canal. It thrived because Thorold was thoroughly corrupt. Just about any night of the week you could see
Thorold's police magistrate, Colonel Donald Munroe, lifting a
glass in some blind pig. Quite naturally then, Munroe was reluc-
tant to convict any bootleggers brought before him. So the local

police gave up, and the town's illegal liquor business was, in the assessment of Detective Inspector William Stringer, "allowed to run unmolested." Which was exactly how Rocco liked it.

Then the OPP dispatched Constable George Stockbridge to Thorold to start enforcing OTA rules. He tried, but he needed the co-operation of the local police force, and that was never guaranteed. On at least one occasion, Stockbridge had to call off a planned raid because the two local constables he'd enlisted to help him were drunk. Stockbridge needed an ally he could rely on, and somehow the OPP convinced the Thorold police force to assign one—a handsome, thirty-six-year-old named Joseph Trueman. An experienced constable, he was new to the Thorold force, and to every pinstriped bootlegger's astonishment, and perhaps Stockbridge's as well, he took his job very seriously.

Together, Trueman and Stockbridge began breaking up known liquor dives. They started arresting people. Suddenly Colonel Munroe had case after case of OTA breaches before him—solid cases built on the corroborating evidence of two constables from different forces. So Munroe found himself, with very apparent reluctance, having to convict some of his friends. The law-abiding citizens of Thorold were thrilled at the sudden enthusiasm of their police department.

This, quite simply, could not stand.

First, Rocco's men tried sending a message. In the wee hours of December 15, 1922, they piled into a seven-passenger touring sedan and drove until they spotted Stockbridge and Trueman on patrol. As they motored past, they fired three shots at the constables without hitting either of them, then sped away before either Trueman or Stockbridge could get a fix on the licence plate.

But that didn't work; the next day, a Saturday, Trueman and Stockbridge were still on the job. So more serious steps had to be taken, and quickly. There were several cases of recently arrested Italian bootleggers due to come before the court. Getting convictions depended on Constable Trueman's supporting testimony. If Trueman couldn't be scared off, he would have to be silenced.

Hunched inside a cold car on a dark street in Thorold, a few of Rocco's men hatched a plan. They knew where Trueman went on his early morning patrols. They would watch for him in a couple of specific locations, and when he appeared, if he was alone, they would signal for a man to come immediately and do the job. Whether they did all this on Rocco's orders, or independently, would never be determined. But someone was willing to pay one hundred dollars for this special assignment, no small sum, so the money had to have come from higher up than the men in this car. And it went to one of Rocco Perri's most reliable soldiers.

SATURDAY night became Sunday morning, and Constable Joseph Trueman made his typical night-shift rounds. It was a night of cold wind and heavy snow. As usual, around 3:45 a.m., Trueman stopped by the depot of the Niagara, St. Catharines and Toronto Railway, the electric passenger rail service that connected the communities of St. Catharines, Welland, Port Colborne and Niagara Falls (although not Toronto, despite the name). In winter, the NS&T depot was a popular place for homeless men looking for shelter, and Trueman's job included rousting the tramps and sending them back out into the storm. As usual, he stayed for a few moments to chat with a friend of his, Tom Morley, the depot's caretaker. Then he stepped outside to resume his patrol, and Morley went into the ladies' washroom to mop the floors. It was 3:53 a.m.

Almost immediately, as he stepped into the street, Trueman spotted someone he recognized and shouted, "What are you doing here?" Shots were fired, the sound of which drew Morley to the window. He saw Trueman chasing a man toward the corner of a hotel and then watched, horrified, as the gunman turned and fired at close range. Trueman threw up his hands in self-defence, then fell as the shooter ran off, swallowed up by the darkness and the blowing snow.

Morley ran out and tried to lift Trueman's head. "Joe, speak to me," he said. "Are you hurt?" But the constable was already dead. He'd been shot once through the right wrist, the .32-calibre bullet travelling up the forearm and out the elbow, and once through the heart.

A Dr. Herod lived in a house on the same intersection, just a few yards away. He came running, along with several other men. Thorold's police station was barely a block away, and the first officer on the scene was a Sergeant Bradley. Together these men carried Trueman's body into Dr. Herod's house. Bradley then wasted precious minutes using Dr. Herod's telephone to call other police, instead of immediately chasing after the killer. The wind-blown snow was already starting to obscure the footprints leading away from the scene. At 4:10 a.m. OPP Constable Stockbridge learned that his colleague had been shot. He came as quickly as he could and soon took up the chase, managing to follow the footprints along the NS&T tracks in the direction of Niagara Falls for about one and three-quarter miles. But by then the snow had done its work, and he lost the trail around the Beaver Board Company manufacturing plant. Of the men who'd sat in the car planning Trueman's death, at least one worked in that plant. If Sergeant Bradley had run after the killer sooner, he might have followed the footprints to its door. But as it stood, there were no clues as to the identity of the man who'd murdered Joseph Trueman. Police searched the first NS&T train that arrived at Niagara Falls, as well as cars on the Grand Trunk and MCR lines, but found nothing.

The OPP immediately assigned Inspector Stringer to the case. He arrived by train that morning, consulted with Constable Stockbridge and made a quick assessment of the motive behind the killing—Trueman and Stockbridge's eager enforcement of the OTA.

His first actions were to arrest two men who seemed suspicious and possibly connected—Frank Young, arrested drunk at the depot, and Domenic Arilotta, pulled out of the home of an alleged prostitute. Arilotta (described in the *St. Catharines Standard* as "a bright looking young Italian") was a particularly hard criminal; he was an associate of the brutal Frank Longo and seemed quite capable of shooting a cop. Stringer determined he'd been with four other men in a Thorold taxi driven by Tony Calabrase a few hours before the murder. The rest of the men had gone missing.

On December 19, Stringer took Stockbridge and another constable around Thorold to raid the local pool rooms. At each place they walked in, ordered everybody up against the wall and searched them for weapons. They found three men worth arresting, including a thug suspected in a recent payroll robbery at Hamilton Steel Works and a gambler from Niagara Falls, New York, who'd been convicted of a holdup at Lewiston. At the station, believing that Trueman had managed to fire a round from his gun, Stringer had all these men, including Arilotta and Young, stripped and searched for fresh bullet wounds, but none were found.

Stringer was told repeatedly that Thorold had been about as dirty as a town could get before Stockbridge and Trueman had started their work. The day he hauled in his pool room suspects, Stringer saw it for himself. That morning a man had been tried for a breach of the Ontario Temperance Act based on information from Constable Stockbridge. The presiding magistrate pulled Stringer aside and asked him whether he should convict. "That is a very improper question," Stringer told him. "As magistrate you should be able to decide yourself on such a simple case."

As he turned over stones and arrested suspects, Stringer heard plenty of rumours about one bootlegger or another having wished Trueman dead. But he came back to the fact that Frank Young and Domenic Arilotta had connections to Rocco Perri. That seemed worth investigating further.

On December 30, Stringer went to Hamilton and interviewed Rocco with the co-operation of the Hamilton police. As usual, Rocco smiled and shrugged and said nothing more than that he knew the two men. In fact, a search of the home of Arilotta's girl-friend turned up an envelope proving that Arilotta had once lived at 166 Bay Street South. He had also worked for Domenic Sciarrone, and he'd been with Sciarrone the night he died. Stringer let Frank Young go—he was just a drunk, and a "Canadian," so apparently beyond suspicion—but he kept Arilotta and others behind bars.

Populated by so many idle yet apparently well-off men, Thorold seemed rich with potential suspects, and Stringer tried on theories to fit several of them. When he learned that the driver of the taxi, Tony Calabrase, was a former chauffeur for Domenic Sciarrone (probably the one stiffed by Joe Sciarrone for his share of robbery loot), he speculated that Calabrase had driven by the rail depot about ten minutes before the shooting and alerted someone at the Beaver Board plant that Trueman was at the depot, alone. But even though Calabrase wasn't finished as a suspect in the case, Stringer had nothing solid to go on. Eventually every one of the men he'd arrested was let go.

On January 24, thoroughly frustrated, Stringer wrote a long report to the OPP's assistant commissioner. He was convinced that Trueman, like several law enforcement officers recently gunned down in Alberta, had been murdered by one or more bootleggers.

"There is no escaping the fact that they are getting bolder," he wrote. "It is quite obvious that the lure of the money to be made by the deliberate breaking of the law steels the hearts of those who succumb to it and murder is often the direct result." But he was forced to admit he'd uncovered not the slightest bit of proof as to who had committed the crime.

Still, the investigation into a cop's murder was never really closed. What Stringer needed was some kind of break—a slip of a tongue, a bit of evidence knocked loose. And he had to be ready when it came.

13

PASSAPORTO
Passport

HERE WAS A CRACK IN FRANK ZANETH'S WORLD. YOU have to peer through formal correspondence and official documents to see it. And even then, it's only the perspective of time that makes its significance clear. In April of 1923, still stationed in Quebec, busting silk smugglers, drug dealers and coin counterfeiters, Frank wrote a letter to his commanding officer. He had handed over his naturalization certificate for some administrative reason some time before and now he needed it back.

He needed it because he was applying for a passport for his wife, Rita. It had become obvious to him that Rita was experiencing difficulties; troubles that were quite beyond either of them to handle without help. He didn't say any of this, of course. In 1923 it wasn't the sort of thing you could talk about, certainly not in an interdepartmental letter. He'd mentioned to his commander something about Rita going back to Italy to visit her mother, but that was as much as he'd revealed. In his mind, Frank surely hoped that a few months back in Italy with her mother would help to soothe

the anguish in Rita. He had lost one wife already, and he didn't want to lose another.

But in his letter, Frank simply said that his wife was leaving in May, heading back to Italy where she would stay, he thought, until the fall. So, could he have his naturalization certificate back, or a copy thereof? The passport authorities were expecting it.

14
COMPLICI
Accomplices

THERE WAS A MONSTER SLEEPING ON THE TORONTO waterfront. While distilleries such as Seagram and Corby's were ramping up production and profiting richly from bootlegging, the enormous Gooderham & Worts distillery sat shuttered and waiting for a buyer. But after two years of turning Corby's into a money machine for Consolidated Distilleries, and getting a solid share of the profits in return, Harry Hatch was ready. He approached William Gooderham to make an offer, and by December 22, 1923, he had a deal. For $1.5 million cobbled together from cash, loans and shares sold to a few select investors, he bought a hulking, aging distillery on sixteen acres of Toronto waterfront. But he also bought a valuable brand. To a legion of whisky drinkers, the Gooderham & Worts name signalled quality. With a long client list of bootleggers ready to buy, all Hatch needed now was some decent aged whisky on which to slap that name.

There was none in the distillery, so he tried to buy some. But at this point demand for Canadian whisky was so great that no distillery had any extra supply they were willing to sell to a competitor.

For Harry Hatch, the only option seemed to be to start up production at Gooderham & Worts and wait for the required two years of aging before beginning to sell. Harry Hatch did not have the money or the patience to wait. But he knew what to do.

Just a few years earlier, in 1920, governments had allowed Canadian distillers a nine-month respite from the aging requirements when they began gearing up production after the war. But Gooderham & Worts had remained closed through that exemption period, so Hatch convinced the government to let that "special privilege" apply now, just for them. From April 1, 1924, to the end of that year Gooderham & Worts was allowed to ship every drop of its production immediately. Very quickly boats began pulling up to the distillery's docks, filling their holds with crates of "G & W Special." One of those boats was the *Aladdin*, a huge luxury yacht belonging to a Michigan millionaire named W. J. Sovereign, whose every stateroom was so crammed with liquor her crew of six had to sleep on the deck. But it was Rocco and Bessie Perri who were arguably Harry Hatch's best customers. As soon as they could in 1924 they met at Hatch's house and worked out a deal.

There was no busier period for the Perri gang. They had customers lined up from North Bay to New York State—within two years there would be more than fifteen hundred blind pigs in Hamilton alone—and they needed vast amounts of supply. So much that it wasn't enough for Bessie to keep up a steady stream of telegrams and phone calls to Hatch & McGuinness, the sales agents for Corby's as well as Gooderham & Worts. They also had to work with partners in Buffalo and Niagara Falls to supply them with raw alcohol that they shipped north, diluted with water and mixed with whisky bought from Canadian distilleries.

And for all of that whisky to flow without too many hiccups, they needed co-operation from the police.

By now, Rocco was openly friendly with the local Hamilton cops, shaking hands and telling jokes whenever circumstances brought them together. Cases of whisky, and more, to the right people engendered a helpful degree of goodwill. But something much deeper than that was going on. It's not that police or OTA inspectors wouldn't raid the Perris' house on occasion; it's that when they did, they wouldn't find anything. The most recent example: a raid on February 13, 1924, when four officers, alerted to a recent liquor delivery, stormed into 166 Bay Street South and began breaking open cupboards while Bessie's maid watched. They found no alcohol at all. It seemed clear that, somehow, Rocco and Bessie were getting help from the inside.

It was a topic of discussion among their rivals. A Hamilton bootlegger named Mildred Cooney Sterling would reveal to an undercover investigator that Rocco "has it on all the big guys in this town. No one would ever go against Rocco Perri. He is entirely too powerful."

That was true even of the man at the very top—Hamilton Police Chief William Whatley. Over the roughly two years since Whatley had thwarted Rocco's naturalization, Rocco and Bessie had convinced the chief to work with them, not against them. How? There were whispers that Bessie had orchestrated a picture showing Whatley drinking in compromising company, but it may not have been that complicated. Money made a powerful argument too, particularly in an era of rampant corruption. At any rate, Whatley and the Perris were now such good friends that it was common, according to Mildred Sterling, to see Chief Whatley and his wife being driven around in Rocco's car. "I remember very well on one occasion," she said, "when Perri stopped at a gas station with his car and Perri made an effort to pay for the gas and Chief Whatley interfered and said to the man at the station, 'Never mind, just charge that to me.'" This would have been only fitting given that, according to Sterling, Rocco had recently bought Whatley a new Studebaker. "It was only one of the many gifts that Perri gave away," she said, "not counting the shut-up money."

Rumours that there was something amiss in Hamilton rustled in the underbrush for about a year when they finally broke into the open on March 13, 1924. A local barrister, Charles S. Morgan, issued two Supreme Court writs for twenty-five thousand dollars against Chief Whatley and his brother-in-law, Norman Nicolson. Morgan claimed persecution and slander, telling a bizarre tale about a conflict with Whatley that was connected with work Morgan had done as solicitor for the Nicolson Sales and Service Company. That conflict, whatever it was, had led to Morgan being arrested on January 25, 1923, and thrown into an asylum for the insane, apparently to keep him quiet. He escaped, hid out for two weeks, then went to the police to make his accusations. But with his wife and father-in-law waiting in police court to help him give evidence, he was again arrested and whisked off to the asylum's homicidal ward. He was held there for ten days until someone in Toronto, likely from the attorney general's office, ordered him released.

Very quickly, questions about lax enforcement of the Ontario Temperance Act, and even the active protection of bootleggers by "certain prominent persons," reached the press. On March 18, Attorney General Nickle admitted to having sent Inspector J. A. Ayearst to the city to conduct a backroom investigation, based on Morgan's accusations. Members of the Hamilton Police Commission, including its chairman, Police Magistrate Jelfs, claimed to know nothing about it, and Hamilton's mayor, Thomas William Jutten, was dismissive. "I know of no good reason," he said, "why an inquiry should be held."

By the evening of March 26, the contents of Ayearst's report were known, not only to Attorney General Nickle but also to Jelfs and to Mayor Jutten. Neither was talking, but Nickle was troubled enough by what he read that he insisted on a full investigation.

Ayearst's report had made clear that the rumours had substance, and the substance was startling. It appeared that Whatley was connected to a complex scheme that allowed Rocco and Bessie Perri, and possibly other bootleggers, to buy protection from prosecution. They did it by purchasing shares in a company, which then funnelled the money to prominent officials. Without evidence, the press didn't dare connect the dots, but the entity in question was the Nicolson Sales and Service Company. Charles Morgan had been directly connected to the sales of those shares, and after a fallout with Whatley he had threatened to go public.

Magistrate Jelfs seemed conflicted, probably because Whatley was a friend and colleague. He claimed to want to get to the truth—"We are anxious to conduct the most open kind of a probe"—but his bias was obvious. "I have no doubt," he said, before any testimony had been heard, "that after the inquiry has been made, the police heads will come out on top." When criticism came swiftly, he found himself having to defend that position. "I have known Chief Whatley for thirteen years," he said. "He is the best Chief of Police Hamilton ever had. Why shouldn't I stand by him, when nothing discreditable has yet been proved against him?"

The probe was to take the form of a hearing of witnesses at a police commission meeting on April 3. Besides Charles Morgan and Whatley's brother-in-law, Norman Nicolson, five men connected with the Nicolson Sales and Service Company scheme were to be called as special witnesses. They included James Lindsay; G. Brown, the company secretary; Sinclair Richardson, company trustee; "well-known tobacconist and sporting man" William Carroll; and Rocco Perri.

Early on, Whatley himself claimed to be unconcerned. He tutted through his thick moustache, saying, "I am quite prepared for any inquiry." But by Saturday, March 31, with the commission meeting just days away and public sentiment turning against him, Whatley felt the need to buff his public image. He ordered police raids on six Hamilton hotels—something he could have done months before if he'd wanted to—looking for liquor above the legal 2.5 percent limit.

Then two days later, Whatley came down with a sudden case of pleurisy. Magistrate Jelfs insisted the meeting proceed without him, and on the evening of April 3, the commissioners and reporters gathered to hear from witnesses. Jelfs opened by coming straight to the point. "It is common knowledge," he said, "that there are certain hints and rumours about—well, I'll put it plainly—the chief of police. There are insinuations." He wanted the people directly connected to the Nicolson firm to explain why "certain others" appeared to be associated with it. He said that, after looking at the evidence presented to the attorney general, "It didn't look good to me."

The lawyer representing the Hamilton police department, a friend of Whatley's named S. F. Washington, stood to say he had tried to meet with the chief but couldn't see him because he was too ill. Dismissing the rumours as "old women's fish tales," he objected to hearing any evidence until Whatley was well enough to attend. Mayor Jutten agreed—the chief should be able to hear the charges. "British fair play demands nothing less."

That gave Jelfs enough reason to adjourn the proceedings until April 17. Having been so confident the probe would be over quickly because there was nothing to find, he had to sheepishly admit to reporters that there was indeed something that needed explanation. For the first time he opened up about Morgan's main charge—that salesmen of the Nicolson Sales and Service Company had been instructed to sell stock to bootleggers.

By April 6, Whatley's pleurisy had apparently become pneumonia in both lungs, and his condition was critical. A week later, at the age of forty-seven, he was pronounced dead. Coming as it did before the resumption of the police commission probe, Whatley's death allowed him to be sent off with full honours on April 15, with eighty uniformed men bearing his Union Jack–draped casket, and his secrets, to the grave.

But maybe not all of his secrets. The day after the funeral a strange scene unfolded in Hamilton police headquarters. Charles Morgan, appearing distraught, came through the heavy oak doors, walked up to a constable and demanded to be placed under arrest. He was beside himself as he was taken to Deputy Magistrate McHattie and appeared to blame himself for Whatley's death. McHattie quickly sent him away, telling him to go and see a doctor.

Why would Morgan blame himself for Whatley dying of pneumonia? Perhaps because it wasn't illness that did him in. Some years later, a different version emerged of the police chief's demise. Published in *Hush*, a Toronto weekly that revelled in rumour, it claimed that Whatley had been caught in a trap. Prompted by Charles Morgan's charges, a provincial officer had arranged for that February 13 OTA raid on Rocco and Bessie's house. Then he'd called Whatley to let him know. With no time to waste, Whatley had driven straight over, parked in the lane behind 166 Bay Street South and helped Rocco's men get rid of the liquor, loading some of it into his own car. That was why the OTA officers who arrived later couldn't find anything. What Whatley didn't know until too late, according to the *Hush* report, was that while he was helping the Perris, the provincial officer was somewhere nearby, watching and taking pictures.

When Whatley knew the truth would come out, this scandalous story suggested, it wasn't pneumonia that killed him. It was a bullet from his own gun.

NOTHING about that private drama affected Rocco and Bessie. They carried on business as usual, because business was booming. And help kept coming from the Hamilton police, even if they didn't always intend it.

Amongst the whisky loads arriving steadily was one that came late in May of 1924—a shipment of about two thousand bottles, which the Perris had delivered directly to their home on Bay Street South and stacked up in their cellar. Immediately after that, Rocco left town for a series of meetings with his top customers in New Jersey and New York, undoubtedly major mob figures Frank Costello and Arnold Rothstein, the man who had, among other things, fixed the 1919 World Series. Rocco was still there the night of May 28 when he called Bessie to fill her in on the day's discussions. They were still talking a little after one in the morning when Bessie was startled by the sound of gunshots.

She told Rocco they sounded close. Instinct told them that if there were men with guns close to the Perri home, then it was probably the gunmen's destination. Someone had found out Rocco was out of the city, and the house was filled with a small fortune in liquor. They couldn't do anything about the cache in the cellar, but Rocco told Bessie to grab all the rolls of cash she kept in the bureau, all the diamonds she kept upstairs, and hide them until she could get them to a safety deposit box at the bank.

Outside, three men in suits and overcoats were running from the police who were chasing them. Constables McGregor and Rolfe, two motorcycle cops, had been dispatched to investigate a report of suspicious prowlers at Hess and Duke streets. When the police spotted the men, they ordered them to stop, then began shooting. The men had split up, and now they were hiding somewhere in the dark about a block and a half from the Perri residence.

As McGregor and Rolfe searched, one of the gangsters, a sharply dressed Ukrainian robber-cum-bootlegger-cum-safecracker named Louis (Jack) Larenchuk hiked himself over a tall wooden fence behind a house on Robinson Street. In his grey suit and silk shirt, he crouched down to hide in the three-foot-high space under the back stoop of the house. A foot or two away sat a hen that had recently laid eight white eggs in her straw nest, and she was not going to budge for anyone.

Inside that house, Mrs. Emma McCallum and her two daughters, woken by the sound of gunfire, had just heard someone climbing over their back fence. Now Mrs. McCallum was on the phone to let the police know. Instantly five more officers, including motorcycle officer Ernest Barrett, were dispatched to the scene.

Minutes later, Constable Barrett dismounted from his cycle and started walking along Robinson Street, a gun in one hand and a flashlight in the other, toward the rear of the McCallum home. As he turned his searchlight on the dark area under the steps leading to the back door, he spotted Jack Larenchuk crouched there, pointing a .38 automatic at him.

Barrett knew if he raised his gun he was dead, so he immediately backed away and called for help. At that moment, Constable McGregor, who'd been searching the yard of the house next door, climbed up onto the fence of the McCallum yard, pointed his flashlight into a dark area under the back door less than five feet away, and spotted Larenchuk crouched under the stoop.

"Throw up your hands!" he ordered. Larenchuk bared his teeth and fired four shots at point-blank range. Two shots glanced off the fence, two more went through and missed McGregor by inches. McGregor returned fire and emptied his gun. Constable Barrett started shooting over the fence from another angle as a third cop, Detective Joseph Chamberlain, crawled forward and handed McGregor his weapon.

One of the cops shouted to Larenchuk that he was surrounded, which just intensified his shooting. An entire residential neighbourhood listened, transfixed, to something that sounded like war. Larenchuk reloaded from a bag of bullets in his pocket and peppered the fence near McGregor's head until he shot away some of the wood, giving him a clear view of his target. McGregor jumped and fired in one motion, and either that shot or one from Constable Barrett struck Larenchuk through the head. Police found him dead, and the nearby hen miraculously unharmed.

About a block and a half away, Bessie Perri listened for a while to the expanding silence, until she decided the danger had passed.

THERE was always danger, though, of one kind or another. If they weren't coming at the bootleggers with guns, they were coming at them with legislation. On June 6, just days after the inquest into Larenchuk's death, Canada and the United States signed the Hughes–Lapointe Treaty to increase co-operation between their governments in the fight against liquor and drug smuggling. Newspaper editorialists seemed relieved. "The operations on the Essex and Niagara borders of rum-runners shame the Canadian people," said the *Globe*, "and are a menace to the morals and the laws of our neighbours." Now customs officials had the ability to deny clearances to vessels "ostensibly clearing for Cuba or some other West Indian island, or perhaps Mexico," that were too small to make the trip. Now law enforcement agencies were obligated to share information with the neighbouring country, alerting officials when known smugglers were headed their way. (A side benefit of this treaty was that signing it made Canada feel quite good about itself, because it had entered into an agreement with the United States like a fully grown-up country—"concrete evidence of the full status being accorded to Canada in the sisterhood of British nations.")

Then on July 19, with the Hamilton police department on its best behaviour in the wake of the Whatley scandal, a combined team of Hamilton and Toronto officers seized a truck carrying 107 cases of whisky. Since it was Gooderham & Worts whisky, this was undoubtedly a Perri gang shipment. Worth about twelve grand, it was one of the largest such seizures ever in Hamilton, and OTA authorities were giddy with the thought that they'd "dealt a death blow" to the organization.

But of course, neither of these complications was insurmountable. The new anti-smuggling treaty made life a little more difficult for Rocco and Bessie. But only a little. The fact was that, as long as distilleries were paying their taxes, there wasn't much incentive for Canadian authorities to help the United States stop the flow of liquor south. And U.S. customs officials were notoriously easy to bribe.

As for the liquor seizure, Rocco was running shipments like that practically every day. Losing one wasn't going to hurt all that much. He'd lost twenty thousand dollars in the Gogo seizure in Toronto nine months before and it hadn't stopped him. He would lose plenty more. A five-thousand-dollar truck shipment here, a grand to bail out a driver there—it was all part of the cost of doing business. Setbacks were temporary; challenges could be overcome. As a newspaper writer said that summer, "Hamilton is the center of the cleverest bootlegging organization that can be found in the province. Desperate, unprincipled men with plenty of means and who will stop at nothing are at the head of it."

And one woman, Bessie might have added.

15

CATTURA
Capture

MONTHS HAD PASSED SINCE CONSTABLE JOSEPH Trueman's murder, and still no one had figured out who'd killed him. At her home in Vancouver, Trueman's sister despaired of knowing the truth. Her husband, H. H. Steen, finally wrote to Ontario's attorney general: "His sister would like to know if the person or persons who committed the foul deed have been apprehended or has the chase been given up."

The chase had not been given up. In fact, for one man the chase had become his life's work.

Sometime early in 1923, OPP Constable George Stockbridge, Trueman's partner in the fight against bootlegging in Thorold, had resigned from the force. Things had not gone well for him in the wake of Trueman's murder. Troubled by his ally's death, he'd become embittered at his treatment, and at the lack of support from his superiors as he tried to carry out his duties. The town council of Thorold cared so little about shutting down bootlegging that it had tried to fill Constable Trueman's position on the force by temporarily appointing E. Taylor, the ex-chief of police, who several years before had been convicted of his own breach of the Ontario Temperance Act. Stockbridge had been as appalled as every other citizen of Thorold, and was frustrated at the failure of investigators to make any real headway in solving the murder. So he'd taken it upon himself to find Trueman's killer. To do that, he descended into the bootleggers' world. He got himself in deep.

The first sign of just how deep came January 14, 1924, when Inspector William Stringer told his superiors that Stockbridge had been arrested in Buffalo for gun toting and had served a term in the Lockport jail. His present whereabouts were unknown, but Stringer also noted that Tony Calabrase, the driver for Thorold's bootlegging gang, was now a "chum of Stockbridge," and he'd been arrested in Buffalo on a shooting charge.

To his former colleagues, it looked like Stockbridge had gone bad. In fact, he'd gone undercover, and he'd done it without any protection or support. Since resigning from the force, Stockbridge had sidled up to Calabrase, trying to befriend him. As a former cop, he had to work hard to earn the gangster's trust. It had taken a year of hanging out with him, visiting blind pigs, liquor dives and gambling dens, playing the role of cop-turned-crook. When Calabrase left Thorold for Buffalo, Stockbridge relocated there himself. He presented himself as a card shark, flashed a gun and got himself arrested, all in the hope of being accepted into Calabrase's circle and spending enough time among them to hear someone, somewhere, reveal a crucial bit of information, as criminals so often did when they got drunk with their pals.

He heard enough while hanging out with Calabrase and his friends that Calabrase told Stockbridge more than once that he knew too much. That he should get out while he could. But Stockbridge hadn't heard what he needed to hear yet, and he wasn't leaving until he did.

On a Sunday night, May 18, 1924, he thought all his effort and risk had finally paid off. As the two men drank in a dingy Buffalo liquor dive, something set Calabrase off. He picked a fight with Stockbridge and pulled a knife, and when Stockbridge pushed him away, Calabrase threatened to do to him "what I did to Trueman." It was exactly what Stockbridge had been waiting for. He left, and that same night composed a loosely punctuated letter to OPP Inspector C. Airey of Niagara Falls. "I am writing you in Reference to Reward offered for the Person or Persons who Killed Constable Trueman of Thorold," he wrote with a fountain pen in lines that curved gently across the page. "I have some valuable information that has taken over a year to get also I have taken some big chances to get I have been warned that should I talk they will get me."

Stockbridge told Airey that he had "mixed with the lowest class of People" and spent time in "the rottenest booze joints in the city" in an effort to get information. Now he was being threatened with a slashed face if he told what he knew, which was, he assured Airey, big. "I think the information I have will be direct evidence against the person who done the job."

Airey thought enough of this to arrange a meeting between himself, Stringer and Stockbridge for Wednesday, May 28, at Buffalo's Hotel Statler, where Stockbridge was staying under the name Frank Olman. A few days before the meeting, Stockbridge sent another letter. He wanted to know up front how much he would be paid for his information. "I have been used rotten by your department and don't think I had any part of a square deal," he wrote. "What I know now I will keep to myself unless I have proof I am going to get used square you know the Italians are hard people to get information out of and I have spent my own money to get what I know from the one according to his story who killed Trueman."

On Wednesday night, Stringer and Airey drove to Buffalo and met Stockbridge at the impressive Hotel Statler. Even though Stringer hadn't much liked the tone of Stockbridge's latest letter, he heard him out and decided he was sincere. He believed Stockbridge when he said Calabrase had revealed that Trueman's murderer had been "well paid" and that, later, had all but boasted that he'd done the deed himself.

But it was hard sometimes, in the criminal world, to distinguish unguarded revelations from pure drunken posturing. Nothing ever came of Stockbridge's effort, brave as it apparently was, because a couple of months later there was another, better lead. It was a lead that pointed to someone Rocco Perri had relied on before to eliminate problems: none other than John Trott.

On July 22, 1924, District Inspector W. T. Moore, stationed in Cobalt, wrote to OPP Assistant Commissioner Alfred Cuddy about a tip he'd received from a local he trusted. It had to do with a man in South Porcupine, a mining town near Timmins, who had been trying to entice a couple of miners to quit their jobs and become bootleggers. When one of them said the police wouldn't allow it, the man said the police could be "fixed." Fixed how? asked the local. "Like I fixed one down in Thorold," said the bootlegger. "I shot him."

Inspector Moore understood this man's name to be "John Trout," but when Inspector Stringer learned about it, he knew immediately it was Trott.

If a name and an overheard boast were all the tipster had offered, it would have sounded like a dozen other tips Stringer had gotten. But Moore had a second piece of vital information—in the midst of crowing about his shoot-out with a cop, Trott had let slip that he had sold the gun he'd used in the murder to another Italian in South Porcupine named James Fera. Stringer knew that if Fera still had the gun, it might be the breakthrough they needed. They had already managed to find one of the bullets fired by the killer, which had lodged in a signboard. Now they could test the gun to see if it had fired that bullet, and if they could prove it, then all they would have to do is find John Trott.

Oh, that was the third piece of information Moore had. He knew where John Trott was living these days—61 Parks Street, Niagara Falls, Ontario.

JOHN Trott (born Trotta) was thirty-eight years old and heavyset. As a younger man he'd had a puckish look, with a small nose, jutting chin and wide light-brown eyes. Some act of violence before 1915 had rid him of the pinky finger on his left hand. Like most gangsters he had a taste for pinstripe suits and shiny ties. An Italian by birth, he'd never managed to learn to read or write in English. In 1915 he'd been arrested in Toronto and sentenced to six months for living off the avails of prostitution. Five years later he'd been fined in Montreal for carrying a revolver. Then he'd found his calling as a bootlegger/hit man in Rocco Perri's organization.

After the shooting that night in Thorold, Trott had escaped to the farm where he was living in Merritton, owned by Jas. R. Emmett who lived in the house next door. But he knew he couldn't stay there long. After Christmas, he drove to Grantham Township in his McLaughlin Special touring car to stay with the Dobrindt family on Carlton Street. Charles and Ada Dobrindt had two daughters, the oldest just seventeen. And after a while, despite his rather blatant lack of prospects, John Trott proposed to young Verva Dobrindt, and she accepted. They were married by a Presbyterian minister on March 30, 1924. Trott claimed he was thirty, and that he worked as a taxi driver. As Verva would one day tell police, her husband often deceived her.

With the tip from Cobalt, an investigation that had lain virtually dormant for a year began to regain momentum. And other revelations began to surface. In the first days of September, an Italian named Adolphe Pedini, who worked at the Beaver Board plant in Thorold, was pestering a married woman whose husband was away. As part of his strategy to get her attention, Pedini told her that he'd been in the car the night Trueman's murder was planned, and in that conversation he revealed that John Trott had been there with him. Perhaps hoping to rid herself of an aggravation, she passed this information on to police.

On September 8, Stringer took the night train to Timmins to meet with District Inspector Moore and hear more about what John Trott had blurted out to a couple of prospective bootleggers in South Porcupine. Then the two of them located James Fera, who ran a picture show in South Porcupine, and obtained the gun Trott had sold him. Trott had taken fifteen dollars for it, Fera explained, because he'd been spending a lot of time in town with prostitutes and needed the cash.

The bullet and the shells found at the scene of Trueman's murder had come from a .32 automatic. The sleek Belgian-made Browning now sitting heavy in Stringer's hand, the gun once owned by John Trott, was a .32 automatic. As far as Stringer was concerned, it was enough for an arrest. He boarded the first train back to Toronto, got his arrest warrant, and from sources in Thorold learned that Trott was now living with his young wife on the New York side of Niagara Falls. The city manager there was able to tell him that the couple likely lived on 16th Street, in a basement apartment in the 500 block. Stringer went from door to door, posing as a census taker—he had no jurisdiction in New York State—until, at 539 16th Street, Verva Trott answered his knock. Feigning a lack of interest, Stringer learned that Trott lived there, but wasn't there at the moment. He thanked Verva, got back in his car, and raced to Niagara Falls police headquarters where he got the assistance and approvals he needed. He returned to see Trott hurrying down the street with a grip in his hand and his wife with him. In his private journal, Stringer wrote that as the car drove up he "pounced on Trott" and hauled him in. "He was enroute to Buffalo, and we nearly missed him." Trott waived his extradition rights and Stringer transported him back to Canada over the lower suspension bridge and stuffed him into the Welland jail.

WORD of Trott's arrest shook southern Ontario's bootlegging fraternity, and almost immediately they convened a meeting. In the same secluded swamp midway between Guelph and Hamilton where Jimmy Loria's body had been found two years before, cars filled with high-ranking mobsters pulled up one by one—a Chandler coupe, Rocco Perri's big Cadillac, three Nash touring cars and more. Out stepped Guelph bootleggers Sam and Mike Sorbara, Domenico Ferraro, Leo Addario and Fred Fazzario; from Welland, mobsters Frank Longo, Domenico Longo, Jimmy Sorbara, and the Marabito brothers Joe, Sam and Domenico; and from Hamilton, Rocco Perri, a hood named "Bulldog" Frank and five of Rocco's men. A Lincoln coupe also drove up from Buffalo with several mobsters including one of the Sacco brothers, but police couldn't get their names.

Regardless of their connection to the crime, they all knew the situation was dangerous. Killing a cop was nothing like killing one of their own, and now that the shooter was caught, they argued about what to do. It was well known—even his wife knew—that Trott talked too much. "Bulldog" Frank in particular was sure Trott was going to "spill his guts," but he didn't much care because he wasn't involved. Frank Longo was evidently very much involved, and he prepared to disappear, as did three others. (James D'Agostino, the baker in Merritton, had already gone underground.)

Rocco agreed to find a lawyer for Trott and pay for his defence (he hired W. M. German, who had worked on Domenic Paparone's case six years before). After that, he said, he would travel to Parry Sound, where apparently some of the witnesses (or accomplices) to Trueman's murder were living, to warn them to stay low and keep quiet.

As they stood around the swamp, the mobsters talked about how to communicate with Trott in jail—to tell him to stay silent, and to assure him they would get him off—and came up with a plan. The police would not allow visitors to talk to a prisoner in Italian, but they could bring him food. So, after the meeting, two of the participants drove back to Welland, cooked a dish of macaroni, and delivered it to Trott in jail. At the bottom of the dish was a note, written in the language Trott understood, telling him to sit tight and keep his mouth shut.

He said not a word.

The Crown had its own plan. It worried about waiting until a trial to get testimony from all of the witnesses on the record—witnesses to mob crimes or confessions had a tendency to forget, or disappear—so it intended to bring them to a preliminary hearing on October 7. Stringer suggested they send a police escort up to South Porcupine to ensure the witnesses' attendance, "and to prevent any interference from sources not in harmony with the administration of justice."

The Crown was also worried about its evidence. The main problem was the expert testimony regarding Trott's gun. On October 12, Stringer took the train to Montreal and the next morning met up with J. Cadham, the sales manager for the Dominion Cartridge Company. Together they drove the forty miles to the factory in

Brownsburg, Quebec, to have the weapon tested by Dominion's in-house expert, S. W. McGibbon. Stringer wanted McGibbon to declare unequivocally that Trott's Browning had fired the .32-calibre shells found at the scene.

He couldn't do it. The bullet that police had found embedded in a sign was flattened on one side, apparently from having first bounced off the road, which had erased many of the "lands" (impressions) and grooves needed to link bullet to gun. The shells, meanwhile, bore no discernible marks or flaws from the gun's firing pin or breechblock. McGibbon was only able to state for certain that, from its weight, the bullet was likely a .32, and that it hadn't been fired from a Colt pistol, because the inner rifling of Colt barrels twisted to the left, the opposite of the markings on the bullet.

Frustrated, Stringer decided the Dominion Cartridge people weren't expert enough to tell him what he needed to hear. He bit his tongue and thanked them for their time, then headed to Montreal's Detective Bureau to get details of Trott's arrest history from Superintendent E. LaFlamme. It was there, while Stringer was grumbling about his Dominion Cartridge disappointment, that LaFlamme told him if it was evidence on guns and bullets he wanted, he needed to talk to Dr. Wilfrid Derome.

Forty-seven years old when Stringer came to see him, and educated in Paris, Dr. Derome was quite possibly the greatest forensics expert on the continent. In 1914 he had founded the *Laboratoire de médecine légale et de police technique*, North America's first forensic science laboratory. Two years after meeting with Stringer, he would invent the microspherometer, a device designed specifically to measure the lands left on bullets by the guns that fired them, and to do it with such precision that the results could be used as scientific evidence in court.

Essentially, Wilfrid Derome invented the science of ballistics.

Though Stringer would later write in his journal that seeing the "great criminologist" was all part of his plan, at the time he had no idea of his luck.

Trott's trial in Welland began on November 11, 1924. Again police gathered up the witnesses they needed—amazingly, they were all still around—and they had in hand Dr. Derome's promise to appear at the trial and state for the record that, from his examination, it was indeed Trott's gun that had fired the bullet found at the scene.

But something went wrong. A number of the jurors asked to be excused from the trial because they knew John Trott, and yet the judge, Justice Mowat, refused. These were the jurors who heard the testimony of the Crown's witnesses—the various Thorold citizens near the scene of the crime; the South Porcupine residents who'd heard Trott talking about the shooting; James Fera, who'd bought Trott's gun; Wilfrid Derome, who attempted to explain the concept of ballistics markings; and Inspector William Stringer himself— and these were the jurors who failed to agree on a verdict. Rocco Perri, who sat in the courtroom every day watching, had managed to arrange an alibi for Trott: a man named Angelo Alfero testified that he'd been with Trott in his house all that night. Nine jurors accepted that alibi; only three voted to convict.

A hung jury meant John Trott had to be tried again. The second time, the following February, they got it right. The Crown managed to discredit Rocco's alibi witness before he could even take the stand. And although Rocco supplied a new witness for the defence, no one believed Domenic Arilotta when he said he saw a strange man sell Trott the Browning *after* the murder. The South Porcupine witnesses, meanwhile, stood up under a tough cross-examination, and Dr. Derome got his ballistics lesson through to the jury. Trott was convicted of manslaughter and sentenced to life in the Kingston Penitentiary.

PART 3

16
PROPAGANDISTA
Propaganda

THERE WERE MEN WHO DIED IN THE BOOTLEGGING business and it was hard, from a distance, to know why. Joe Basile was one of those. On the evening of May 29, 1924, the restaurateur from Hamilton's James Street North—brother, coincidentally, of Harry Basile, the stranger a frantic Olive Rutledge had asked to watch over her baby—was gunned down in Buffalo. Two men had approached him at the corner of Front Avenue and Carolina Street, pulled out their guns and put five slugs into him, then ran to a car and sped away. "He was evidently a marked man," said the *Hamilton Herald*. Evidently.

Five and a half months later, two other men with possible connections to bootlegging were found slain, in ways that suggested a message was being sent. The first was Joseph Boitowicz, a Polish immigrant who had been murdered on July 31 in the basement of his Gage Avenue home. Boitowicz was a gambler, and he had been killed with a blow to the head that was strong enough to partly remove it. Then his body was wrapped in a blanket and dumped over the side of Hamilton Mountain at Albion Falls. His gruesome form—his head now a short distance from his body—was discovered on November 8.

It was found by several intrepid Boy Scouts who were out looking, in fact, for a different body, that of Fred Genesee, a jitney driver who had gone missing in late October. Genesee's body was discovered a week after Boitowicz's in another spot on the mountain a couple of miles to the east, somewhat less decomposed, but equally mutilated (he had been strangled with a cord, the side of his face had been smashed with a heavy instrument, and his left eye had come loose). After the discovery of Genesee's body, the *Toronto Daily Star* harkened back to past bootlegging deaths and, reaching deep into its kit of metaphors, compared the escarpment to the stone altars of ancient Aztec priests: "Hamilton Mountain has become a place of skulls, a mountain of human sacrifice."

Hamilton police quite naturally preferred to downplay the significance of Hamilton as a headquarters for murder or bootlegging, and Inspector of Detectives Gooderham (no apparent relation to the William Gooderham family) dismissed the idea that Fred Genesee had anything to do with the illegal liquor racket. But the provincial police had taken the lead in the investigations, and they had a feeling that, although the methods used were different, these two violent murders had links to the murder of Joe Basile. Apparently Basile knew both men and, before he died, had given a certain ring of Hamilton bootleggers some reason to be angry. And who could miss the scent of enmity in the most recent murders? When Fred Genesee went missing, a message of warning was left in the form of a dagger shoved to the hilt through the centre of a wooden table in his house.

It seemed a powerful man was imposing rule. And A. H. Lyle of the Hamilton Temperance Federation had no doubt who it was. "It is no exaggeration to say that the king of the bootleggers in the province lives in Hamilton," he said to a reporter, apparently loath to utter the man's name, "and for many months the police have been trying to obtain evidence that would convict him. He is an Italian. A few years ago he was only an ordinary fruit seller . . . Now he has his motor cars and lives in luxury."

Lyle went on. He spoke of the number of times "this Hamilton man" had been found in the vicinity of liquor seizures and "shooting affrays." He spoke of the Gogo incident, which had happened little more than a month before, and of tips the police received in advance of bootlegging activities, only to arrive and find "the King of the Bootleggers at the threatened spot in time to prevent arrests and confiscations." He noted the number of times police had raided the man's home but found no liquor. "The fact of the matter seems to be that he is too clever for the authorities."

The young reporter, David B. Rogers, who was just out of New York's Columbia University School of Journalism, thanked Lyle for his remarks and returned to the *Star*'s King Street West offices. He showed his editors what he had, and then he did an extraordinary thing. Perhaps driven by a sense of competition with that rising young reporter Ernest Hemingway, who seemed to be specializing in stories of vice and depravity for the *Star*, Rogers convinced his editors to let him go back to Hamilton and attempt to interview the man A. H. Lyle was speaking about. It had never been done before, and the editors agreed, it was time. Later the next day, November 18, Rogers arrived at 166 Bay Street South in Hamilton, made note of the "plain" and "unpretentious" brick edifice in which his subject lived, then knocked on the door to interview the allegedly murderous Rocco Perri.

Even more astonishing than the pluck of David Rogers in trying for this interview was the willingness of Rocco to give it. Perhaps it was hubris. If there is anything more corrupting than power it's flattering press, and after hearing himself called "King of the Bootleggers" and "too clever for the authorities," perhaps Rocco was feeling magnanimous.

Or maybe he and Bessie realized that he was starting to get too much of the wrong kind of attention—the quick assumption that he was behind every unexplained Italian murder—which could only lead to more invasive and constricting police scrutiny. Perhaps it was time for a little counter-propaganda, to show the world he wasn't so dangerous after all. So he and Bessie got dressed to impress and welcomed the journalist in.

Rogers wasted no time. The trio seated themselves in the home's sumptuous parlor, and after the initial pleasantries, Rogers put his first question to Rocco: "Who killed Joe Boitowicz and Fred Genesee?"

Rocco Perri, self-styled 'king of the bootleggers,' suave, immaculate and unperturbed, leaned far back into the luxurious cushions of the chesterfield. There was a quick flash of sparkling white teeth; black eyes shone with sudden amusement; a carefully groomed pair of shoulders rose slowly in a gesture of perfect Italian indifference and then he spoke.

"Who knows?" he said with apparent puzzlement and then looked smilingly across at his charming Italian [*sic*] wife. 'Rocco Perri did it,' I suppose. Everything that happens they blame on Rocco Perri. Why is it? Maybe because my name is so easy to say; I don't know. It is amusing."

Rocco and Bessie then laughed softly at the amusement.

Rogers didn't ease up. He flattered Rocco as "the recognized leader of the Italian population of Hamilton" and pressed for some theory to explain the "extraordinary sequence of murders."

Signor Perri's face took on a more serious expression. "How came these two men to be killed?" he repeated. "I know not, but from what I have heard and from what I have read, I would say that Joe Boitowicz was put out of the way because he was a squealer. He was a Pollack. I have been told that he was a stool pigeon. There was a case some time ago in which he helped the police. There may have been others. He said too much. He has paid the price. That's what I think, but I don't know."

Whether or not Rocco had something to do with Boitowicz's murder—and time would show he probably didn't—there was nothing wrong with delivering a stern warning about squealing. "And Fred Genesee?" prompted Rogers.

"Fred Genesee, yes but I do not know him. Maybe I have seen him. I don't remember. But he was not a bootlegger, I don't think. I have not heard that he was. Why was he killed? I don't know, but I think there was a woman in the case. I think it was spite."

The voice of Mrs. Perri slipped naturally into the conversation. "Ah, yes, a woman, there must have been a woman. It would not be the first time that man went to his death because of a woman, nor will it be the last."

Now that Bessie had spoken, she seemed to warm to the conversation, particularly when a troublesome subject came up. This was a time of some challenge for the Perris. At least one rival bootlegging gang, maybe more, had recently begun getting pushy around Hamilton. One of Rocco's men had just had his face slashed from one ear to the other. Another had been injured when his sabotaged truck lost a wheel. When Rogers raised the suggestion that Boitowicz and Genesee had been killed in connection with a bootleg war, Bessie may have considered this dangerous territory for Rocco, so she set the tone.

"Bootleg war, that is funny." She reached toward her silent husband and patted him easily on the back. "You tell them Rocco, that there is no war. You are the king of the bootleggers. That is what they say. You should know."

Mr. Perri was quick to respond. "There is no bootleg war," he declared with abrupt emphasis. "Next they will be saying that it is the blackhand or the vendetta."

Rogers asked Rocco to describe the difference between the two. Rocco answered, but Bessie found a way to change the conversation's direction.

"The blackhand—that is to put away a man if demands for money are not met. The vendetta—that is to kill a man for revenge."

From across the richly furnished parlor of the Perri home at 166 Bay Street south, one of Hamilton's finest residential sections, came the soothing symphony of a stringed orchestra. "It is New York," Mrs. Perri explained, stepping lightly toward an elaborate radio cabinet. "You would like something else, perhaps? But no, you are here to talk, and you must not be interrupted."

Rogers moved on to the subject of bootlegging, and Rocco basked for a moment in the title King of the Bootleggers. "The uncrowned king," he said with a chuckle. A month before, the

Ontario government had held a referendum that had (barely) reaffirmed the Ontario Temperance Act, and Rogers said Rocco must be pleased. "No, no I am just the opposite from pleased," said Rocco. "I am sorry that the OTA was not put away. With government control it would be far better."

It had been rumoured that the Perris were so anxious for the temperance movement to win, to maintain the profitable status quo, that they had contributed thirty thousand to the Dry campaign. A. H. Lyle of the Hamilton Temperance Foundation had already quashed that notion when Rogers put it to him the day before, and when Rogers raised it again, Bessie stepped in. "Oh, it is to laugh," she said. "Rocco helping them with the OTA. No, no, he was sick in bed all day when they voted and when I told him that it was to remain dry, he was sorry."

Rogers tried to understand the logic. Could you, he asked Rocco, do just as well as a bootlegger with liquor under government control?

Signor Perri placed the palms of his painstakingly manicured hands together as if to lend weight to what he was about to say. "Better," he ruled without hesitation. "I say that my business would not be harmed. Look at Quebec, look at the other provinces. It would be better all around. There would be less crime."

"Why?"

"Because there would be no moonshine, because there would be no stools. Now what have you? Many hundreds of cheap bootleggers selling poison liquor. That is bad. It drives men crazy. They commit crimes. It kills them. And besides there is so much cut-throat competition. The little bootleggers, they try to get protection by telling on each other. They are stools. You have them in your ward, hundreds of them, Jews. They have no principles, they will sell anything, they will do anything to get the business of their competitor. That makes more crime.

"There are the boys and girls to be considered. Under the OTA they visit the dives because they think it is clever and smart. But how many of them would enter the authorized stores under a system of government control?"

No one could argue with much of Rocco's assessment, although it's impossible to know if Bessie was bothered by her husband's easy disparagement of Jews. Rogers observed her fiddling with the shiny black knobs of the radio as Rocco spoke, and saw that it was the word *principles* that seemed to ignite her. She turned toward them.

"You have heard that there is honour among thieves," she said, "but maybe you do not know that there is such a thing as principle among bootleggers. Yes, we admit that we are bootleggers but we do our business on the level."

Rocco took up the theme. "My men," he said, "do not carry guns. If I find that they do, I get rid of them. It is not necessary. I provide them with high-powered cars. That is enough. If they cannot run away from the police it is their own fault. But guns make trouble. My men do not use them."

Here a phone began to ring in another room, and Bessie left to answer it as Rocco continued. "There is no business," he said, "I don't care what you name, in which honesty is a more important factor than in the bootlegging business."

Rocco's remarks were so rational and straightforward that Rogers imagined himself attending a lecture on business administration. Rocco even took pains to emphasize that he was speaking of "accredited" bootlegging, and he delivered a message to his upstart rivals.

"The man who does not play the game as it should be played will not get far," he said. "Pure liquor, fair prices and square dealing. Those are the requisites of the trade. I have played the game and—" Here Rocco made a show of looking around the room at all the trappings of wealth he had acquired.

Something about the Bootleg King's self-satisfaction prompted young David Rogers to take a more judgmental stance. "You think you have a right to carry on an illicit traffic in liquor?" he asked.

Near where Rocco was sitting lay a strategically placed copy of the *Toronto Daily Star* from the previous Friday, open to a huge story about the former provincial treasurer Peter Smith, who was beginning his three-year term in Kingston Penitentiary for conspiracy and theft in the Home Bank deposit scandal. Rocco had been waiting for the journalist's tone to turn disapproving. He pointed to the paper.

"Am I doing more wrong than men like Peter Smith and Aemilius Jarvis?" he asked, referring as well to the scion of the wealthy and respected Jarvis family, equally implicated in the scandal. "I at least play square with my customers."

Rogers again tried to prod Rocco—"There is a law against selling liquor," he said—and Rocco responded.

"The law, what is the law?" he asked scornfully. "They don't want it in the cities. They voted against it. It is forced upon them. It is an unjust law. I have a right to violate it if I can get away with it. Men do it in what you call legitimate business until they get caught. I shall do it in my business until I get caught. Am I a criminal because I violate a law which the people do not want?"

"And if you get caught?" asked Rogers.

Rocco laughed like a man perfectly at ease. "We will not cross that bridge just yet," he said. "But one can fight the law and win sometimes." He was thinking back to just a week before, when it had been so easy to work the system to get a mistrial for John Trott. "They tried to put the blame on a poor innocent boy," said Rocco. "He did not kill Constable Trueman. We fought them with the instruments of the law. I was at the trial myself. The jury disagreed—nine were for acquittal. Next time he will go free. The boy is innocent; he did not do the killing."

Rogers asked the follow-up question that would naturally occur to anyone who considered himself bound by the obligations of a law-abiding society. "If you knew who killed Trueman," he asked, "do you not think it would be your duty to notify the authorities?"

Rocco thought about this for a moment. "No, I don't think so," he said. "If I knew, and someone else was about to suffer the penalty I might tell, but it is up to the police to find the guilty man."

The subject of informing police naturally led Rocco to a related idea—the notion of squealing—and, unprompted by Rogers, he then offered an unprecedented (if somewhat sanitized) view into the mind of the 1920s Italian mobster.

He went on to say that if a man "squealed" on him . . . "I would not kill him; I would punish him. That is the law of the Italians. We do not go to the police and complain. That is useless. We take the law into our own hands. I would kill a man on a question of honour, but not if he merely informed on me. We believe that we have a right to inflict our own penalties. Sometimes it is necessary to kill a man. But I have never done it, and I don't want to."

Of course, he didn't need to. Not personally.

Rogers turned to the subject of the Ontario Temperance Act, and this time appealed to the mobster's ego. Did Rocco, he wondered, find it difficult to evade the OTA?

Again the king of the bootleggers laughed. "They are like a lot of schoolboys learning to play ball, those who are trying to enforce the OTA," he said. "Now, everything that happens which they cannot solve they place at the doors of the bootlegger. If there is a crime that they cannot explain, then it is the bootlegger's fault—and usually they find Rocco Perri to blame. Murders, bank robberies, burglaries—they say that Rocco Perri is at the bottom of it all. I laugh at them.

"What would they do if they did not have the bootlegger to blame, I wonder? I suppose they would say that it was the blackhand. But now they declare that we are to blame for all of these different offenses. It is ridiculous. But they must find someone to blame—and so we suffer."

After the recent referendum, the OPP had announced it was stepping up enforcement of the OTA. Rogers asked Rocco if he had found it more difficult to operate. "I have not noticed it yet," he said. "I have heard that they are imposing $1,000 fines in Toronto. That is no good. What is a thousand dollars? They can never enforce the act by increasing the fines."

What if jail sentences were added?

"That would help. That would do a lot, but always there will be bootleggers. If I am put out of business tomorrow there will be others to take my place."

Then Rocco, again a model of reason, offered some unsolicited advice for the provincial authorities. "They must stop the manufacture and exportation. That is what they must do if they want to enforce prohibition. And even then there will be leaks from other sources which they will have trouble in plugging."

It had reached 10 p.m., according to the rich chime of a clock in the Perri home. Rogers, with a deadline looming, decided it was time to leave. Getting to his feet, hardly able to believe how well the interview had gone, he checked to make sure Rocco had no objections to having his statements published.

"You may say to the people what I have told you," said Rocco, and he offered Rogers his hand. "They blame everything on me now anyway. I have no good name to lose. My reputation is long since blackened. I am a bootlegger. I am not ashamed to admit it. And a bootlegger I shall remain."

As Bessie came to say goodbye—"petite, prettily gowned and smiling gaily," wrote Rogers—Rocco showed the reporter to the door and sent him off with a bow. "Good evening," he said. "Come again when I can help you."

Rogers had been thoroughly charmed, and Rocco, so deft at reading people, knew it. The reporter left readers with a final impression of the mobster that could hardly have been more flattering: "Debonaire [*sic*], polished and confident, he remained bowing in the doorway as *The Star* passed out into the night."

WHEN Rogers got back to the *Star*'s offices with his notes, his editors almost choked on their good fortune. They had what appeared to be an unreserved confession, and so much more, from the country's most notorious bootlegger. No one in Canada, perhaps in North America, had published anything like it before.

But when it was set in type, the story looked almost too good to be true. City Editor Harry Hindmarsh began to have qualms. What if the rookie reporter had gotten it wrong? What if he'd imagined some of what he'd heard, embellished a few of those quotes? What if the police got involved and the mobster accused them of fabricating the whole thing? A major scoop could suddenly turn sour.

Hindmarsh sent the reporter back to Hamilton to get Rocco's signature on galley proofs of the two-page story. With the pages rolled up under his arm, Rogers knocked on the Perris' front door and explained the situation. The Perris examined the story and asked for a couple of small additions. And just like that, Rogers would later remember, "That vain little man signed my proofs."

The story ran the next day with a picture of Rocco as the personification of wealth and respectability, seated with his arm resting on a throne-like chair, in an expensive suit, wearing what appeared to be a large diamond ring and a diamond stud in his tie. The headline above continued the theme: "'King of Bootleggers' Won't Stand for Guns." It also ran with a byline for David. B. Rogers. It was his first credited story. In an age when most newspaper stories ran anonymously, it amounted to an editorial pat on the back.

The November 19, 1924, *Toronto Daily Star* was a sensation. The first edition sold out immediately at two cents a copy and before long hawkers were demanding as much as two dollars each. Other papers, hoping for a piece of this action, scrambled to catch up, sending reporters to the Perri residence, where Rocco "obligingly" consented to answer more questions.

In these follow-up interviews, first with the *Hamilton Spectator*, then with the *Hamilton Herald*, Rocco and Bessie stuck to the main themes: Prohibition encouraged crime; the government should do away with the OTA; Rocco was happy to proclaim himself a bootlegger; and it was time for the false accusations against him and his men to stop. He added a couple of new messages too. He was a charitable man, a benevolent leader. "If an Italian comes to my home and wants help," he said, "I give it to him."

Bessie liked this message, insisting they gave money to everyone. "If Rocco Perri went away tomorrow this city would be worse than it is," she said. "For you have no idea how many people come here with pitiful tales of being out of work and having no food or heat or clothing, and Rocco gives them money to keep them until they could get a job." All of this was true. It may even have been a little irksome to Bessie just how much her husband was willing to do for countless destitute people. But to a *Herald* reporter, Bessie warned that Rocco's giving was not just an unalloyed good, it was a hedge against chaos. "If he didn't give them money some of those men might get desperate and rob you and might even kill you, if you resisted." Speaking of the poor it was too bad, said Rocco, that the government had chosen to continue the OTA. "The very ones it is supposed to protect are the ones who now spend all their money buying poisonous moonshine and such stuff and this awful canned heat," he said. "I would like to see the days before 1916 back so that the poor man might buy a glass of beer or one of whisky, if he wanted, for a reasonable price. It would be better than now. Now the rich have all they want and the poor have to do without or buy poison."

Rocco saw an opportunity to direct the government's attention away from his organization and toward the smaller bootleggers that had recently been trying to muscle in on his territory. So he came back again and again to notions of quality. He was discriminating in his clientele, he said. His customers were prominent citizens. "We do not sell to every man who wants it, no matter how much money he might be prepared to spend."

Having such rarefied clientele meant "I sell only the real, good liquor." And he was able to get that liquor because he was a bootlegger who dealt in large volumes, someone who delivered orders of up to three hundred cases at a time, through distribution centres in Rochester, Detroit and Syracuse (he made no mention of his main route through Buffalo and Niagara Falls), to buyers who were mostly in the United States (no mention of his enormous Ontario market, except to say that he was doing very little business locally). He said all this to set up a contrast with his smaller competitors. "Small bootleggers do not sell good liquor," he said. "Most of it is poison, and a man goes home and beats his wife and children after he drinks it."

Of course, Rocco had once been a small-time seller himself. "When I started a long time ago I was the only one in the business; in fact I was the only one in this district. Now there are thousands behind me. Yes, I admit I am a bootlegger. Why deny it? Instead of sneaking around at night, why not come out and be honest about it? We're not crooks. We do not peddle from door to door and we don't have to go up and down the street selling. [As apparently others were doing.] . . . It's eight years now since I became known, and because I have not been convicted, everything has been put down to me."

And now that he had the province's ear, Rocco claimed, of all things, that he was ready to retire. The *Spectator*, perhaps not believing it themselves, reported this revelation indirectly. But the *Herald* quoted Rocco, just days after he'd told the *Star* that he would remain a bootlegger, sounding almost wistful. "I'm practically out of the business now," he said. "People haven't got the money now to buy liquor like they used to. But for my trade in American cities I would be doing very little business." This was far from true, although he and Bessie were definitely developing other revenue streams, including narcotics, which would become more important.

Over the course of all his interviews, during what had turned into a veritable public relations blitz, Rocco painted a picture of himself as a fair dealer and a forgiving man.

He was forgiving of his employees, "Sometimes it is not the fault of the men if they don't deliver a shipment," he said. "They can't succeed all the time. And I don't dismiss them if it's not their fault." He was forgiving of the press. "Of course, we can't blame you newspapers for getting things wrong, because you get it from the police."

He was forgiving even of the police. "They're not to blame because they're often fooled by false reports sent in by people who want to make trouble." (By this, Rocco meant the rival gangs, and his forgiveness didn't quite extend to them. Immediately after the *Toronto Daily Star*'s big story came out, a reporter from the *Toronto Evening Telegram* delivered a copy to Rocco at the Hamilton General Hospital, where he was at the bedside of the man who'd been hurt in the crash of his sabotaged delivery truck. Apparently Rocco hadn't seen the *Star* edition yet because he'd been busy. That morning, the *Telegram* reported, two men had gone to the Hamilton police asking for protection after being threatened by a "foreign bootlegging gang," the typical euphemism for the Perri outfit.)

Finally, Rocco wanted it to be known that he was a man who played by the rules—and he expected the authorities to do the same. "I know that selling liquor is not within the law, but it's like a game," he said. "If they ever catch me I'll admit that I'm beaten at the game. I want to be caught fairly though, and not framed. I've heard of cases where the officers 'plant' bottles of liquor in houses and cars. I don't want that to happen to me."

ALL in all it was a masterful performance, a seminal bit of PR wizardry, and official reactions were predictable. "It was the most shameful confession I ever read in a newspaper," said Reverend W. A. McIlroy, moderator of the Hamilton Presbytery. "Brazen-faced effrontery" was the phrase A. H. Lyle chose, and the secretary of the Hamilton Temperance Federation wanted something done about it. "If I were in a position of authority, I would feel it my duty to go to the limit to secure a conviction."

As for why no one had yet, Reverend G. K. Bradshaw, chairman of the Hamilton Methodist Conference, wondered whether rumours that Perri had the local police in his pocket were true: "True or not, his statement justifies public suspicion of it. He is boasting that he has hoodwinked and outwitted the authorities of this country. So it is up to those authorities to get him."

The authorities were apparently trying to do just that. The day after the *Star*'s big story, officials in the attorney general's office spent the morning in conference. Attorney General Nickle and OPP Chief Brigadier General Williams called in "several newspapermen" to grill them on what Rocco had said, then hinted some action would follow.

But by November 30, eleven days after the interview that had captured so much attention, no action had come, and the legal reasons were clear. "A man can say anything he likes about himself," said Nickle. "Even if he says he is a criminal the Crown would have to secure proof that he was before it could put him on his defence."

Hamilton Police Chief David Coulter and Crown Attorney Ballard declined to make any statement, although the police did briefly step up their searches of the homes of suspected bootleggers, just as Rocco had hoped. According to Inspector MacCready, one of them complained, "Rocco Perri, he talk too much; busta de biz."

Magistrate Jelfs took the opportunity to shovel dirt on any lingering hints of corruption near him: He was all for deporting Rocco Perri. At a meeting of the Ministerial Association, churchmen and prohibitionists seemed very taken with the idea. "How will we go about it?" asked a Reverend R. M. Dickey. "Will you work with us?"

"A petition would have to be got up," said Jelfs.

"Could you ask the chief to look into a thing of this nature?" inquired another reverend.

"Yes," said the magistrate, who made a suggestion: "Go out and get a petition signed by the leading citizens, asking for his deportation."

Oh, came the reaction, *we* have to do the work? "We are very busy men," harrumphed the Reverend Dickey. "We could not do that."

Jelfs shrugged. "The proof of good intentions is the manner in which you work for them." (It was just two days later that Attorney General Nickle, without giving any reason, asked the seventy-two-year-old magistrate to resign from the bench. Jelfs, true to form, refused, demanding a proper explanation, and Hamilton's legal community rallied around him. After a meeting with Nickle and Premier Howard Ferguson, Jelfs won a reprieve and stayed on the bench until nearly the end of the decade.)

Rocco had known all along what he could get away with. Nothing ever came of the shock and indignation he'd provoked, but he'd bought himself some legal elbow room.

There was only one aspect of what Rocco had said to reporters that he may have regretted, and that was focusing so much on the quality of his liquor. Yes, in hindsight, that focus was soon going to look deeply, tragically ironic.

17

VELENO
Poison

AROUND THE TIME ROCCO WAS TELLING THE WORLD he was getting out of the bootlegging business, he was actually nearing the peak of his wealth and power as a bootlegger. By the end of 1924, a majority of the illegal beer and liquor drunk in southern Ontario, and much of the Canadian liquor drunk in the northeastern United States, came through the Perri gang.

But a majority was not all, and Rocco and Bessie wanted all. That meant they had to deal with certain independent operators. A Hamilton bootlegger named Alf Wheat who bought his beer from the Kuntz Brewery suddenly found his trucks being run off the road until he agreed to work for the Perris instead of against them. And then there was John Ben Kerr.

Now here was a headache. Ben Kerr was not only running his own loads—eighty cases at a time—from the Gooderham & Worts dock into Hamilton, he was taking other loads into Buffalo and actively undercutting the Perri gang's prices. Rocco was furious, not just with Kerr but with Gooderham & Worts for supplying a competitor.

Any other mob leader might simply have had Kerr killed. But to Rocco this was a business problem, and it called for a business solution. He had the leverage; the Perri gang was such an important partner to Gooderham & Worts that Rocco could establish new rules. One day in the spring of 1925—as avid readers were beginning to pore over F. Scott Fitzgerald's account of a similarly self-made man, the great Jay Gatsby—Rocco motored into Toronto for a meeting with Harry Hatch. It was rare to see Rocco angry, but he was angry in this meeting. Hatch later admitted they had a "row." Rocco made his demands clear: G & W had to stop selling to Ben Kerr. From that day forward, Kerr would have to buy his liquor either from the Perris or with the approval of the Perris.

Ben Kerr was a go-getter, no question about that. He didn't join the Perris but apparently he came to heel, and with Rocco's help he gained a new employee—Alf Wheat—and actually expanded his operation that summer to three boats. And it seems the Perris profited from every drop of G & W liquor he sold.

~~~~~~~~~~~~~~~~~~~~~~~~~~~~~~~~~~~~~~

FRANK ZANETH HAD DONE ALL HE COULD DO IN Quebec. One of his last acts was to assist a court of inquiry into the conduct of the superintendent of Valcartier Camp, a Canadian Forces base north of Quebec City. In the process he impressed a colonel in the Department of National Defence, who told RCMP Commissioner Cortlandt Starnes that Zaneth was "courteous, zealous and at all times ready to fulfill our every requirement and wish." Now it was time to move on.

In March 1926, he was transferred to the RCMP's biggest division—O division, headquartered in Toronto but responsible for federal policing throughout Ontario—where he would be a special investigator. Frank took the opportunity to make a clean break of it. He sold or gave away almost everything he owned, making sure to let his commanding officer know that by *not* bringing two thousand pounds worth of personal effects with him to his new home, he had saved the force $20.10 in shipping costs.

There's no sign that his wife, Rita, was involved in that decision. But maybe Frank was clearing away the past in order to embark on a new life with her. By that summer she had recovered enough from the troubles that had taken her to Italy that he was making arrangements for her to live with him again. In July, the Niagara Falls detachment lost one of its key men, Sergeant Birtwistle, to temporary customs department duty, and Frank Zaneth, still working undercover, was seconded to fill in. Money was still an issue for the Zaneths, and so H. M. Newson, the superintendent commanding the western Ontario district, asked the commissioner for his okay to let Frank and his wife stay in a spare room in the Birtwistles' home. "My object in making this recommendation is to assist him financially," wrote Newson, "and it will not interfere in any way with his usefulness in the force."

Divested of most of their personal belongings, Frank and Rita moved into the Birtwistles' spare room at 347 River Road in Niagara Falls, just a few minutes' drive from the falls, if Frank ever allowed himself the time to go and look. It's pleasant to imagine they found some measure of contentment there—undercover, in a sense, from their own lives, without any tangible reminders of who they were, or where they'd come from. But if they did, if there was any joy for them in a life stripped of history and identity, it wouldn't last.

‖‖‖‖‖‖‖‖‖‖‖‖‖‖‖‖‖‖‖‖‖‖‖‖‖

ROCCO WAS RIGHT ABOUT PROHIBITION: IT MADE drinking practically *de rigueur*, and subterfuge heightened the enjoyment. A growing number of downtown stores sold shiny hip flasks for smuggling liquor into theatres and restaurants. In Sarnia, customers for moonshine signalled their interest by walking along the street with a white handkerchief dangling out of their pockets. Young people in particular enjoyed the *frisson* of breaking the law. Around Hamilton it was popular to drive out in dad's Studebaker Special Six and hold raucous drinking parties along hitherto quiet rural roads. (In Washington, DC, drinkers and bootleggers met to whoop it up late at night in government office buildings, which led to one inebriated young woman breaking her leg in a jump from a senator's second-storey window.) And for several years running, southern Ontario's many dance halls were decried as incubators of immorality. Young men in cream-coloured flannel trousers and flappers in satin crêpe waggled their feet to the Charleston as the liquor flowed freely. To the dismay of church leaders and editorialists, both sexes were "in the habit of indulging in it to their befuddlement."

Another kind of subterfuge added to the fun: The poor quality of much of the liquor mothered the invention of new cocktails, as bartenders at high-end establishments devised ways to hide the taste, adding fruit juices, bitters and sweet liqueurs, then giving their concoctions winking names—"Mule's Hind Leg," "Sidecar," "Frankenjack," "Alexander's Sister," "Bees Knees," "Gin Rickey."

But Prohibition also put the most desperate drinkers at risk, particularly in the United States where supply was so tight. In July of 1923, it was revealed that of the eighty thousand samples taken from seized liquor loads over the previous twelve months, only 1 percent was found to be genuine. The next year, Roy Haynes, the U.S. Prohibition commissioner, proudly announced that in a "victory of law and order over outlawed liquor traffickers," the sources for unadulterated spirits in America had been effectively cut off. That victory had consequences.

There are different kinds of alcohol, but for drinkers the stuff that matters is ethyl alcohol, produced by fermentation, when a specific yeast consumes the sugar or starch in fruit, vegetables or grain, and pumps out alcohol and carbon dioxide as waste. Distill that mixture and you get the spirits found in whisky, rum and gin. Distill it further until it's nearly pure, and it becomes industrially useful as solvent or fuel.

Prohibition hadn't ended the production of industrial alcohol—factories couldn't do without it—but that presented governments with a problem. Distilled from the cheapest starchy mash, it was far less expensive to produce than carefully blended and aged liquors, and it was easily available. One could, theoretically, take raw industrial alcohol, dilute it dramatically with water and drink it like vodka. Bootleggers could use it to stretch their supply of whisky. Even ostensibly legitimate whisky producers weren't above this. In *Booze*, his look at whisky's history in the Canadian prairies, James Gray described how Saskatchewan's Bronfman brothers famously bought one-thousand-gallon redwood vats, then into each of them poured one hundred gallons of real, aged rye whisky, 318 gallons of overpoof raw alcohol, and 382 gallons of water. Then they coloured the batch with caramel. That turned a hundred gallons of good whisky into eight hundred gallons of ersatz whisky with a much higher profit margin. (Unfortunately for the Bronfmans, the first time they did this something else got into the vats, which turned the fake whisky a bluish-black colour. Being businessmen, they didn't toss the ruined liquor, they portioned it out into future batches.)

In an effort to prevent people from drinking industrial alcohol, the government stipulated that it be "denatured"—made unfit for consumption—by adding lethal poisons. In the days of Prohibition, one of those poisons was methanol made from wood, just an ounce of which could cause death. The amount of methanol used in denatured alcohol was small, about 2 percent, but that combined with other additives—sometimes formaldehyde, kerosene or benzoyl—made the stuff sufficiently dangerous to keep most drinkers away.

The system worked—right up until denatured alcohol became the only alcohol many people could find or afford. In the spring of 1924, for example, thirteen people in Toledo, Ohio, died from imbibing "canned heat"—the jellied denatured alcohol called Sterno used as a heating fuel—after squeezing it through socks or cheesecloth to turn it liquid (which is why the drink was sometimes called "squeeze"). Those tragedies kept piling up, and toward the end of 1924, a United Press survey of coroners, bureaus of vital statistics and other officials found that over the course of just nine months, poison alcohol had directly killed two thousand people in the United States, and had contributed to scores of additional deaths.

Not that this death toll dissuaded bootleggers and pharmaceutical companies from trying to make denatured alcohol drinkable. There was just so much delicious profit potential in it. So they bought huge quantities of industrial alcohol, at $1.10 a gallon, and then, to the best of their dubious ability, filtered and redistilled it to remove the additives. To this raw, unpalatable alcohol they added water, caramel syrup and a dash of (poisonous) fusel oil to make ersatz whisky. For faux rum, they stirred in rum caramel and blackstrap molasses. Then they sold the result for more than twelve times what it cost to make.

Contrary to what Rocco told the newspapers in November 1924, he dealt in plenty of low-quality *renatured* liquor. But he was confident in his product because he trusted his source. In August of 1922, the Jopp Drug Company in Buffalo had applied to the U.S. Bureau of Prohibition for a permit to make "toilet water"—then the common English phrase for *eau de toilette*, a light perfume—which was granted a couple of months later. Ever since then, it had operated on Michigan Avenue, redistilling thousands of gallons of denatured alcohol to supply bootleggers with a steady flow of cheap raw booze.

In Niagara Falls, New York, the second leg of this organization—the Falls Tonic Manufacturing Company—applied for a similar permit within a week of Jopp, but had to wait more than a year for its approval. As of November 1923, however, it too was ordering huge amounts of government-issued denatured alcohol—specifically formulas 39-A and 39-B—and turning it into money.

The deliveries arrived at an enormous, secret facility. Inside what had once been the National Theater at 326-13th Street in Niagara Falls—chosen for its high ceilings and paucity of windows—workmen had installed a huge five-hundred-gallon still, a couple of 250-gallon stills, two five-thousand-gallon vats and more. The product that issued from this redistilling plant was housed in barrels and cans in a two-storey building next door, alongside some scenery and seats that had been ripped out of the theatre to make room. That building was connected via tunnel to the Third Ward Political Club at 328-13th Street, where the Falls Tonic Company kept its offices. On the streets outside, no one could have noticed anything amiss, except perhaps for the extra wires that ran from the power lines into the two-storey building at the rear of the Third Ward Political Club, and from there into the National Theater, which were stealing the power needed to run the facility.

Behind all this sat a smart, Philadelphia-born Sicilian named Joseph Henry Sottile, who ran the Falls Tonic Company with the help of his brother-in-law Joseph Spallino, and supplied dozens of bootleggers, including Rocco, Ben Kerr, James Sacco in Niagara Falls, Ontario, and Max Wortzman in Toronto.

Sottile was a long-time criminal; in 1916, as a twenty-five-year-old in New York City, he'd been imprisoned for armed robbery. Since then he had become aligned with Don Simone in Niagara Falls, New York, and risen in Italian crime circles to the point that some American police officials believed he was the head of the Black Hand.

For Rocco he was a powerful ally, and their relationship helped make both of them rich. Rocco would ship some of his precious high-quality Canadian whisky from the G & W dock across the lake to Port Dalhousie, Ontario, then slip it over the border to Sottile. In return, Sottile paid Rocco with money and with raw booze that he could use to inflate the volume and profitability of the "whisky" he could sell. In one of his most lucrative schemes, Sottile diluted the good Canadian whisky with his own raw alcohol, then shipped it to St. Pierre and Miquelon for temporary storage. From there, a New Brunswicker named James Lavallée took it by ship to Rum Row off the eastern U.S. coast. Lavallée slipped his vessel in amongst the Scottish ships and sold Sottile's bastardized whisky as if it were the real thing. Rum Row lasted until the summer of 1925, when the feeble American and Canadian coast guards finally stiffened sufficiently to crack down, but until then Sottile and Lavallée made a fortune; in one particular deal they grossed $184,000.

Well-educated but ruthless, Sottile tolerated no impediments. In 1925, when a U.S. special agent named Orville Preuster worked in Niagara Falls, New York, to stem the flow of liquor into the United States, Sottile and another of Rocco's friends, Joe Serianni, arranged for his murder by car bomb. But Sottile could also be politically deft. Already equipped with an American passport, he decided in October 1925 to become a Canadian citizen too, just in case. He applied, hired New Brunswick lawyers who wrote a friendly letter on behalf of this "chap named Joseph Henry Sottile [who is] . . . in business here and wants to take a trip to England, France and Belgium." Eventually, when his need to be Canadian became urgent, he sent cash to two Liberal MPs—one of them Montreal MP Samuel Jacobs, the other apparently Edward Mortimer Macdonald, a member of Cabinet. "They took advantage of the situation and charge[d] plenty" wrote Sottile in a letter to James Lavallée (one of several Italian letters translated for the OPP by Frank Zaneth).

Sottile was also smart enough to know that it was important to keep his customers alive. So he paid trained chemists to regularly test the liquor produced by his redistillery. In that way, he kept the lethality of Falls Tonic's secret product to a minimum, bootleggers kept buying and distributing it, and the profits kept coming. The lives of countless drinkers on both sides of the border depended on this system continuing to hum along.

Then over a few weeks in 1926, it all went very wrong. On May 13, a special Prohibition agent named Mark H. Crehan Jr. obtained a warrant to search the Third Ward Political Club, and the next day he led a team of eleven agents through the doors. They seized all of the equipment, along with five thousand gallons of whisky and twelve thousand gallons of raw alcohol. They ordered Joseph Spallino to open his desk and pulled out ledgers and chequebooks. Shortly after, the agents broke into the safe they'd found and pulled out other documents. Together, the haul of evidence defined the contours of a vast, multi-million-dollar bootlegging network reaching from Rum Row to Hamilton and as far west as Detroit.

In an instant, one of the chief suppliers of drinkable raw alcohol had been shut down, an untenable shortage of that alcohol had been created, and the fuse of an unprecedented health crisis had been lit.

Sottile scrammed north. First, a priest who bootlegged sacramental wine helped him across the border. Then Rocco shuttled him to Max Wortzman's house at 230 Beverley Street in Toronto. Two weeks after the raid on Sottile's illegal redistillery, MP Samuel Jacobs sent a nudging note to the undersecretary of state for immigration to help "facilitate" the granting of Joseph Henry Sottile's certificate of naturalization. On June 8, even as Agent Crehan was putting together his twenty-four-page report on Sottile's connection to a "gigantic conspiracy," Sottile was parlaying his investment in Canadian politicians into a special citizenship hearing. Before Judge Emerson Coatsworth in Toronto, he swore allegiance to King George V and all his heirs and successors, and just eight days later, Canada's undersecretary of state confirmed that Sottile had his certificate in hand. By then he had travelled east, to Saint John, New Brunswick, where he knew James Lavallée would help keep him out of sight until the trouble passed. Some weeks later, Sottile wrote a letter to a contact in Thorold. He planned to leave for Italy soon, he said, and he was hoping Rocco Perri would accompany him.

Apparently Rocco declined that invitation. Sottile soon boarded a ship, escaped to Liverpool under an alias and continued on to Sicily. By leaving, he managed to miss the real drama.

Bootleggers in southern Ontario and New York State quickly ran out of the raw booze they needed as the base for their fake whisky and began clamouring for more. Someone had to fill that need. In Buffalo, a well-manicured, thirty-year-old bootlegger named James Voelker, who lived in a finely appointed home on Amherst Street, saw an opportunity. Voelker was a cog in the organization that linked Sottile with Don Simone, and by then he'd built his bank account to about fifty thousand dollars. But with a chance to supply many of Sottile's customers he could make much more. If only he could get some liquor.

It took some time, but then Voelker learned that two other Buffalo links in the chain, David Goldberg and Nate Sapowich, partners with New York City's "Davey" Burden, had lined up a huge shipment of alcohol from a source apparently in Germany. That July, Voelker put in an order for twelve hundred gallons, to be shipped in twenty sixty-gallon drums.

When they arrived, Voelker had samples taken and sent these to the chemist, John J. Nesterowicz, at the Babcock testing laboratory. Nesterowicz applied the necessary chemicals to the samples and then went home to dinner. It was July 17, a Saturday, and as far as Nesterowicz knew, the results weren't needed until early the next week. Clearly he had no idea how desperate these people were. Either Voelker or someone who worked for him went to the lab for the results. Not finding Nesterowicz, he called the chemist at home. Nesterowicz, no doubt eyeing his dinner on the table, told the caller to look at the samples in the rack: If they were cloudy, the alcohol was poison; if they were clear, the batch was fine. The man on the telephone judged the samples clear and hung up. Immediately Voelker shipped the drums off to all of the waiting customers. Two of those sixty-gallon drums were split up into one- and five-gallon cans, hidden in trucks labelled as coal, and smuggled into Ontario.

When Nesterowicz finally returned to the lab and looked at the test samples, he saw they were cloudy. In fact, they were nearly 94 percent wood alcohol. They were pure poison. The chemist tried to warn the bootleggers, but no one would listen.

On Wednesday, July 21, three men in Allanburg, a tiny community within Thorold on the Welland Canal, went out and bought a gallon can of cheap liquor from a local bootlegger. Late that night they got into it and kept the neighbours up with their blasted shouts and singing. As the morning broke, those same neighbours woke to the men screaming. Two of the drinkers, John MacDonald and Reuben Upper, who lived together in a bachelor apartment, were dead by 9:10 a.m. The third, Charles Durham, a widower who lived with his children across the road, perished later that day. All three suffered horribly.

In Oakville, a bootlegger named George Gill, who lived in a shack on the Seventh Line, surrounded on all sides by scrub meadow, got a new liquor delivery from his supplier, who'd driven up from Hamilton. One of the first things he did was let the Lyons brothers know. Gill was brother-in-law to the Lyons brothers— six aging men who lived together in a rough house over on the Sixth Line—and usually supplied them with their liquor. One of the Lyons men came to buy a few bottles, and on Thursday night three of them—John, Thomas and Patrick—poured themselves some drinks.

Very shortly, one by one, they took ill. John, weakened by rheumatism, died in his bed at one in the morning. On Friday night the eldest, sixty-two-year-old Thomas, died with his lungs full of bloody, frothy fluid. Patrick was rushed to hospital and managed to survive, but George Gill, having gotten into his own supply, wasn't so fortunate. A doctor who went to see him Friday evening found Gill in a cold sweat, his pupils dilated and his lips and ears turning blue. He was dead two hours later.

While this was going on, another drama was unfolding. Earlier in the week two young Toronto women, Mrs. Olive Guertin and Mrs. Elsie Louise Fairbanks, had taken a bus to Oakville to visit their friend William Maybee, a short, wavy-haired bootlegger who often got his liquor by the gallon can from George Gill. Maybee had two teenage sons and a young wife named Ruth, who wasn't much older. Confined to walking with crutches for the past sixteen years, he made money any way he could, manning a filling station, selling maple syrup in the spring and running a dart game at fall fairs. The liquor angle was fairly new and his clientele was small, but he showed people a good time. Maybee's customers liked the rich whisky hue of his liquor, which he achieved by diluting the raw alcohol with water and mixing it with burnt sugar, or sometimes caramel syrup bought at a nearby pharmacy. He would convert a gallon of alcohol bought from Gill for fifteen dollars into twelve or thirteen bottles that sold for four dollars each, hiding them under a culvert about a mile and a half from the house until needed. Truth be told, he drank up a lot of the profits himself.

By midweek it was turning into what people liked to call a liquor orgy over at the Maybee place. That was something an Oakville war veteran named James Johnston could not resist. Johnston was Maybee's father-in-law, and despite the pleas and protests of his wife, Ida, he left his house on Wednesday, July 21, to join the fun. If Maybee was worried his liquor supply was running low, his concerns were allayed when a Hamilton bootlegger dropped by in his car with a new gallon can. Maybee bought one, had his sons mix it up as usual, and the revelry continued. It was so crowded at Maybee's place, James Johnston had to sleep outside on the grass.

At a certain point on Friday, July 23, the party had wound down and it was time for the Maybee family to drive their guests back to Toronto. Maybee told one of his sons to pack a couple of the new bottles in the car. James Johnston had at least one drink for the road and then returned home.

James didn't say hello to his wife when he got in, because she was out doing laundry in the back, but she knew he was home because she could hear him vomiting. He vomited about a dozen times, and after that he felt too weak to stand. "Come and help me lie down on the floor," he said. But Ida fixed up a stretcher for him instead and helped him to it. A little later he asked his wife where she was.

"Right here," she said.

"I can't see you," said her husband. His eyes looked ghastly white.

"Jim," said his wife, "you have been poisoned."

"I guess I've had something I shouldn't have," he gasped. Ida knew he'd been at Maybee's place, but James wouldn't tell his wife where the liquor came from. "No, I'm done for, I guess. And I won't squeal. I don't blame anybody but myself." Finally he vomited a black, inky substance and died wretchedly as the sun came up.

By Saturday morning there were nine dead in Ontario and the authorities were awakening to the crisis. Oakville's coroner opened an inquest into the tragedy and police in that city and in Hamilton began searching for culprits. From the initial analysis of the bodies and the alcohol containers, it looked as though all of the dead, with the possible exception of John Lyons, had been killed by wood alcohol poisoning (methanol contains corrosive formic acid, which attacks the optic nerve).

The first arrests came Saturday morning. In Hamilton, Detective Crocker collared the bootlegger who'd supplied both George Gill and William Maybee. He was Bert D'Angelo, a middleman in the bootlegging chain. By ten o'clock Oakville Chief of Police David Kerr had tracked down William Maybee at Olive and Elsie's home on Balmuto Street in Toronto. The partyers had been playing poker most of the night, but Maybee had begun vomiting and had to lie down. Now he was in so much pain the police had to carry him to the car. They took Ruth and Maybee's two teenage sons to the station as well and all five, the Maybees and D'Angelo, were charged with manslaughter.

Within an hour or two, Olive Guertin began to feel unwell. Though it was a beautiful, sunny day the light seemed murky to Olive. She peered out the window at the trees and told her housemate, "Look, the leaves are black." She felt worse when police picked her up as a witness, and in the middle of questioning she had to be rushed to the hospital.

By Monday, the death toll was thirteen, including four in the north end of Hamilton. Olive Guertin, who had told police she was a nurse and didn't need help, had died frothing bloody foam at the mouth. By the time William Maybee died, he had turned blue down to his thighs.

Bert D'Angelo commanded a lot of police attention. Many people knew him as a fruit peddler, but he had become well-known in Oakville for his regular liquor deliveries. Over the weekend he confessed to buying the poison liquor at a house in Hamilton and delivering two gallon cans of it to George Gill. He also mentioned the name Sullivan. But he gave no further details.

"I am reasonably certain," said Police Chief Kerr, "that D'Angelo knows more than he is telling." Kerr was also certain that the matter was closed and there would be no more deaths.

By that evening, eighteen more people were announced dead, most of those in Buffalo and Lockport, New York, and the details of their deaths told the same woeful story as the others. The *Toronto Daily Star* did not shrink from the opportunity for sensation:

TRAIL OF DEATH ACROSS PROVINCE
FOLLOWS BUFFALO-TORONTO ROAD
VICTIMS BLINDED AND DIE IN AGONY

Police released the surviving Maybee family and charged Bert D'Angelo with the deaths of Thomas Lyons and George Gill.

But looking at D'Angelo, one would never have guessed his dire situation. Short, dark-haired and athletic, with the rough clothes and cap of a labourer, he seemed cheerful, smiling brightly as he smoked cigarette after cigarette. A reporter tagged along as police drove D'Angelo to the Halton County jail in Milton, Ontario, and the suspect was as happy to answer questions as he was skilled at giving nothing important away.

Where had he gotten the liquor? "I got it from different people," he said. "I'm not going to tell you who they are. There were lots of them." Police had determined by the smaller gallon cans found at every site that the liquor had arrived first in Hamilton from somewhere over the U.S. border, and D'Angelo didn't deny it. But as far as he was concerned, the fault for everything lay with the government. "There'd never have been any trouble like this at all if it wasn't for the laws here. Why don't they have it like they do in Quebec?"

In Buffalo, police closed twenty "soft drink" stands and arrested Carl Maischoss, a "soft drink" dealer who'd used the poisoned alcohol to make ersatz gin, which he'd bottled and labelled "Gordon" and "High and Dry." Maischoss pointed police in the direction of the wholesale distributor who'd supplied him—James Voelker.

By the time police got to Voelker's door he was gone, having sped away in his big car after one of his distributors, Joseph Banos, tried to return 240 gallons of his deadly liquor. In the meantime, police ransacked Voelker's home looking for evidence and found, among other things, phone records linking him to Louis Sylvester, one of Rocco's men in Thorold.

At 10 a.m. on Tuesday, July 27, with thirty-four dead, James Voelker walked into police headquarters with his lawyer and surrendered to the authorities. From the look of bewilderment in his "thoughtful, dark eyes," he seemed thoroughly shaken.

"Heartbroken" was the term his jailer would later use. There were reports that someone high up had hired a team of Detroit hit men to deal with anyone likely to squeal, and the day before he turned himself in, someone had driven up to Voelker on the street and tried to lure him into a car. He figured he'd be safer in custody.

While police south of the border were bringing suspects in, Inspector William Stringer of the OPP's department of criminal investigation had begun looking into the connections between the deaths. No one had any doubt that Rocco Perri was somehow involved—his name came up often in the documents seized from the Falls Tonic safe—so naturally Stringer drove to Hamilton. There he teamed up with Detective Joe Crocker, who'd known Rocco and Bessie since their first days in the prostitution business.

They needed someone they could squeeze for information that would link Rocco to the deaths, so they sent an informant to lean on Edward (Red) Miller, a twenty-year-old who lived with his mother on Tisdale Street North in Hamilton and sat low in the organizational command chain. Miller had been involved in distributing some of the poison liquor, and he was worried the gang would finger him. "They are not going to use me as a goat," he said. So the cops hauled him into the station, sat him down in a chair and got him to spill what he knew.

In his signed statement Miller admitted to working for Harry Sullivan, a bootlegger who lived on Main Street East (and who may have been related to Fort Erie's Jim Sullivan, a.k.a. Sullirano). "About two weeks ago," he said, "Harry Sullivan told me that Bert D'Angelo wanted three gallons of alcohol and told me to go and get it from Joe Romeo."

Joe Romeo, one of Rocco's cousins, lived with his brother Frank and Frank's wife at 25 Railway Street. Sullivan had told Miller to go and pick up three cans of alcohol from his garage, so Miller drove over in his Ford and loaded up. "I took the three cans to Bert D'Angelo, on Ferrie St., and delivered the alcohol to him personally," said Miller. "He paid me $33 for the alcohol. I then went over to 25 Railway St. and paid Mrs. F. Romeo $30 for the alcohol received by Harry Sullivan from Joe Romeo."

Stringer and Crocker arrested Joe Romeo on the afternoon of July 27, noting that he was a man with no visible means of support, yet owned a Studebaker Big Six touring car. For the time being they held Romeo and Miller on charges of vagrancy.

As the week progressed, the subjects of bootlegging and poison liquor touched nearly every corner of the political and legal systems of two nations. On Wednesday, the inquests into the deaths of the Ontario victims began. In Buffalo, where eleven people were now under arrest, James Voelker entered a plea of Not Guilty to a charge of first-degree murder, even as his lawyers hinted that he was going to name names. And in Sarnia, the scandal made it into a campaign speech by William Lyon Mackenzie King, who pointed out that because Arthur Meighen had become prime minister on June 29, the poison liquor had been smuggled into Canada while the Conservatives were in charge. The Conservatives were appalled at the insinuation.

The next day, Prohibition authorities in New York State acted on the information they'd found two months before in the safe at the Third Ward Political Club. A grand jury in Jamestown, New York, issued ninety indictments, as the press revelled in the details: a network of bootleggers backed by close to $15 million in capital, an organization that was "as well-oiled a machine as the average corporation, boasting its legal bureau, its fleet of sea-going and river-going boats; its flotilla of automobiles and its extensive system of vats and cleaning apparatus."

Joseph Henry Sottile had gotten away, but all of his customers and associates were named in those indictments. That included his partner Joseph Spallino. It included Arthur. J. Jopp, president of the Jopp Drug Company in Buffalo, who was one of the first to be arrested. And it included at least thirteen people in Canada—among them, Harry Sullivan, Louis Sylvester, Fannie Shulman, Max Wortzman, Harry Goldstein, Ben Kerr and, of course, Rocco Perri.

Quickly police on both sides of the border picked up those named in the indictment list. Major Eugene Roberts Jr., of the Buffalo division of the Bureau of Prohibition, made it clear that this action was separate from any investigation into the poisoned liquor deaths. "In my opinion," he said, "the two are entirely different problems." But they touched many of the same people. In Toronto, Max Wortzman and Harry Goldstein gave themselves up, while police arrested fifty-two-year-old Fannie Shulman at her store on Maria Street. In Hamilton, police collared Ben Kerr at one-thirty in the morning, grabbed Harry Sullivan around the same time and locked them up with Miller and Romeo.

As Rocco had become aware of people dying from what one bootlegger called "bunk hootch," he'd sent out orders that no one was to talk; Ed Miller had received threats. So when Joe Romeo arrived in handcuffs he kept his mouth shut. No one had to worry about Ben Kerr, he was his usual uncooperative self. Among the new arrivals, only Harry Sullivan seemed willing to help the cops. But perhaps Romeo, from his corner of the station, got Sullivan's attention, because suddenly Sullivan showed "considerable reticence and an unwillingness to answer the questions of the officers."

When all four appeared in police court, Magistrate Jelfs remanded them for eight days without bail, meaning they would stay in custody. Michael J. O'Reilly, acting as lawyer for Sullivan but speaking for all, complained loudly. "You are punishing them first and trying them afterwards by doing this," he said and hinted at repercussions. "I feel sorry for the officers who threw them in jail."

The prize, of course, was Rocco, and the papers eagerly anticipated his capture. "Net Closing Around Boss of Liquor Ring," the *Spectator* panted. But when OPP inspectors Hammond and Boyd arrived at the house on Bay Street South, one of Rocco's men answered the door. He didn't know where Mr. Perri was and couldn't say when he'd be back.

By Friday, July 30, there were forty-four dead, and the chemical analysis of the dark-coloured alcohol in D'Angelo's cans came back with the same results as Voelker's lab: 93.9 percent pure wood alcohol. Professors at the Ontario College of Pharmacy described it as "the most terrible ever heard of . . . a beverage so powerful that it would cause a poison if applied to the skin externally."

ALL this time, Rocco was hiding, huddling with Bessie and his men, consulting with his lawyer. How exposed was he? What were the chances that he could do time for all these deaths? When he became convinced that he would come away unscathed, he agreed to give himself up. On the clear-skied morning of Saturday, July 31, looking the dapper gentleman in a bright straw hat and a grey, glen-check suit, he walked into Hamilton police headquarters. With his lawyer—and recently elected Hamilton West MP—Charles W. Bell beside him, he approached the desk sergeant with the ease of a man ordering a soda and asked for Detective Crocker. "I heard that I was wanted," he said, smiling. "So here I am."

Someone went to fetch Crocker, who came and read out the arrest warrant—that Rocco did "unlawfully slay and kill one John Lyons and others." From that point on he treated Rocco like an honoured guest. He led him into the muggy detectives' room and gave him a chair by an open window. Someone brought a fan to augment its cooling breeze. There Rocco waited comfortably, smoking a cigarette, for the few minutes until his name was called in police court. His appearance in court was but a brief interruption—his name was called, he was escorted in, Jelfs remanded his case for a week—before he was returned efficiently to the comfort of his cool seat among the detectives.

For a few minutes he chatted easily with the cops he knew, until OPP inspectors Boyd and Ward came in to question him. They smiled; he smiled. He rose, shook hands and offered to give up his seat but, no, that wasn't necessary. When Crocker was ready he joined them and closed the door, and, as far as anyone could tell, the conversation continued just as amiably as it had begun.

Before the police led Rocco off to his jail cell, they gave the waiting reporters a moment to ask him a few questions. But Rocco knew better than to talk to the press this time. "You had better see my lawyer," he told them. "He'll do my talking for me." When they persisted—just a few questions?—he shook his head. "I don't feel much like talking this morning. I've got a headache."

But how, they asked, had Rocco known he was wanted?

He shrugged. "I knew. That's enough."

Where had he been over the past few days, somewhere in the city?

He grinned. "That's up to me."

Then he was taken to the detention cells on the lower level, and shortly after that a wagon arrived to convey him to the jail on Barton Street.

Authorities on both sides of the border kept up the pressure. In New York State, twenty-five federal agents combed through Rochester alone, looking for poison liquor. Frank J. Hale, the chief of the alcohol division of the Bureau of Prohibition, arrived in Buffalo from Washington to underline the national importance of the investigation. Police had determined that the more than four thousand gallons of wood alcohol that had flooded Ontario and New York had been part of a shipment purchased in Germany for just sixteen cents a gallon, plus customs charges. It seemed that "Davey" Burden, Nathan Sapowich and former Hamiltonian David Goldberg had thought they were getting an amazing deal. "It is quite possible the German manufacturers put one over on them," said an official.

The trio was said to be hiding out at Forest Lake, north of Albany. A few days later, the underworld buzzed with the news that Sapowich had been murdered, perhaps taking the brunt of a bad decision. For his part, James Voelker, by all accounts a likable man, seemed to be calming down in prison. His jailer, who'd wondered whether the prisoner would ever pull himself together, now observed that he was "much more composed."

By August 3, Ontario's provincial force had arrested a total of sixteen suspects. Meanwhile, three new charges, relating to illegal importation, tax evasion and smuggling, were laid on the five men in the Barton Street jail—Rocco, Kerr, Romeo, Sullivan and Miller. Each new charge brought a possible sentence of seven years, on top of the maximum sentence of life in prison for manslaughter.

Their situation seemed not to trouble the men in the least. They rested quietly in their cells, comforted by the "downy pillows, white sheets and fine blankets" brought to them by friends. For an hour each day they went outside into the jail yard to soak up the summer sun and chat. When someone noted that T-bone steaks seemed to have been added to the menu for these special guests, Hamilton's jail officials insisted that their meals were the same as any other prisoner's—porridge and coffee or tea in the morning, beef and potatoes with tea at midday and a light supper in the evening. And their lights went out at eight o'clock, as for everyone. Smoking was banned, so Rocco couldn't indulge in his cigars. Nevertheless, he retained "his pleasant smile and debonair manner."

With the expected arrests made and the suspects largely in hand, authorities turned their attention to gathering the evidence needed to put them away for good. But here they had a problem. No one was talking, and other forms of proof seemed to evaporate. In Hamilton, police searched the Perri home and seized all of the documents and account books they could find. The books revealed a lavish lifestyle—expensive cars, inlaid mahogany radio sets, thick Persian rugs, a nineteen-dollar pair of French calfskin boots—but no references to liquor. Instead of a fortune made in whisky or even raw alcohol, the books Bessie had kept showed them doing a huge business in macaroni and manila rope.

Thus began the game of legal dithering. On Saturday, August 7, the five Hamilton prisoners were marched back into police court where the Crown asked for another remand and the defence demanded the prisoners be released on bail. Magistrate Jelfs intimated that someone higher up in the judicial system had ordered him not to grant bail in this case—"They may have their reasons," he said—so he issued the remand. Rocco's lawyer, Michael J. O'Reilly, could hardly contain himself. "We understood last week that there would be no more remands," he fumed. "It is disgraceful keeping these men in jail like this."

Ben Kerr's lawyer hadn't appeared in court that morning, so that gave Kerr a chance to speak for himself, which he loved to do. "I would like to state that I have never in my life tasted, sold, carted, bought or had in my possession at any time any kind of alcohol," he said. He complained that police had destroyed his property—"torn up my floors in my house and office, dug up my lawn"—without finding a shred of evidence against him. He was still proclaiming his innocence as he was led out of the courtroom.

The frustrations of the bootleggers and their lawyers had barely even begun.

By August 11, four coroner's inquests had issued verdicts on the deaths of Thomas Lyons, James Johnston, George Gill, William Maybee and Olive Guertin. All of them named Bert D'Angelo, and only Bert D'Angelo, as the source of the poison that had killed them. In Niagara Falls, the court released all seven of Rocco's associates on bail, and still Rocco, Kerr and the three other Hamilton bootleggers stayed behind bars.

At some point, dissatisfied with the work of the OPP, Attorney General Nickle contacted the Pinkerton's detective agency. He arranged for an undercover operative to try to infiltrate the Hamilton underworld to gather information. Soon, an agent with the initials J. C. S. showed up in a local poolroom and started making friends. At a blind pig on Mulberry Street he met a bootlegger named Mildred Sterling who bragged of having "driven many a load" in her Marmon and had no love for the Perris.

Sterling was clearly infatuated with J. C. S. "Mildred Sterling and I became mutual friends and drinks were served," he reported. She called him and met him repeatedly, and assured him she was not actually married to Harry Sterling, the American underworld figure from whom she'd taken her last name. Not seeing him anymore either. Through with him, really. The more the two met, the more she talked, with J. C. S. showing the most interest when she talked about Rocco. "Rocco Perri and his strong-arm men" had the city petrified, Sterling told him, especially since the poisoning crisis. According to her, Rocco could get away with anything in Hamilton; he just had to give the sign and Magistrate Jelfs wouldn't touch him. "Rocco Perri has this fellow tied around his little finger," she said. "Rocco can get anything done. All he has to do is flash the high ball . . . and the works are in."

But she also doubted that Rocco had had any knowledge of the bad liquor. "Rocco Perri and other millionaire rum-runners do not have to handle poisonous liquor," she said, "because they can make more money with less trouble by handling the straight goods.".

On Saturday, August 14, Rocco waited in the dock in Hamilton's police court, along with Kerr, Romeo, Sullivan and Miller. As a clutch of lawyers argued in front of Magistrate Jelfs, Rocco chatted with a police officer next to him, and smiled at Bessie sitting nearby. Special Federal Prosecutor Peter White made the smuggling case against granting bail, and Crown Attorney G. W. Ballard argued against it on the manslaughter side. But once the lawyers for Rocco and Kerr were done, Jelfs relented. He set bail at the enormous sum of thirty thousand dollars for each of the five men, and when the lawyers objected to that, he wilted to twenty thousand. Rocco was first out the door, and by the end of the day all five men had been released.

In theory, the case against them was still being prepared. But when the prosecution returned to court on August 28, White and Ballard had to admit they were no closer to being ready. Jelfs released the five men from any obligation until they were needed. Rocco met Bessie and a few of his men at the entrance and grinned. "I guess they don't want us anymore."

It wasn't quite over yet. On October 6, the OPP searched the empty premises of 27 Railway Street, next to the house of Frank Romeo, brother to Joe. There they found 130 cans of alcohol, although they didn't know how long it had been there and couldn't prove it belonged to the Romeos. At the same time, they were working the Red Miller case, trying to get informants to link him to Rocco. On October 9, it was time for the court to see what progress they'd made.

By now, a team of eight Crown attorneys involved in the various cases in Toronto, Niagara Falls and Hamilton had been taken over by two special prosecutors: McGregor Young, handling the manslaughter cases, and Peter White, working on the federal customs charges. On this Saturday, Young had decided to make public Miller's signed statement to Detective Crocker—he admitted it was the only piece of evidence he had—and apparently a lot of Hamiltonians wanted to hear what Miller had revealed about the bootlegging organization that seemed to run their city.

It was so crowded that when two men entered the room late, by separate doors, they were both forced to stand at the back. Peter White found a spot near the prisoner's dock. Rocco Perri, very curious to hear what Miller had told police, found a place not far away and leaned against the wall. A Hamilton constable, sizing up the situation, went to the press box. As reporters complained loudly, he grabbed a chair from them and carried it toward the back. And he kept walking, past the federal prosecutor, to the most important man in the room.

"Here, Mr. Perri," he said. "Here is a chair for you. Won't you sit down?"

Peter White had never seen anything like it. "Nice place this," he said. "Give the prisoner a seat before the counsel." And off he went to find his own chair.

But it became clear that young Red Miller had, wisely, revealed very little, and nothing about Rocco. On December 4, 1926, Magistrate Jelfs determined that the Crown would never manage to pull together enough evidence against either Rocco or Kerr, and that to keep them under the weight of a heavy bail was tantamount to keeping them "in a condition of slavery." He dismissed both manslaughter cases and put Peter White on the clock to produce enough evidence to proceed with the customs and smuggling charges the following week.

He couldn't. Police had cheques linking Kerr to thousands of dollars' worth of alcohol purchases from the Third Ward Political Club in Niagara Falls, New York, but American officials had refused to release the original books to complete the connection. On December 13, Jelfs dismissed all charges against Kerr, and a month later Edward Miller and Harry Sullivan were acquitted on manslaughter charges. Gradually the cases against almost all of the other men—and one woman, Fannie Shulman—were dismissed or dropped by the Crown.

In the end, forty-five people died as a result of drinking from that shipment of wood alcohol. Twenty-one were in Ontario, an extraordinary number given that only 10 percent of the original shipment had come into the province. One hundred thousand dollars had been spent in Ontario, and much more in New York State, to arrest and prosecute 123 people. All of this effort resulted in just two convictions: At midnight on December 21, a Buffalo jury found James Voelker guilty of manslaughter; he got fifteen years in Auburn Prison. In Ontario, Bert D'Angelo was sentenced to four years in Kingston Penitentiary for manslaughter but spent only sixteen months behind bars; a judge overturned his conviction because there had been no intent to injure the victims. No evidence but hearsay ever emerged to tie Rocco Perri, Ben Kerr, Joseph Henry Sottile or any of the others to the deaths.

But it wasn't as if nothing came of this whole affair. The mood had changed. Innocents had died in numbers that could not be ignored. Sensing the shift, Ontario Premier George Howard Ferguson called an election and campaigned on getting rid of the Ontario Temperance Act and turning liquor sales entirely over to government control. Nickle ran against him to preserve the OTA, and on December 1, Ferguson won. His new attorney general, William H. Price, immediately began the work of rewriting the province's liquor laws. In the United States, the government announced that it would find another way to discourage the drinking of industrial alcohol. Poisoning it had turned out to be "ill advised."

Neither the dismantling of the Niagara–Buffalo liquor ring nor the end of the OTA was good news for Rocco. Both made his job of getting richer and staying on top that much tougher, and had the potential to force him down dangerous paths.

Just as significant, the events of the summer of 1926 cast more light on the enormous amount of money involved in the cross-border movement of liquor—and therefore, from the federal government's perspective, how much tax revenue was being lost. Already, in the beginning of that year, political pressure had begun mounting to investigate flagrant corruption in the Quebec branch of the customs department. The Tories wanted to drape scandal around the necks of the Mackenzie King Liberals, and with men like Jacques Bureau and Joseph Bisaillon running things in Montreal, there was yards of it. (Bureau, as minister of Customs and Excise, was accused of having nine filing cabinets full of incriminating government documents destroyed; Bisaillon, the chief preventive officer of customs in Quebec, seemed far wealthier than his salary should have allowed and may well have been what MP Harry Stevens called him in the House: "the chief smuggler of the ring, a perjurer and a thief.")

In response, the federal government formed a special committee to investigate the accusations of unfettered liquor smuggling and political cover-up. In June 1926, that smuggling committee (which, with wonderful irony, included Rocco's lawyer, Hamilton West MP Charles W. Bell) recommended a clean-up of the customs department and a thorough audit of Canadian distilleries. The poison-liquor crisis, the U.S. grand jury indictments and the exposure of the Niagara–Buffalo bootlegging ring threw gas onto this fire, and ensured that Rocco and Bessie Perri would be central figures in what came next.

Downtown Hamilton, looking north toward the bay, during its early industrial boom, circa 1910.

Hamilton's busy James Street, circa 1908, looking north to city hall.

The *Hattie C* at Toronto's Ashbridges Bay in 1923, after police fired on members of the Perri gang unloading its whisky cargo.

Mugshot of Rocco Perri, charged with manslaughter during the poison liquor crisis of 1926.

In 1917, alone and broke, Frank Zaneth applied to join the Royal North West Mounted Police.

Hamilton Police Chief William Whatley, a tall, tactful Brit, became ensnared in Rocco's schemes.

George Frederick Jelfs lasted thirty-six years as Hamilton's colourful police magistrate.

The multi-talented Charles W. Bell, Rocco's criminal lawyer, was also a politician and a Broadway playwright.

General manager of Corby's distillery, then president of Gooderham & Worts, Harry Hatch was one of Rocco's most important suppliers.

With a fierce mind for business, the auburn-haired Bessie Starkman was a perfect partner for Rocco.

Olive Rutledge first attracted Rocco's attention in 1917. Their relationship came to a tragic end in 1922.

The Hotel Stroud, where Olive Rutledge would begin her tumultuous last few days in Hamilton.

OPP Inspector William Stringer, circa 1923, a year before he captured murderer John Trott.

Mugshot of John Trott, circa 1924, arrested for the murder of Constable Joseph Trueman.

The Gooderham & Worts distillery, which became an important source of supply for the Perri gang.

A. H. Lyle (far left) led the Hamilton Temperance Foundation and spoke out angrily against Rocco Perri.

Rocco bobbed and weaved during his 1927 testimony at the Royal Commission on Customs and Excise.

The daring rumrunner and Perri rival Ben Kerr (seated, far left), before his wedding in 1912.

From the front page of the *Toronto Daily Star*, July 26, 1926: (1) Bootlegger and poisoning victim William Maybee; (2) his young wife, Ruth Maybee; (3) Oakville's Chief Kerr, taking Bert D'Angelo into custody; (4) D'Angelo, shown with his two young sons; (5) poisoning victim George Gill; (6) sixteen-year-old Nora Connelly, who was hospitalized but survived.

From the front page of the *Toronto Daily Star*, June 15, 1927: Rocco and Bessie surrender to the authorities in the Toronto office of Assistant Crown Attorney Ed Murphy (seated), accompanied by their long-time lawyer, Michael J. O'Reilly (standing, left).

In the papers Bessie Starkman became an icon of fashion, even as she steered the Perri gang toward narcotics.

Self-Styled Bootleg King's Wife Shot by Gunmen

From the pages of the *Toronto Daily Star*, August 14, 1930: This portrait of Bessie, taken prior to her 1927 testimony at the Royal Commission on Customs and Excise, ran again in the wake of her murder.

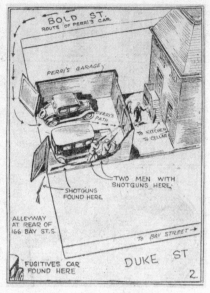

From the pages of the *Toronto Daily Star*, August 14, 1930: Rocco and Bessie's home at 166 Bay Street South. (Note that the attached townhouse on the right was erased by the *Star* for clarity.)

From the pages of the *Toronto Daily Star*, August 14, 1930: An artist's depiction of the murder; the street layout is not to scale.

The bloody scene in the Perri garage shortly after Bessie Perri's murder by shotgun.

In the days leading up to Bessie's funeral, at least ten thousand people streamed through the Perri home to view her body.

COURTESY OF LOCAL HISTORY & ARCHIVES, HAMILTON PUBLIC LIBRARY

Bessie's daughters, Lily and Gertie, struggled in the oppressive sun and the heaving crowd at their mother's burial.

FROM THE *TORONTO DAILY STAR*, COURTESY OF THE TORONTO PUBLIC LIBRARY

Perri gang lieutenants Tony and Frank Ross had reasons to want Bessie eliminated.

FROM THE *TORONTO DAILY STAR*, COURTESY OF THE TORONTO PUBLIC LIBRARY

Rocco's cousin Mike Serge (left) was allowed a day pass from jail to attend Bessie's funeral.

COURTESY OF LOCAL HISTORY & ARCHIVES, HAMILTON PUBLIC LIBRARY

A bereft and exhausted Rocco, supported by Perri gang members, after his collapse at Bessie's grave.

The crowd swarmed the pall bearers at Bessie Perri's funeral. (Note that this archival copy of the *Toronto Daily Star* photo was cut to remove the image of one of the underworld attendees.)

Frank Zaneth (left), here with a fellow officer, didn't look like the typical Mountie, which helped him avoid suspicion while undercover.

This detail from a group photo of RCMP officers, circa mid-1940s, shows Zaneth (centre) seated next to Commissioner Stuart Taylor Wood (left).

As the Mounties' first undercover operative, Zaneth posed as a Communist, a bootlegger and a Chicago drug dealer.

Rocco's mid-1930s gambling expansion led to a pushback. In March 1938, a bomb ruined the front porch of his Bay Street South home.

Police inspect Rocco's bombed-out DeSoto after another attempt on his life in November 1938.

Charged with conspiracy to bribe customs officials and evade duties, Rocco wasn't the least bit worried on his way to a court appearance in Windsor, 1939.

Rocco (in front of the window) with fellow internees at the Petawawa internment camp, 1942. As Internee No. P298, he spent three years behind barbed wire.

By the time he reached age fifty, Rocco had already outlived many of his underworld contemporaries. But his disappearance a few years later would remain a lasting mystery.

18

INDAGINE

Investigation

O NCE A ROW OF DOMINOES BEGINS TO FALL, IT BECOMES unstoppable. It wasn't obvious yet, but with the launch of the Commons committee investigation into smuggling Canada was headed toward a political crisis. Given the events that unfolded over the next few months, it's hardly an exaggeration to say that as two of the leading figures in bootlegging, Rocco and Bessie Perri played a role in bringing down the federal government. The repercussions would not leave them unscathed.

The Commons committee ultimately heard from 224 witnesses. Its findings weren't a complete surprise; even Prime Minister King knew the customs department was, in his words, "a sink of iniquity." But when the committee made its sweeping recommendations— which included dismissing half a dozen top customs officials, reorganizing its preventive service, ordering an audit of distillery export practices and imposing excise and sales taxes on all exported Canadian liquor—it triggered a kind of political avalanche.

The committee's submission of its report to the House of Commons on June 18, 1926, provoked a series of dramatic political manoeuvres. Conservative MP Harry Stevens, the chair of the committee, attempted to amend the report to include an official censure of the minority Mackenzie King government. Hoping to avoid censure and the parliamentary defeat it would bring, the government proposed a Royal Commission to investigate the customs mess. That led to further manoeuvres and more drama, as MPs from the Progressive Party, which had been propping up King's Liberals, began to peel away. Amendments and sub-amendments competed for votes. One suggested that the House adopt a version of the report that included both a Royal Commission *and* censure. The press described the political mood as "heated and dangerous."

Ultimately the machinations brought Prime Minister King to the doorstep of Lord Byng, the governor general. To King it seemed now that an election was his best option; there was at least a chance his Liberals could win it outright. So, over tea and buttered bread, he asked Byng to order the dissolution of Parliament. Traditionally, a governor general acceded to such a request, and King argued for it forcefully, but Byng refused. He thought the Conservative Party—which actually had more seats than the Liberals—deserved the chance to govern. This was the infamous "King–Byng" affair, which led to King's resignation and the very brief Conservative government led by Arthur Meighen.

All of those events, from the introduction of the smuggling committee's report to the change of government and the swearing-in of a new prime minster, took just eleven days. And through that entire crisis, as well as through the general election that soon followed (which Mackenzie King's Liberals did win), one thing survived: the demand for a Royal Commission into bootlegging, border corruption and distillery shenanigans. The Royal Commission on Customs and Excise got under way officially on November 17, 1926.

Had they been aware of the commission's early progress, through Ottawa, Victoria and Vancouver, Rocco and Bessie might have been amused at all the political commotion. If they took any notice as its three judges and battery of lawyers compiled thousands of pages of testimony during winter hearings in Calgary, Regina and Winnipeg, the royal couple of bootlegging might have allowed themselves a moment of concern. But when winter begat spring and the commission arrived in Toronto, they almost certainly got down to strategizing. Things were taking a serious turn.

Among the first witnesses called in Toronto were represent-atives of O'Keefe's Beverages, who were ordered to bring their financial records for examination. The O'Keefe's men immediately had to apologize to the commission. Sadly, they had somehow lost all of those records—by loading them into a large, dark car and sending it speeding off into the night. Also missing: a number of O'Keefe's executives, who had flown the country rather than test-ify. Commission Chairman James Thomas Brown, a Saskatchewan judge, threatened the cancellation of O'Keefe's licence unless the various missing pieces began to appear.

It was around then, when Rocco knew that his main supplier—Harry Hatch, president and general manager of Gooderham & Worts—was going to take the stand, that he decided to make him-self scarce as well.

Besides James Thomas Brown there were two judges on the commission—William Henry Wright, from Ontario, and Ernest Roy, from Quebec. Two lawyers acted as commission counsel, con-ducting most of the questioning—Chief Counsel Newton Wesley Rowell, KC, who had once campaigned for prohibition as leader of Ontario's Liberal Party, and a Montreal lawyer named R. L. Calder, KC. It was Calder who, on March 28, 1927, interviewed Harry Hatch.

Prior to the investigations of the Commons smuggling committee, it had been assumed, by politicians and civilians alike, that it was illegal for Canadian distilleries to export liquor to the United States. So people were astonished when the committee revealed that, over the fiscal year that had ended March 31, some three-quarters of a million gallons of liquor and three million gallons of beer had been cleared for export to U.S. destinations. Calder tried to get Hatch to admit that, because of the Volstead Act, his distillery's contributions to that number had been somehow against the law.

"We are not strictly interested in the Volstead Act," said Hatch. "I never saw it. Don't know anything about it. I know there is such an animal over there."

"You also know," said Calder, "that that animal prevents your exporting without considerable danger."

"No it does not," Hatch said. "It does not prevent us exporting at all. It prevents somebody there importing." If Americans wanted to break the law, it was fine with him.

The commission also wanted to know more about the practice of short-circuiting. Witnesses had revealed that some of those exports to the United States and other countries had wound up illegally back in Canada. Hatch was happy to talk because, again, he was sure the company had done nothing wrong. He explained that the distillery often got telephone orders from Canadian cities, such as Hamilton or Toronto. They would come in to G & W's head of shipping, Lionel Sinclair, who would then relay them to an American border city. Sinclair would call the telegraph office in, say, Niagara Falls, New York, dictate a U.S. address, an amount and the name of a consignee, and ask them to send that order in by telegraph, so that the order could be registered as having come from the United States. That way, said Hatch, when an OTA inspector showed up accusing G & W of an illegal shipment to

Ontario, "We would throw this in his face and say, 'There is the order for it.'"

The point was to obey the strict letter of the OTA rules. "Let me make myself clear," said Hatch. "We accept orders in our office by telephone, by telegraph, and by letter; we don't care where they come from so long as the goods are for shipment to a legal point—the United States or anywhere else."

Once the liquor was loaded onto the boat with all the customs paperwork filled out, including all five copies of the B-13 form, Gooderham & Worts considered its responsibility complete. "We do not ship the goods if they are not for export," said Hatch. But they couldn't be held responsible for what happened to them after that.

Right at the end of his examination of Hatch, after an exhaustive series of questions about bookkeeping practices and shipping procedures, Calder slipped in this apparent afterthought: "Do you know a man called Rocco Perri?"

"Yes, sir," said Hatch.

"Do you know Mrs. Rocco Perri?"

"No," said Hatch. Of course, he knew Bessie Starkman very well, but that wasn't the question he'd been asked.

And that was it. But there was so much more to come.

LIONEL Sinclair was sworn in next, and Calder asked him about the Perris. Did Sinclair know Rocco? Did he know Rocco's wife? Had he ever spoken to anyone he thought was Mrs. Rocco Perri on the telephone? To each of these questions Sinclair answered no or "Not that I know of." But when Sinclair was asked if he had ever received orders from Mrs. Perri, the answer "not that I know of" didn't satisfy Calder.

"You must know, is it either no or yes?"

And here, Sinclair broke, just a little: "Not under her name, no."

That opened the door for Calder to get at the real object of his interest. "Who is the person who has a credit in your book, or an account in your book, called Penna?" He was referring to "Joe Penna," the front name used on most of Rocco and Bessie's G & W orders.

"He is a consignee of ours in the United States," said Sinclair. "As far as I know."

"Where is he, at what point in the United States?"

"His goods are sent to Wilson, New York," he said, referring to a small lakeside town near Niagara Falls.

"Where does he order them from—where do the orders to you come from?"

"They might come from any place," said Sinclair.

"Don't they come from Hamilton?"

"Some of them might, yes, not all." They came by telephone, Sinclair admitted.

"And is it a woman's voice who . . . speaks to you on the telephone?"

"Sometimes."

"Nearly all the time?" pressed Calder.

"I don't know how frequent it is, but it is sometimes."

Calder knew he was dealing with a clerk, someone he could gently bully. "Most frequently?" he asked.

"It may be."

"The majority of the calls are from Hamilton in a woman's voice?"

"They may be."

"Aren't they?"

"They may be."

"Are they?"

"I don't know," said Sinclair. "I couldn't say whether the majority is or not."

Calder moved on. Slowly he got Sinclair to admit that when "Penna" orders came from Hamilton, Sinclair would telephone the Postal Telegraph Company in Niagara Falls, New York. He would ask them to send in a wired order, signed according to the name Sinclair provided. The orders directed G & W to ship on specific boats, one of which was the large *Atun*, capable of holding as many as five hundred cases. As various G & W personnel came to testify, Calder went through the names of fishing boats, motor boats, Cruisers, pleasure boats and, lastly, American boats—more than two dozen vessels in all.

Shortly after that, he questioned Joseph Burke, the owner of Port Credit's Lakeview Inn and of two fishing vessels—*Patricia* and *Meredith*—that the mysterious Penna had chartered to ship his liquor, ostensibly to the United States.

"Do you know Penna personally?" Calder asked.

"No. I met him only once," said Burke.

"Is he an Italian?"

"I think he is an American," said Burke. "He is Americanized."

Joe Penna was actually real, a Buffalo resident whom Rocco and Bessie paid to allow them to use his name. But at this point Calder was still operating under the assumption that "Penna" was an alias Rocco used.

"Is not his real name Rocco Perri?" Calder asked.

"No."

"You are sure of that?"

"Positive."

At this point, Justice Wright spoke up. "If you don't know him, why are you so positive that 'Rocco Perri' is not his correct name?"

"Because I know Perri," said Burke, "and I only met Penna once."

"You know Rocco Perri?" Wright asked.

"You bet."

Calder took over. "Where does Rocco Perri live?"

Burke knew he was treading on dangerous ground. "I don't want to answer anything about Rocco Perri. I want to answer only about my own personal affairs."

"Where does Rocco Perri live?" Calder persisted. "In Hamilton?"

"Yes."

"And you swear that Penna is not Rocco Perri?"

"Positively. You bet."

"And you will also swear that he is not acting for Rocco Perri?"

"Yes," said Burke. "I will stake my life on it."

It was probably a fair assessment of his situation. "Just now," said Calder wryly, "it will be sufficient if you swear to it."

BEHIND the scenes, authorities had been trying for more than a week to find Rocco in order to subpoena him. But he was staying ahead of them, moving around from address to address in Welland, St. Catharines and elsewhere. He was buying time. Undoubtedly his lawyer, Charles W. Bell, who had an insider's view of the process, had advised Rocco that he couldn't avoid testifying. But what he could do was delay the inevitable, long enough to force the commission to question others close to him first—besides Hatch and Burke there was Ben Kerr, who was his usual voluble self and, most important, Bessie. That would give Rocco an insight into what the commissioners were after and, in the case of Bessie, it would allow them to test out the strategy they'd devised to handle the questioning.

On an unseasonably cold Tuesday, March 29, Bessie arrived at the courthouse wearing the epitome of 1920s fashion—a brown spring coat trimmed with thick white fur at the cuffs and collar, sand-coloured gloves, stockings and modish shoes, and an orange, asymmetrical cloche hat. To everyone watching she seemed calm, self-assured. She stopped briefly, with hands together, holding her purse at the waist, so the newspaper photographers could get their shot. Then she went in and, when it came her turn, took the stand with that same self-possessed air and allowed herself to be sworn in, still dressed in her coat, her head practically swallowed by her fur collar.

"You live in Hamilton?" Calder asked.

"Yes, sir."

"At what address?"

"166 Bay Street South."

"What is your telephone number?" Phone calls were to be a very big part of Bessie's testimony, so this was important.

"Regent 8267."

Then Calder asked where Rocco was.

"I couldn't say," said Bessie. "He was supposed to go to Ottawa." That was ten days ago, Bessie explained, and she hadn't heard from him since.

Calder asked her what business Rocco was in.

"He used to have a store."

"What is his business now?"

"At present, nothing."

"When did he give up the store?"

"He gave up the store on account of my health; I have been sick." For the past few years, she said, Rocco had been "travelling" for a macaroni firm whose name she didn't know.

"As a matter of fact, Mrs. Perri," said Calder, "does not Mr. Perri go about the United States and Ontario taking orders for liquor?"

"I couldn't say that."

Calder asked if she would state, under oath, that he didn't.

"I couldn't tell you," said Bessie. "Because he never tells me his business."

"Are you yourself engaged in business?"

"No."

"Do you act for your husband in any business?"

"No, sir."

"Is it not a fact that you are in the liquor business yourself?"

"No, sir."

"Is it not a fact that you are in the liquor business under the name of 'Penna'?"

"No."

"Did you ever telephone Gooderham & Worts over the long distance telephone?"

"No, sir."

This was the Bessie strategy, to deny the yes-or-no questions. For everything else, she would claim to be in the dark. Who knew what a husband and his friends got up to? But she had to set this up properly, and when Calder told her he was getting telephone records delivered the next day, she took her opportunity.

"Lots of people can come into my house and telephone," she volunteered.

"Did they telephone to Gooderham & Worts?"

"I couldn't say that they telephoned to Gooderham & Worts, but I can tell you other places." Toronto, for instance, was one place she knew that friends called.

"Who are these people who came and telephoned to Toronto from your house?" asked Calder.

"I couldn't say; lots of friends from the United States come to my house."

"Are these friends rum-runners?"

"I couldn't say that."

"You don't know what their business is?"

"No."

Calder couldn't hide his irritation. "You won't mind if I say," he began, pressing each word, "that you are the most incurious woman I have ever met?"

"I don't know their business," repeated Bessie.

Mr. Justice Roy leaned forward. "Do you say that they are your friends and that you don't know their business?"

"They are my husband's friends," said Bessie. "The men are not my friends."

"Are they always men?" asked the chairman.

"Always men," she said, "coming to see my husband."

To Calder's many questions about her possible dealings with Gooderham & Worts, Bessie answered no as often as possible. Eventually Calder perceived the strategy in Bessie's persistent denials.

"Do you know Mr. Herbert Hatch?" he asked her.

"No, sir."

"Do you know Mr. McGuinness?"

"No, sir."

"You know neither of them?"

"No."

"You never made any payments to Mr. Hatch—?"

"No."

"You say 'no' before I have completed my question."

"I never make payments to anybody," said Bessie.

"You made some payments to somebody sometime."

"I don't know."

"You don't know if you have made payments in your life—"

"I might pay the stores."

"You had better wait until I finish my questions," said Calder.

"Otherwise I shall have the impression that you are prepared to say 'no' to everything I ask you."

When it came to questions about her bank accounts, Bessie gave as little information as possible. She admitted to having one bank account with perhaps eight hundred or a thousand dollars in it. When it came to telephone calls from her house, she admitted to calling her two grown daughters in Toronto almost every day.

"So that would explain every Toronto call?" said Calder. He smirked. "That is convenient."

Even more convenient for Bessie was that, apparently, all the other calls placed from her phone in the dining room of her home were made by her husband's friends, some of whom she didn't know.

"I don't interfere with my husband's friends, you know," said Bessie. "They are his friends; he is an Italian and so are they. They are his friends."

Calder began, "Mrs. Penna, will you give me—"

"Not 'Mrs. Penna,'" said Bessie.

"I beg your pardon," said Calder. He led Bessie into a long back-and-forth over the use of her telephone, which appeared to have been used by anyone who walked through their front door.

Justice Roy seemed quite perplexed by Bessie's testimony. "What kind of a home is your home?" he asked. "Is it a boarding house?"

"No."

"I don't understand why so many people would go into your place and use your telephone."

"Italians are different," said Bessie. "Italians have a lot of friends always coming in."

But Bessie's claimed indifference to the use of her telephone stood at odds with a fact Calder revealed—that she had recently gone to the phone company and asked for all of her call records.

"Why did you ask them for their call records?" asked Calder.

"Because I always got them from years ago."

"Why did you do it?" said the commission chairman.

"For no reason," said Bessie. "I don't know; no reason at all."

"You had some reason."

"No," said Bessie, staying on course. "No reason at all. Just because I done that for years."

"You are the only person I have heard of in all my life who did that," said Calder.

"I don't know about that."

"I suggest to you," said Calder, "that you wanted the company's call records in order to destroy all traces of your calls."

"No."

"You swear that?"

"I swear that."

The following day, evidence from the Hamilton district manager for Bell Telephone put three "substantial" bundles of telephone slips into Calder's hands that showed almost daily station-to-station calls from the Perri home to Gooderham & Worts and to other distilleries and breweries. Calder thumbed through one of the bundles, saying, "In this one parcel alone there are—I've lost count of the number. You'd require a bank teller."

The calls represented by the slips had taken place over two periods, between April and July of 1926 and from October of that year to February of 1927. When Bessie was recalled to the stand, she could tell the commissioners nothing about those calls. The commission chairman asked her specifically about the calls between April and July.

"Were you living in Hamilton during that period?"

"No," said Bessie. "In the summer I go out. I have been in Buffalo."

"Where were you between these dates?"

"I couldn't tell you, sir."

"Yes, you know perfectly well; that was not long ago. Give her the dates again."

She stayed in Crystal Beach, she said. She came and went. She would stay for a week at the beach, come back for a day, then leave the next morning.

The chairman had all but taken over the questioning at this point. "You never stayed for a week at home?"

"I might," said Bessie. "But I don't know about—"

Justice Roy broke in. "Why not say the truth and answer clearly?"

"This is the truth."

"You ought to remember that," said Roy.

"I don't phone to those places," said Bessie.

"Never mind the phone," barked Roy. "We are just testing you about your stay at home, if you did stay at home or not in those months."

"I would not stay at home the whole summer," said Bessie. "I would be going out for a while. I don't stay to look at those numbers or who would call, because I am only a woman. I am not concerned to go and look to the people who phoned." And even if she was at home, Bessie explained, "I am in the kitchen downstairs and would not listen upstairs to people telephoning."

The lawyers and commissioners failed to pick up on the contradiction in Bessie's testimony. The day before, she had said the phone was in the dining room. Apparently it moved according to her location, remaining always out of earshot.

Questions about telephone calls, and who might have made them, took up most of Bessie's second day of testimony. If a man had made the call, it must have been one of Rocco's friends—why, there were three strange men from Buffalo in her house just last night. And if the call was placed by a woman, then it might have been the housekeeper.

"It is your housekeeper calling up Gooderham & Worts?" said Calder.

"I am just saying maybe she put the call," said Bessie. "Did they see my pictures through the phone that it was me?"

"Don't be silly," said Calder. "It is sufficient that you are clever."

Finally, Bessie agreed to let the commission's auditors examine her bank account, the one at the Canadian Bank of Commerce, which she knew contained very little money.

"I will go with them," she offered.

But then Justice Wright suggested they just bring the records to the hearings. Bessie agreed to that as well, and then Calder drew her into agreeing to further examinations, including one Bessie may not have intended.

"And to examine all the accounts that you may have in the bank?"

"Yes."

"Or any of its branches?"

"Yes."

"Or any of the banks?"

"Yes."

It was that final agreement, a subtle change in wording to open up the investigation to any bank in which she had an account, that set the stage for some dramatic revelations in the days to come.

That night, the authorities got another break. RCMP officers had been following Rocco's movements, waiting for the chance to serve him a subpoena. Rocco wasn't in Ottawa at all, as Bessie had said; he was in Hamilton. He was there to support and advise Bessie as she gave her testimony, and he had to deal with a problem—one of his men, Frank Di Pietro, had just been arrested on the highway to Dundas, driving a truck containing eighty cases of Three Star Seagram rye whisky and five cases of Old Tom gin. The consignee on the shipment: J. Penna. At the moment, Di Pietro was sitting in jail, awaiting his trial in police court, and no doubt Rocco was arranging a lawyer for him. That plus the commission—he had a lot on his mind.

Subpoenas had to be served in person, preferably by placing the document in the witness's hands, and the RCMP had been trying for days. But however busy he was, Rocco was smart enough never to answer the door or make himself otherwise accessible. The Mounties finally decided they needed the help of the Hamilton police. The local cops knew their way around the Perri property. At the back of the house was a set of stairs that led down from the kitchen to a door into the garage. On Thursday night, when they knew Rocco was home, meeting with Mike Romeo, they snuck into the garage. Once they'd stationed themselves near the door, they kicked up some noise. For a moment, distracted by other concerns, Rocco let down his guard. Instead of sending Romeo to see what the commotion was, he went down himself from the kitchen and opened the door to the garage. The minute he did, the cops shoved the subpoena into his hands, along with a five-dollar bill for travel expenses. Rocco tried to refuse the money, but he was still bound to appear.

ON the following Monday afternoon, he did just that. Hair neatly combed, wearing a dark suit, striped tie and winning smile, Rocco stood comfortably amid the polished wood of the city hall courtroom and laid bare the terrible frailty of his memory.

Oh, how he wished he could help the commission in its quest to find answers. Sadly, it was not to be. Early on in the examination, when the hopes of the judges and the commission counsel, Newton Rowell, were still bright, Rocco recalled having once been the owner of a fruit store. Then he was a traveller, dealing in Italian olive oil and groceries. And for a while, he recalled, he was in the export business. But that was a long time ago. With a glance toward Bessie, who was sitting in the courtroom, he said they now lived on "a little rent coming to us."

"When did you stop the export business?" asked Rowell.

"A long time."

"Tell me the year."

"I cannot remember," said Rocco. "I am not quite sure. I don't say that because I don't want to tell you; if I remembered I would tell you." Pressed, Rocco offered that it was a year or two before the *Star* had visited, whenever that was.

"The *Star* interview, I understand, was in 1924?" said Rowell

"You know better than me then."

Rowell happened to have a copy of the interview in his bag. "Do you remember giving the interview?"

"I remember two or three boys were there."

"And you remember signing the interview?"

Yes, Rocco did remember that. But whatever he had said to the reporters, "I was not telling them the truth, but was telling them a little story to get them away from my door."

Rowell pointed out that Rocco had signed a statement saying he was a bootlegger. "Did you sign a false statement?"

"I did not sign a false statement," said Rocco. "I said I was not doing anything at the time I signed the paper."

"Did you sign a statement that you were engaged in the bootlegging business?"

"Not at present," said Rocco. "Not when I signed the paper."

"Did you call yourself the 'King of the Bootleggers'?"

"We had done a pretty good business in mail order," Rocco admitted. The business began in 1918 or 1919, he said, and stopped long before the *Star* interview.

"How long before?"

"I don't remember."

"Just try," prompted Rowell.

"No; there is no use my trying," Rocco insisted, "because it is impossible for me to tell you. You mention the date and I can remember it, perhaps."

"You have a better brain than you really want us to believe," said Rowell.

"Maybe I look that way, but I don't think I have."

Rowell indicated the newspaper. "You didn't say in this interview that you had gone out of business."

"I said I was out of the business long before that."

"No."

"They didn't say it there," said Rocco. "I said I was out of the business a long time before I gave that interview." In fact, Rocco was remembering something he'd said to one of the reporters who'd come after David Rogers of the *Star*.

Rowell scanned the paper in his hands. "I'm just trying to see if I can find it in this report of the interview."

"I hope you find it," said Rocco.

Rowell read. "You said, 'There is no business—I don't care what you name—in which honesty is a more important factor than in the bootlegging business.'"

"I never said that," said Rocco. "I could not explain it like that if I wanted to."

The problem, he explained, was that he had a very poor grasp of English. This is why he signed a document that said untrue things.

"What's that?" the chairman interjected.

"I don't read English very good," said Rocco.

"Now you say you did not understand what you were signing?"

"I don't say I don't understand it," said Rocco. "The boys read it out to me, and I signed it; but I don't read very good English."

"You want us to believe," said Justice Roy, "that you have signed a document without knowing what was in it?"

"They read it to me but I could not understand what they say."

"You understand English," said Justice Roy.

"Not to read and write," said Rocco. "I could not understand it very good." And even as he explained his inability, Rocco's grasp of English seemed to falter. "I could not understand what he say the words." Part of the trouble, he explained, was that "the wife was playing the piano."

"And you couldn't hear?"

"I could hear, but I could not understand exactly every word, what was explained."

Eventually Rowell moved on to other matters, such as where Rocco had been for the past two weeks.

"I have been in Welland a few days, St. Catharines, and been home; went down to Ottawa."

"How many days have you been in Hamilton during the past two weeks?"

"I don't remember when I come home—I was in Hamilton two or three times I think in the past two weeks."

Rowell informed Rocco that the police had observed him in Hamilton for several days. Rocco admitted he was there for a few hours perhaps, here and there. But he was also out of the country. He couldn't remember details.

"I want you to try and think," said Rowell. "It's only two weeks back."

"If you ask me where I was yesterday I could not tell you."

"Nobody believes you when you make a statement like that."

"I have a very poor memory to remember things," Rocco lamented. "You don't believe it; I know it is pretty hard for you."

The chairman stepped in. "You know where you were yesterday, you know we are not so childish as that."

"I was in Welland yesterday," Rocco said.

"You swore a moment ago you couldn't remember," exclaimed Rowell. "You cannot fool with this commission in that way."

Rowell moved on to try and get Rocco to tell them when he had last slept at his house in Hamilton. He had no luck here, either.

"I hardly remember," said Rocco, "because I went out many times and I come back so many times, it is pretty hard for me to remember."

"I want you to test that failing and fragile memory of yours a little bit," persisted Rowell, "and tell me when was the last occasion prior to Thursday night that you slept in your own home."

Rocco shook his head. "I could not tell you sir. If I tried to, I cannot remember; I would tell you the wrong day, the wrong night."

"Try it and let's see."

"I cannot. It is impossible."

After a few more minutes of this, Justice Wright warned Rocco that he had taken an oath, and that he would be punished for lying. As they tried to establish his movements over the previous couple of weeks, Rocco admitted to visiting friends in Welland, going up to Ottawa for a while, and visiting a friend in Port Weller. He remembered staying in St. Catharines for a couple of nights, sleeping in a home whose address he recalled as 83 Geneva Street, very close to the address of the home in which he'd housed Olive Rutledge and their children.

After that, his memory failed again. To questions of where, he could not remember. Questions of when, he could not remember. Even the times he saw Bessie—Did he see her Monday? Did he see her Tuesday?—no longer registered. What about driving together—did he come down to Toronto with her?

Rocco admitted that maybe he'd come to Toronto with Bessie three or four weeks ago.

"Did you come down with her last week?" asked Rowell.

"I don't remember; I cannot remember if I saw her last week."

"That is ridiculous," thundered the chairman. "A child would remember that."

"I know it is ridiculous," said Rocco. "But I cannot remember."

Rowell asked Rocco if he knew whether or not Bessie had been subpoenaed as a commission witness. With a roll of the eyes, the chairman answered for him: "He cannot remember."

In the midst of an extended back-and-forth about whether or not Rocco knew his wife had been subpoenaed, and whether the two of them had discussed her testimony, something occurred to Justice Roy. He interrupted the examination.

"Is it Mrs. Perri?" he asked Rocco.

"Yes."

"Is she your wife?"

"Yes."

"When did you get married?"

"I live with her about fifteen years," said Rocco.

"When were you married?"

"We are not married."

Since Rocco and Bessie weren't officially married, there was a chance Bessie could be compelled to testify against Rocco, which meant she couldn't be allowed to hear his testimony. "I think Mrs. Perri had better be excluded while we are continuing the examination," said Rowell. For a moment the proceedings paused as Bessie was shown out of the courtroom.

Rowell was finally about to get to the meat—the matter of the Perris' telephone, as much an instrument of transgression, apparently, as any weapon.

"Who uses that telephone?" asked Rowell.

"Sometimes I use it and sometimes the wife use it," said Rocco. "Sometimes a friend come in and they use it."

"Who uses it besides you and Mrs. Perri?

"There are a lot of friends of mine come in, and they use it."

"I want to know who," said Rowell, "and I am going to follow it. I want you to give me the names of the people you say use your phone."

"There are a lot of outside people use it."

"I want the names of the people and where they live."

Rocco could see that his memory would need to improve, if only briefly. He proceeded to give the names of men who were safely outside the country. "Mr. Joe Penna uses it," he began, explaining that Penna lived at 13 State Street in Buffalo, but had used the phone a lot in the summer and fall of the previous year, mostly to call up Gooderham & Worts. There was Nino Sacco, said Rocco, also of Buffalo, who came and called up the same distillery to find out the price of whisky. There was also his brother from Chicago, Domenic Sacco, who came up to Hamilton often . . . to use the telephone.

"Where does Domenic live?"

"Now you got me here in this address," said Rocco. "I can't remember this address, your honour. You got to remember the States, there is big number over there. I can't remember."

Rowell wouldn't have it. He insisted Rocco answer the question. So Rocco sighed, pulled out a notebook from his pocket, and leafed through it.

"Number 914 South Halsted Street, Chicago."

"And who else called up?"

Rocco had found a business card in his notebook. He held it up. "This fellow here. He called up the distillery." His name was Rocco Pizzimenti, who lived in the heart of New York City's Italian section, at 139 Mulberry Street. He'd called the distillery and also Kuntz Brewery, but just to ask for their prices.

"Then who else called up?"

Rocco laughed. "There was a lot of fellows that I couldn't remember now."

"Oh, yes, you do," said Rowell. "Come on now. Give me the others you have got there in your notebook."

"I got some. I don't know if they called up."

"Now, give them to me," Rowell demanded. "You have your notebook there. I want their names! Perhaps all the rest of the calls are your own, are they?"

Rocco could not be bullied. "No," he said. "The rest, Mr. Penna. I told you he put in over one hundred calls there. I don't know how many—I wouldn't say over one hundred. I wouldn't say nothing."

And then came an exchange that could easily have been the original inspiration for "Who's On First?" the Abbott and Costello routine that would become famous a decade later.

"How much did you get a case?" Rowell asked.

"A case for what?"

"For the goods ordered over the phone?"

"I never ordered no stuff over the phone."

"How much did these men pay you a case?"

"What men?"

"These men who ordered over the phone."

"What you mean, the distillery?"

"No, paid you."

"The distillery pay me?"

"How much were you paid a case by anybody?"

"I never pay nobody a case."

"I asked you how much you were paid."

"I never buy any liquor."

"How much were you paid?"

"Paid to whom?"

"Paid by Penna, or any distillery in respect of the calls put through on the phone."

"How much I paid Penna for using the telephone?"

"How much were you paid?"

"All I pay, or they pay me?"

"They pay you."

"Who?"

"Penna!"

"Penna pay me?"

"Yes."

"What for?"

"I told you what for!" shouted Rowell. "Answer my question!"

Rocco had had his fun. Now he smiled and gave a relaxed, expansive answer. "Penna come down here like a friend, and he use my phone whatever he pleased, and he called up my distillery. He never pay me a case of whisky or anything at all. He pay me for my call, that is all he pay me for."

Rowell handed a stack of call slips to Rocco indicating calls to the Kuntz Brewery. "Who made those calls?"

"I can't remember who made them calls. Maybe I made them myself. Maybe some friends of mine made them."

"What would you make them for?"

"Friends of mine, they want to go up there and see them from the States."

"Some friends of yours wanted to go up and see them, and you put in the call and arrange the appointment?"

"No," said Rocco, "I don't arrange the appointments. I asked if the manager would be there, that the people from the States want to see them, that is all."

Rowell hammered away at Rocco, repeatedly asking him about the calls on the stack of slips. "Look over all those and tell me who made any of them."

"What I know about this?" said Rocco. "I don't know anything about this."

Besides the calls to Gooderham & Worts and Kuntz, there were calls to Maine and to Brantford. There were thirty calls from Rocco's phone to the home of Charlie Muir, a customs officer in Fort Erie, the smuggling implications being very clear.

"I am telling you I don't know him," said Rocco. "I don't know the man."

There were other calls to Fort Erie, and calls to Hagersville, and to Niagara Falls, Ontario, and to North Bay.

"What were you phoning to North Bay about?" asked Rowell.

"Let me see," said Rocco. "What was it? Ah! A fellow had an accident in North Bay. We see a notice in the paper and we call up to see how that fellow is." Suddenly Rocco's memory had become astonishingly clear. "The fellow had an accident was Delfino."

There were a lot of calls to Joe Burke in Port Credit. And there was a large number, Rowell noted, to someone in Port Colborne.

"That is a friend of mine over there," said Rocco. "Frank Ross." Frank Ross was the alias for a twenty-eight-year-old associate also known as Frank Sylvester, or Sylvestro, who was becoming an important part of the mob chain that linked Perri's gang to cities in New York State. Arrested during the poison liquor crisis and then, like so many others, released, he was destined to become a pivotal figure in the lives of Rocco and Bessie Perri. But in his testimony, all Rocco said was that Frank Ross had a store in Port Colborne, selling cigars, cigarettes, candy and ice cream. There were other calls to Port Colborne, and Rocco offered a reason: "I want to put a poolroom over there."

He called someone named Secorza in St. Catharines. Who was that? "Oh, he is my godfather," said Rocco. The many calls to Thorold went to a cousin who was a baker, Rocco said. The sixty-four calls to the Waterloo Club? Joe Penna made those, trying to do business with Seagram. And there were forty-eight calls in a short period to the brutal, wife-threatening Frank Longo in Welland. Rocco had a reasonable, in fact troublingly plausible, answer for those too.

"I will tell you," he began. "His wife was down in the hospital, operated by Hamilton doctors and we generally used to call pretty near every day because she had a bad operation. When she went home we used to call pretty near every day to find out how she was."

For these several minutes, Rocco had seemed unconcerned about mentioning the names of people he knew; either the context was innocent or the men were safely out of reach. But something fascinating occurred when Rowell asked about the many calls to someone named Bernardo. On the stand, Rocco seemed to stiffen a little, and Rowell appeared to pick up on it.

"Mike Bernardo is it?"

Rocco gave no answer. And there was a reason: Mike Bernardo wasn't out of harm's way. He was in the courtroom at that moment, watching.

"Do you know Mike Bernardo?"

"No," said Rocco, suddenly circumspect.

"Now steady," said Rowell. Rocco stayed silent. "Do you know Mike Bernardo?"

"I don't think so."

Rowell addressed the courtroom. "Mike Bernardo, please stand up." Bernardo slowly rose from his seat. Rowell turned back to Rocco. "Do you know that man?"

"I know him now," said Rocco.

"What were you calling Mike Bernardo about?"

"I don't call Mike Bernardo."

"Why do you call him?"

"I said I don't call him . . . A fellow from Rochester came down there and said he knew Mike Bernardo for a long time, and he called him up."

Rowell then moved on to the last subject of significance: bank accounts. Where did Rocco keep his, Rowell wanted to know.

"I have not got any bank account," said Rocco. "I had a bank account about seven or eight years ago at the Imperial Bank." He had not had one since, he said, because Mrs. Perri kept an account and he gave his money to her.

"All your money?"

"Not all. I keep some for myself."

"Where do you keep your own money?"

"In my pocket," said Rocco.

The mention of Mrs. Perri prompted Rowell to ask, "Who was the woman who was calling from your house in Hamilton?"

"Maybe the operator call," said Rocco. ". . . Unless it was Mr. Penn's wife."

Rocco may in fact have said "Penna," but both the court stenographer and Justice Wright heard "Penn." From his seat on the bench, Wright asked, "Are Penna and Penn the same man?"

"Oh, no," said Rocco, enjoying the confusion.

"Are you sure?"

"I am sure."

"Will you produce him for us?" said Rowell.

"If I had the power to do it I would do it," said Rocco. "Why don't you send a couple of people over there to investigate? I will give you the name and address and telephone number if you want it."

"Didn't Mrs. Perri put through the calls for the shipments which were sent in the name of J. Penna?" Rowell asked a moment later.

"No, sir."

"How do you know she didn't?"

"I know, because we don't do that. If Mrs. Perri knew I touched any liquor, she would leave me tomorrow."

Rowell asked Rocco about the Jopp Drug Company in New York State, whose records showed that it had delivered large quantities of denatured alcohol to him. That was a mistake, said Rocco; he'd never received any alcohol from them. Indignantly, he suggested that someone else was using his name.

"If I knew who was using my name I would have him punished," he said. "I would have him arrested."

"You would have him arrested?"

"You bet your life I would, for using my name to bring alcohol over here."

Rowell asked about the Third Ward Political Club too, where Rocco's name had been on the books since 1924. The trouble, explained Rocco, was that people used his name all the time for their own purposes.

"They know I was well known at that time, and if they go over there and say, 'Perri sent me here to get some liquor,' they would treat them good." As for Rocco himself, he had nothing to do with denatured alcohol. "I did not know the people who bought it and I don't know the people who sell it. I have not been to the Falls for six or seven years." And when the name Louis Sylvester came up, and Rowell suggested he was Rocco's agent in bootlegging, the last words from Rocco's mouth were, "No, sir. You have made a mistake. How many calls have you got from my telephone to Sylvester there?"

It was time to call a halt to this performance, and Rowell asked Rocco to stand down. No doubt the experience had been draining for one of them, and R. L. Calder was standing by to call Bessie back to the stand. It was time for the next step in exposing her bank records.

A moment later, when she was standing before him in the same spot Rocco had just vacated, Calder got right to it.

"Have you got the bank book you were to produce?"

"Yes." She handed it over.

Calder described it for the record—a bank book for savings account 4761 in the Canadian Bank of Commerce, King and James streets, Hamilton branch, with a solitary entry, dated March 9, 1927, for a balance of $98.78. Calder looked up at Bessie in astonishment.

"Where is the bank book before that?"

"I don't know," she said. "I may have left it at home."

"You did leave it at home, as a matter of fact."

"No."

"And you brought only this book with one entry in it?"

"That is all I have got."

Bessie swore that was her only account, under any name. When Calder asked her for the letter she'd promised to sign, authorizing the accounting firm of Clarkson, Gordon & Dilworth to draw any bank books from any accounts she might have, Bessie said her lawyer had it, and she pointed to Michael J. O'Reilly. When O'Reilly brought it to Calder, the commission lawyer noticed it wasn't signed.

"She can sign it here," said O'Reilly. Apparently resigned to this process, she did, and the letter was handed to Albert Nash, the auditor for Clarkson, Gordon & Dilworth.

When Nash returned to the commission hearings, some weeks

later, to report on what he'd found, a picture of the Perris' hidden wealth emerged. Nash had found eight distinct bank accounts in Hamilton that had all been opened under the name of Bessie Perri or Bessie Starkman, at some point between 1916 and 1927. Into these accounts money had flowed in the following amounts: $20,000 in a Royal Bank account; $25,000 in a Bank of Toronto account; approximately $34,000 in a Bank of Montreal account; approximately $50,000 in an Imperial Bank account; approximately $240,000 in two Canadian Bank of Commerce accounts; and roughly $525,000 in two Standard Bank accounts—a total of $894,000. A few months later, apparently after further investigation, the *Globe* put the amount the Perris had deposited into various banks over the years at $960,000, or the equivalent of nearly $14 million in today's dollars.

THERE was more to be learned about the operations of Gooderham & Worts, and this time the commission ordered Herbert Hatch to talk about his work as a partner of Hatch & McGuinness, the sales arm of G & W.

Hatch's testimony made it clear that Hatch & McGuinness was a loose and shady affair. Hatch's sales territory was "any place I feel like going." His Ontario buyers came from "any place I can find a man to buy for delivery outside." Who acted as the firm's bookkeeper? "Any of us that are handy." He admitted taking liquor orders that were possibly for the Perris, but under the name of Penna. Hatch told the commission that Penna lived in Niagara Falls, but he had taken orders from him, in person, in Rocco's house in Hamilton.

Other Perri contacts were questioned. Bessie's bank records had offered up cheques with the names of men she'd paid or received money from—eight hundred dollars to George Hardy for the use of his boat, for example, and $7,275 to Mike Bernardo, who was working with the Perris' partner Jim Sullivan to ship as much as forty tons of whisky at a time from St. Pierre and Miquelon to Port Colborne.

Toward the third week of April, the hearings left Toronto and headed to Windsor. By the time the commissioners arrived back in Hamilton in May, wanting to talk to the Perris again, Rocco and Bessie had decided to disappear.

In their absence, there were still more revelations. And if it wasn't obvious yet how deeply integrated into the financial side of the business Bessie was, it became clear as more of the Perris' Hamilton associates testified. Both Mike Romeo and a fruit store owner named Rosario Carboni (who'd been living at Bay Street South in 1922 when he was arrested for having a gun in his "grip") admitted to depositing thousands of dollars for Bessie. Customer Louis Mascia, one of the partners in the Mascia Brothers grocery in Hamilton, talked about how his orders of Seagram and Gooderham & Worts whisky would arrive half an hour after he called her. "Generally we gave the order to the woman," he said. "It was through the woman that does the business."

Most damning was the testimony from two men who worked closely with two of the Perri's biggest suppliers. Bart Moriarty, the accountant for Grant's Spring Brewery (located ten blocks away from Rocco and Bessie, on Bay Street North), admitted to receiving a series of cheques from "Bessie Starkman," along with an untold number of cash payments, amounting to as much as twenty-five grand a year. And when a man named Samuel J. Low took the stand, commission lawyers revealed that he had endorsed cheques from Bessie showing that she'd paid about eleven thousand dollars for shipments from the Seagram Distillery in March 1927 alone.

Far from being retired as bootleggers, here was proof that Rocco and Bessie were doing a steady business even as the commission was investigating them.

As the Hamilton hearings came to a close, commission counsel R. L. Calder turned to the judges and asked them to direct that perjury charges be laid against Rocco and Bessie Perri. Rocco had sworn that he was not in the liquor business, and testimony had abundantly proved that he was in that business extensively. Mrs. Perri had asserted that she had only ever had one bank account, with just ninety-odd dollars, when in fact she had a large number of accounts. And that was just the beginning.

"The whole tenor of their testimony is perjury," said Calder.

"We quite agree," said the chairman. "What we have learned since they gave their evidence at Toronto has satisfied us that they are guilty of most flagrant perjury . . . If these people are still in the jurisdiction, then they should be prosecuted and brought to justice at once."

Now it was just a matter of finding them.

19

SPERGIURO

Perjury

F OR A WHILE THE RUMOURS SAID THAT ROCCO AND Bessie had fled to the United States, or possibly Italy. But neither seemed very likely. They had too many reasons to stay. True, the bootlegging business was facing the end of its heyday. On June 1, 1927, with the ardour for Prohibition abated, the Ontario government brought in the Liquor Control Act, and the era of government-run liquor stores began. But they were mean, bureaucratized affairs that hid the merchandise and required customers to register for permits and submit to reproachful stares from government clerks. And there were only eighteen stores for the entire province when the new system began, plenty of communities voted to remain dry, the government booze was taxed and expensive, and it was still illegal to buy booze by the glass. All of which meant a continuing demand for what Rocco and Bessie offered. On top of that, the United States was still six years away from repealing the Volstead Act, so there were plenty of customers below the border too. The Perris' money tap still flowed.

No, the Perris were definitely somewhere close, and now legal cords were tightening around them. The books of the Taylor and Bate Brewery in St. Catharines were found to be filled with references to "R. Perri." RCMP Constable Graham told commissioners that Perri had smuggled at least sixty-eight thousand dollars' worth of liquor across the Niagara River the previous year—and there was ample opportunity for more, because just two mounted officers patrolled an eight-mile stretch of frontier.

The suppliers who had worked so closely with the Perris began to feel the weight of the Royal Commission pressing down. During testimony in Hamilton, the commissioners learned that Waterloo's Kuntz Brewery had hidden hundreds of barrels of strong beer in railway carloads of scrap leather, auto tires and contractors' equipment in order to ship them to the United States without detection, a crime punishable under the Criminal Code. The Hamilton Brewing Association had shipped beer to Ohio under baled hay, and the association's president, George Russell, admitted that in an effort to avoid prosecution, he'd paid about five thousand dollars in protection money. The money had gone into a waterfront "rat fund" for William Egan, a Windsor prosecutor with ties to the Liberal Party who had demanded payments from a number of breweries. He wasn't alone in this. "There were certain lawyers who specialized in taking care of the exporters," Albert Healy, a former MP for Essex South, told the commission. "It was street talk in the border cities that they were making fabulous money."

On May 23, the Crown launched a suit against Gooderham & Worts for unpaid sales tax plus interest from December 1924 to March 1927, totaling $439,744.05. That was equivalent to fully half of the company's annual net earnings. It was a suit that would figure crucially in Rocco and Bessie's own legal battle.

Also in May, commission counsel Newton Rowell summarized his findings against twenty-eight breweries that had been investigated, of which all but one had fraudulently evaded the gallonage and sales taxes payable on domestic sales. He called for immediate action to end the organized corruption of customs agents, railway officials and police; the switching and camouflaging of railway cars filled with beer bound for the United States; the forgery and misuse of customs and shipping documents; the sale of strong beer within Ontario and the falsification of records to conceal those sales.

The commission still had a few more stops to make before the show concluded its run, but its stars were already established, and on June 15 Rocco and Bessie came out of hiding to take their bows.

They had decided to give themselves up, rather than wait to be caught, probably because surrendering made bail a certainty. So early on a cool Wednesday, they drove into Toronto where they met Michael J. O'Reilly, their steady counsel. O'Reilly walked them into city hall to meet with Assistant Crown Attorney Ed Murphy.

It had all been prearranged. Murphy, an up-and-comer who was eager for the publicity, had even made sure that the press was waiting in his office. When O'Reilly entered with his two clients, they were surprised. "This is to be a quiet little affair," O'Reilly said. Bessie wasn't feeling well that day and didn't want to pose for pictures, but when the photographers complained, O'Reilly suggested they might as well get it over with. Bessie agreed as long as the lawyers posed with them, so the foursome gathered around Murphy's desk. Dressed in an elegant black satin coat, bright spring gown and dark blue "picture hat," Bessie sat and faced the cameras. Rocco, standing next to her in a grey three-piece suit and black Oxfords, took off his "new straw" and looked quietly pleased. The fifty-four-year-old O'Reilly struck a distinguished pose in the background, and Murphy, seated front and centre, positively beamed.

O'Reilly had come with two certified cheques for the ten-thousand-dollar bail, each ready to be signed, but neither he nor Murphy had a pen, so the Hamilton lawyer borrowed a fountain pen from a reporter, then signed the cheques himself. Then a police officer was called in to make the Perris' surrender official. When Detective Sergeant Albert Johns arrived in Murphy's office, he had a question. Eleven days before, while police across Canada had been on the alert for the Perris, Toronto officers had spotted and seized one of the big Perri-owned Marmons as it drove out of Toronto's Thorncliffe horse-racing track carrying four Perri gang members. Now that the Perris were here, Detective Sergeant Johns wanted to know if they should give them back their Marmon.

"I see no reason why we shouldn't," Murphy said.

"She's a peach of a car," said Johns, handing over the keys. "You can roll along at fifty-five an hour and not know you're moving."

Rocco grinned. He loved that Marmon. "I drove twenty-seven thousand miles on those tires," he said, "and gave it some pretty rough treatment at that."

After a brief appearance in court to hear sixteen charges of perjury read into the record and see the case remanded to July 28, Bessie returned to Hamilton. Rocco picked up the Marmon and drove off to spend the afternoon at the Long Branch Racetrack.

In at least one legal arena, the Perris were shown to play strictly by the rules: They paid their water bill early. Tax records in Hamilton also indicated they were fully paid up on their income taxes. Not that they'd paid very much. In the 1924 tax year, Rocco's assessment had called for the payment of a paltry $13.30. Bessie had paid much more—$96.43, on declared income of $2,900. Rocco's assessment for the following year pegged his taxes at $66 on income of $2,000, and for 1926 he had claimed income of $3,000. A city councillor wondered if authorities shouldn't look into that a bit further. As the weather warmed they did, and they read up on the commission testimony as well, then reassessed Rocco's income at

$28,000—equivalent to roughly 3 percent annual bank interest on the Perris' supposed $960,000 fortune. Rocco wasn't just going to accept that. With O'Reilly, more than half a foot taller, again at his side, he appeared in court in July to protest the revision and swear that he had no income at all. When Judge Snider asked him how he lived and who kept him, Rocco declared, "My wife." A decision was pushed off for some months.

The perjury charges, a much graver matter with the potential for a sentence of fourteen years, bounced along as well. The Crown needed the Royal Commission's court reporters to testify as witnesses, so it had to wait while the commission continued its hearings. When the first remand date of July 28 came, Rocco and Bessie arrived at the courtroom in fine spirits and high fashion. Apparently Bessie liked the way the black coat had looked on the newspaper's front page, so now, for summer, she appeared in a lustrous black satin dress, with a black picture hat set off with a scarlet ribbon. The two of them smiled through their brief appearance before the judge, and, after the case was remanded for another month, Rocco tucked his arm through Bessie's and strolled with her out of court.

After that, the appearances and remands became a monthly affair, and the press took to reporting them, in August, September and October, with a kind of star-struck glee. No story failed to mention Rocco's cheerful smile or what became Bessie's signature court attire—the black dress and hat with the splash of red.

October was a busy month. On October 5, Hamilton's Court of Revision compromised on Rocco's 1926 income and fixed it at fourteen thousand dollars. Rocco, for the sake of the coming perjury trial, appealed that as well. As for the perjury trial itself, the remands were coming more frequently now, and so the Perris appeared in Toronto a few days later on the 8th and again on the 20th—still happy (Rocco "as is his usual wont, treated the whole proceeding as a most excellent joke"), and still marvellously dressed (for fall, Bessie wore a "stunning" brown coat with a thick grey fur collar). Finally, on the 22nd of the month, Rocco's tax tussle concluded exactly as he'd hoped (and maybe even arranged) when Judge Evans of the Court of Revision, following the absolutes of the law against a tide of logic, found for the record that Rocco Perri had no income whatsoever, and had to pay no tax at all.

With the Royal Commission hearings concluded, the Crown was free to proceed with its perjury case. On Friday, November 18, Bessie and Rocco arrived to be committed for trial on eight counts of perjury each. Rocco wore a favourite navy blue tie with his suit; Bessie's health looked much better than it had in June. As the proceedings began, their Toronto counsel, A. G. Slaght, rose and told the court, "We elect for a preliminary inquiry. Plead not guilty."

This was a subtle but deft legal manoeuvre—proof again that Rocco and Bessie had some of the best legal minds in Canada working for them. By requesting a preliminary inquiry, Slaght was demanding that the Crown prove it had enough evidence to proceed with a trial against his clients. It seemed an unnecessary formality—anyone who'd followed the Royal Commission hearings knew there was more than enough evidence. But Slaght had strategic reasons that would become clear only later.

First came the payoff for Michael J. O'Reilly's work knocking down Rocco's income to nothing in the Court of Revision. After the court reporters from the Royal Commission swore to the veracity of the Perris' testimony transcripts, and after reporter David Rogers had taken the stand to attest to the truth of his 1924 *Toronto Daily Star* interview, Slaght rose to speak. It was being suggested that his client had amassed a fortune as a bootlegger—the audited figure was set at $861,000 in deposits from 1922 to 1927. But, said Slaght, "What evidence is there as to Rocco Perri's income?"

History doesn't record whether Magistrate Jones rolled his eyes, but he may have. "You would know enough," he said, "if you knew bootleggers as I know them."

WITH the preliminary inquiry under way there was nothing more to be done on the perjury case until the grand jury had pored over the Royal Commission's transcripts and decided whether or not to proceed. Of course, it was a foregone conclusion that it would, so why had Slaght put everyone through the exercise?

It turned out that requesting a hearing allowed enough time for the other pending legal action involving the Perris—the Gooderham & Worts trial—to unfold. That was important, because the Dominion government had a lot riding on that test case: at least $5 million in revenue from the many tax-dodging distilleries and breweries that had been outed during the commission hearings. As witnesses against the millionaire Hatch brothers, Rocco and Bessie were better positioned than anyone to help the government prove its case. That gave them bargaining power and a chance to negotiate lighter sentences in the perjury trial.

But the strategy depended on Rocco and Bessie giving truthful testimony at Osgoode Hall when the time came. For two people who had a tendency to disappear, or to lie under oath, that was no sure thing. On December 8, 1927, the arrangement seemed in immediate jeopardy when Bessie failed to appear after she was called to the stand three times. Newton Rowell, who had stepped straight into this case from the hearings, and who knew the Perris all too well, called for the bench to issue a warrant.

The next day, anyone who heard the sudden hubbub in the courtroom didn't even need to look up to know that both Rocco and Bessie had arrived, with Bessie flaunting a luxurious mink coat.

Rocco took the stand first. Before he spoke, his lawyer requested the protection of the court—meaning the evidence Rocco gave couldn't be used against him in another trial—and this was granted. But perhaps Rocco hadn't heard; he wanted to be sure. So before he answered the first question he said, "I want the protection of the court." It was granted again, and from that moment it was as if a key had been turned inside Rocco.

In short, concise sentences, he admitted to his and Bessie's history as customers of Gooderham & Worts. Their first trans-actions—"two or three loads of whisky"—had come in 1924. The bulk of their business came between April or May of 1925 until March 1927. They worked through the distillery's sales agency, Hatch & McGuinness, dealing primarily with Larry McGuinness in all of their transactions. Rocco admitted to getting most of the liquor from Gooderham & Worts by boat, and to purchasing under the name J. Penna of Wilson, New York.

"Mr. McGuinness told me I must have a name on the other side to protect my shipments," Rocco explained. "So I saw my friend Joe Penna in the States and arranged to use his name." The system of telegraphing orders from Niagara Falls, New York, had also been imposed by their sales agent. "Mr. McGuinness told me that every order had to have a telegram."

Beginning in 1926, after "I got into trouble over some poison alcohol," Rocco had begun using the name J. Johnson on his orders. "There was too much Penna," he said. To make sure police couldn't link the Johnson name to him, Rocco said, "I had to go out and phone from a pay phone to the Postal Telegraph and ask for a boy to take a message. We would tell them to wire for a certain ship-ment and sign name of J. Johnson."

Early in their working relationship, Rocco visited the distil-lery to make payments. But then Hatch & McGuinness did their best to make life easy for their important customers. "Mr. Hatch or McGuinness would come up to the house sometimes, once every two weeks and get the money," said Rocco.

If it seemed as though Rocco was ratting on a supplier to save Bessie and himself, that was arguably true. Although turnabout was fair play—just the day before, Herbert Hatch had testified that it was the Perris who had paid him for all shipments to J. Penna and J. Johnson. And if Rocco understood anything, it was the economics of personal gain. By this point, he didn't need Gooderham & Worts; since their relationship had ended in March, other distillers, such as Seagram, had stepped in to supply the Perris with liquor. Finally, because everyone now knew the broad outlines, and many of the details, of what he and Bessie had been involved in with G & W, that information was a depreciating asset. The only place it had any real value was here. He was going to use it.

It wasn't as if there had been a great deal of goodwill between Rocco and this particular supplier. Prompted by Rowell, he spoke briefly about the complaints he'd made to Hatch & McGuinness about selling to Ben Kerr. "When we first started in 1925 I told them I'd buy from them if they sold to nobody else in Hamilton," said Rocco. When it was clear they were selling to Kerr in 1926, "I went to see McGuinness and Hatch and told them they must stop."

For the first time, Rocco mentioned his partner Jim Sullivan of Fort Erie, who was deeply involved in moving their liquor into the United States. (According to reports from U.S. Coast Guard agent Bill Kelly, uncovered by historian C. W. Hunt, Sullivan—or Sullirano—moved about twelve hundred cases of whisky and ale per day from Bridgeburg to the U.S. on his boat the *Maroma*.) Between 1925 and the spring of 1927, Rocco admitted, Sullivan and the Perris had split liquor proceeds fifty-fifty. But Rocco became less co-operative, more cagey, as the Hatches' lawyer William N. Tilley pressed him about visiting the United States, which would have given weight to Gooderham & Worts's contention that their shipments actually ended up there.

Rocco claimed he was no longer able to cross the border into the United States. "I can't get across. They won't let me."

"Did you ever try?" Tilley asked him.

"Yes, lots of times. But every time they send me back."

"How many times?"

"I don't know," said Rocco, "maybe a thousand times."

If anyone was involved in selling liquor into the United States, said Rocco, it was his old partner, Jim Sullivan. "Maybe he sold it direct," said Rocco. "Or maybe he went over and talked to somebody." But when Tilley tried to press down on this point—"He went because of dealings in liquor"—Rocco waved it all away. "Oh, no, just with his wife. He had a good time . . . He never sold liquor."

The more Rocco talked, the slipperier his testimony became— he was *never* in the boats carrying liquor / he *was* in the boats and Sullivan wasn't / *both* Sullivan and he went in the boats. Eventually Tilley suspected that there was an arrangement between Rocco and the Crown in return for talking. "I suppose you gave a statement of this evidence to the Crown?" he asked. When Rocco denied it, Tilley asked if he'd spoken to his solicitor about it.

"He told me to tell the truth," said Rocco. "Nobody asked me for any statement, so why would I give one?"

"You are still under another charge at present?"

"Perjury," Rocco admitted. "For evidence before the Royal Commission. I refused to tell the truth."

"What did you say at that time?"

"I said I knew nothing about liquor shipments."

And then, as if reminded of how he usually handled situations like this, Rocco began to have trouble with his memory again. For five or ten minutes, Tilley asked questions that elicited only "I don't know" or "I can't remember" answers. It was as if Rocco had tired of telling the truth, or a version of it. He had done his bit to help these people out; he wasn't going to be a martyr about it.

Eventually, Rocco was excused, and the Crown called Bessie to the stand. She admitted to being part of Rocco's bootlegging business, as someone who phoned orders and paid money.

"You were the cashier?" asked Rowell.

Bessie laughed at that. "I suppose so."

"When did you get the money?" the judge asked.

"From my husband," said Bessie. "I got the money and paid Hatch or McGuinness."

"But after the sales?"

"I got it."

"How about Sullivan? Did you handle his?"

"Well, he received only from the profits." Whenever cash came in from liquor sales, Bessie explained, she split the proceeds equally.

Bessie came clean about her "Bessie Perri" bank accounts in the Imperial, Commerce and Royal banks, and her much larger "Bessie Starkman" accounts in the Commerce and Standard. She threw a bit of light on how the process of payments worked.

"Sometimes I paid Hatch or McGuinness and sometimes we would come down to the distillery and pay them or Mr. Sinclair, the cashier. Sometimes when we gave it to Hatch or McGuinness they would give it to Sinclair."

"Who do you mean by 'we' went to the distillery?"

"Mr. Perri and I."

She admitted that sometimes it was Rocco who called in the orders, and sometimes Mrs. Sullivan. "The boys," meanwhile, regularly gave her money. "They take the liquor and give me cheques." Then, sometime in 1926, she explained, Herbert Hatch stopped accepting cheques made out by other people as payment. So, apart from a few special cases, she stopped taking cheques as well. "I used to get a lot of cheques until I quit it. Then, after I quit taking cheques, I made people give me cash money."

For a while, Jim Sullivan had been intricately tied to the finances of the business. Usually the sales agents came from Toronto for money about once a week. But, Bessie explained, "Sometimes Mr. Hatch or Mr. McGuinness would come for some money when I wouldn't have any, and Mr. Sullivan would give me some." These loans would be as much as three or four thousand dollars. She kept a record of them in her books—books that, to answer Tilley's next question, she no longer had.

"Where are they?" he asked.

"I don't know."

Later testimony, from other witnesses, exposed Gooderham & Worts's bogus shipments to something called the Mexico Export Company and other tax dodges. And it uncovered something else too. Between 1924 and 1927, over nine hundred cases of various kinds of Gooderham & Worts liquors had been confiscated by police or OTA officers, from hotels, houses and off the backs of trucks. A large portion of these would have been Rocco Perri and Jim Sullivan shipments. And what happened to all that liquor? Apparently the government had held those cases until the advent of government-run liquor stores, when they began a remarkable practice. William Johnstone, the warehouse superintendent of the Liquor Control Board, revealed that he personally tested and disposed of anything that was not fit to drink. His workers then poured the rest—whether they were bottles of Special Rye, Hyde Park Gin, Old Judge Bourbon or any of the others—into vats called "dumps." Then they redistilled it and sold it in government stores.

"We dumped all which was found to be good into one dump," said Johnstone, "and called it rye."

Near the end of the trial, Judge Grant admitted to being overwhelmed by the mounds of evidence and asked for the assistance of both counsel in coming to a judgment. "The evidence is so voluminous," he said, "in fact so great that I could not peruse it inside of a week, that I might feel I might be overlooking something." He adjourned the case until Monday, December 19.

ALL three legal proceedings that involved the Perris—the Royal Commission, the Gooderham & Worts trial and the perjury trial—found closure over the next few months.

The Royal Commission came first. Its official Final Report was tabled in the House of Commons on the afternoon of January 27, 1928, and outlined a plethora of recommendations to clean up the corruption at the border and tighten the restraints against commercial smuggling, to make rum-running more hazardous and bootlegging more expensive, and to overhaul the Department of National Revenue. A longer "interim" report, tabled separately, went into greater detail about the findings of corruption and incompetence in the Department of Customs and Excise, and it specifically mentioned Rocco and Bessie. "They have been engaged in the liquor trade on a very large scale, purchasing their stock from different breweries and distilleries. The sales were made in Canada, partly for consumption therein, and partly to be smuggled into the United States . . . The Commission has recommended prosecution for perjury."

Spring brought resolution to the Gooderham & Worts trial. Judge Grant dealt with the heaps of evidence in a judgment that went on for 118 pages. The key issue was Gooderham & Worts's efforts to evade paying sales tax on all goods sold in Canada by presenting those sales as exports, which were exempt from such tax. And Judge Grant had been struck by the fact that, of the forty-four "export" transactions he had been given to look at, not a single through bill of lading from Toronto to any foreign port or city had been found. In one case, he noted, a winter shipment bound for Mexico City had been loaded aboard a motorboat.

As for Rocco and Bessie, Judge Grant was impressed. Their testimony had been "unshaken by the cross-examination by skillful counsel" and corroborated by documentary evidence. He ruled that Gooderham & Worts had to pay $439,744 in taxes owing, plus interest. The Dominion government, which had already launched twenty other claims against brewers and distillers, rubbed its hands together in glee.

Last came the perjury trial. Rocco was officially charged on seven counts, Bessie on nine. On April 23, 1928, when the matter finally came before Toronto Magistrate Emerson Coatsworth—the judge who'd been so quick to grant citizenship to Joseph H. Sottile—most of the action had already taken place back in Assistant Crown Attorney Murphy's office. As they had arranged, Rocco pleaded guilty to one count of perjury, and all the charges against Bessie were dismissed. Even so, Bessie had seemed nervous, and when she came off the stand, Rocco gave her a comforting pat on the shoulder.

When it came to the ruling on how much time Rocco would have to serve—potentially as much as fourteen years—the forty-year-old Perri sat expectantly, his fingers twitching slightly with nerves. But the assistance he'd given to the government had convinced Judge Coatsworth that "he should have only a nominal sentence." Coatsworth even gave him a choice: "Six months at the jail farm, or six months definite and one month indeterminate if he be sent to the Ontario Reformatory. Which would your client prefer?"

"Does the Ontario Reformatory mean that he would be sent to Guelph?" asked Slaght.

"Either Guelph or Burwash." There were, at the time, about nine hundred prisoners at the Guelph Reformatory and roughly five hundred at the Burwash Industrial Farm.

"Very well. He would rather be sent to the Ontario Reformatory."

Rocco had been doing his best to keep a smile showing throughout the proceeding, but now relief washed over his face. At least, in Guelph, he would be among friends.

PART 4

20

SOLDI
Money

A s long as Frank Zaneth had worked for H. M. Newson, superintendent of O division, Newson had tried to look out for him. It was Newson, back in July of 1926, who had recommended Zaneth be stationed undercover at the Niagara Falls detachment, to work on customs and narcotics cases. And when Zaneth complained of being short of cash, it was Newson who had tried to help by arranging to let Frank and Rita stay in the spare room of the house on River Road.

But now it was October 1927, and Frank Zaneth was costing Newson money. At least he seemed to be—Zaneth was still working undercover, so it was impossible to examine his spending closely. However, it looked bad enough that Newson decided to let Commissioner Cortlandt Starnes know. "Not that I wish to suggest that he is profiting by his expenditures," Newson hastened to add, "but I consider that they are very high whatever the results may be that will be accomplished."

Zaneth was working the drug racket in conjunction with the U.S. Secret Service. He'd connected with a dope peddler named

Pat Drouillard, but nothing could be done on Drouillard just then because the American authorities were involved. Besides that, Zaneth was working on two other suspects, and accomplishing nothing very much as far as Newson was concerned. And for all that, Zaneth had spent nearly twelve hundred dollars over the past three months on incidentals and car repairs. What the devil was going on with Zaneth's car? Newson had officially called him in—"paraded" him—and let him know his expenses were too bloody high. And now Newson was asking the commissioner whether Zaneth might be better deployed elsewhere, perhaps more in the open, which would allow him to appear in court if necessary. If not that, said Newson, then maybe it would be "more economical to tie him down to a set figure for expenses which must not be exceeded."

Zaneth wasn't the kind of man who would misappropriate funds, but there's no doubt he was living under great financial pressures. Anything he could reasonably charge to the force, he would. The troubles of his wife, Rita, which had lifted long enough for her to live with him in Niagara Falls, had become an illness that required treatment. Frank had paid for her to return to Italy, and she lived now in Lacchiarella, a village half an hour's drive south of Milan. According to a letter from his C division commander, sent to the commissioner on Zaneth's behalf, Frank was her sole support, paying an average of seventy dollars a month for her care.

Two months later, on December 5, an internal communications extract regarding Zaneth indicated his expenses were still an issue: "The commissioner further states that the high operating costs of this N.C.O.'s car is difficult to understand."

And then, suddenly, Zaneth's car expenses hardly mattered. A Canadian immigration officer stationed in France had uncovered what looked to be an international immigration racket involving forged permits. Within days of the car expenses complaint, the

RCMP assigned its now unencumbered detective sergeant to an investigation that would take him to Ottawa, Winnipeg, Italy—and Rocco Perri's Hamilton. With his wife gone, and his world shrunk to the task set before him, Zaneth attacked that investigation as only someone with nothing else in his life could do.

〰〰〰〰〰〰〰〰〰〰〰

LONG BEFORE BOOTLEGGED ALCOHOL, THERE WAS TRADE in narcotics. In the early 1800s, Britain's economy thrived on exports of opium to China, and opium dens became a dark fixture of the Victorian age. During the American Civil War, wounded soldiers were soothed by applications of morphine, giving rise to the addiction known as "soldier's disease." In the 1880s, half a dozen factories in Vancouver and Victoria manufactured crude gum opium for smoking. In 1895 the German chemical company Bayer introduced heroin as a morphine substitute. By 1905, cocaine was being smuggled across borders and snorted. In Ottawa in 1911, Mackenzie King, as minister of labour, won approval for "drastic" legislation to stop the importation, manufacture, sale and use of narcotics. In this bill, said the minister, Parliament was striving for nothing less than "the conservation of human life and human well-being."

All of this is to say that in 1920s North America, drug trafficking wasn't a new phenomenon. But for Bessie Perri, it was a convenient one.

No one knows precisely what happened to the hundreds of thousands of dollars discovered in those bank accounts, but it's almost certain that after the Royal Commission, Bessie converted the fortune into unregistered bonds that were hidden in safety deposit boxes in American banks. There was a later report that she took a vacation south of the border in the company of nine hundred thousand dollars, which she left safely behind. But storing the cash in the States made it harder to get at when it was needed.

Running the liquor business proved difficult without Rocco around to supervise the truck and boat shipments, the loading and unloading, the customs payoffs. With the end of the Perris' relationship with Gooderham & Worts, their most reliable whisky stream had dried up. At the same time, the preventive service branch of the federal customs department had dramatically increased its force—from a single officer in the early 1920s up to the current fifty-five—leading to the brief seizure of one of the Perri gang's boats, the *Uncas*. And the U.S. Coast Guard, which had successfully shut down Rum Row off the Atlantic coast, had shifted nearly 250 of its patrol vessels to the Great Lakes. Soon they were nabbing at least one rum boat a week, more than ever before. Complicating matters further, competition from other bootleggers was getting increasingly dangerous, especially when the Staud family, a band of violent brothers backed by the Bronfmans, began running booze from Port Hope, Ontario, to Rochester, New York.

All of this affected the returns on a bootlegger's investment. The summer and autumn flow of liquor cases across the Detroit River from Windsor fell from 150,000 in 1928 to just fifty thousand in 1929. In the eastern section of the Great Lakes it was no different. By one estimate, the Perris' liquor profits plunged to less than a fifth of what they'd once been. At some point while Rocco was behind bars, money became so tight that Bessie was forced to borrow twenty-five hundred dollars from a Hamilton dentist, William T. Griffin, by taking out a mortgage on the house on Bay Street South.

Some millionaire liquor men—including Windsor bootlegger Harry Low—sized up the situation and started investing their money elsewhere, like real estate. Bessie Perri knew nothing about real estate, but she did know dope. With Rocco biding his time in Guelph, she decided this business would be hers. "She reached out for the easy greenbacks," said an acquaintance of Rocco's. "She did this even after they were very wealthy."

BESSIE Perri had certain loves in her life. She loved Rocco, of course—although his philandering (there were other women besides Olive) had hardened her to him.

She deeply loved her two daughters in Toronto, Gertie and Lily. As they'd grown up Bessie had made it possible for them to attend a private school and take business courses. "Mother arranged and paid for it all," said Gertie. And after her daughters married and gave birth, she loved her two grandchildren. Gertie became Mrs. Maidenberg of Euclid Avenue and had a boy named Stanley. Lily became Mrs. Shime of Robert Street and had a child of her own. Bessie doted on both children, and Gertie and Lily often brought them to Hamilton for visits.

She loved money, too, and money had never let Bessie down. Since its arrival, it had only brought her pleasures.

One of her greatest pleasures was diamonds. Her jeweller, Thomas C. Binkley, of Klein & Binkley in Hamilton, called Bessie "a diamond fiend—she almost had a mania for them." She loved most her six-thousand-dollar four-karat square-cut solitaire diamond ring, but also her three-karat round diamond solitaire, and her set of three 1.5-karat diamond rings, and her diamond pendant necklace with three large stones, and her diamond bar-pin, and her diamond bracelet, and the ring even her jeweller thought was too large, featuring a solid one-inch-by-three-quarters-of-an-inch blaze of diamonds that seemed almost to catch fire under the light. She amassed a collection that Thomas Binkley estimated to be worth fifteen thousand dollars, and she came to his James Street North store frequently with an eye to add to her collection. "She wasn't interested in anything but diamonds," he said. "They seemed to fascinate her strangely."

And last, Bessie loved the growing power and fortune that dealing in drugs brought her.

She and Rocco may have dabbled in the drug trade before. In 1921, a narcotics investigator revealed that Hamilton had become one of the chief drug trafficking centres in Ontario. OPP Inspector John Miller viewed the issue as a largely "Anglo-Saxon" problem. "I have found, from observation, that the foreigners do not use drugs," he said. But when their man Bruno Attilio was picked up by police in March 1922 and found in possession of cocaine, heroin and morphine, with a stash of drugs in his house on Bay Street North, it was an indication that Rocco and Bessie might have had at least some piece of this action. (A further indication came during Inspector John Miller's investigation into the murder of Joe Sciarrone, when he noted in an aside that Perri gang member Charles Bordonaro had switched from bootlegging to selling narcotics.) A year later, another Perri gang member named Giusto Tobaccharo was caught with narcotics and convicted. Still, compared with the volume of documented evidence regarding the Perri bootlegging operation, this was a blip, and hardly conclusive.

Rocco had never been keen on the drug racket. Perhaps, having achieved his goals with liquor, he saw no need to get into it. But he must also have known that the authorities viewed narcotics far more negatively than liquor, so that any involvement with them would attract much more onerous scrutiny. No need and too much trouble—the combination was enough to keep Rocco mostly out of narcotics for a while.

By 1926, however, with the end of Prohibition nigh in Ontario, it seems clear that Bessie convinced Rocco they needed another revenue stream. Drugs were, at the very least, far easier to smuggle than alcohol. Small amounts were sometimes mailed, hidden in the middle of hollowed-out books. Larger amounts came mostly from Germany, Italy and Switzerland, often concealed in shipments of cocoa and chocolate. Montreal was a frequent port of entry; so was Toronto. From there the shipments sometimes travelled south. The same month that police picked up Tobaccharo, a former Canadian soldier named James Wadsworth was arrested as part of a drug ring that smuggled narcotics from a blind pig in Toronto into the United States with the help of two Buffalo doctors. Wadsworth typically pinned small paper sacks into the inside of his clothes then took the steamer ship *Cayuga* to Lewiston, New York.

The drugs that stayed in Canada passed to users through dealers like Attilio, who sometimes carried their merchandise in the hollowed-out heels of their shoes. Shipped in ounces, the drugs were then broken down into "grains" that could be melted and injected. An ounce of morphine, bought by a dealer for twenty or thirty dollars, became 110 small white cubes each weighing a few grains and packaged in one-dollar "decks." An ounce of cocaine or heroin became 480 "shots," each a grain, which sold for a dollar or more in small packets of folded paper. Wealthy users obtained their drugs, more expensively, through doctors who profited handsomely (one Hamilton doctor was rumoured to have made $250,000 a year) and injected them with proper hypodermics. Many addicts, however, jabbed their veins with the same small instruments used to fill fountain pens with ink. Before the ballpoint pen became commonplace, there were plenty of those.

By 1926, a gang of Italian dope peddlers had established itself in western Pennsylvania. The core of the gang hung out at a Pittsburgh confectionery store and sold the drugs into

Westmoreland and Fayette counties for as much as sixty-five dollars an ounce. In March 1926, Rocco sent a letter to one of the members of that gang, Joe Pandillo (alias Pandaglio). It was intercepted by a U.S. narcotics agent named William T. Duffy, who was investigating the Pennsylvania gang. On March 12, 1926, he contacted the RCMP for information.

It fell to Corporal R. E. R. Webster of the RCMP's Hamilton detachment to respond. On March 23, he sat down at his desk and composed a letter for Superintendent H. M. Newson—Frank Zaneth's boss—summing up what the local detachment knew about "Rocco Perri or Perry of 166 Bay St. South," a.k.a. "Rocco Susino."

"This man is the biggest liquor smuggler in this district and at the same time is believed to be concerned in the smuggling of narcotic drugs, though there is no direct evidence of this," Webster wrote. He described Rocco's large network of Italians. "The members of his gang are frequently changed, Perry using them as he sees fit, thereby keeping them all under his thumb. There is not an Italian in Hamilton who will give this man away."

Webster warmed to his task as he typed, perhaps aware that he was going to receive an extra dollar in his next pay packet for his efforts: "Perry is a clever and dangerous crook exercising an extraordinary influence over the men in his employ, and any who are not in his employ are afraid of him. He is the 'King-pin' directing all operations, but the members of his gang when caught shoulder the responsibility and pay the penalty.

"In Hamilton during the last few years there have been several bombing outrages and murders among the Italians, and it is freely stated that these have all been in connection with the members of Perry's gang of smugglers, who are desperate men and will stop at nothing. Again the directing hand is stated to be Perry."

He closed with a list of the full or partial names of fifteen known Perri associates, with descriptions of several who'd been convicted of crimes. "Most of these men," finished Webster, "have large and powerful Touring cars registered in their name, or did have last year, but in reality these cars are said to belong to Rocco Perry."

Superintendent Newson forwarded Webster's letter to William T. Duffy, who continued his work of trying to break the ring. Some twenty months later, in November of 1927, nineteen members of the Joe Pandillo drug ring in Pennsylvania were charged and, by May of 1928, most of them were convicted and sentenced to two years in prison. At one point, American authorities were fairly sure that Rocco had been supplying the ring with drugs, but nothing more came of his connection. It's possible that Rocco severed his association when the gang was arrested, and perhaps he vowed to make better choices in his drug associations in the future, or to swear off the whole bad business.

But then came the perjury conviction, when Rocco was trucked off to prison and Bessie Perri was left to her own devices. For five months, until Rocco was released (a month early) on September 27, 1928, Bessie was left alone—with her mahogany radio, her jewels and furs, and her husband's gang of underemployed hoods—to indulge her own entrepreneurial impulses and establish a new business model.

21

STUPEFACENTI
Narcotics

CORPORAL WEBSTER GOT THAT EXTRA DOLLAR FOR HIS painstakingly compiled report on Rocco Perri's criminal activities. But obviously neither Superintendent H. M. Newson nor anyone else at the higher levels of RCMP command paid it much attention before they sent it on to Pittsburgh. Webster's report, written in March of 1926, very clearly mentioned the possibility that Rocco was smuggling narcotics. But two years later, in April of 1928, when western Ontario district commander Inspector Charles Deering LaNauze received a letter from the Department of Justice in Pittsburgh that confirmed it—"[we] are in possession of evidence showing that Pandaglio has . . . received narcotics from Rocco Perry" it said—he replied, "This is the first we have heard of Rocco Perry being engaged in the narcotic drug traffic." Then, so as not to sound utterly naïve, he added, "I am not surprised."

Once this information was laid in the laps of the RCMP commanders, they rushed off to do nothing about it. For a week or two, the notion of "Rocco Perri and drugs" lingered in the air at the RCMP, wafting from office to office in memo form. Detective

Sergeant H. Darling became aware of it. So did Commissioner Cortlandt Starnes. But it seems they perceived the information as little more than a rumour, something with no substance, giving them nothing to act on. Perhaps, in a time of limited resources, they took comfort from the fact that Rocco was just then being transferred to the Ontario Reformatory to begin serving his sentence for perjury. Whatever the reason, the impetus to look into Rocco Perri's drug connections slipped away into a quiet, bureaucratic corner, where it waited for its moment to arise.

That moment came about a year later, in the summer of 1929.

Parts of downtown Toronto were a chaos of steel beams and construction towers as work continued on a series of railway underpasses and the massive waterfront viaduct extending from the new Union Station. On June 11, a cavalcade of dignitaries arrived for the official opening of the Royal York Hotel, while in homes and offices throughout the land, ordinary clerks and secretaries were riveted to news of the financial markets and debated stock picks as if they were veterans of the trading floor. About a week later, New York State's attorney general attended a bankers' banquet at the Royal York, and told the assembled that this time of wealth and plenty would be a true test of character. "How much better can we stand prosperity than any race ever did before?"

Frank Zaneth was certainly prospering. He had cracked the forgery ring that had been churning out immigration permits for big profits, and he'd sent the leader, a Toronto businessman named Frank Wise, up for thirty months in prison. Afterward, a lawyer in the case said of Zaneth, "He is one of the best officers I have ever seen."

One of the key figures in the forgery case was a man in Hamilton named Flavio Masi, a slightly rotund and expensively suited Italian with a truncated black moustache who was working with a corrupt official at the Italian consulate in Ottawa (and whom OPP Inspector John Miller had suspected of selling drugs in 1922). That gave Zaneth a reason to visit Hamilton for the first time. Posing as a representative from the consulate, he obtained information from Masi's wife, and he began the process of developing informants in the city. He didn't cross paths with Rocco, but since every Italian in Hamilton spoke highly of the little boss, he surely became aware of his influence.

For the time being, whatever he might have heard about Rocco, Zaneth had to file it away. The forgery case sent him on a chase after Flavio Masi that took him to Italy, through Milan (where he had the opportunity to visit briefly with Rita). It also required an extra level of secrecy, so he began to sign his reports "Operative No. 1." It was the code name he would use from then on, whenever he was undercover, and he put it to use almost immediately as he began investigations into the Toronto drug world.

Zaneth was a master now at slipping into identities that gave him access to exactly the information he needed. If he lacked the sexy charm that had allowed the Pinkerton's operative, J. C. S., to seduce bootlegger Mildred Sterling into spilling about Rocco, he had other assets: a willingness to put himself in harm's way, and an ability to work doggedly until he was ready to drop. The Pinkerton's agent had typically signed off duty every night at around ten o'clock. Frank Zaneth was never off duty. "There is nothing this man cannot 'Tackle,'" said a memo that circulated within O division. "He is a lone worker and afraid of nothing."

By June of 1929, Zaneth was working to build drug connections in Toronto's gritty core. According to authors James Dubro and Robin Rowland, one of the undercover agents he'd developed was Ernest Tomlinson, a twenty-seven-year-old ex-drug user, thief and pimp who'd spent two years in Kingston Penitentiary. It was with the help of Tomlinson—essentially a freelancer who was paid a monthly wage—that Zaneth had found a twenty-three-year-old drug runner named Tony Defalco, who hung out at a Bay Street taxi stand. Tomlinson had bought small amounts of morphine from Defalco already, using the RCMP's marked bills (officers either marked each bill discreetly with ink or recorded its serial number in a notebook in advance). One day, posing as a Montreal drug dealer, Zaneth drove an unmarked police car to meet with Defalco and initiate a large drug buy of his own.

Defalco told Zaneth the prices—twenty-five dollars an ounce for cocaine, thirty for morphine. Zaneth said he thought those prices were high but agreed, and the next day they drove together to the Marathon and Enosis Club, a poolroom and gambling hangout near Yonge Street on Dundas East. There Defalco introduced Zaneth to Tony Roma, a forty-year-old gangster who ran the club and controlled access to the drugs. Zaneth handed over $210 in marked bills for six ounces of cocaine and two ounces of morphine, then got back in his car along with Roma and another Italian, Tony Brassi, who told him to drive west along Dundas.

After a few minutes they pulled up in front of the house of Ned Italiano at 887 Dundas Street West. Roma and Brassi told Zaneth to wait in the car while they went in, and when they emerged a minute later to say the drugs would be ready soon, Zaneth handed over the key to his trunk. A few minutes later, Brassi came out with a paper bag, which they placed in the back of the car. As Roma handed the key back to Zaneth he leaned in. "Don't go to Defalco anymore when you want drugs," he said. "Come straight to me."

So Zaneth now had evidence connecting four men to a major drug ring in Toronto. But questions remained: Where were the drugs coming from? Who was the supplier? Zaneth didn't know that Ned Italiano had lived in Hamilton, and that several of his young male relatives were Perri employees. He didn't know that fifty-one-year-old Tony Brassi ran a blind pig just east of Hamilton, in Stoney Creek, and had his own ties to Rocco. But he had noticed that whenever drugs were bought from the Roma group, they were wrapped up in pages from a Hamilton newspaper. So the day after he made his buy, he followed his investigation down the highway.

He hadn't been in Hamilton very long when he encountered one of his informants, Joe Scime, a steamship agent with Italian connections who'd been useful in the forged permits investigation. Scime needed money and Zaneth had told him that if he kept his eyes open he might earn a few dollars. Now Scime had some information he thought Zaneth would like to hear: He was certain that Rocco Perri was the "big gun" in narcotics smuggling and distribution in Ontario.

As Zaneth listened, Scime talked about a Hamilton garage that Rocco rented at 108 Merrick Street, at the corner of Bay Street North, which was possibly the headquarters of the operation. And he mentioned that an Italian named Frank Ross was now Rocco's first lieutenant and handled the distribution of the drugs.

This jibed with what Zaneth already knew about the lean and cruelly handsome Ross—that he "drives very expensive cars, never works and lives the life of a millionaire." And it fit neatly beside the facts of his Toronto investigations: Tony Defalco, Tony Roma and Ned Italiano had all originated in Calabria, like Rocco Perri. Zaneth knew full well that Calabrians "generally stick together."

Zaneth reported all this to his new commander, Superintendent George L. Jennings, and the timing was opportune. Two days before, while he'd been going through the work on his desk, Jennings had come to a report from some operatives in Windsor. They'd been working on an opium buy from two drug dealers, one of them a former Medal of Valour winner named Archie McFarlane, when whose name should surface but Rocco Perri's.

That combination of reports, from two disparate cities, was what finally convinced the RCMP that "Rocco Perri and drugs" was something worth looking into. Jennings immediately sent a note to RCMP Commissioner Starnes. "It would appear from recent information that Rocco Perri is now in the drug game," he wrote. He mentioned the Toronto drug investigation but said that, as important as that case was, the Hamilton case seemed even more so. "To this end I am employing Sgt. Zaneth for the purpose of cleaning up this ring which we have stumbled upon."

The operation began inauspiciously. During his time among the Toronto drug dealers, Zaneth had noticed one of them driving an Overland sedan. So on the evening of June 17, with a new shipment of drugs expected to arrive in Hamilton, Zaneth made the hour-and-a-half drive in from Toronto with Detective Sergeant H. Darling to see if they could spot the Overland somewhere in the vicinity of Rocco's garage, or near Frank Ross's house at 255 Barton Street West. They stationed a shadow at both locations and, for almost five hours on that unusually warm June night, they drove back and forth and around the city in an unmarked McLaughlin-Buick police car. There was no sign of the Overland.

At some point during this frustrating hunt, Zaneth and Darling decided to check out the home of Rocco Perri himself. They turned south and drove slowly through Rocco's neighbourhood after midnight. For one tantalizing moment, they got close enough in the dark to 166 Bay Street South to get a clear look at the porch. But they saw men stationed there, apparently acting as lookouts, so it was impossible to set up a watch. The two RCMP detectives finally made it back to Toronto, no wiser, at two-thirty in the morning.

Four days later, the RCMP conducted two simultaneous raids

in Toronto. Still undercover, having slept hardly at all for ten days, Zaneth had arranged to be at the Marathon and Enosis Club making another buy as police busted in. They gathered up the drugs, money and a revolver, and arrested both Zaneth and Tony Roma. At the same time, about thirty blocks west, a second team of officers surrounded Ned Italiano's house. When police announced their presence at the front door, Tony Brassi and Italiano—with $1,010 in his pockets—tried to bolt out the back.

They didn't make it, and in the search that followed—which included ripping up floor boards while Mrs. Italiano implored police not to tear her house down—officers found some of Zaneth's marked bills, along with six different kinds of ammunition, and about three pounds of morphine and cocaine. At the time, it was the largest drug seizure in Toronto's history.

And then came a strange stroke of luck. As the police were wrapping up their two-hour search of Italiano's house, who should walk in but Bessie Perri, dressed in her jewels and finery, carrying hundreds of dollars in cash. (So much cash, in rolls, that she couldn't tell the police how much it was.) She'd arrived on one of her rounds, collecting the money her dealers owed her. As the detectives began to search her, she calmly explained, in her deceptively gentle voice, that she was simply visiting her good friend Ned. And since she was carrying no drugs or weapons, and none of her bills were marked, there was nothing to prove she was doing anything else.

But now the connection was clear.

ON a cloudy Thursday, July 4, as rowing fans were taking in the news that the London Boat Club had defeated the Toronto Argonauts during a smashing day of races at England's famous Henley-on-Thames, Frank Zaneth motored toward Hamilton for a drug buy.

In the passenger seat sat Hugh Mathewson, a young detective constable who'd been working with Zaneth, learning from the best, during his narcotics investigations. The day before, Zaneth had ordered Mathewson to set up the buy by calling a man in Hamilton named Jimmy Curwood.

Curwood was an ex-convict who existed on the fringes of the Hamilton drug world. Anticipating an investigation, Zaneth had found and recruited him to work, like Ernest Tomlinson, as an undercover agent. In his reports, to keep Curwood's identity secret, Zaneth referred to him by a code name, "Informant Q," but like Tomlinson, Curwood was more than strictly an informant. His job was to act as a conduit, a way into the drug ring Zaneth hoped to infiltrate. He too was likely paid a monthly wage for his efforts— not as much as an officer, but enough to keep him on task.

Curwood's task was to tell a Hamilton drug dealer that he knew a Jewish mobster named "Arthur Anderson" (Zaneth) who was coming in from Chicago. He was to let the dealer know that Anderson wanted to inspect some drugs and make an immediate purchase of about thirty ounces. Curwood had done that, approaching someone Zaneth described in his report as "a certain Negro, by the name of Gordon Goins," who was a go-between connected to the drug ring. Curwood told Goins that Anderson would have a large roll of cash on him along with a "rod" (gun).

Since Anderson was supposed to be coming from Chicago, Zaneth and Mathewson made a stop in Brantford a little before sunset so that Zaneth could board the 8:58 p.m. train into Hamilton. Mathewson continued into Hamilton so that he could shadow Zaneth's movements, from the train station where Curwood would be meeting him to the King George Hotel at the corner of MacNab and Market streets, where Anderson was supposed to be staying.

The train pulled into Hamilton at 9:45. Though he'd been

through this countless times by now, Zaneth must have felt the slight quickening of anticipation. He stepped down onto the platform, dressed in the pinstripe suit and pearl-grey fedora of the 1920s mobster. He breathed the warm evening air, which still held some dampness from the day's taste of rain. Then he spotted Curwood, and Goins next to him. After cursory introductions, Curwood hailed a taxi and told the driver to take them to the King George.

In the back of the cab, Curwood told Goins again, as if he hadn't before, that his pal Arthur Anderson was a big-time Chicago gangster. As they rumbled through the streets, from the unlit northwest corner of Hamilton toward the brighter, busier market district, Zaneth did his part, dropping the names of several known gunmen as his friends. Once they'd arrived at the hotel and made their way to Anderson's room, Curwood gave Zaneth a chance to show off his gun, prompting him about the "good rod" he must have on him. "My best one," said Zaneth, pulling it out. When Goins seemed amazed, and a little intimidated, Zaneth said, "Well, I'm in a strange city; I'm carrying about five grand and I am not taking any chances." Zaneth then produced a large roll of about three hundred dollars in American bills that he'd obtained from a Hamilton bank. He'd put a fifty on the outside, a twenty underneath, and filled out the roll with a large number of one- and five-dollar bills in the centre.

Curwood had bought a case of beer and a bottle of liquor to help them pass the time until their drug buy, and the three men sat around drinking for a while. Zaneth bided his time, careful not to rush things, but after a few drinks he probed Goins about who he was going to be dealing with. Goins clearly knew who the important players were—he mentioned the thirty-year-old Frank Ross, his older brother Tony Ross, Frank Romeo and finally, the magic words, Rocco Perri.

After another drink or two, Goins decided it was time to leave. They went downstairs, hailed a cab, and Goins took Zaneth and Curwood to a blind pig owned by Tony Ross at 72 Sheaffe Street, halfway between Caroline Street and Bay Street North. When they climbed out of the cab, Zaneth took in as much of his surroundings as he could see in the light coming from the houses. Like most of the north end of Hamilton, Sheaffe was a street of modest frame buildings. Directly across the street a man sat out on his front steps, almost as if he were keeping watch.

Inside the blind pig it was dark and smoky. When an unnamed Italian approached them, Goins asked Zaneth to take off his hat so the man could see his face. "Here's the boss himself from Chicago," said Goins in Italian. "He wants to see the stuff by tomorrow morning." The unnamed Italian recoiled. "I haven't got it now," he said, alarmed. "What I was talking to you about was shirts."

Goins laughed. "Never mind," he said. "We'll be back in the morning."

Zaneth sensed that Goins didn't have the confidence of these dealers that he'd suggested to Curwood he had. Without revealing that he also spoke Italian and had understood the whole exchange, he began to act annoyed. As far as he was concerned, he'd "come a long way to meet a bunch of suckers." They'd never even seen thirty ounces of drugs, he said. Their limit was a two-dollar deck, otherwise they would have been here to make the deal.

Goins assured him he would take him to the "big boss." They took a taxi to the house of Frank Romeo and asked for Frank Ross. But Romeo said he didn't know where he was. As they left, Goins tried to impress the man he was showing around. "Did you see that fellow?" he said, meaning Romeo. "Well, he is worth three million dollars." Zaneth snarled that he hadn't come from Chicago to find out how much money his friend had, he was here to purchase drugs.

He told Goins he had only a few more hours to "produce the goods or get out of my sight." Goins pleaded for more time. Things were done differently in Canada, he said, assuring him that everyone was acting in good faith and he wouldn't be disappointed.

It proved to be a long night.

By about 2 a.m., having driven from one address to another trying to find either of the Ross brothers, they were back at the hotel. Curwood was now feeling some pressure himself and began to press Goins on why he'd said his people could supply thirty ounces when it seemed obvious they couldn't. Goins was starting to look scared. Caught in the middle, he put it down to the gun Anderson was carrying. All the talk about the gun had made the Italians wary.

Zaneth could see he'd played that card too strongly. He told Goins to let his friends know he'd either leave the gun at the hotel or turn it over to one of them until the deal was over. All he wanted was to meet them, wherever they liked, and examine ten ounces.

Goins left to find someone and returned around three-thirty with John Flynn. Looking at him, Zaneth realized he was the same man who'd been sitting out on his front steps across the street from Tony Ross's liquor joint. Flynn established his credentials with Zaneth. He was an addict who'd been buying drugs from Tony and Frank Ross since 1923, sometimes acting as their runner. Just yesterday, he said, Frank had told him to try to sell six ounces of cocaine and ten ounces of morphine. He promised to talk to the Ross brothers first thing in the morning and set up a meeting with Zaneth at nine o'clock. By then he was sure he'd have drugs for Zaneth to examine.

After Goins and Flynn had gone, Zaneth walked a few blocks east along a lamplit King Street to the Royal Connaught Hotel at the corner of King and James. That's where Mathewson was staying. He ordered Mathewson to get a search warrant for 72 and 73

Sheaffe Street so they'd have it when they needed it. Mathewson said sure, but then he reminded Zaneth that before the office would issue a warrant, they would have to inform the Hamilton police.

Now there was a problem. Zaneth had big doubts about the cops in a city controlled by Rocco Perri, and where two of Rocco's right-hand men, Frank and Tony Ross, had been operating for years without being caught. But if the local cops had to be informed, there was nothing he could do but hope for the best.

The next morning, Zaneth and Curwood drove to Sheaffe Street to meet with John Flynn. Mathewson shadowed them from a distance. As soon as they arrived, Flynn crossed the street to the blind pig, returning almost immediately to say he'd been told to speak directly to Tony Ross. He dialled Ross on his telephone, spoke briefly, and about twenty minutes later, Ross pulled up in a Chevrolet coupe.

As Zaneth watched Flynn and Curwood talking to Tony Ross in his car, he could tell something was wrong. A moment later, inside the house, Flynn pulled Zaneth out of Goins's earshot to tell him the Ross brothers had shut everything down. They weren't selling to anyone, because they were wary of him. A guy with a big rod and a big roll shows up all of a sudden out of Chicago? It wasn't that the Ross brothers suspected Anderson of being a cop, Flynn assured him, but they didn't like it. And they didn't believe that Gordon Goins, who was only a "deck man," had connections to a Chicago gangster with five grand in cash.

Zaneth was quietly furious. He'd relied on his informant to set up a proper connection, and Curwood had obviously placed far too much confidence in Goins. Now the whole operation was in jeopardy. In front of Curwood and Flynn, he told Goins he was disgusted, that he'd come a long way for nothing. He ordered the kid to get out of his sight.

His best hope now was John Flynn. Luckily Flynn seemed to have convinced himself he was going to make a couple of hundred dollars if a deal went through, so he was motivated to keep helping him. As they talked, Flynn told Zaneth that Tony and Frank Ross had two separate caches of drugs, but that Frank Romeo and Rocco Perri were the real bosses. Flynn suggested they let the matter stand for a few hours. In the meantime, he'd talk with another drug runner called "Spot" who might be able to convince Tony Ross to come through with the goods.

It wasn't until about 4:20 in the afternoon that they finally got word that Spot would be able to bring five ounces of morphine to the hotel, as a trial sell. From there, they might be able to get more, in increments of five or ten ounces, until Zaneth had received his thirty ounces.

Zaneth quickly made his way to the Connaught, where Mathewson was awaiting orders. Figuring the drugs would cost between thirty and thirty-five dollars an ounce, the two sat at a table and marked $175 in U.S. bills. Zaneth had been told that, on each run, either Tony or Frank Ross would be driving Flynn and Spot to the hotel. The goal now was to get one of the Rosses on the second purchase.

A deal seemed fairly certain, so Zaneth phoned Toronto headquarters. Apparently all the protocol had been followed and his warrant was granted. Now he needed a police car and two men to drive into Hamilton with the warrant and assist him in searching. He intended to call in the city police to help search as well, as a matter of courtesy. But that would let the dealers know an arrest was imminent, so he decided not to call the local cops "until the last moment."

They waited. By six-thirty Friday night nothing had happened, so he sent Curwood off to find out what was going on. He returned a half hour later, with a disappointed John Flynn, to say that the Ross brothers had refused to sell even a deck for fear they would be trailed to their caches. But Flynn was sure that in a few days he'd be able to approach them again.

Zaneth wanted to keep the chances of a deal alive, but he didn't want to look like a putz. In front of Flynn, he let Curwood know he was going to Montreal to try to get a load. He invented a drug-using girlfriend, saying he'd dropped her off in Windsor on the way in from Chicago, and asked Curwood to give her a call to let her know he'd be delayed. This allowed him to drop another name for Flynn's benefit. If his girl needed anything, Zaneth said, Curwood was to tell her to call "Mug Moren." It seems pretty clear that he meant Chicago gangster "Bugs Moran," whose outfit had been Al Capone's target in the St. Valentine's Day Massacre a few months before. Whether this was a mistake Zaneth made typing the report, or one he actually said aloud, Flynn was apparently convinced enough that he offered to mail the fictional girlfriend five decks of morphine. Zaneth declined. Then a few hours later, beneath an unsettled sky, he and Mathewson drove back to Toronto.

In the city they left, at 166 Bay Street South, Rocco and Bessie—and probably Frank Romeo and one or both of the Ross brothers—talked about what to make of Arthur Anderson. It's possible that Rocco put in a call to one of his Chicago pals, to see if anyone had ever heard of him.

They knew one thing: they had to be more careful. The moment Bessie had walked into Ned Italiano's place and been patted down, she knew the police weren't just looking for drugs; they were looking for marked money. That meant one of their men had already sold drugs to an undercover cop. They'd let down their guard and it couldn't happen again. So for now, no one was selling to Anderson or to anybody they didn't know like family, until they had proof he was on the level.

OVER the next few days, Zaneth and Curwood worked several angles. Saturday morning, Zaneth had someone in the RCMP's Montreal division send a telegram from Arthur Anderson to Jimmy Curwood at the King George Hotel, telling him he was detained in Montreal because he was making a "large deal." The whole of Sunday, Hamilton was drenched in rain and nothing moved, but on Monday, July 8, Curwood showed the telegram to John Flynn and Frank Ross. Then he let Zaneth know it looked as if he might be able to make a deal the next day. Late Tuesday morning, Zaneth arrived as if he'd just driven in from Montreal; however, Flynn could not be found. But they met yet another hood, a bookmaker and drug buyer named Jim Crawford, and someone else named Matt Hayes. An assurance of a deal, a phone call, and still nothing materialized but another spit of rain. Zaneth was back in Toronto by late afternoon Tuesday, no further ahead.

"Tony Ross, Frank Ross, Frank Romeo and Rocco Perri are not the usual type of men found engaged in the distribution of narcotic drugs," Zaneth wrote in his July 8 report. "These people are always on the alert, and do not deal with anyone at all. These people also gather data from newspapers of any drug cases in the Province, and whatever they learn from there, they use to their advantage."

In hindsight, it seemed to Zaneth as if their chances had been blown early on. The raid at Ned Italiano's, the need to advise the Hamilton police of their search warrant request, the fact that Rocco Perri's name had featured so prominently in court after the Archie McFarlane drug buy in Windsor—any of these were enough to have caused the ring to shut down their operations. On top of that,

Zaneth blamed himself. For all his experience, he was still fairly new to the layered workings of Italian mobsters. "I might have been over zealous in getting close to Rocco Perri," he admitted. "When the Negro failed us I should have dropped the matter."

On July 11, 1929, Inspector LaNauze of O division recommended to the commissioner that they put a temporary halt to their Rocco Perri operation. "This man is, as you know, exceedingly alert." That very day, Zaneth was forced to appear in court to testify about the RCMP's Toronto investigations in the preliminary hearing for Ned Italiano, Tony Brassi, Tony Defalco and Tony Roma. With their Hamilton investigations on hold, the force seemed unconcerned about Zaneth showing his face to the men in the dock, or to onlookers in the gallery, but there's no doubt the Perri ring learned more about the extent of the investigations. By the end of the day, Defalco and Brassi were unable to raise bail and had to remain in jail, but Roma and Italiano were released, on bail of ten thousand and twenty-five thousand dollars, respectively.

Despite their release, things weren't entirely happy inside the Perri drug ring. It used to be that the Perri syndicate helped its men when they ran into legal trouble; but the fact that both Defalco and Brassi were still sitting in jail indicated a shift. Bessie had more power now, and she was far less inclined to help than Rocco. Both Roma and Italiano had had to post some of their own money for bail; Italiano in particular was said to be bitter about it. And it had troubled Tony Roma's waters too.

Some days or weeks after he was released—no one will ever know precisely when—Roma and the woman he called his wife, Helen Groves, visited a woman they knew in Thorold. Her name was Mrs. Frada, and she was the wife of a fruit dealer and known Black Hand extortionist. The couple knew her well enough to talk openly in front of her.

The trial for Roma, Italiano and the other men was scheduled for September, and Tony Roma was thinking about fleeing the country long before that day came. As they visited in Mrs. Frada's kitchen, Tony and Helen began to argue.

"What a fine friend Rocco Perri turned out to be," said Helen. "After he asked you to stop doing business with Jimmy [a.k.a. Frank D'Agostino of Merritton] and buy from him, in time of trouble he refuses to help you."

Tony tried to calm her down. "The reason why I stopped buying from Jimmy is because Perri gave it to us much cheaper," he said. As far as having to cover bail himself, he claimed not to be bothered. "Rocco has too much money and can't take a chance to show his hand in this thing."

"At least he could have helped you financially to pull through your trial," said Helen. "Now you must leave the country."

"The reason why I am leaving is not the question of money," insisted Tony, "but because I am wanted in Montreal on a murder charge, and it will be better for the rest if I do go away."

It would have helped Zaneth had he heard about this conversation shortly after it happened. Unfortunately Mrs. Frada didn't come forward with it until months later.

A FEW days after the July 11 hearing, Curwood contacted Zaneth to assure him that no one in the Perri gang suspected him of being a cop. That was a relief, although it still appeared as though Rocco had shut down operations until the court cases in Toronto and Windsor were concluded. But a shutdown meant no one was making any money, so Zaneth waited for a break. On the morning of July 20, it came: Curwood called in to say that apparently the Ross brothers had gotten impatient and sold John Flynn several decks of narcotics. It seemed operations had resumed.

On July 24, Inspector LaNauze sent a secret memo to update the commissioner and underline the importance of pursuing Rocco. "Rocco Perri is the leader of the drug ring in this Province," LaNauze wrote. "I believe that by concentrating on the Hamilton angle we might, with a little luck, get Perri either with marked money or by fingerprints."

LaNauze laid it on thick—"by getting Perri we can safely say it will be the biggest scoop we ever had in this Division insofar as the illegal traffic in drugs is concerned"—because he was about to ask the department to spend some extra money. He enumerated his needs:

1. A motorcar, possibly one bought in Illinois. It didn't need to be expensive, necessarily, but it had to be "decent enough to give colour to the suggestion that Operative No. 1 is a drug runner from Chicago."
2. Illinois licence plates for the motorcar.
3. Exclusive use of the motorcar. No lending it out for other cases.

The issue of the motorcar became a point of internal debate at the RCMP. Should a new motorcar be bought for this operation? If so, what motorcar was best? Money was tight, so someone suggested an economical new Ford. This idea was raised with Zaneth, who was horrified. Gangsters didn't drive Fords; they drove expensive cars such as Packards and Marmons and Buicks. Zaneth knew this because he was out in the field. He had visions of the whole operation falling apart because some desk man couldn't be convinced not to buy him a Model A.

Inside the RCMP's criminal investigation branch in Ottawa, Zaneth had the support of a staffer named W. W. Watson, who agreed that in choosing a motorcar for an operative trying to pass himself off as an important gangster, ideas didn't come much worse than "a new Ford." Luckily he convinced the decision makers of a simple solution: Use the McLaughlin-Buick that was already in the RCMP's Toronto garage. Have Zaneth drive it to Chicago to pick up plates. Put them on when he gets near Hamilton and let the man get to work. Zaneth later sent Watson a personal note: "Thank you very much for having straightened up that tangle about the car."

THE stakes were rising. On the morning of July 30, Zaneth drove into Hamilton to see Curwood, who told him that Jim Harris, a bootlegger since 1916 with close connections to Perri, was waiting to meet with "Arthur Anderson" in the home of another unnamed bootlegger. A little while later, the men met over drinks, and Harris gave Zaneth some good news and some bad news.

The good: Harris had what he called the biggest connection in the country for narcotic drugs, which Zaneth took to mean Rocco Perri. The bad: Before he would do business with him, Harris had to satisfy himself that Anderson was a bona fide drug runner. And Harris found it highly suspicious that a Chicago man needed to come all the way to Hamilton or Montreal to get drugs. Why didn't he make his buys in Chicago, or even Detroit?

Zaneth had an explanation ready. He told Harris the drugs in Chicago and Detroit were badly cut. Sure, the price was cheap at between seventeen and nineteen dollars an ounce, but he would rather go to Montreal and pay twenty-five or twenty-eight dollars and get pure goods. If there was any cutting to be done, he wanted to do it himself.

Then Harris did something unexpected. He pulled out a note-book and asked Anderson for the names and addresses of two or three men in Chicago or Detroit who could vouch for him. For a tense moment, Zaneth froze. "I was taken by surprise," he admitted later, "and for a second did not know just what to say." Then he said . . . no. He told Harris he wasn't going to give him the name or address of any friend because Harris was a stranger. Harris was insistent, so to buy time Zaneth said he'd have to get the consent of his friends first. Harris said he would wait.

Later, safe in a private location, Zaneth and Curwood brain-stormed about who they could find in Detroit or Chicago's under-world to vouch for him. Since Zaneth already had plans to drive to Chicago, Curwood suggested Zaneth take him along and drop him off in Detroit, where he could look up some possibilities. He also had an acquaintance in Chicago and a brother in Hamilton, Ohio, Curwood said, whom he could contact and "wise up to this scheme."

Back in Toronto, Zaneth got LaNauze's permission to take Curwood to Detroit. But the RCMP would not be laying out extra per diems to cover it—the usual three dollars per day in "legitimate expenses" was all he could expect. Like Superintendent Newson two years earlier, LaNauze was fed up with Zaneth's constant demands for more money and his wild, undocumented expenses while he was undercover. During a 1928 Halifax investigation into possible drug smuggling via Dutch flower bulbs, Zaneth's commander had advanced him $660 that he'd blown through in a matter of weeks. "As you may have gathered," LaNauze wrote to the commissioner, "money and this man part company very quickly . . . This Operative is very well paid, and I do not consider that he should be given any further leeway along these lines."

One unusual bit of investigative paperwork remained. When

police had seized that cache of narcotics at Ned Italiano's, they'd found that each of the small tins of morphine was wrapped in a special red paper. The experts in Ottawa wanted to study one of those wrappers to see if they could lift Rocco Perri's prints from it. LaNauze had one shipped on July 29.

About a week later, Ottawa let him know it was hopeless. The experts couldn't develop any prints from the morphine wrapper. Zaneth would have to link Perri to the drugs himself. Everything depended on his Detroit-Chicago trip to establish his credentials.

22

CONFIDENZA
Trust

O<small>N THE EVENING OF</small> J<small>ULY</small> 31, <small>THE SAME DAY</small> G<small>EORGE</small> Frederick Jelfs finally retired as Hamilton's police magistrate after thirty-six years—"I'm glad I'm through," he said— Zaneth drove into Hamilton from Toronto on the first leg of his Chicago trip. He'd hoped to talk to Jim Curwood that evening, but he was nowhere to be found. The next morning the sun rose at 5:05 and after breakfast Zaneth pulled up to the front of Curwood's house in the McLaughlin-Buick. They were scheduled to leave together on their trip at 8 a.m., but "Informant Q" didn't show up until 9:15, driving a car belonging to Jim Harris. Now it all became clear. Obviously Curwood worked for Harris as a bootlegger and he'd been out all night on a job. It was an excellent cover, Zaneth had to admit, even if Curwood did deny it when he was asked.

To this point, Zaneth had kept his personal opinions about Informant Q out of his reports. He was used to dealing with all manner of lowlife; as long as Curwood did what was expected of him for the money he was paid, Zaneth had no complaints. But the frustrations of the investigation so far, and now having to wait around for the man to show up, had worn Zaneth's patience thin. He wasn't happy either with LaNauze's decision on the expenses for this operation. So when it was clear Curwood expected extra money for his scouting trip to Detroit, Zaneth told him to forget it. "I did not feel like paying his expenses," he reported to LaNauze, "in view of your instructions on the matter." The only thing Curwood was getting out of his trip to Detroit, said Zaneth, was a lift back to Hamilton.

But all he had on him was $1.50, said Curwood. Zaneth had to give him *something* to cover his costs. Well, then, Zaneth wanted to know: Who exactly did Curwood have in mind to vouch for him in Detroit? Now Curwood could only offer some vague reference to relatives in Chatham, Ontario; he knew nobody in Detroit at all. Zaneth left him at the curb and drove off to Chicago alone. It was a lousy way to start his crucial trip.

He arrived in Chicago at 8 p.m. on August 2. The next morning, a Saturday, he walked into the U.S. Treasury Department. He had a list of possible contacts in the intelligence unit and found one—Clarence L. Converse—who was willing to do all he could to help.

It would take Zaneth ten days to get "Illinois markers" the normal way, Converse told him, because the application had to be sent to Springfield. Instead, Converse took Zaneth to Chicago's central police station and introduced him to Deputy Commissioner John Stege. Soon Zaneth was talking with a Lieutenant William Cox in the stolen cars department, who promised to have a pair of untraceable markers for him on Monday.

With plates taken care of, the next task was finding a couple of Chicago gangsters to vouch for him. Converse knew just where to go. He took Zaneth deep into Al Capone's territory, to a bootlegger's joint and dance hall at 60 East 30th Street, known as the

Garage Café. Inside he met Patrick Horan, who ran the place in partnership with a Sicilian mobster named Sam Constantino (a.k.a. Frank Galgano). Zaneth must have assumed Horan was Converse's version of Jimmy Curwood, an underworld figure recruited as an agent. In a quiet corner, Converse explained Zaneth's needs, and Horan agreed. He would tell anyone who asked that he'd known Arthur Anderson for years, running some sort of racket that he didn't know about. Horan asked only that Zaneth come back in the evening, because Constantino wasn't around just then, and Horan wanted the two men to meet.

That evening, Zaneth returned alone to the speakeasy. Horan introduced him to Constantino and laid out how they were going to tell anyone who asked that Anderson was a known Chicago gangster. To prove their good faith, as Zaneth sat at the bar, Horan and Constantino proceeded to convince every racketeer who came into the place that they had known Anderson for years.

It seemed almost too good to be true and, in a way, it was. What Zaneth didn't know, and what no one could tell him, was that the Garage Café was an elaborate ruse. A Chicago business- man, Robert Isham Randolph, had become tired of the way Al Capone was taking over the city. Through his position as head of the Chicago Association of Commerce, Randolph organized a few like-minded businessmen into a shadowy group that became known, unofficially, as the Secret Six. The group tried various ways to push back against Capone, and the Garage Café was one of those ways. Randolph's group spent about twelve thousand dollars to set up the joint as a speakeasy, illegally selling beer and liquor with the co-operation of the federal authorities. They used the Garage Café as a honey pot to attract real gangsters and gather intelligence, pay- ing disgruntled members of Capone's gang as much as a thousand dollars for useful information. Randolph himself had hired Horan and Constantino to run the place. Constantino was a real gangster who obviously had no love for Capone, but the bartender, Patrick Horan, was a cop working deep undercover. The café operated for perhaps a year, until Constantino learned that Capone had found out what he was doing. He gave Randolph his keys to the place and told him he was "takin' it on the lam" before Capone's gang "took him for a ride." But the Secret Six, in eventually helping to put Al Capone away, inspired books and at least one Hollywood movie, a 1931 gangster flick starring Wallace Beery, Jean Harlow and Clark Gable.

In the course of contributing to Canadian history, Frank Zaneth had walked into the midst of American history being made. He came away from a second night at the Garage Café sensing that something was going on under the surface, but at least feeling sure that Constantino and Horan would vouch for him: "They seem to be in debt to Mr. Converse over something."

On Monday, August 5, Zaneth picked up his free Illinois markers as well as a city licence—which, he noted for LaNauze's benefit, normally cost ten and eight dollars, respectively—and telegraphed Curwood to let him know he'd be back in Hamilton on Wednesday afternoon. Before he arrived, he pulled onto a country road outside of Brantford, took the Ontario plates off the McLaughlin-Buick and put on the Chicago markers. Then he drove into Hamilton, now firmly established as a Chicago heavy.

The careful game of narcotics cat-and-mouse began to intensify. Curwood had warned Zaneth that even with the new credentials he'd supplied to Harris, the dealer would not do business with him directly for some time. He offered to be a go-between, taking money from Zaneth to buy from Harris. When Zaneth rejected that—he would buy direct or not at all—Curwood implored him not to be too difficult to work with.

The game took enormous patience. Zaneth had established the story that he was running drugs from Montreal to Chicago, driving back and forth between the cities, and so he would arrive in Hamilton every few days as if making a midway stop. For weeks, Harris repeatedly told Zaneth that this or that contact who was currently out of reach—a man at a race meet in Windsor, a man in Montreal, a man in New York—would soon be able to provide drugs. Then the connection would fall through. Early on, thinking a drop was imminent, Zaneth set up surveillance with another Toronto undercover officer to observe a rendezvous between Harris and his supplier, supposedly bringing drugs from Switzerland and Germany. He wanted the officer to see who the important players were so he'd know who to capture and interrogate "when the pinch comes," only to learn that the man—"wearing a straw hat and a blue suit" according to Curwood—had come and gone before the officer could get into position.

By the middle of the month, Zaneth was pressing Harris on whether he was going to do business with him or not. "I am not going to string you along," Harris said. But that was exactly what he was doing. It seemed to Zaneth as though the ring was just going to "beat time" until the cases against Italiano and the others came up for trial.

As the waiting continued, Zaneth's informant went from being a tenuous asset to a tangible liability. His drinking was one problem—on a morning when "the Informant was not feeling up to the mark," Zaneth suggested it might be best for him to keep out of sight for a while. To facilitate that he planted a story that Curwood had gone with Anderson to Montreal.

But worse than Curwood's drinking was the dubiousness of

his acquaintanceship with someone as apparently well-connected as Arthur Anderson. As far as the Perri gang was concerned, Curwood was the sort who typically associated with "riff-raff," and once he had a few drinks in him he started to talk. People began to have suspicions, and on August 21, Jim Harris pulled Zaneth aside. He said he was "very surprised" that a heavyweight like Anderson would associate with the likes of Jim Curwood. Harris said he had no doubts now about Anderson's standing in the underworld—he and his men were quite satisfied, particularly when Zaneth gave them Clarence Converse's Chicago address as his own—but they were less and less sure about Curwood. Harris warned Anderson to "be on the alert."

The next day, after Zaneth informed headquarters, Superintendent G. L. Jennings let the commissioner know that Informant Q had outlived his usefulness in Hamilton. He wasn't proposing that they abandon him—it was better to keep him "in a good frame of mind"—but he wanted him shipped north with Detective Constable Mathewson, to assist in his narcotics investigations in one of the far-flung regions of the country, well out of the way.

The next time Zaneth arrived in Hamilton, on August 26, the Curwood problem was still chafing at Harris, and Zaneth washed his hands of him. Curwood wasn't to be trusted, he admitted, and he was through using him as a go-between. In fact, he had "turned him loose in Montreal to fare for himself." Harris approved. Keep away from Curwood, he warned. The guy was very likely "a stool for someone."

But aside from the Curwood hiccup, and the small lingering matter of not being able to make a deal happen, Zaneth began to feel optimistic about his chances. Harris took him along on a drive to a location near Vineland, Ontario, to meet two friends from the Beaver Board factory—that spawning ground for Perri henchmen around Thorold. Once "Alfred" and "Charlie" were in the car, the four of them drove back together and chatted about the price of drugs and the various methods dealers could use to avoid detection, then they hung out at Harris's house, drinking together like old friends, until four in the morning.

"They are making certain that I am a bona fide drug runner," Zaneth reported. It was astonishing to him the lengths they were willing to go to, the time they were willing to take. But he sensed his chances of a deal improving. Perhaps it was wishful thinking, because the fact was his time was running out. The trial for Ned Italiano and the three Tonys was coming up soon, and it was very likely Zaneth was going to have to testify publicly again. Over the course of a trial, rather than a short hearing, the chances were much greater that his cover could be blown.

Before Zaneth left that morning, bleary eyed, Jim Harris asked him for a favour. The next time he was coming through from Montreal to Chicago, could he give him a lift into Detroit? There was someone there he needed to see. Zaneth knew he would have to get special permission from his bosses to make another trip, so he told Harris he wasn't sure. But as soon as he got back to Toronto, he banged out a request to Superintendent Jennings: "I am convinced it would be in the best interest of this investigation for me to oblige Mr. Harris and take him into Detroit. Possibly it would be advisable for me to continue on to Chicago in case they have a shadow on me."

Jennings went along with it. He estimated Zaneth had maybe twelve days before the beginning of the Italiano trial. "We are nearing the end of this investigation," he told the commissioner, "and no chance can be taken which might prejudice our efforts."

Saturday afternoon, August 31, Zaneth was at the wheel of the McLaughlin-Buick, driving west out of Hamilton with Jim Harris in the passenger seat. They didn't say very much to each other until they were near Woodstock. Zaneth's mind was surely focused on how to make good on this opportunity, spending extended time with a drug-dealing bootlegger one or two levels away from Rocco Perri. In the trunk of his car—since he was supposed to be on a drug run himself—he had props: two leather club bags, which he hoped Jim Harris wouldn't ask to look inside, because whatever they contained, it wasn't drugs.

As they entered the outskirts of Woodstock, Harris saw a gas station coming up and told Zaneth to pull in. This was unexpected. As Zaneth rolled to a stop, he saw two men and a woman waiting in a parked Buick sedan with New York plates. Harris got out of the car, walked over to the Buick and leaned in for a brief word. A moment later he came back and asked Zaneth to come and meet his friends.

The bootlegger said that he'd decided to go back to Hamilton, but these new people were the ones Zaneth had to impress. These were the people he'd be doing business with, once they were satisfied. He introduced "Arthur Anderson" to all three people in the Buick, but apparently the most important one was the man at the wheel: Frank Poles.

Once again Zaneth had to adjust on the fly. He must have felt like a bouncing ball—here was another set of unknowns, another group of personalities to figure out on the way to Chicago. But after a moment's conversation in the August sun, Zaneth agreed that he would meet Frank Poles and his friends in a few hours at the Windsor ferry terminal. Poles obviously wanted to see how Zaneth got his drugs over the border.

As soon as he arrived in downtown Windsor, Zaneth drove to the Crawford House Hotel, a grand, chandeliered edifice at the corner of Ferry Street and Sandwich Street (before it was renamed

Riverside Drive West). There, he checked one of his club bags, then continued on to the ferry dock.

When they were standing together on the ferry as it slowly made its way across the Detroit River, Frank Poles asked Zaneth the question he'd been expecting: How was he going to get his drugs into the United States without being detected? Zaneth told him the drugs were coming across the river by speedboat. They would be transferred from the club bag into a wooden box, and he had a man waiting to take them over.

The foursome spent the night in Detroit, Zaneth somewhere on his own, presumably receiving his drugs, and the Poles trio out drinking, or so they said. He didn't see them until noon the next day, but once they were together the trio wanted Zaneth to stay with them. Avoid the heavy midday traffic, they suggested. Wait and we'll leave together this evening. They didn't leave Detroit until 8:50 p.m., then stopped for the night in Coldwater, Michigan. In the morning, the group made a side trip to see some "Italian friends of theirs" in the Chicago suburb of Cicero. It was a long visit; they didn't pull into Chicago until after 11 p.m.

Everyone was tired, and Zaneth wanted to break away from the group for the night, but they wouldn't let him. They wanted Zaneth to take them for a drink at his friend Patrick Horan's joint, the Garage Café.

Even late at night, the city was clogged with traffic, and as Zaneth made his way to 60 East 30th Street, he had plenty of time to worry about whether his efforts to establish an identity there would pay off. "I knew perfectly well that the drinks were used as an excuse," he reported. "What they wanted to know was if I knew Pat Horan and if I were allowed with strangers in such a place." To Zaneth's relief, as he reached the entrance with his three watchful guests, "The negro who guarded it gave me the high sign and said,

'Hello, Arthur. Pat wants to see you.'" After a few drinks, Poles asked Zaneth to get them some beer and a bottle of liquor to take back to the hotel. From Horan he was able to get a pint of bourbon and four bottles of draught beer, and he gave them to Poles and his friends once they got to the Great Northern, an enormous sixteen-storey, five-hundred-room hotel that had made its name during the 1893 World's Fair. That's where Zaneth finally left them, supposedly to sleep in his own bed. This was Arthur Anderson's home base, after all.

For the next two days, Zaneth saw the trio as little as possible. He had other cases he was working on with Clarence Converse at the Treasury Department, and as he came and went he had to make sure he wasn't followed. He also wanted to minimize the amount of time he left himself open to prying questions. Poles, who lived in Welland or Thorold, seemed to be a cousin of Rocco Perri, and his favourite conversation topic was Zaneth's informant, Jim Curwood. Whenever he had a chance, he carefully probed Zaneth about Curwood, asking how long he'd known the man, whether he had ever lived in Windsor, ever worked for someone in Ottawa with the Mounted Police. They seemed to be certain Curwood was connected to the police somehow. Zaneth tried to offer believable explanations for why they'd been working together—Curwood had been a decent dealer, had sold Zaneth drugs a few times without trouble—while distancing himself from him as much as possible.

Finally, they agreed to leave as a foursome on the morning of Thursday, September 5. Zaneth picked up his now "empty" club bag in Windsor and they arrived back in Hamilton around suppertime on Friday.

Zaneth felt good about the trip. As Anderson, he'd portrayed himself as Jewish and never given away that he understood Italian, so he'd been able to pick up nuances from remarks between Poles and his friends. He knew they'd come to Chicago for no other reason than "to trail me, watch my actions and see just whom I would get in touch with. I believe that I have played my part carefully."

His only worry was the ongoing Curwood problem. But he'd seemed to weather that as well. And Superintendent Jennings was doing his best to ensure Curwood stayed out of Hamilton. At the moment he was in Toronto, where he'd been ordered to stay. And just in case, Jennings had assigned their Toronto agent, Ernest Tomlinson, to keep him under surveillance.

Before Zaneth left Hamilton that Friday, he told Harris that on his way back from Montreal the following Wednesday, September 11, he expected a definitive answer. Both Harris and Poles insisted they would have good news.

WHAT they had for Zaneth the following Wednesday was a surprise.

Zaneth arrived in Hamilton around lunchtime, pressing for a deal—the Italiano trial was just days away—and Harris spent the day telling him to be patient. There was someone who still had to look him over, to be satisfied he was safe to do business with. After it got dark, things started to happen.

At around 10 p.m., Harris took Zaneth to the Athletic Hotel in Market Square—"a splendid rendezvous for underworld characters," in Zaneth's opinion—and introduced him to Joe Murphy, the proprietor. By now, the name "Anderson" had become familiar to people in the Perri organization. Murphy, who was a bookmaker for Rocco and had his hands in other illegal pots, told Zaneth he'd heard of him—and he recognized him too, as someone who'd been seen with Harris.

From the hotel they went to a place near the corner of Barton Street and James Street North and met up with bootlegger Matt

Hayes. Here was someone else who recognized Arthur Anderson—Hayes had met him back in early July when Anderson and Curwood had discussed a possible deal with Jim Crawford.

All this time, all this effort and patience—it was paying off. Arthur Anderson, the drug dealer from Chicago, was becoming accepted.

That night, at eleven-thirty, Hayes, Murphy and Harris asked Zaneth to accompany them to Bessie's, a roadhouse just outside Hamilton on Lakeshore Road. Inside, they introduced him to the owner, Teddy Bone. And Murphy told Bone that any time Arthur Anderson stopped at his place he should be given a room out of the way, as the man didn't want to be observed. Ensconced in their private room, they ordered drinks. Then, twenty minutes after they'd arrived, Matt Hayes pushed back his chair, walked over to the telephone and called someone.

Close by, Bessie Perri had been waiting for the signal. Immediately she roared up, alone, in a maroon Marmon sport roadster with a tan top. When she entered the roadhouse, Teddy Bone escorted her back to the private room. And there Frank Zaneth, Operative No. 1, was formally introduced to Mrs. Rocco Perri, the wife, he was told, of "the biggest man in Ontario." They had a brief conversation. Bessie was there only to get a good look at Arthur Anderson, to judge the man for herself. She asked him if he was Jewish, and Zaneth said he was. "Fortunately," he wrote later, "she did not speak the Jewish language to me." She stayed for one soft drink—Bessie never touched alcohol—then left.

As far as Zaneth could tell, this had been the ultimate test, and he had passed. "This woman must have been satisfied, otherwise she would have shown it right there and then, as she is just the type that would not hesitate to say what she thought."

Before he left that night, Zaneth told Harris that he thought they were putting him "through a rather stiff process, and that I was taking a big chance in stopping there to have all these people giving me the 'once-over,' not knowing who they were." But now that he had gone through that, it seemed as though anything might be possible. It seemed realistic to imagine getting evidence that would lead to shutting down arguably the biggest narcotics ring in the country. But there wasn't much time. The schedule for the Italiano trial called for Operative No. 1 to testify on September 23. Zaneth asked his superiors to let him stay on the investigation until the last possible moment.

On the evening of Wednesday, September 18, Murphy and Harris met again with Zaneth in their private room at Bessie's. Zaneth had spent much of the day with Murphy, who'd asked him to drive him into Toronto to deliver a small club bag to someone at an Italian restaurant in the heart of the Ward. Now, with drinks in their hands and cigarette smoke in the air, Harris told Zaneth the only thing in the way of a deal with him was Jim Curwood. See, explained Harris, Curwood was in Windsor before. He'd tried to make a case there against someone connected to the Perri gang— that was the Archie McFarlane case—and now he was working with Arthur Anderson, who wanted so badly to make a deal with the same gang. It seemed fishy.

Zaneth protested as strongly as he could. He said that he had completely severed his connection with Jim Curwood. He had nothing to do with him. This business was just between the two of them, Arthur Anderson and Jim Harris. "Curwood didn't enter into it in any way shape or form."

Harris got up to make a phone call. Twenty minutes later he was signalled, stepped out of the room, and came back in with half an ounce of cubed morphine, identical to the goods seized at Ned Italiano's place. He set it in front of Zaneth and told him to give it a good look. If he was satisfied, then on his way back from Montreal on Monday or Tuesday, they would be able to make a deal at twenty-five dollars an ounce.

That was no good. On Monday, Zaneth would be taking the stand as a witness. He played it cool, saying he had commitments next week with his connection in Montreal. But if they were willing to sell to him tomorrow, he would be there. Harris said he would do what he could. But the next day, he told Zaneth the big boss was out of town. They would have to wait until next week.

Back in Toronto, Zaneth tried to figure out how he could make this work. "If it is at all possible for me to return to Hamilton on Monday morning on a hurried trip, I would like to do so," he wrote. "I would be able to be back in Toronto on the afternoon of the same day and if my testimony is not required until the next day it would be in the interests of this investigation."

But it wasn't possible. In a Toronto courtroom, on Monday, September 23, a plain brown-leather suitcase was set on the table in front of prosecutor T. N. Phelan, KC. He opened the lid to reveal a $3,630 cache of drugs: thirty-three small, brick-shaped packages, each wrapped in red paper and tied with yellow string, each package containing 110 one-dollar cubes of morphine. Zaneth took the stand and testified that his undercover agent had introduced him to Tony Defalco, who introduced him to Tony Roma, who in turn introduced him to Ned Italiano. He talked about giving marked money to Tony Roma for six ounces of cocaine and two ounces of morphine, money subsequently found during a raid four hours later. As he spoke, which wasn't for long, he was surely scanning the courtroom for people who might recognize him.

Zaneth's testimony, as well as that from other witnesses, including Ernest Tomlinson and Detective Constable Mathewson, was enough to put away Tony Defalco and Ned Italiano for six months each. Fifty-one-year-old Tony Brassi, who had been living in Italiano's house, tried to take the brunt of the penalty by pleading guilty to five counts of illegal possession of morphine and cocaine. He got three years in Portsmouth Penitentiary. "It would have been a longer sentence if he were a younger man," said the judge.

Tony Roma, having jumped bail, failed to show his face at the trial that day. No doubt Frank Zaneth wished he could have done the same. He drove back to Hamilton that evening, arriving at 7:10 p.m. It was a gutsy, risky decision, to try to keep the deception going after he'd revealed himself at the trial. Harris asked him to come to Matt Hayes's place at ten o'clock, and when Zaneth got there he found Harris, Murphy and Hayes deep in conversation. When they greeted him, they were pleasant enough, but something had changed. "They seemed cold and uninterested," Zaneth reported, "and it appeared that something was weighing heavily on their minds."

Their connection was lost, Harris told him. Their "New York man had flown the coop" (an allusion to Tony Roma, who'd absconded to New York State) and they couldn't say when, if ever, they'd be able to do a deal. For a while they talked about Jim Curwood—Harris claimed to have "positive proof" that he was employed by the RCMP in Toronto. And Zaneth surmised that Curwood had let something leak. "This informant, while under the influence of liquor, would say most anything and I fear that it was during one of his drunken bouts that he let out who he was and also probably who I was."

Zaneth was convinced his appearance in court had not been what soured the deal, but Superintendent Jennings wasn't so sure. "After his appearance in court on Monday I am quite satisfied that those connected with the ring in Hamilton were posted as to his identity," Jennings typed at the bottom of Zaneth's report. If this was true, then it was equally possible that Zaneth's identity had been blown at the preliminary hearing; that the Perri gang had known all along and had toyed with him, just to see what they could learn about the RCMP's investigation.

Jennings wanted the commissioner to know he was eager to put someone else on the case as soon as possible, but he was frankly at a loss as to who it would be. "At the moment I know of no one who could follow up this investigation effectively." One thing he could do, in the meantime, was fire the informant, Jim Curwood. "Q's services are no longer required and he can be paid off at the end of this month." He also wanted to comment, for the record, about the fine work done by Operative No. 1. "It is through no fault of his own that he is unable to bring [this investigation] to a successful conclusion. He has taken great risks and he has shown considerable initiative in following up this case."

Staring at the end of his investigation, Zaneth wasn't just frustrated and disappointed. He was also impressed. "There is no doubt this is the cleverest gang of drug runners in the country," he wrote. "Every one of these men used to be employed by Rocco Perri in rum running and when the liquor racket was exhausted they turned to narcotic drugs. I may also say that Mrs. Perri is the brains of the whole gang and nothing is being done without her consent."

Zaneth may have understated Rocco's authority as the head of the gang, and even his brains, given that for all his efforts Zaneth had never managed to meet him. But there was no doubt about Bessie's influence over the drug racket, and her smarts in staying safe from prosecution.

Funny thing about smarts, though: events will sometimes prove they don't always work to one's advantage. Given what was coming, it would have been much better for Bessie Perri had she been caught and put away.

23

AGGUATO
Ambush

No matter what Helen Groves said to Tony Roma in Mrs. Frada's kitchen, Rocco didn't abandon his friends. That wasn't good for business. It's true he couldn't show his hand in the September drug trial, couldn't allow himself to be connected to Italiano and the rest by showing up in court or having Bessie sign for bail, things he'd been happy to do in the past. But he could help in other ways.

A new RCMP informant named Pietro Licastro, who worked in construction in Hamilton, had his ears open to the workings of the Perri syndicate and knew that Roma was a key man for Rocco in the drug trade. So it was no accident that Roma (along with Italiano) managed to find the money to pay his own bail after his arrest in June. Licastro told the RCMP that Rocco often "furnished Roma with sufficient funds to keep him going from time to time and also assisted on the providing of bail for the arrested parties." And since it would weaken the cases against the other men if Roma never appeared for trial, Rocco arranged to get him out of the country, and probably helped "Mrs. Roma" join him some time later.

Money well spent, Rocco would have said. As long as he had

the backs of his men, they had his. He had a knack for thinking ahead. He took his time, never acted precipitously. No matter what his immediate interests, he kept the bigger picture in mind. It was true with his men; it was true with the official palms he greased. In a moment of reflection he would one day say, "I have never done anyone a bad turn in my life. I always paid. That is why I was the king of the bootleggers." It was the kind of thinking that allowed some Sicilians and Neapolitans to trust him almost as much as his Calabrian kin. It allowed politicians to consider him an asset. In October of 1929, people were saying that if the Ontario Liberals won the next provincial election, interim leader William Edmund Newton Sinclair would put Rocco on the Liquor Control Board, to act as his "strong man." People in positions of power knew they could work with Rocco Perri.

This kind of thinking didn't come as naturally to Bessie. She had a way, said a Perri insider, of "upsetting the applecart, so far as fixing the police was concerned." Once, a police official who was throwing a party had someone call the Perris to get three cases of whisky. Bessie answered the phone, and when she heard the request she told him to go hell. "I can't afford to hand out whisky anymore to the police," she said.

Rocco smoothed that one over by sending the official five cases of whisky and promising more whenever he asked, and he tried again to convince Bessie of the value in keeping the police happy. But she would not change.

||||||||||||||||||||||||||||||||||||

F RANK ZANETH KEPT WORKING ON THE PERRI FILE, EVEN AS the world around him neared a crisis. In mid-September, the New York stock market was seen to be "staggering under the weight" of frenzied investors, many of whom had borrowed money to get into the market, some taking out mortgages on their homes to buy shares on margin. By the beginning of October, even Britain's chancellor of the exchequer was voicing concern over the "orgy of speculation." On Wednesday, October 23, Strathearn Boyd Thomson, the editor and publisher of Toronto's *Hush* tabloid, sent his October 24 issue to the printer, telling his readers to "Get Out of Wall Street Now."

They would have had to act quickly. The first major panic hit the morning of October 24, as an avalanche of selling wiped about $3 billion off the books. It was, wrote the Associated Press, "the most terrifying stampede of selling ever experienced on the New York Stock Exchange." And it wasn't over. Some 12.9 million shares had sold on what became known as Black Thursday. Then came Black Monday, four days later, with more than nine million sold, and the "blind panic" of Black Tuesday, as investors dumped a record 16.4 million shares. That two-day plunge alone constituted a drop of about 25 percent of the market and meant a loss of over $30 billion. Stock markets around the world quickly followed suit.

Throughout the crash and the tumultuous aftermath, Frank Zaneth—who hadn't the time nor the money to worry about the stock market—continued to field reports of the various ways in which the Perri gang was getting its drugs. Superintendent R. Y. Douglas, director of the RCMP's criminal investigations branch, asked Zaneth to come to Ottawa to brief everyone on how the Perri narcotics were being funnelled through Bridgeburg, Ontario. As far as Douglas was concerned, nothing was more important than rounding up the Perri gang, and he wanted Operative No. 1 on it full time. "He is to be detailed entirely to this investigation," Douglas directed. He gave Zaneth full authority. How long to go at it, how deep, when to lay off, whom to enlist as agents, whether to buy drugs in order to establish his credentials—it was all up to him. And Douglas directed the commander of O division in Toronto to give Zaneth his full co-operation. "He is to be given the assistance of members of your command when circumstances require it and is to be furnished with the necessary motor transport upon request." No more haggling over the damn McLaughlin-Buick.

Tony Roma seemed to be a crucial cog in the organization, and Zaneth tracked sightings of him from Thorold to Bridgeburg to Buffalo. He drove to New York City and roamed poolrooms and blind pigs in the Italian section, showing Roma's picture in every low-down dive. He chased a rumour to Newark, New Jersey, where Roma's son owned a bakery. But wherever Zaneth went, Roma had already been and gone.

A breakthrough came in April 1930 when information Zaneth put together from several sources led him to Philadelphia. It seemed that Roma was sequestered in a house somewhere in the city's Italian section. With the help of two Philly detectives and some local federal investigators, Zaneth eventually found a source who placed Roma on or near South Seventh Street. There was a restaurant nearby, so he began to stake it out, observing the comings and goings of waiters, cooks and customers. One of Zaneth's strengths was an ability to recognize faces quickly. Before long, he caught a glimpse of Helen Groves and tailed her straight to the house where Roma was staying. For one heart-pounding moment, he actually spotted Roma in his hideout, obscured by a set of curtains.

But not all, in fact maybe none, of the gumshoes helping Zaneth were on the level. At the time, American federal narcotics operatives were notoriously corrupt. It seems that their interference prevented Roma's arrest.

That close call, the threat of Zaneth's persistence, and the fact that by now he was fed up with running were enough to prompt

Roma to offer Zaneth a bribe to quit chasing him. The offer came to Zaneth through one of the crooked Philly cops, and if Zaneth had been a different kind of man, he might have taken it. But he proudly refused, telling them "nothing in this world" would push him off the hunt. And so Tony Roma kept running and eluded his pursuer for a while longer.

The rest of O division kept looking into how the Perri gang was getting its narcotics. Informant Pietro Licastro had them coming in via Rocco's old bootlegging network, through Joseph Serianni in Niagara Falls. The assistant director of investigation for Canadian National Railways, J. P. Scott, reported opium moving by passenger train from Vancouver to Bridgeburg. There the opium was transferred to motorboats that took it across Lake Erie and returned from the United States with loads of morphine and heroin. A newspaper reporter digging into the gang's activities informed the Mounties that some of its drugs were coming from the United States by air—first via seaplanes landing on the lake near Burlington, then by silk parachutes dropping into an old Hamilton flying field. Later, Zaneth learned from the same source that the Perri gang was getting drugs shipped in tins hidden in coal bunkers on Canada Steamship Lines barges, which unloaded at the north Hamilton docks of the Steel Company of Canada or the United Fuel Investments Company.

Any or all of these routes may have been used. Rocco may even have been bringing in drugs via an underwater cable system (although that tip came from an informant named "Baldy" Nicholson and seemed to Mathewson more like a "yarn"). The significant fact was that the drugs were coming steadily from some powerful people—probably including the New York narcotics ring that had been run by Arnold Rothstein before his 1928 murder—and flowing through the Perri network to every corner of Ontario.

The other fact that began to impress itself more and more upon authorities and those associated with the Perri gang was that, where narcotics were concerned, Bessie was in charge. She had important connections—first to Rothstein and then to Jack (Legs) Diamond, a flamboyant bootlegger and drug trafficker with whom Bessie was apparently seen dining at the Morrison Winter Garden in Chicago. ("Legs told me she was the slickest woman he had ever known," said the man who saw them. "But he was always leery about trusting her.")

Bessie used her ability to move in glamorous circles to gain access to prestigious new narcotics markets. She hosted banquets in her home's ostentatious dining room beneath a crystal chandelier that set off the buffet of diamonds around her neck. She was said to supply personally at least one Toronto society doctor who was rumoured to deliver drugs hidden in boxes of chocolates to wealthy Rosedale women. If she could never be one of the women invited to tea with Lady Eaton at Ardwold, the Eaton mansion high on the Davenport Hill, she could at least profit from their weaknesses. For a once-impoverished Jew from the Ward, this was its own kind of victory.

Most of the money, however, came through an expanding network of dealers selling to addicts in the general population. That meant she had to deal with the gang members, and here her style was very different from Rocco's.

The practice of taking care of his men and their families while they did time in jail ended when Bessie made the decisions. Some of those wives and children went hungry—Ned Italiano's family was one of those affected—and her stinginess made Bessie no friends. It didn't help that she had no buffer of goodwill. Rocco treated his boys like cousins and friends because that's what they were. Keeping the *paesani* happy and toeing the line was far more challenging for someone who wasn't of the culture. Over the years, for instance, Bessie had done her best to learn Italian. But when gang members came to the house, they would often slip into dialects she could not decipher. It infuriated her and she insisted they speak a language she could understand. "She could not fit in with Italians," said one of them. No matter how important she was to the success of the gang, writer Antonio Nicaso has observed, Bessie remained in their eyes a *fimmina*, Calabrian for "woman." Maybe this is why the adjective "overbearing," or its Calabrian equivalent, came to be applied to Bessie. Rocco was loved. She was not.

At the same time, under Bessie the Perri gang added more fear and intimidation to its methodology. A Port Colborne liquor exporter was walked at gunpoint through a hotel lobby into a waiting car, and a Niagara Falls man saw his house broken into, his furniture busted up and his dog killed—all, it was said, because they had turned down the opportunity to help Bessie move her product.

The more Bessie took control of the gang, moving it away from bootlegging and toward drug trafficking, the more the men complained to Rocco. The more he deferred to Bessie, the more he risked losing their respect. The growing rumours of Bessie's own infidelity—not just during her solo trips to the United States, but certainly then—heated the friction between them. In the summer of 1930, Bessie confided to Mae Rosen, a close friend and the daughter of Rabbi S. Levine of the Hess Street Synagogue, that she and Rocco were fighting constantly.

One of those arguments had to do with a recent trip to Chicago, when Bessie had resisted taking on a new supply of dope that was far more powerful than usual. Bessie worried about the drug's effect. Rocco, who knew all about watering down hard liquor, and about working with suppliers, wanted her to accept the drug they were offering. He knew that if they didn't, their suppliers could easily find someone else to work with, or worse.

And there was another problem, linked to the product they had once controlled. The United States, still locked under Prohibition, continued to thirst for Canadian liquor—to the tune of about $26 million worth smuggled over the border every year. But the beefed-up U.S. Coast Guard had made it harder for the smaller, less organized bootleggers to get it. Successful rum-running required the coordination that only bigger players could manage. In June 1929, a *Toronto Daily Star* reporter learned that "a giant combine of Great Lakes rum runners" had made plans to work together, creating a system to shift liquor runs to Lake Erie, Lake Huron or Lake Ontario to avoid the interference of law enforcement.

Increasingly, it also required firepower. That same June, a Detroit rum boat fired on a U.S. Coast Guard vessel, forcing it to turn back. The following month, the Coast Guard came gunning, unleashing about five thousand rounds, from rifles and machine guns, at rum-runners on the Detroit River and the western end of Lake Erie. The number of arrests and seizures climbed, and as Canadian customs worked more diligently to catch boats trying to bring liquor back into Ontario, rum-runners had to dump more and more of their loads. On one particularly bad day, according to historian C. W. Hunt, three thousand cases of bottles in burlap bags went over the side into Lake Erie.

The hardest blow came when the Dominion government put a serious legislative stopper in the flow of liquor across the border. A major amendment to the Canada Export Act, which became law on June 1, 1930, finally made it illegal to export liquor to countries under Prohibition. That meant boats could no longer get clearance papers for shipments to the United States, and any boats ostensibly taking loads to a country like Cuba had to put up double bonds, which wouldn't be paid back until the liquor had reached its destination. Suddenly bootlegging was not only more dangerous, it was more costly.

All things considered, the game had changed. "The amateurs are out now, with things so strict," said the proprietor of a St. Catharines speakeasy. It was a contest for serious players only—gangs with big bankrolls and big guns, like Detroit's ruthless Licavoli Squad or the Purple Gang in the western part of the Great Lakes. To the east, it took people like the Staud brothers of Rochester, who were willing and able to equip their fifty-foot cruiser, the *Dorothy*, with two twelve-cylinder airplane engines and a .50-calibre machine gun.

On the other hand, perhaps it took someone like Rocco Perri.

The greater need for co-operation between bootlegging gangs required a certain mindset and a particular set of skills—the very things at which Rocco excelled. He had proved his ability to form alliances, and demonstrated his willingness to avoid regional hostilities in the pursuit of profit. If anyone could act as the calm centre of a multifaceted organization, it was Rocco.

It seems that others recognized this. Judging from hints and clues buried in newspaper and police reports, it appears that pressure began to build—both from inside the gang and from outside—to pull Rocco and his outfit away from Bessie's narcotics dealings, and back into large-scale bootlegging. One of those trying to convince him may have been Frank Ross. In the year since his name surfaced so often in Frank Zaneth's investigations as a Perri lieutenant in the drug game, Ross (a.k.a. Frank Sylvestro) had developed into a competitor. He'd bought a large home at 196 MacNab Street North and built his local dealings in dope and prostitution to the point where they were said to rival the Perris'. Now he would have wanted the Perri gang to focus on liquor so that the drug racket could be his alone.

Whoever it was who wanted to convince Rocco to return full time to the liquor game, Rocco himself seemed willing; he'd always preferred bootlegging to drugs. It was a chance to regain his power and prominence. The only impediment was Bessie, who was adamantly opposed.

As the heat of the summer of 1930 grew, so did the pressures. Rocco's apparent acquiescence to his wife contributed to a perception of weakness, and one or more of the gangs eyeing the Perri territory began to get bold. There was a night in July when Bessie had just done a collection run and come back loaded with cash. Occasionally the Perris would hide this money overnight at the Bay Street North home of Rocco's cousin Mike Serge and his wife, Mary—they used the kitchen stove—but that night Bessie had it with her at their home. Several men, knowing Rocco's personal distaste for guns, waited until they knew the Perris were alone. With the only other protection on the property, a vicious German shepherd guard dog named Rex, safely behind a picket fence by the garage, the men forced Rocco and Bessie into the basement, then robbed them of ten thousand dollars.

A week or two later someone—likely the same gang—tipped off police about a liquor delivery Rocco was due to make with Mike Serge. He was still serving some of his loyal customers, and on the night of August 2, OPP officers were waiting in the far north end of Hamilton, watching for Rocco's seven-passenger Marmon sedan. In his bootlegging heyday, Rocco would never have been at the wheel of the delivery vehicle, but this time he was. When he pulled up in front of a corner grocery store at Bayfield Avenue and Beach Road, Mike Serge got out to unload. Just as he lifted a load of ten one-gallon cans of alcohol out of the car, a police vehicle pulled up beside them. Only luck, or a history of goodwill, prevented Rocco from being caught with the liquor still in his trunk. He stayed calm at the wheel, while Serge, facing his second liquor charge, ran until they captured him.

In between those two related events came a murder. On July 22, the body of Philip Rumbold, a realtor from Tonawanda, New York, was discovered in the back of his Franklin coupe, which had been abandoned on a road near Port Credit, Ontario. Rumbold's violent death—by rope strangulation and a crushing blow to the back of the head—seemed to fit Port Credit, which boasted a disproportionate number of rough roadhouses. But as OPP investigators, including Inspector William Stringer, pieced together the evidence, it emerged that Rumbold had been involved in bootlegging and narcotics and had made a number of trips into Ontario. The night before his body was found, he had come to Hamilton for a meeting. The person Rumbold thought he was meeting never showed, and an hour or two later he was killed, in Hamilton, before his body was thrown into the back seat of his car and driven to Port Credit by two men.

Rumbold's murder may have been further evidence of a gang trying to push its way in, or a sign of Bessie Perri pushing back. Or perhaps it was a message to Rocco, to return to liquor full time or else. Whatever it was, it meant trouble, and there was more to come.

Two weeks after Rumbold's murder, Tony Ross was driving along the Niagara highway near Grimsby. As he motored along, someone took aim at him and fired two shots. He said later that the slugs had barely missed him, and it shook him so badly that for several days he refused to show his face. "He has been sick and had to remain in bed," his wife said. If Frank Ross was muscling in on Bessie Perri, targeting his brother could have been her way of telling him to back off.

This succession of events, combined with the animosity that was building between Bessie and Rocco, not to mention between Bessie and their men, put Bessie on her guard. One night, during an agitated conversation with Mae Rosen, she told her friend all about her troubles with the Chicago mob over the dope supply, and even admitted that she expected someone to try to get rid of her. She seemed to know instinctively what Renaissance philosopher Niccolò Machiavelli had once warned: that beloved leaders were safe, because conspirators would lack to the courage to harm them, but hated leaders ought to fear everything and everyone.

Don't be surprised, Bessie told Mae, if you hear that I have been killed.

EARLY on Tuesday, August 12, Rocco appeared in court with Mike Serge on the August 2 liquor charges. He had a new lawyer—a few months earlier, his faithful advocate, Michael J. O'Reilly, had risen from his chair in front of the magistrate and dropped dead of a heart attack. Now he was defended by a Conservative MPP named William R. Morrison, KC, who convinced the judge there was no evidence against his client. Mike Serge had pleaded guilty and said that Rocco hadn't even known what was in the package in his trunk. Serge was sentenced to three months in the Barton Street jail, and everyone knew he'd taken the rap for his friend.

It was an entirely routine court appearance. Rocco even made a joke during the proceedings that had everyone laughing, and one would have thought that afterward he would have been his normal, smiling self. But later that day, just before three o'clock, someone saw Rocco in the back of a grey touring car driving through the intersection of King and James streets. Two young men in the front appeared carefree, but Rocco, in the back seat, looked "haggard and worn." It was as if he was caught in the middle of something deeply troubling.

That night, Bessie and Rocco were at home expecting a narcotics shipment from Rochester. Given the complex network that linked elements of the underworld, the drugs were probably from Charles (Lucky) Luciano, the Sicilian gangster who was now running Rothstein's New York organization, and they were likely being delivered by men from the Stefano Magaddino gang. When three of Magaddino's men arrived at Rocco's house, they handed over the package and waited for payment. Then, according to reliable information that Frank Zaneth received, something unexpected happened.

Maybe Bessie had already paid for the drugs and Magaddino's men didn't believe her. Or maybe Luciano wanted to establish new terms. Maybe it had already been agreed that from here on in Bessie had to cut Frank Ross in on their trade, and now she was reneging on the deal. Whatever the reason, when the men insisted on payment she refused. She told them that if they wanted money for this dope, they could "go to the law."

Rocco was enraged. He knew these men. He knew what Bessie's defiance could mean. He insisted she pay, and the two of them argued furiously. But Bessie wouldn't budge and ordered the three men out of her house. Who knows what thoughts raced through Rocco's mind as he watched the men from Rochester drive away.

THE next day came decidedly cool for a mid-August Wednesday. The temperature rose barely to the mid-seventies, then dropped as the day progressed. It was a good day to get things done.

At one o'clock, the Perris got ready to leave the house. Bessie wore a light, fur-trimmed tweed coat over a white silk dress. She had on peach-colored stockings and white shoes. And of course she wore her diamonds; on her fingers and around her neck, ten thousand dollars' worth. She couldn't help herself.

She and Rocco walked through their white enameled kitchen, down the stairs at the back of the house and through the screen door into the double garage. Rocco walked between the cars, the big Marmon sedan on the south side to the left, where it had been sitting since Rocco's most recent arrest, and the sporty Marmon roadster on the right. He went to unlock the garage door and swung the north half open wide. After they climbed into the roadster, Rocco stepped on the clutch, brought the engine to life, and backed down the property into the lane. They drove off, leaving the sedan where it was parked and the garage door open.

They headed up the lane to Bold Street, turned right and then left, heading about eleven blocks north to pick up Mary Serge at her home at 163 Bay Street North. From there, along with a friend named Tony Marini, they went to see Mike Serge in the Barton Street jail. Rocco didn't intend to let his brother-in-law and cousin rot in that lousy place. He told Mike he was going to have him moved to the jail farm, "where he would be more comfortable." After the visit, the group drove to William Morrison's office so that Rocco could discuss that matter and settle up their legal bill. Morrison happened to be out and wasn't due back until four o'clock, so Bessie and Mary went shopping while Rocco waited in the office.

Once the errands were accomplished, they returned to the Serge house. Rocco later recalled that Bessie had bought a new dress, and that she modelled it for him. Apparently the friction of the night before had passed. He told Bessie that she looked beautiful. Then, by Rocco's account, he hugged her, kissed her and said that he loved her. After all their recent fighting, this was unexpected. For Bessie, it must have been a moment of joy and relief.

"Roc," she said, "do you mean it?"

At some point late in the afternoon, Rocco left with Tony Marini for Sheaffe Street. There was an empty grass lot on Sheaffe and Rocco would later explain that he'd gone there wanting to play *bocce*. Maybe he did. But other things could have drawn him there. His twenty-eight-year-old brother, Mike, who had been living at Rocco and Bessie's place since coming over from Italy some months earlier, now had a room on Sheaffe Street. Rocco might have been going there for a visit. But then, there'd be no reason to lie about that.

The other possible destination—one Rocco would have wanted to keep private—was Tony Ross's blind pig. Maybe Rocco left the Serges' house because he had things to discuss with Ross, trouble to smooth over, perhaps, or arrangements to make. He would go there twice that day, once in the afternoon, and again later around supper—both times, he would tell police, to do some lawn bowling—so something needed his attention.

Eventually they all settled down at the Serge residence for a night of cards. Bessie and Rocco were just into their forties and, at least according to Rocco, this is how they spent their evenings now, playing cards at the Serges' house. Rocco would say later that "we used to go there every night, pretty near." That night it was Mary Serge, Tony Marini and one or two others at the table with the Perris. The tall and wavy-haired Mike Perri could have joined them, but recently he had been spending a lot of his evenings back at 166 Bay Street South, getting to know the Perris' pretty new live-in maid, Mary Latyka. That's where he was now, apparently taking advantage of their few hours alone.

The card players sipped tea and ginger ale while Bessie glittered in her fortune in diamonds. At a little before eleven, the Perris decided it was time to go. Bessie went to the telephone to call

Mary Latyka. "I am coming home," she told her maid. Perhaps she intended to interrupt whatever Mike and the girl might be getting up to, or maybe it was her signal to Mary to get her bed ready. It turned out that, when she called, Mike was sitting in the bathtub; he didn't get to take baths where he was staying.

A short while later, with Bessie in the Marmon's passenger seat, Rocco drove south along Bay. In the few minutes they had, Rocco would recall, they talked about whether it was time to trade in their Marmons for new ones. The huge new Marmon Sixteen was said to be the most advanced car in the world, capable of reaching one hundred miles per hour. Rocco thought they were likely to lose a lot of money on the sale, but Bessie scoffed. What was two or three hundred dollars to them?

They crossed King Street, where Rocco lifted a friendly hand to a policeman standing on the corner, and five blocks later turned west on Bold Street. Immediately Rocco swung the roadster left to head down the unlit laneway running behind the Bay Street houses from Bold toward Duke Street. At the end of the lane, on Duke, there was a car idling in the darkness.

At 166 Bay Street South, on the second floor, Mike Perri called from the bathroom to ask Mary Latyka for a towel.

At about 11:20, Rocco steered the roadster off the lane, up and neatly through the open door of the garage. He pulled the car in tight to the north side, to give Bessie room to open her door without dinging the side of the sedan parked to the right. He kept the roadster's headlights shining against the front wall, and as Bessie climbed out he handed her the key to the house and said, "Put the light on." He meant the garage light—there was a switch at the top of the stairs, by the kitchen. He slid across the seat after her and stood between the cars as she walked toward the door at the front of the garage.

In the house, on the second floor, Mary Latyka reached through the bathroom door to hand Mike Perri his towel. Below, in the garage, lit up by the roadster's headlights, Bessie Perri was walking around the front fender of the big Marmon, past a cluttered area that included part of an old stove, tire chains and a long rectangular tin for planting ferns hanging on the wall. She was about to lift her hand to pull open the screen door.

A thunderous shotgun blast hit the wall near her head. It was a missed shot, knocking the tin off its nail. Either Bessie or Rocco, or both of them, screamed.

Two more blasts came, from two guns. The first tore through Bessie's neck and jaw by her right ear, exiting under the lobe of her left and plastering bits of skin, blood, bone and hair against the brick wall. The second shot hit her low in the right shoulder blade and ripped through her ribs and right lung. As the garage filled with gun smoke, she fell back, dead, on top of the gardening tin, her head near the front wheel of the sedan, her feet toward the screen door she had almost reached.

And Rocco—what did he do, as his wife was being killed? It's hard to be sure; each time he was asked, by the police or the press, he described the events and his actions slightly differently.

When the first blast came, Rocco told the *Toronto Daily Star*, "I had just started towards the [rear garage] doors." Which meant he had to turn back. "I ran towards Bessie and grabbed her coat, trying to push her into the doorway."

Hamilton Police Detective Digby Sharpe told the subsequent inquest that Rocco had told him, "He was alongside of her when the shot was fired. Thinking she had got in the door he immediately turned around and ran out of the garage."

A third version, described by OPP Inspector John Miller, who interviewed Rocco early the following day, put Rocco three or four feet from Bessie when he heard the first shot. "He reacted by trying to grab for her, intending to pull her back so that they might get out of the rear of the garage, which was still open, and reached her but was only able to get two fingers on the sleeve of her coat when he heard the second shot fired."

At the inquest on September 5, Rocco's account went like this:

Q: "She got out of the car and as she stepped out what did she do?"
Rocco: "She started to walk to open the screen door."
Q: "How far did she go?"
Rocco: "Went about two steps away from me."
Q: "When did you get out?"
Rocco: "As soon as she got out I started to get out."
Q: "What was the next thing you saw her do?"
Rocco: "I heard a shot."
Q: ". . . You heard the shot, what did you do?"
Rocco: "I turned around and screamed."
Q: ". . . Which way were you facing when the shot was fired?"
Rocco: "Facing the back door, the garage door."
Q: ". . . What did you see when you turned?"
Rocco: "Saw Mrs. Perri standing there yet. I tried to grab her, I thought she might attempt to move."

In John Miller's report, he said that when Rocco heard the second shot, "he ran out the garage door yelling for help."

Rocco told the *Star*, "There was a second shot and she stumbled, but I thought she was protected and I turned and ran to the back again. There was a third shot but when I got to the alley I could see no car."

To a reporter from the *Evening Telegram*, Rocco said, "I thought she had slipped in the screen door and was safe. I ran out the back of the garage and tried to catch whoever shot at us."

At the inquest, regarding events after the first shot, Rocco said:

Q: ". . . How long before the second [shot] was fired?
Rocco: "About two seconds."
Q: ". . . And when the second shot was fired what happened?"
Rocco: "When the second shot was fired I started to go out and when the third shot was fired I was right in front door of garage."
Q: ". . . You didn't see her fall?"
Rocco: "No, the garage was full of smoke when I left."
Q: "You heard the first shot and turned round and she was standing there?"
Rocco: "Yes, she was standing."
Q: "And when the second shot was fired you started towards her or going to get away."
Rocco: "The second shot I was going to go away."

Whether he ran toward Bessie and tried to push her through the screen door or pull her back through the rear doors to safety, whether he saw her fall or thought she was unharmed, whether he ran away from the shooting or bravely toward where he thought the shooters were, it's a certainty that Rocco ran into the alley. He ran south in the darkness to Duke Street and there turned east, past the killers' waiting getaway car. Running frantically he passed Bay and ran toward Park Street, then seemed to change his mind and turned back. He would tell Inspector Miller that he'd remembered he had a key to the front door, and he ran up Bay toward his house. "He seemed completely out of his head," said a neighbour.

As he ran, the two men who had been hiding along the far side of the Marmon sedan, squeezed into a space barely a foot wide between the car and the red brick wall, emerged into the smoke-filled garage. One of them must have checked the body as the other calmly wiped his 12-gauge shotgun clean of fingerprints with a small towel, then leaned his weapon against the back south corner of the garage. The first man took his rifle into the alley, wiped it down, set it by the dog fence and dropped the towel next to it. Then they hustled to the waiting car. But before getting in, they bent down and removed the New York licence plates that had been wired in place over the car's existing markers. Once they were in, the wheelman gunned the engine, so much so that the car briefly hopped the curb and drove along the sidewalk for a second, before heading off, barely missing a tree. They turned south down Caroline. Four blocks later they turned onto Markland and heaved a carton of unused shotgun shells out the window. As they crossed Bay, they tossed out the New York plates. From there, they probably turned south onto James Street to head up the escarpment and out of the city.

Running up Bay Street, toward his house, Rocco saw a man out walking his dog. Was it that he'd spotted this man, and not that he'd remembered a key in his pocket, that caused Rocco to turn and run toward him? The man's name was David Robbins. He'd been standing by a drinking fountain at Bay and Bold streets when he'd heard shots and wandered down toward the sound. Rocco raced up to him, apparently wild with fear, barely able to speak. "They've shot my girl!" he cried.

"Rocco seemed awfully scared," said Robbins later.

"There was a young fellow in front with a dog and I asked him to go in with me," Rocco would explain. It's hard to imagine why he would ask a stranger to come into his home immediately after a shooting, unless he wanted a corroborating witness to the scene, and to his own great distress. Incredibly, Robbins agreed.

He had to tie his dog to the veranda before coming in, and he was shaking so badly with adrenaline he had trouble doing it. In the meantime, Rocco opened the front door with his key and made his way through the house and down the cement stairs from the kitchen to the garage below. He saw Bessie's body and, he told the inquest, "tried to lift her to get her to speak to me." When he knew she was dead, he came up the stairs and told Mary to call the police. Before she did that, Mary let David Robbins in the front door.

As Robbins stepped into the house, he saw Mike Perri, dressed in shirtsleeves, running down the stairs from the second floor. Robbins made his way to the kitchen. "They were all excited and scared," he remembered. "They seemed to think they might still be there with the guns and they were afraid to go down the stairs." Yet Robbins was willing, and Rocco, having just come up, moved aside to let him descend. "The first thing I saw," he said, "was Mrs. Perri, all dressed in white I thought, and wearing marvellous jewels, lying there in a pool of blood."

24

DOPO
Aftermath

ERE MINUTES AFTER THE SHOOTING, THE HOUSE
began filling with people. Rocco had called one or more
of his closest lieutenants; word had spread to friends and
acquaintances, and to the press. They all came. Mike Romeo was
there quickly. So, apparently, was Frank Ross. Two women by the
front door embraced—"She's gone!"—others cried hysterically,
clutches of men in the hallway muttered dark theories about why
Bessie had been slain. "I do not know," whispered Mike Romeo,
"but I have a thought." He didn't elaborate.

Rocco, who staggered through the house, his face wet with
tears, seemed sure of the motive. But from the mind of someone
so savvy in the ways of the underworld, it was an incongruous one.

"I am sure they intended to rob her," he said. He said this
while holding in his right hand ten thousand dollars' worth of
diamonds—rings, a pin, a necklace, an elaborate watch—that had
been left untouched by the murderers, jewellery that he had helped
Hamilton Police Constable Kingerly remove from his wife's body
before it was transported to the morgue.

Someone needed to tell Bessie's daughters what had happened, and Mary Latyka made the call to Toronto. When she reached Gertie at her house on Euclid Avenue, she blurted : "Gertie, someone killed your mother." Gertie's scream through the phone could be heard by others in the room.

"Oh, why did you tell her that?" cried Rocco. "Poor girls, oh, the poor girls. It will kill them. They'll die on the way."

For hours after the event, Rocco presented a dual front to the friends and press around him; he was both a figure of inconsolable grief and a determined spokesman. He sobbed, he buried his face in his hands, he sat limp and slack-jawed on the chesterfield. But he forced himself to describe, again and again, his version of the events of the night—the card game, the drive home, the shooting, the running through the streets—as well as the shape of his life with the woman he had loved. "Bessie and I worked together like pals for years," he said. "All we have she helped me make."

Several reporters, awed by the luxury of the home in which they found themselves ("palatial" said the Toronto papers; "pretentious" declared the *Hamilton Spectator*), thought to ask Rocco—not even an hour after his wife had been slain—about the fortune he and Bessie had built together. "What good is that to me now?" he exclaimed to one of them. "She is dead." He sobbed to another, "If only I could have Bessie with me again I would not care if I did not have a cent. The wealth we have made is nothing to me now. I have lost my best friend."

Whenever he was asked, Rocco repeated his theory. "They were after her diamonds," he said, two days later. "She was crazy about diamonds. They may have figured too that we were carrying big money rolls as often we do." Even after Hamilton's Deputy Chief Goodman had publicly dismissed the notion of robbery as the motive, and even after denying the report that he and Bessie had recently been held up in their basement, Rocco stuck to that line. No one used the press better than Rocco Perri, and no one believed more firmly that gangsters settled their own affairs. With every word, every repetition, he was telling the murderers that what had happened would remain between him and them.

Even if few believed the robbery theory, most who witnessed Rocco's grief found it genuine and moving. The little man seemed utterly bereft. "I wish I was going with her, wish I was in that casket instead of her," he sobbed to Gertie. "What will I do now that she is gone?" Even Inspector John Miller, sixty-two years old and hardened from having worked through far too many such scenes, took it at face value when he put Rocco through a lengthy interview the next afternoon. "From the present outlook Rocco takes the matter very hard," he typed into his report, "and it would look as if the Killers were after him as well as her."

By the end of the following day, August 15, Miller's opinion had evolved. The shotgun shells—both in the guns and in the carton police found—had been altered. Someone had traced around each of the cartridges with the point of a knife, creasing and occasionally cutting through the casing to weaken it. Initially commentators thought this had been done to widen the shotgun blast so as to cover a larger area, perhaps making it easier for the gunmen to kill Bessie and Rocco both. But no. Gun experts explained that such weakening of the shell casing actually worked to narrow and compress the blast. It was a technique hunters used to shoot more precisely. And, indeed, Bessie's two shotgun wounds had been relatively small—the one through her neck little more than an inch in diameter; the one in her back not much bigger. It indicated the killers had wanted to avoid stray pellets; they had had a very specific target.

Miller had also spoken at length with RCMP Detective Constable Mathewson, the man trained by Frank Zaneth. They agreed that it was something about Bessie's connection to the boot-legging and dope racket that had killed her, and they knew her murder had not been a spur-of-the-moment decision but the end of a well-executed plan. The New York licence plates used to disguise the getaway car had been acquired on August 10, the Sunday prior to the murder—stolen off a wrecked Pontiac that had been sitting for months in the yard of the Auto Electric service garage in the northwest part of Hamilton. They also knew that Tony Papalia, ostensibly one of Rocco's men, had brought his Studebaker into the garage that same Sunday afternoon. The car had needed work on a few loose or missing bolts—bolts that, because they were fastened with lock washers, could only have been loosened deliberately. Papalia had come in with another man no one recognized, who had wandered off in the vicinity of the wrecked vehicle. What Miller didn't note in his report, and may not have known, was that Papalia happened to be a cousin of the embittered Ned Italiano, and he had links to Stefano Magaddino.

Miller and another detective took Papalia in for questioning but got nothing out of him. Rocco himself, questioned for hours the morning of August 15 in the upstairs of the house, assured the inspector that Papalia was a friend who would never do him harm. "We do not seem to be able to escape from the fact," wrote Miller, "but that Rocco Perri himself knows more about the crime than he wishes to divulge."

The inspector's investigation was also hampered by the huge numbers of people who were now streaming through the Perri residence: "We are unable to get anywhere with our inquiry with regard to Perri and those who live with him," Miller complained, "because of the great crowd hanging around the place." Earlier that day, Bessie's body had been released from the morgue. Dressed in a white shroud that exposed only her pale, still face, she now lay beneath a lacy silk veil in a gleaming three-thousand-dollar silver and bronze casket—similar, said the undertaker, to the one in which movie idol Rudolph Valentino had been buried. Hour after hour, hundreds of people came through the Perris' front drawing room to pay their respects, catch a glimpse of the murdered celebrity and ogle the luxury in which she'd lived.

The more people who came, the more the room filled with flowers. What had started as just two wreaths from close friends the night after the murder, and a huge pillow of roses, orchids and gladioli from Rocco, became dozens and then hundreds of wreaths—flower horseshoes, a flower harp, a flower chair, a blanket of flowers draped across her casket—stacked to the ceiling by two of Rocco's young cousins, who first carefully removed the cards so that thank-yous could be written and sent.

Rocco proclaimed that the waves of mourners proved how much Bessie was loved. "My people, the Italian people, worshipped her and loved her," he told a reporter late Saturday evening. "If you had been in this house since six tonight you would have seen for yourself what my people think about Bess. There must have been two thousand people here since tea time. They just poured in."

The number was roughly true, the love—mostly wishful thinking. A clock of flowers, for example, pointing to the time of Bessie's death, had been sent by "Leo and Friends," which very likely meant Jessie Leo, a Sudbury bootlegger and brothel-runner Rocco had been seeing romantically since the previous May. It was almost as if the clock was pointing to the time at which Rocco had been set free.

In fact, most of the flowers were implicit expressions of love and loyalty for Rocco. ("He is so kind to the poor," said a woman, heartbroken for him. "When anyone is sick or in trouble he gives all his heart.") In bestowing this affection upon Bessie, he may have been trying to repudiate the recent statements and actions of those who had once been closest to her. Only hours after her death, reporters had tracked down her husband, Harry Toben, now a Toronto pawn-broker, who revelled bitterly in her fate. "She died as she deserved to die," Toben said in his doorway. "Seventeen years ago she left me with two small children. She means nothing to me . . . I was kind to her, and I had a good job. I was driving a wagon. She just vanished one day, stored the furniture, and left the two little children on the streets." He shook his head, muttering, "Terrible, terrible. What has it to do with me? I don't want to talk. I won't talk." Two days later, when a reporter suggested that he might be in for a windfall from Bessie's estate, his mood changed. "Now I will be able to enjoy life," he crowed. "How soon can I get my lawyer?"

When reporters came to the door of Mrs. Bella Wexler in Toronto, she admitted to being Bessie's sister but said, "I haven't seen her in years. We have had nothing to do with her." That was apparently true for all of her siblings. Although again, when the subject of Bessie's estate arose, so did Mrs. Wexler's interest: "Do you think I would get any money, being a sister?"

Even Hamilton's Jewish community seemed to turn its back on her. Rocco wanted to do right by Bessie, and her daughters, by giving Bessie a traditional Jewish burial. But he seemed to be thwarted at every turn. Jewish leaders at first denied his request for a burial plot, even when he offered a thousand dollars to which-ever synagogue would accept her. When finally the Hess Street Synagogue relented and offered a small plot in Ohev Zedek, a small, sun-parched cemetery four miles from the city, they set it at the edge, away from the faithful. And as for the service, Rabbi Levine refused to have anything to do with it. "I do not want to be mixed up in this whatever," said the father of Bessie's good friend, Mae Rosen. "I do not want my name associated with it. I am not going to be there." A rabbi from North Carolina, who had once lived in Hamilton and happened to be visiting, agreed to officiate in his place.

In the lead-up to the Sunday funeral, the papers worked every angle. Via telegraph, a *Toronto Daily Star* editor berated his reporters in Hamilton for letting up on the competition—"WE SLACKENED UP AFTER BELTING *TELEGRAM* FIRST DAY AND MUST NOT REPEAT"—and pages filled with a lurid mixture of pathos and bloody intrigue. Mike Perri gave a reporter a tour of the murder scene, wiping tears from his eyes. Every heavy sigh from her grieving daughters, every expression of Rocco's love and any speculation linked to the shooting found new life in print. A rumour emerged that police had been given advance warning of an attempt on the Perris' lives, which Detective Crocker denied. Reporters wanted Rocco's reaction to Harry Toben's statements. ("INTERVIEW ROCCO TO GET LIFE STORY AND TELL WHY HE STOLE ANOTHER MANS WIFE . . . SPARE NO PAINS TO GET THIS COMPLETELY AND COLOURFULLY" cabled the editor.) "That man in Toronto can say what he likes," said a downcast Rocco. "I loved that woman." Someone who looked like Bessie was said to have bought shotgun shells just days before the murder and for several days readers and even police wondered: had Bessie herself bought the tools of her demise? It seemed plausible until Rocco told Inspector Miller to forget it: Italians were schooled not to trust women in anything connected to guns. Eventually the woman who had actually bought the shells came forward.

A *Daily Star* reporter named Athol Gow was sitting at the Perris' kitchen table when a tear-choked Gertie asked Rocco, "Did you see where the city of Hamilton is offering a thousand-dollar reward for the killers?"

Rocco, garbed in black, turned to Gow. "Is that true?"

"Yes," said Gow, his mind working, "and why don't you offer a reward?"

"I will do that," said Rocco. "I will make it two thousand."

Gow prodded Rocco to "make it worthwhile." The number became five grand, and the next day the headline "Perri Puts $5,000 Price on Slayers' Heads" stretched across the front page.

Every story spurred more people to come to Bay Street South. Bessie had been murdered just as athletes and spectators were gathering in Hamilton for the British Empire Games, which had been years in the planning. Now, even as crowds flocked to the Games' August 16 opening ceremonies, swelling numbers of the curious came to the street where Bessie had lived, from six-thirty in the morning to long past midnight, to play a game of Spot the Gangster. As the funeral approached, imposing cars from Chicago, Buffalo, Montreal, Detroit and Toronto pulled up with growing frequency to disgorge swaggering, diamond-studded men and their attractive companions. They came to pay their respects, along with poor and loyal Italians from Hamilton, Welland, the Niagara Peninsula and beyond. Mary Serge estimated that over the course of three and a half days, ten thousand people walked over the hardwood floors of the drawing room past Bessie's casket.

By Sunday, it was a mob. In the rising August heat, streets, sidewalks and neighbouring lawns thickened with rabid onlookers. Here and there amongst the sea of heads were known gangsters, plainclothes policemen and working pickpockets. Strangers filled the Perri garage to ogle the murder scene. On the streets around the Perri residence, the cars of the procession—twelve for the flowers alone—tried to inch through the crush in order to take their positions. Most of them were blocked. The last thousand or so well-wishers, the majority of them women, crowded up the front steps and inside along the hallway into the drawing room. As the hour of the service approached, the strain and tension grew. One young man tried to lift the white silk veil suspended over the casket

to get a better look before a guard named Sardo grabbed his arm—
"*Don't do that!*"—and ushered him from the room. Fifteen minutes
before the service was set to begin, the mourners wanted the strangers out and the doors closed, and several men had to hold the door
against people trying to push their way in. "Close the door tight,"
Rocco shouted. "Plenty have seen. It is enough." The bay window
of the drawing room was open in an attempt to get air into the
flower-scented room, and as the ruckus outside grew, guards and
police took up position on the veranda to keep people—some of
them reporters—from climbing through.

Inside the sweltering drawing room, its grey wallpaper tinted
pink by the lampshades and the light filtering through rose-hued
curtains, heat and exhaustion took their toll. As the scuffling and
shoving outside grew more intense, Gertie Maidenberg, Bessie's
eldest daughter, gave a small moan, collapsed, and had to be carried from the room. A few minutes later the visiting rabbi, Isadore
Freund, in a blue suit and grey fedora, took his position near the
enormous casket, by a candelabrum of three burning tapers, and
the mourners gathered around. Gertie, barely recovered, and
her sister Lily were helped back in for a last look. Rocco, who
had avoided looking at Bessie's body since the night of the murder—"I might break down," he explained, "I am trying to keep
myself together"—now entered the room, stood with his hands
on the casket, and shook with silent sobs.

Besides Bessie's daughters and their husbands and children, the
chief mourners included Rocco's cousin Mike Romeo, one of the
men Bessie had trusted most, and his wife; Mike Serge, who as a
favour to Rocco had been granted a day pass to attend the funeral,
along with Mary Serge and Mike's brother Joe and his wife. A married niece of Rocco's had arrived from Detroit. Somewhere in the
background stood Inspector John Miller. Before the service began

Rocco asked for his hat so that he could conform to Jewish tradition. After a brief flurry of searching, it was found and passed to
him, and the other men who had their hats handy put them on.

Rabbi Freund spoke briefly, trying to ignore the frequent shouts
of "Order! Keep that door shut!" and the incessant barking of the
guard dog in the basement. Once the service was complete, the
great job of carrying flowers out to the cars began. Twenty minutes later the tuxedoed pallbearers took their place, and Joe Romeo,
Tony Serge, Anthony Marando, Jules Speranza, Matthew Restivo
and Sam Calubro, all wearing grey silk gloves, began the struggle to
carry Bessie's casket to the waiting hearse.

The crowd outside gasped and murmured "Hush!" when the
casket appeared, and pressed in on the pallbearers as they moved.
So thick was the crush they couldn't turn to place the casket in the
hearse, and the vehicle had to be driven forward several feet to give
them room.

Some thirty thousand people lined the four-mile route to the
cemetery. Somewhere in the procession was a Calabrian named
Stefano Speranza, attending the funeral on behalf of Al Capone.
Later Speranza would write in his diary, "I never saw so many
people at a funeral, not even in the United States." In places, the
spectators stood three and four deep, some smoking cigarettes
as they waited. With the weather turned hot and dry, grass fires
broke out along the route. As the procession passed, dozens of men
stomped and beat on the flames.

Hundreds of vehicles rolled slowly along in advance of the
cortège—many of them taxis paid for by Rocco—while Rocco,
Bessie's daughters and their husbands sat behind the closed curtains
of a vehicle driven by Frank Romeo. The combination of the heat and
the slow climb up the escarpment proved too much for the hearse.
Shortly after it crested the brow, it broke down. By luck, the sheriff's

officer responsible for getting Mike Serge back to his jail cell had a rope in his Dodge and rigged up a tow. But the arrangement forced repeated stops for rope adjustments, and at each delay people pressed in on the mourners' cars, trying to peer inside.

Once at the cemetery, the cars full of flowers, unwelcome at a Jewish burial, drove past the entrance and another large grass fire that threatened a parked car. As the iron gates opened to allow in the mourners, onlookers poured in to secure a prime viewing perch. Those who couldn't get in at the gate ran to climb the fence, some breaking away pickets in order to squeeze through. From the hearse Bessie's casket was carried first into a dilapidated wood-frame holy house for inspection by the synagogue officials. Inside, as the lid of Bessie's casket was lifted, a brief crisis arose. Something about the preparation of Bessie's corpse (perhaps the body had been embalmed, contrary to Jewish custom) seemed to anger or offend the officials. "Get it out of here!" someone shouted as the lid was closed. "Get it out to the grave."

That was far easier said than done. The crowd was too thick and energized, and there were no police. To get to the graveside, the pallbearers had to fight through a pushing, jostling swarm. It got uglier as each minute passed. People trampled graves, men wrestled each other for position, women were shoved and hurt. The mourners could not get through. Rocco and Bessie's daughters were still trapped in the mayhem as the casket was being lowered into the ground. "I have never seen anything so pitifully terrible," wrote an appalled reporter.

The casket was set in a pine box in deference to Jewish tradition, and as the box began to sink past ground level, Bessie's family finally made it to her side. It was four o'clock. By then the struggle and the oppressive beating sun had drained them of all strength. As the crowd pressed in, the daughters fainted. Rocco collapsed with exhaustion and had to be saved from falling into the grave. A small unidentified man frantically fought back the crowd around Gertie and Lily while Charlie Bordonaro, Mike Serge and others grabbed Rocco under the arms and held him up. They opened his shirt and tugged loose his collar to give him air, then formed a phalanx to half carry him, nearly unconscious, to the safety of his car. "Where is Lillian? Where is Gertie?" he cried as they pushed him inside.

None of Bessie's family saw the final rituals of her internment. And according to Jewish custom, none of her diamonds went with her to the grave.

THE funeral was over, but not the investigation. At eleven-thirty the next morning, with the crowd finally dispersed, three police cars pulled up in front of Rocco's house and nine detectives emerged— an OPP contingent led by Inspector John Miller and a local group headed by now-Inspector Joseph Crocker. No doubt Miller had told Crocker how his men had already balled up the investigation— in the immediate aftermath of the murder, the Hamilton police had gathered up Bessie's jewels, money and her handbag with all her papers and notes. "And without looking over them for possible evidence," Miller would later report, "they turned the whole thing over to Rocco Perri." This unannounced search was an attempt to repair the mistake.

They spent an hour in the home. While detectives combed the house, Miller and Crocker sat with Rocco, made him go over the events of that night and tried to get him to open up about who might have wanted his wife dead. Rocco had had very little sleep over the previous four days. Concerned, Mary Serge described him as "fidgety and fretful," and he showed such signs of exhaustion that his doctor warned that without rest soon he could get very sick. Still, in the face of Miller's questioning, Rocco held fast to his ignorance. "He maintains that he does not know anything about the matter other than to say that it is an Italian gang, and that they were after him as well as her," Miller reported. "He stoutly denies that he himself did it, or would have any reason for doing so, as she was the best for him that ever lived."

Rocco also revealed—to the extent that detectives could believe him, given that he was still insisting he and Bessie had never been involved in peddling dope—that whatever money issues had existed between him and Bessie had been resolved four or five years before. It was then that their lawyer, Michael J. O'Reilly, had suggested to Bessie that they should have something in writing to protect the estate, in case anything happened to either of them.

Since her death, all the papers had been speculating about Bessie's will. When it finally came to light, it showed only a fraction of the wealth she'd amassed with Rocco—just $44,866.19, of which a mere $3,000 went to each of her daughters, and the rest, $38,866, to Rocco. Real estate accounted for $14,500 of the estate; besides the house on Bay Street South, there were two other houses in Bessie's name—a $3,000 house at 56 North Street, St. Catharines, and a $6,000 farm in Thorold. She also held four mortgages on other properties, valued at $14,215.71, and a promissory note of $2,049. Furniture worth $2,500 was mentioned in the will, and cars worth $3,500. Her jewellery was undervalued at $8,000. In the bank, just $101.29 in cash. The rest of the fortune lay somewhere hidden—exactly where, and whether Rocco could get at it, remained a mystery.

The more immediate riddle, the one that concerned police, seemed just as elusive, and Miller and Crocker were anxious to pursue all possible leads while they were fresh. As he submitted to their questions, Rocco quietly counselled the two officers to take a more Italian approach. "He says we are to[o] impatient. We want to get things quick, when it cannot be done," Miller reported. "When Italians kill like that they are pretty well covered up, and it will take time to uncover."

The following day, Inspector William Stringer joined the investigation and went with Miller to question Sidney Gogo. Given his son's death, his financial struggle after the loss of his boat and Bessie's heartless refusal to help, "he has good reason to feel hard against them," Miller wrote. But Gogo told them he had a steady job, was now happily married to Verva Dobrindt, once the wife of murderer John Trott, and had put the past behind him.

In his digging, Miller uncovered the story about Bessie's argument with the Chicago mob. He learned about her fearful confession to Mae Rosen, the daughter of Rabbi Levine, and how Levine had become so convinced another murder was coming he wouldn't touch the Bessie Perri funeral. And the more Miller looked into the men and activities of the Perri gang, the more darkly impressed he became. The dope running, the prostitution, the fear that kept people silent: "Perri has gathered a band of the toughest . . . crooks [and] murderers that ever congregated in Canada."

As to whether Rocco himself was behind Bessie's murder, Miller was clearly torn. The more he and Stringer talked to people in the area, the more he sensed that Rocco was at least capable of it, and the recent conflict between the couple gave him a motive. On top of that, Miller learned about Rocco's romantic link to the Sudbury bootlegger Jessie Leo. It seemed a telling coincidence that Leo's own husband, Joe Leo, had disappeared mysteriously in May, around the time the affair between Rocco and Jessie was supposed to have begun. Even more telling, Joe Leo had left a note before he disappeared, saying that he expected to be killed for "my woman and the money," and that if he was killed, it would be at the hand of Domenico D'Agostino, who was then one of Rocco's men.

The trouble was that nothing Miller got ever turned out to be solid. "One lead after another we follow," he wrote, "only to find nothing at the end to help us."

For several days Miller criss-crossed Rocco's southern territory, driving from St. Catharines to Niagara Falls to Bridgeburg, Fort Erie and Erie Beach. He built up a list of people he could connect to the Perri gang as current or former members—a string of some forty-five names, including Charlie Bordonaro, Frank Corde, Tony Papalia, Joe and Mike Romeo, Mike and Joe Serge, Frank Ross, Frank Longo, several others in Welland and more than a dozen in Niagara Falls. Though far from complete, it was a bigger list than anyone had put together before. But even that wasn't encouraging. "Many of the above have been interviewed," Miller reported, "and they tell us we will never find out who killed Bessie."

One thing Miller did manage to accomplish, during his many conversations with Rocco, was to get him to concede that Tony Papalia might have been involved. Miller had tried raising different subjects and ideas with Rocco to "start him thinking," and "nothing started him so much," he reported, as the matter of the New York licence plates. Miller had learned that Papalia was linked to Frank Ross's growing gang in Hamilton, along with Papalia's cousin Ned Italiano, Tony Roma, Tony Brassi—and Domenico D'Agostino, who had apparently fallen in with Ross fairly recently. He'd also learned that Bessie had angered the gang by the way she'd denied support to Italiano's family while he was in jail.

Miller raised all of this with Rocco, and then pointed out that Papalia and his cousin, Domenic Pulice, had been in the Auto Electric garage on the day the plates were stolen, and they were the likeliest ones to have done it. After thinking about it for a moment,

Rocco admitted he'd never thought of it in that light, and agreed "there might be something to it."

But he was probably just humouring Miller. Rocco must already have known all of that, just as he probably knew, even if Miller didn't, that Frank Ross stored his car in that same Napier Street garage. And it wouldn't have been long before someone mentioned to Rocco that Frank Ross, who had come to the house so quickly that terrible night, had been seen driving north on James Street moments after the murder, and that he had circled around, arriving at Bay Street South almost as quickly as the police, as if he had known without being told. (It was Milford Smith, a *Toronto Daily Star* editor devoted to the underworld beat, who gathered these bits of intelligence about Frank Ross. One of his confidential sources told him explicitly: The gunmen had driven straight from the Niagara Hotel in Buffalo, hired by Frank Ross through Charles Bordonaro. Smith tried to convince his bosses to run with the story, but it was never published.)

Before Miller left that day, just a few hours before what would prove to be a fruitless inquest into the death of Bessie Perri, Rocco told the detective something else. He said that he didn't expect to live long, and that he would probably die the same way Bessie had. In fact, he'd even gone to his lawyer's son and partner, John P. O'Reilly, and had his own will drawn up. Handwritten on legal-sized foolscap, it dictated that the bulk of his estate be left to his brother Mike, with one thousand dollars and a diamond ring to Mary Serge, and the same amount of cash to each of Bessie's daughters. And he was careful to add the following instruction: "I direct that in the event of my death occurring under any un-natural circumstances that my executor investigate same and if any of my beneficiaries are in any was [*sic*] suspected of having anything to do with my un-natural death their share of my estate shall be forfeited."

It certainly seemed to be the action of a man worried about forces working against him. What Rocco didn't mention to Inspector Miller was that later that night, after the inquest, Jessie Leo arrived from Sudbury to console Rocco in his time of grief.

PART 5

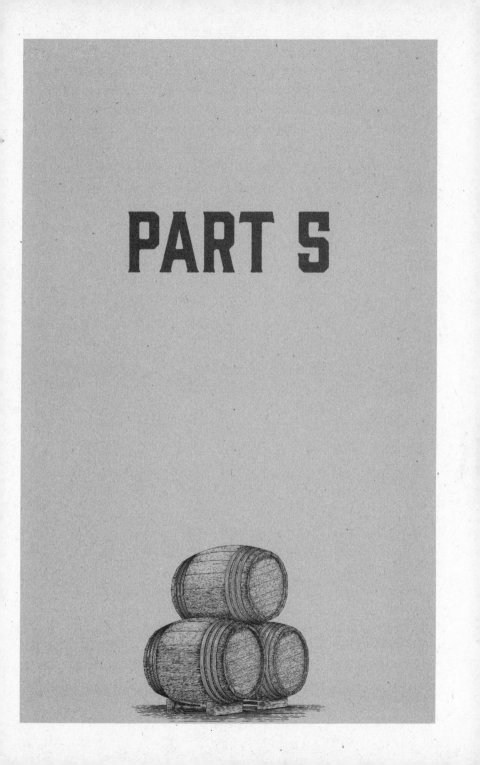

25

CAMBIAMENTO
Upheaval

FOR MONTHS AFTER BESSIE'S FUNERAL, EXHAUSTED and possibly sick with pneumonia, Rocco mostly stayed holed up inside the house on Bay Street. When he went out, he was surrounded by bodyguards—on October 15, 1930, a motorcycle officer pulled Rocco's car over because he had three other men with him in the front seat, one of them the trusty Frank Di Pietro, who took the blame.

His apparent weakness opened the door to opportunists. "Writs innumerable are being hurled at him from all quarters," wrote the tabloid *Hush*. "The little Italian is prostrated." A few years earlier, for example, the Perris had taken on a $17,550 debt with Hatch & McGuinness. Rocco himself had signed a promissory note on January 17, 1927, because Bessie had refused Harry Hatch's request. Somehow that debt had gone unpaid, and on November 3, Hatch & McGuinness sued Rocco for the debt plus interest, a total of $21,508.55. Within a few weeks, two more suits were filed against him—one by a Toronto man named Charles Calarco for $14,032, another by a former Perri driver, Andrea

Catanzariti, for a $5,636.84 promissory note. Other creditors waited in the background for Rocco to remember his obligations to them; one was Henry Corti, a Toronto printer to whom Rocco owed five hundred dollars. Some of that was for expenses Corti had incurred when Rocco, upset about the unflattering way Bessie had been portrayed in the press, had asked Corti to consult a libel lawyer for him.

Things got particularly bleak when, on December 8, in the midst of the lawsuits, Rocco's own lawyer, William Morrison, who was acting for Andrea Catanzariti, forced the seizure of Rocco's Bay Street house to cover the promissory note. A $2,100 piano, five Oriental rugs, mahogany tables and many more furnishings—even Perri's guard dog—were on the sheriff's list. Rocco was furious, no less so when Charles Calarco's lawyer tried to get in on that seizure as well, and claimed rights to some of the proceeds of any sale.

Rocco and his lawyers had to get creative. He may have investigated the possibility of taking out a thirty-thousand-dollar life insurance policy from which to borrow to pay his bills. Rocco denied that—"It's a lie!" he said. "I don't need to borrow on insurance to cover the writ"—but that's probably because he came up with a better solution. With the help of John P. O'Reilly, he raised part of the money to pay his debts by cleverly selling his house to Frank Calarco, the brother of the man suing him, for $8,600. (He remained as a tenant until February 1937 when, in a nifty bit of business, he bought the house back at the bottom of the market for less than three thousand dollars.) The Hatch & McGuinness suit took longer, but eventually Charles W. Bell successfully argued that the promissory note was invalid, because the original transaction— for whisky intended for U.S. export—had been "a conspiracy to violate the laws of the United States."

The news of Rocco's battles over his finances led the press to take liberties in other personal matters. Greatly intrigued by the prospect of an affair between Perri and Sudbury's Jessie Leo, reporters pestered them about the prospect of marriage. They published rumours that Leo had sold her luxurious twenty-thousand-dollar Sudbury home, along with her Kirkland Lake and Cochrane properties, in preparation for a move to Hamilton. Reached on the phone, Leo admitted she'd known Rocco for ten years, and that he'd visited her recently in Sudbury. But, she huffed, "How should I know whether I am going to marry him or not? He has never asked me yet."

Rocco smirked at the idea of people talking about a wedding. "They know more about it than I do." Three days later he was more definitive. "I will always be single," he said. "I decided many years ago never to marry and there is no reason now why I should."

Perhaps spoiled by all the talk of marriage, Rocco's affair with Jessie Leo cooled. In truth, he missed Bessie. It's said that he filled some of the emptiness at the house by inviting Mike Serge's brother Tony to live there with his wife, Angelina. But he still thought about his partner, the mother of his son, and he refused to abandon her in her rude grave at the edge of Ohev Zedek cemetery. In May of 1931, he assigned a man he trusted, Rosario Carboni, to buy up land next to Bessie's grave. Then he paid for a new iron fence that redefined the cemetery's shape and gave Bessie pride of place nearer the middle. A few months later, when the year required by Jewish custom had passed, he had a marble grave cover installed, and marked it with a tall and regal headstone that featured a plaque with Bessie's picture. On the anniversary of her death, wearing a black armband, he drove up the Caledonia highway to the cemetery, and laid wreaths on the grave.

But money, as you would expect for a gangster, remained the pressing issue. With Bessie gone, Rocco was all but out of the narcotics racket; it mostly belonged to Frank Ross now. That left liquor and gambling.

Bootlegging presented immediate challenges on two fronts: supply and demand. Distilleries were selling less to bootleggers because of the changes to the Export Act. And there were fewer customers. Hamilton had been hit hard by the crash of 1929. Men who had averaged forty-five weeks of work a year in 1921 now averaged thirty-eight. By December 1930, the city's textile mills were operating at 60 percent capacity. At the worst point, a quarter of the city's families were subsisting on government handouts. Things weren't much better in the rest of the province. "Times are very bad," Rocco said. "People who go to bootleggers have very little money."

Needing to keep his prices low, Rocco had to find a cheap supply, so he became a liquor manufacturer. In 1931 and '32, he had his men set up several enormous stills—it was probably more accurate to call them small distilleries—in secret locations. One example, discovered by police thanks to a tipoff, showed just how serious an operation this was. Housed in an old Concession Street mansion, and assembled without the knowledge of any of its well-to-do neighbours, it began in the cellar with five eight-hundred-gallon vats of bubbling sugar mash, heated by a state-of-the-art oil-fuelled boiler. From there the copper apparatus rose through the torn-out first floor, its arm reaching up thirty-five feet through a section of ripped-out boards on the second floor and farther into the third-floor garret, then worming down again with nearly a mile of copper tubing leading to the second-floor rectifier and condensers. There, 170-proof spirits poured like water from a kitchen tap into waiting tanks. The entire structure, expertly made and professionally assembled by steamfitters, plumbers and electricians, had an estimated value of twenty-five thousand dollars and produced six hundred gallons of high-quality liquor—generating profits of as much as $3,500—per day.

In this once-stately building, guarded by Rocco's German shepherd and hidden behind shuttered windows covered on the inside by blankets and thick velour curtains, three people in their twenties monitored the operation of this still. One of these was Mary Latyka. Two years after Bessie's murder, the maid who'd once turned down her mistress's bed was now a full-fledged member of the Perri gang. The police who rounded up the occupants noticed that the only room that hadn't been ruined by the still's construction and operation was Mary's bedroom. There she kept her furniture and lingerie perfectly tidy and clean.

A BOBCAYGEON BOOTLEGGER, A VACATIONING CNR CLERK, a ladies' man who enjoyed parties—Zaneth took on any number of roles as he investigated illegal liquor manufacturers, drug smugglers and a New York fur racket in the early 1930s. Then he was transferred to Montreal, put in charge of non-commissioned officers and constables, and given an overarching mandate to get the city's leaders of organized crime. Thus it fell to Zaneth, at the beginning of 1933, to take down Harry Davis, head of the biggest drug ring in Quebec.

Based on what he'd learned trying to get at Rocco and Bessie Perri, Zaneth knew that Davis, "one of the barons of the Montreal underworld," would be insulated from the actual crimes being committed. So from the beginning he chose a different tack—he set out to prove the *conspiracy* to commit a crime, which was a crime itself.

Now in his forties, living alone and occasionally eating in the RCMP mess, Frank Zaneth had two chief pastimes: watching pro wrestling—which he loved to the point of personally getting to know many of the wrestlers at the Montreal Forum—and studying the Canadian Criminal Code. He knew, based on precedent established long before in a British court, that conspiracy was committed the moment two or more people had agreed to do something illegal. As he would later explain in a 1937 article written for the RCMP *Quarterly*, it wasn't even necessary for the criminals to follow through on the crime they'd conceived. "The conspirators may repent and stop," he wrote, quoting a judge's ruling, "or may have no opportunity, or may be prevented, or may fail. Nevertheless the crime is complete; it was completed when they agreed." He was one of the very first RCMP investigators to take this approach.

The key was to prove the conspiracy by finding circumstantial evidence of the decision made, be it a telegram, a notebook notation, a telephone call, a bank deposit. Over the next weeks in Montreal, Zaneth pulled in fifty-six informants to tell him what they knew, then carefully analyzed their statements. The proof that ultimately tied Harry Davis to the trafficking of a million dollars' worth of narcotics came down to a small revelation by one of those informants, a man named Charlie Feigenbaum. Three years before, two Montreal drug dealers had sold a couple of pounds of morphine to undercover cops. The drugs had come from Harry Davis, and been intended for a buyer in New York City. Davis had sold the package to the two Montreal dealers only because the cubes were too big to be sold in New York. When the Montreal dealers were arrested, Davis ruefully admitted the cube-size problem to Feigenbaum.

Feigenbaum mentioned this in his interview with Zaneth three years later. Zaneth then located the seized morphine cubes in the RCMP's evidence storage. That morphine was matched to another shipment tied to Davis, and a few days later he was arrested.

To assist the Crown prosecutors, Zaneth put together a complete brief on the case, laying out every aspect of the evidence, the fifty-six informants and the various conspiracies involved. The lawyers were amazed by its thoroughness—Quebec's attorney general was moved to ask who had prepared the brief—and used it over the course of a five-day trial in October 1933, to convict Davis of nine counts of conspiracy to traffic narcotics. He was sentenced to fourteen years in prison. It was, to that point, the biggest victory against a major crime boss in Canadian history.

RCMP brass in Montreal could not say enough about Zaneth after that. "Only Staff Sergeant Zaneth's experience and devotion," wrote Inspector H. Royal Gagnon, "made it possible to have the brief ready in such a short time." The commander of the Quebec division, F. J. Mead, tried to convince the RCMP's new commissioner, Sir James Howden MacBrien, to give Zaneth a special award of money for his effort. He knew Zaneth needed the cash—Rita, officially an invalid, was now in the care of an Italian mental institution. When MacBrien said no to the award, Zaneth's response was to try harder. He followed up Davis's conviction with an investigation that led to the arrest, five months later, of Davis's main partner, Pincus Brecher, a former Montrealer who'd become one of the biggest narcotics bosses in New York City. The capture won enormous praise for the Canadian justice system and prodded the U.S. Bureau of Narcotics into one of its first major clean-up efforts against drug trafficking. Three days after the arrest, Commissioner MacBrien created a new rank, and made Zaneth the RCMP's first-ever detective inspector in charge of criminal investigations. "He is," wrote MacBrien, "one of the outstanding detectives of the Force."

ONCE you've nabbed two of the biggest drug kings in North America, what do you, a freshly minted detective inspector in 1934 Montreal, do for an encore? You go after the kings of Montreal bootlegging.

You go after the Bronfman brothers.

With the repeal of the Eighteenth Amendment on December 5, 1933, America's thirteen years of Prohibition under the Constitution had officially ended, but not bootlegging. Even after repeal, nineteen states were still legally dry, and many others still imposed restrictions. And where "wet" rule prevailed, there were practical obstacles. Initially the liquor that came through official channels was in very short supply, and some of it was nearly undrinkable—odious concoctions of real whisky mixed with raw alcohol and colourings that sometimes included coal tar. So bootlegging thrived as much as it ever had—even twenty-five years after repeal it would account for 20 percent of American spirits consumption.

No one was better equipped to profit from this situation than the Bronfmans. In 1934 the supply and capacity of their company, Distillers Corporation-Seagram Ltd., was bested only by that of Harry Hatch's Hiram Walker-Gooderham & Worts Ltd. The Bronfmans had a well-established distribution scheme that channelled liquor to the United States through the French islands of St. Pierre and Miquelon. Their bottled whisky blends—5 Crown, 7 Crown and VO—were recognized and trusted by American customers (by the end of the year, 5 Crown would be the biggest selling brand in the United States). And the Bronfmans had already proven their ability to beat the RCMP, when Harry Bronfman was arrested in 1929—and subsequently acquitted—for trying to bribe a Saskatchewan customs official.

For an RCMP investigative team led by Frank Zaneth, no organization in eastern Canada had a bigger target on its back.

Zaneth began by travelling to St. John's, Newfoundland, and ana-
lyzing the transactions of an import-export company called Eastern
Trading. He traced its connection to a Halifax company called Atlas
Shipping, run by a woman named Evelyn Carline. Soon Zaneth and
two local RCMP officers were inside Carline's house, opening her
cupboards and drawers. As they looked through Atlas Shipping's
records—including code books, schooner expense accounts and a
handwritten instruction to "destroy everything"—Zaneth realized
he'd uncovered a vast rum-running operation. "Enough incriminating evidence was found," he reported to Montreal, "to show nefari-
ous activities of the Bronfmans since 1926."

It was a long, complicated road from this eureka moment, taking Zaneth and his men through more searches, trips to Montreal
and Halifax and discoveries of money laundering in records from
the Bank of Montreal. At one memorable point in October, the
investigation took Zaneth to the Montreal offices of Distillers
Corporation-Seagram Ltd., where he met Sam Bronfman himself.

There's no proof of what happened next, but one account,
reported by authors Dubro and Rowland in the book *Undercover*,
says that while Zaneth was looking for important financial records
Sam Bronfman offered him a large bound ledger, suggesting he take
it away and give it a thorough perusal. According to what Zaneth
later told a friend, the ledger was stuffed with cash. Hundreds of
thousands of dollars? A million, as Zaneth's friend claimed? Either
way, if the account is true, the cash would have solved all of his
money problems in an instant. But Zaneth could not be bought. He
turned the ledger and cash over to RCMP headquarters and wanted
to press bribery charges. But there had been no witnesses, and nothing more ever came of that event; perhaps the RCMP was happy for
the infusion of funds. The larger investigation, however, continued.

Finally, as the year came to a close, Zaneth thought he had

all the evidence he needed. The Quebec division commander, Superintendent F. J. Mead, faced reporters at his first-ever press conference to announce a $5-million liquor-smuggling conspiracy that reverberated from British Columbia to Prince Edward Island. "This affair," he said, "has indications of being the biggest case in the history of the Royal Canadian Mounted Police." On Monday, December 18, Zaneth arrested Sam Bronfman and his brother Allan at an RCMP building on Sherbrooke Street—the arrests of Abe and Harry Bronfman, and other Seagram executives, came half an hour later—and photographers vied to get shots of the Bronfman brothers, freshly fingerprinted, being led away to court, where they were released on one hundred thousand dollars' bail each.

Ultimately sixty-one people were charged. Fifty-one of those, and their dozen lawyers, took up half the courtroom on the first day of the preliminary hearing, January 11, 1935, forcing the press to sit in the jury box. Many of the accused were from the Maritimes, but once the trial got under way, legal logistics narrowed the focus to the Bronfmans and their Montreal coterie.

The trial, before Justice Jules Desmarais, lasted six months. But it took only a few days of argument to understand that the Crown's case was fatally flawed. Zaneth travelled to New York in search of more proof that Bronfman vessels had been smuggling into U.S. waters. But while he was doing that, the Bronfmans were applying political and financial persuasion in Ottawa, with promises of million-dollar campaign donations if the proceedings were dropped. Frank Zaneth may have been able to resist temptation, but it seemed unlikely the political class could.

On February 4, Judge Desmarais laid down a ruling that knocked the legs from under the Crown's case. Despite the fact that the Canada Export Act now prohibited exporting liquor into countries where liquor imports were illegal, he decided it wasn't actually an indictable offence. Therefore there was no smuggling conspiracy. On June 14, 1935, Desmarais dismissed all charges.

Zaneth was incensed. As far as he was concerned, the Crown had proved conspiracy. "We proved an 'agreement,'" he wrote to Commissioner MacBrien. "'Common design' and 'common means.'" If he could console himself with one thing, it was that he now had a wealth of knowledge and experience in conspiracy cases—what strengthened them, what weakened them, and what helped them stick. All he needed was a chance to use that knowledge against another worthy opponent.

IN THE DEPTHS OF THE GREAT DEPRESSION, ROCCO found his next great love. And like so many of his paramours (with the exception of Olive Rutledge), the new woman had a criminal mind.

Shorter than Bessie, but considered by some to be just as elegant and beautiful, Anne Newman had arrived in Canada from Poland and settled in Toronto's Ward in 1907. When Rocco met her—she was living at 677 Richmond Street West at the time—she was a mid-forties dish with platinum blonde hair and "the cold, blue eyes of a killer." In her love of fashion finery and parties, as well as her shrewd intelligence, she must have reminded Rocco of Bessie. There were other similarities too. "Very good-looking but greedy," one gang member called her. She made Rocco happy though, and she learned to handle his books. By the end of 1933 they were a committed couple, and before long Annie had moved in at 166 Bay Street South, along with her plump, aging Pekingese dog, Fifi.

Thus revived, Rocco poured much of his renewed energy into his revamped liquor racket. With the end of Prohibition in the United States, it was now Ontario drinkers who suffered comparatively from regulation. They wanted access to the booze that began to flow south of the border, and with mob sources in Detroit and Chicago, and a gang of seasoned rum-runners, Rocco was there to help.

Improved policing had made it risky to boat the booze across lakes and rivers, so cars—specifically Ford and Dodge coupes—became the smuggling mode of choice. With beefed-up suspensions, each coupe could hold hundreds of gallons of liquor, packed neatly in cans. The problem was getting those cars through the border checkpoints.

The solution was a system of coordinated bribery.

In this, Anne Newman proved herself invaluable. The system required hiring and managing teams of drivers and corrupt customs officials. Annie organized the men, arranged the buys in Chicago, and managed the bribe payments like a mob shipping dispatcher. By 1934, Rocco Perri's gang had arguably as much control over the entry points of the Ambassador Bridge and the Detroit–Windsor tunnel as did the Canadian government.

The first of those corrupt customs examiners was twenty-five-year-old David Armaly. A husband and already a father of four, Armaly was also an addicted gambler—he especially liked craps and horses—which gave him a constant need for cash. At age twenty-one he'd embezzled money from a Windsor shoe store where he worked. When he was fired from that job and began working at the border in 1929, his habits didn't change.

In 1933, while he was playing at an illegal Windsor gambling joint, Armaly bounced a cheque and wound up thirty dollars in debt to Sam Miller, the owner. "A smooth duck," Miller was into liquor smuggling as much as he was gambling, selling most of what he snuck over the border to Rocco Perri. So he gave Armaly an easy way to pay off the debt. Since Armaly was then working as an inspector at the Walkerville ferry dock, all he had to do was pass a few of Miller's liquor-laden cars through the customs checkpoint.

A few became many. In the time he worked at the ferry, Armaly passed at least a hundred of Sam Miller's liquor loads through customs, some of them driven by Miller's nineteen-year-old son, and Miller paid him twenty-five dollars for each car that he passed. Miller would let him know when he had a car ready and give him the licence plate number to look out for. Armaly would tell Miller when he would be on duty, and which ferry to take. He also waved through four trucks loaded with gambling equipment and parts for an illegal still. Each of those trucks earned Armaly two hundred dollars.

With business booming, David Armaly recruited two other customs officers to work with him, and eventually attracted the attention of people who worked even more closely with Rocco. One early spring afternoon in 1936, a "short Jewish man with glasses," who was likely Toronto rum-runner Milton (German) Goldhart, came to Armaly's house. Armaly knew the man as a gambler at Sam Miller's joint, but that day he'd come on another mission—to suggest Armaly work for Anne Newman. Armaly wasn't keen on the idea of working for a woman, but he agreed to go outside to a parked car where Newman was waiting. In the fresh air of a Windsor thaw, she told Armaly that by working for her he'd be working for Rocco Perri, "the best man in the alcohol racket," and when she agreed to pay Armaly the going rate, twenty-five dollars per car, he signed on. That arrangement didn't last long. One of the Sam Miller trucks that Armaly had passed was seized and searched, and when the Department of National Revenue traced it back to Armaly, he was fired. After that, he became what might be called a full-time corruption coordinator.

On behalf of the Perri gang, Armaly lined up at least four customs officials—Carl Gough, Eddie Mansell, Wilfred Fletcher and Norman LePain—the first two at the Walkerville ferry dock, the other two on the Ambassador Bridge. The costs were higher now—Armaly had no other income and had to be paid—so for each car, Anne Newman gave Armaly forty dollars, and from this he paid his customs men twenty-five per, often using his wife, Marie, to deliver the envelopes of cash. The arrangements were usually made by phone, sometimes telegram, between Armaly and either Newman or Rocco himself. After each trip Armaly would meet Annie at the corner of Wyandotte Street and Ouellette Avenue, near the mouth of the Detroit–Windsor tunnel, and get the money in cash. In typical Perri-gang fashion, they took extra precautions, including using coded language—a liquor load was referred to as a shipment of "birds," the drivers of rum-running cars were "auntie and uncle."

In addition to his work for the Perris, Armaly provided the same service for a lean, sharply dressed Windsor bootlegger named Sammy Motruk. He even began to drive some of Sam Miller's loads himself, taking booze-packed cars from Chicago to Detroit, where he'd hand them off to other drivers who took the cars across. For this, Armaly earned fifty dollars per trip. In the early part of 1937, when Milton Goldhart heard about the money Armaly was making with Miller, he went to Anne Newman and got a job driving loads from Chicago all the way to Hamilton, via border crossings arranged by Armaly.

The first significant hitch in all this came on July 2, 1937—the same day aviator Amelia Earhart, attempting to circumnavigate the globe, disappeared somewhere in the southwestern Pacific. Rocco had instructed Milton Goldhart to drive a car loaded with what was probably Perri-manufactured alcohol to Detroit, then take the car to Chicago and pick up another load, paying for it with the five hundred dollars Anne Newman had given him. Driving west and nearing Chatham, Goldhart was arrested. Anne Newman paid his fine, but according to Rocco's rules he was now finished as an employee, since a conviction made him a prime target for future arrests. With no other option, he became an independent contractor, driving loads that he would buy himself and sell to the Perris, meeting Rocco on the Dundas highway between midnight and five in the morning. Rocco told him there were no limits—he would buy any amount at any time. That arrangement lasted until a large still, possibly owned by Rocco himself and housed secretly on Front Street in Toronto, undercut Goldhart's terms. "The still put me out of business," he later admitted. "[Rocco] would no longer pay the original price."

To supplement his bootlegging proceeds, Rocco began to beef up his gambling operation in partnership with John Taglierino, the Black Hand leader he'd worked with before. In the mid-1930s, Toronto was considered wide open for gambling. It met the main conditions that would draw the big-shot American players like Eddie Massie, Doc Brady and Johnnie Boyd. "In the first place there must be plenty of dough," said a Detroit detective, and there was. Even in the midst of the Depression, a steady stream of narcotics from Toronto to Detroit and Chicago returned a flow of dirty money that fuelled gambling. "In the second, things must be 'set'—'fixed' with someone so that they get the tip-off." Rocco and Taglierino could handle that as well.

But the Perri/Taglierino expansion—setting up bookmakers in little shops and dives across Toronto and other districts—encroached on an already established racket. When Rocco began offering more money to entice some of those rival bookmakers to join him, and shaking down others with the help of criminals like John (The Bug) Brown and Donald (Mickey) McDonald, something had to give.

In the attic of Rocco's house, two men sat at telephones at all hours, clearing bets called in by Perri agents. This arrangement worked just fine until January 14, 1938, when police raided the house and arrested John Mostacci and Jay Honigman, the brother-in-law of Jack Borovoy, who owned a drugstore at York and MacNab streets that Rocco had long supplied with liquor. Those two were found guilty, but despite having the bookmaking setup *in his house*, Rocco miraculously escaped any charge.

A few days later, police busted in again. This time the raid came at a Perri/Taglierino gambling house on York Street in Hamilton that took a steady rake off a regular craps game and handled bets on boxing matches. Eighteen "found-ins" were charged, including Taglierino's brother, Ben.

One raid might have been bad luck; two raids in quick succession indicated a rival gambling gang pushing back. Other moves seemed inevitable, and when they came they were unmistakable.

On the night of March 16, as a lightning storm crashed over Hamilton, someone set a package of dynamite against the back door of Taglierino's Simcoe Street home. It burned for a minute or two, then exploded. Taglierino and his wife weren't home, but their fifteen-month-old baby, her eighteen-year-old nursemaid, Irene, and Irene's boyfriend were. The blast knocked Irene to the floor and sent the back door and shards of window glass flying over her head; everyone else was unharmed. John Taglierino, who rushed home to check on his child, told police, "They're trying to get me!" But he wouldn't say who, or why.

Four days later, it was Rocco's turn. On the night of Sunday,

March 20, just before ten, a maroon coupe with two men inside stopped for a moment in front of his house. Then it drove away. A few minutes later, an explosion tore through the veranda of 166 Bay Street South. It shattered the floor, steps and railing, blew apart the cellar door underneath the veranda, sent shards of glass over Rocco's billiard table and damaged one of the veranda's heavy pillars, blowing the bricks past a mounted stag's head and through the ceiling. It smashed the windows of some of Rocco's neighbours too. But Rocco was lucky. He'd been at Jack Borovoy's drugstore when a young man ran in to tell him what had happened. Rocco arrived at the house just as a fire truck was pulling away. He looked genuinely stunned, but speaking with police and reporters amid the lingering smell of dynamite he stayed as cool as ever. "I had a headache and was taking a bromo," he said. "When I got home I saw this mess. Now I don't feel any better." Then he picked up a bit of debris and entered the house through his wrecked front door, walked through to the kitchen and telephoned Annie, telling her only that they had had visitors. At his feet, the now fourteen-year-old Fifi, who had been resting in the kitchen, seemed unperturbed.

From the placement of the dynamite, it was obvious no one had intended to kill Rocco with that blast; it was meant to send a message. And whoever sent it wasn't done.

<hr />

I T IS ONE OF THE GREAT IRONIES OF FRANK ZANETH'S life that as he worked to bring millionaires to justice—refusing the bribes that could have made him wealthy—he often scraped for pennies to survive. Was it because he was Italian that his superiors often begrudged him his due? Or was he was poor at the art of glad-handing the high command? John Marrett, a man who knew Zaneth in his later years, once said that the detective wasn't popular with "some of the brass" in the RCMP. Zaneth was, said Marrett, "not necessarily the most diplomatic person. Frank was a very direct individual." There's no doubt that when rewards and remuneration were being handed out by the people above him, Zaneth was often overlooked.

After promoting him to detective inspector, for instance, the RCMP didn't just give Zaneth the financial bonus that always came with such promotions, he had to ask for it: "I have the honour respectfully to request that I be granted the usual One Hundred and Fifty Dollars, ($150.00) gratuity, upon my appointment to Commissioned Rank." And he only asked for that money in order to buy a new uniform.

The next month—two weeks after the infamous Bonnie Parker and Clyde Barrow were riddled with bullets by a southern posse on a country road in Louisiana—Zaneth was on an investigation in Montreal. As he was poking around an equipment yard, he pulled the plug from a metal drum and had his suit and shoes splashed with motor oil and ruined. That same day, he came back to head-quarters to find himself scolded for continuing to draw a ten-cent-per-diem telephone allowance. As a commissioned officer now, he wasn't supposed to receive that money. He had to give it back.

If that weren't indignity enough, he was constantly disbelieved regarding his identity as an RCMP officer. Years before, he'd lost his ID card in a Greek restaurant in Montreal and requested a replacement. Now he tried again: "I have the honour to request that I be furnished with an identification card, as I have found it difficult, on a number of occasions, to identify myself."

But if any administrative matter came to vex Frank Zaneth at the height of his career, it was the issue of the four-dollar daily living allowance. He fit the criteria: married, not occupying government quarters, and not drawing rations. According to General Order No. 2548, paragraph 2, issued June 15, 1935, he was entitled like any married officer to see his living allowance increased from three dollars per day to four. So he wrote the commissioner to ask for it, concluding: "I trust this application will receive your kind consideration."

It did not. "The Commissioner does not approve" came the reply three days later. It was signed by Adjutant Superintendent V. A. M. Kemp, who was no ally to Zaneth in these matters.

Six months later, in January of 1936, the division commander, F. J. Mead, tried to make Zaneth's case, explaining to the commissioner that Zaneth had been sending seventy dollars a month to Italy for his wife's care since 1927. It took an entire year, until February 1937, for Superintendent Kemp to finally approve Zaneth's one-dollar raise. That should have meant he was due the raise retroactively, but when Zaneth tried to get the money owed to him, he was told he was out of luck.

By April 11, 1938—the day he was ordered to reimburse the RCMP thirty-five cents for a telegram he'd sent from Regina— Frank Zaneth had had enough. There was a new commissioner in the chair now; James MacBrien had died just a month before, and was replaced by Stuart Taylor Wood. Thinking that perhaps now, finally, he might receive fair treatment, Zaneth sat down at his typewriter and brought all of his evidentiary powers to bear on the issue of the extra one dollar per diem. The retroactive pay amounted to $681, and in a three-page memo, which he titled "For The Perusal of the Commissioner, Please," he spelled out why he was entitled to it, and why the decision to deny him "would constitute an injustice if allowed to stand."

Maybe Commissioner Wood—a tight-jawed officer whose father had joined the North West Mounted Police in 1885, served under the famous Sam Steele and risen himself to become acting commissioner—was wary of establishing a reputation for being a pushover so early in his tenure. He didn't just deny the claim, he squashed it. At the end of a detailed reply, he asked, "Can Inspector Zaneth name any other officer of equal rank who received this $4.00 per diem prior to the 1st of February 1937?" If not, said Wood, "the matter is to be closed."

              ||||||||||||||||||||||||||||||

I n Europe, it was looking like war. By the fall of 1938, Hitler had already annexed Austria. He had managed to back Britain and France into the Munich Agreement, handing Germany chunks of Czechoslovakia. In early November, Kristallnacht began in the Jewish quarters of many German cities, and soon Italian troops were massing on the Pyrenees frontier of Spain. In the Ontario underworld, meanwhile, another kind of hostility was brewing.

Rocco had gotten hints that something bad might be coming. But he couldn't live his life in fear. So on the evening of Tuesday, November 29, he was at one of his regular card parties at John Rosso's house on Hughson Street North, just a few doors from the house of Joe Romeo, where he and Annie were staying while the Bay Street house was repaired. Out front he'd parked his new car, a sleek DeSoto Business Coupe registered in Annie's name.

In the darkness, someone crouched down at the rear of the car and set an explosive near the tailpipe, then strung a wire from the detonator to the rear right tail light. A while later, Rocco came out with Frank Di Pietro and Fred Condillo. They chatted for a minute as Rocco used his car lighter to give Di Pietro a light for his pipe. When he was ready to go, he closed the car's door and stepped on the starter.

"Next I remember," said Rocco, "I was in the back of the car. It was upside down and starting to burn."

The bomb had flipped the DeSoto over its nose, flinging Rocco into the rear, and the exploded gas tank had sent flames everywhere. Still conscious, but trapped now in a hulk of burning wreckage, Rocco had to crawl out to safety. "I saw the fire start all around me and got out somehow," he said. "I don't know how I did it." Amazingly, except for cuts to his forehead and burns on his left wrist, he had hardly been touched. Frank Di Pietro, standing on the sidewalk, had taken the worst of it, with serious injuries to his left leg including the loss of three toes of his left foot and the possible amputation of the remaining two. Condillo received treatment for wounds to his left leg, arm and back. But all three of them could have been killed. The "pineapple" had blown a hole in the pavement and sent parts of the upended DeSoto the distance of a football field up the street. Nearby power lines were downed, neighbours' windows were broken, and the car's rear wheels were blown to opposite sides of the street; part of the right one had smashed through the front door of Joe Romeo's house and wound up in the kitchen.

Once Rocco was safely inside Romeo's place, with a crowd of onlookers and reporters gathering, someone sent for Dr. Vincenzo Agro. Rocco's personal physician, Agro was, in the words of a government report, a "shrewd and well-educated Italian." Born in Sicily, he had arrived in Canada in 1926 and immediately taken up with the rackets. For mercenary gain, it was said, he would commit "any criminal act." Within a few minutes, Agro arrived and began dressing the wound on Rocco's forehead. With his clothes still smattered with upholstery fluff from the explosion, Rocco sat and kept his head still while a reporter in the room angled for a quote for the morning paper.

"It seems that every time we meet," he said, "you have a peck of trouble."

Rocco gave a little smile. "I am okay, and you get your living out of it."

"He's got nine lives," said one of Rocco's friends.

THE night after Rocco's car blew up, even as he was resting at home, still touching the unfamiliar bandage on his forehead, David Armaly was waiting on a street corner in Detroit, wondering where the hell two of his drivers were. Bill (The Butcher) Leuchter, the twenty-six-year-old son of a kosher meat shop owner, was supposed to be driving back from Chicago with his partner, Michael Mikoda. "Auntie and Uncle" were due to meet with Armaly the night of November 30 and find out what lane to take over the bridge the next day, but they were late. Finally, after checking his watch one last time, Armaly gave up and drove home. That's when he got a call from Anne Newman.

They'd almost made it. Leuchter and Mikoda had loaded the Dodge coupe with at least 250 gallons of alcohol, weighing fifteen hundred pounds, in five-gallon and one-gallon tins. Around 10:15 p.m. they were driving fast along a highway outside of Ann Arbor, Michigan, when somehow they crashed into the back of a slow-moving oil truck. Some of the alcohol ignited and turned the car into an exploding ball of fire. For a while no one could get near as cans continued to burst and spray flames. Inside, Leuchter and Mikoda were incinerated to the point that investigators weren't sure at first whether the bodies were male or female.

The fiery death of Bill Leuchter and Michael Mikoda, in a car full of bootleg alcohol, was not the event that caused Canadian officials to believe that something not quite right was going on with their Windsor customs examiners. But it definitely heightened their sense of urgency about goings-on at the border. Just two days later, RCMP Commissioner Stuart Wood sent a personal note to Assistant Commissioner F. J. Mead, asking if there was any way they could get Frank Zaneth on this.

The answer was yes, but it involved some bureaucratic wiggling. So on December 19, 1938, under section 134A of the Customs Act, Minister of National Revenue James Ilsley authorized RCMP Detective Inspector Frank Zaneth to conduct "any inquiry or investigation into matters relating to the Customs."

Which meant that, whether he knew it at the time or not, Frank Zaneth was going to get his second shot at Rocco Perri.

26

COSPIRAZIONE

Conspiracy

THE GEARS OF THE WINDSOR BORDER INVESTIGATION took some time to catch. Zaneth and his RCMP investigators didn't know yet what they were dealing with. Nothing appeared improper in the way customs officials were doing their work. So over the spring of 1939, Rocco's smuggling operation ran as smoothly as ever through its greased customs portal. David Armaly sent telegrams to Annie: "OPEN FOR BUSINESS IMMEDI-ATELY CALL MY HOME SEVEN PM" said one in March; "LEAVE TEN PM TONIGHT WITH FORTY BEST BIRDS FOR SHOW" said another in May. Anne Newman visited Armaly's home five or six times, and met his wife, Marie. Rocco came at least three times himself to see Armaly. When he met Armaly's wife, Rocco was always polite but didn't introduce himself, and Armaly only referred to Annie and Rocco as "friends." It took Marie months to figure out who they were, because she was not in the habit of asking her husband questions. Not even when he asked her to hand envelopes of money to customs officials, or when she went with him to Chicago and stood in the garage while big rectangular tins of alcohol were wrapped in newspaper and loaded in the back of their car, did she probe the details of what her husband was into.

But Marie Armaly may have had something to do with the customs scheme finally coming to an end. When asked later, she did admit talking to her husband, so perhaps, rather than ask questions, she expressed concern. Maybe she hinted at what it would mean for their four children if their father went to jail. Or maybe it was just the whispers in Windsor that the RCMP had begun nosing around that gave the man pause. Whatever the reason, David Armaly's conscience began to gnaw at him.

In May, Commissioner of Customs H. D. Scully asked the Mounties to look into some suspicious activity that had nothing to do with bootleggers. A man named Richard Albert Madden (ironically from Hamilton) was bringing used cars in through Windsor without a customs permit, to sell them. He was arrested on May 26, after which RCMP officers questioned customs employees to find out whether anyone had helped Madden. That couldn't have been good for Armaly's peace of mind.

Then in June, while the RCMP were poking around, bootlegger Sammy Motruk had a falling-out with one of his drivers, a man named Victor Bernat. Now Bernat was making noises about calling the RCMP and filling them in on just how Motruk was getting his loads over the boarder. When Armaly caught wind of this, he called one of his customs men, Carl Gough, and together Armaly and Gough went to pay Bernat a visit.

At the corner of Parent Avenue and Erie Street in Windsor, they pulled Bernat into the car and told him about all the trouble his squawking would cause for a bunch of customs men who'd never done him any wrong—customs men who had families, who were all "good sports." And then Gough, perhaps a lesser sport, told Bernat that if any harm came to him because Bernat had spoken out of turn, Gough would see that he was taken care of.

By the end of June, David Armaly's conscience was apparently a wreck. Coincidentally, on June 28, Customs Commissioner Scully wrote to his RCMP counterpart, Commissioner Stuart Wood. He wanted to thank the force for their help on the Madden affair and, oblivious to the irony, to say how "gratifying" it was to learn that his staff was beyond reproach. The very next day, David Armaly could no longer hold back his moral horses. He went to the RCMP's Windsor headquarters, sat down with Detective Sergeant F. W. Davis, lit a Philip Morris cigarette and confessed everything. He would later say that he had become disgusted with himself and wanted done with his life of crime, but perhaps it was merely survival instinct that had forced his hand. It would have occurred to Armaly that, if the RCMP were going to find out soon anyway, turning King's evidence might help him stay out of jail.

Frank Zaneth was already headed to Ottawa to meet with Commissioner Scully about the Madden matter when he learned about Armaly's revelations, and it was Zaneth who gave the head of customs the bad news. In his chagrin, Scully granted Zaneth carte blanche to interrogate any Windsor official he wanted.

On July 4, 1939, as Lou Gehrig, diagnosed with amyotrophic lateral sclerosis, stood at a microphone at Yankee Stadium, telling fans he was the "luckiest man on the face of the earth," Frank Zaneth was in Toronto, sitting down at an interview table with David Armaly and a police stenographer. He had the confession Armaly had given to Detective Sergeant Davis, but he had to get everything fresh. He adjusted his glasses and began.

"What is your name in full?"

"I was baptized Joseph David Michael Armaly," said the thirty-two-year-old, as if referencing his religious foundation might make the next hours a little easier. Then he paused and told "Mr. Zaneth" that he wanted the protection of the Canada Evidence Act.

"Mr. Armaly," said Zaneth, "the protection of the Canada Evidence Act is afforded to you provided you tell the truth, all of the truth and nothing but the truth. Of course you understand that should you commit perjury, the Canada Evidence Act cannot protect you in any way." Armaly said he understood, and then he and Zaneth proceeded to unpack the details of his story.

Armaly described his beginnings with Sam Miller, first taking bribes to let Miller's cars through, then driving some over from Detroit himself. Perhaps twenty minutes into the interview, Zaneth asked, "Was Miller the only man you were dealing with during that period?"

"No."

"Who else?"

"Rocco Perri."

Now Armaly really had Zaneth's attention. Because Rocco worked at a remove, Armaly couldn't share much about him, but then he mentioned Anne Newman.

"Can you describe this woman?" Zaneth asked.

"I would say she was about five feet in height, a woman approximately around forty-four or forty-five, fair complexion, would weigh about 130 pounds."

"What colour hair did she sport at the time?"

"At this time it was sort of light."

"Would you call her a peroxide blonde?"

"Right."

Gradually Zaneth learned all the names of the customs officers who wound up colluding with Armaly, and all the nuances of the system they used, signalling which tunnel lane to take, which ferry or when to cross over the bridge. He learned about Newman's and

Miller's trips to Chicago, and Armaly's meetings with Newman in Detroit. He learned about Milton Goldhart, bootlegger Sam Motruk and his partner Victor Bernat, about drivers named "Beaver" and "Jimmy" and René Charron, and at least half a dozen other names.

He learned about the code words and envelopes of money, about meetings and transfers of cars and merchandise, outside hotels, on street corners, in garages and YMCA parking lots. He learned how Rocco had calmed Armaly after Goldhart was arrested, and how Newman had told him not to worry when Leuchter and Mikado were burned up. He learned enough from his Armaly interrogation—and another the next day with Victor Bernat, who was finally getting his opportunity to talk—to know he had the beginning of something solid. He was already thinking ahead to the trial. When a lawyer named E. C. Bogart seemed poised to be appointed Crown counsel on the case, Zaneth wrote an internal memo about it. "This lawyer does not appear to be very strong," he wrote, "but we think that our evidence is good enough in this case to warrant a conviction under any circumstances."

He proceeded carefully, not wanting to tip off the customs inspectors who were still taking bribes. A discreet search of bootlegger Sam Motruk's place found some important physical evidence—slips of paper with alcohol sales, notebooks with names, letters to Motruk from two competing suppliers named Morris and Kelly, who were trying to do business with him: "I am now loading two cars each twice a week clean merchandise and also with moon. If you are in bad need of merchandise write to me," wrote Morris. "Don't forget Sam if you are going to buy from Morris then write to me and I will let you know what he paid for it here in Chicago," wrote Kelly.

Zaneth was travelling between Windsor, Ottawa, Toronto and Montreal, dealing with two separate government institutions and making sure everyone appreciated "the delicate nature of this enquiry." Finally on July 24, it was time for him to sit down with Milton Goldhart. Zaneth had more information in his pocket now—including Armaly's contention that it was Goldhart who had introduced him to Anne Newman—but he needed corroboration. Years later, Goldhart remembered Zaneth from this encounter, describing him as "a dandy Dan with spectacles." From the start, he didn't like the detective inspector's tone. "Zaneth called me a rat the first time I met him," Goldhart said. "I felt like zapping him."

In the interrogation room, Zaneth began. "Do you know Dave Armaly of Windsor?"

"Yes I do."

"When did you meet him?"

"I met him in 1937."

"Who introduced you to him?"

"No one introduced me."

"How did you meet him?"

"With Anne Newman."

"Did Mrs. Newman introduce you to him?"

"No, she didn't."

"Did you go to his house?"

"No, I didn't."

"Did you not go to his house and call him outside to speak to Mrs. Newman who was in the car?"

"I was parked around the corner."

"Who got him out of the house?"

"I think she, Mrs. Newman, I'm not sure."

"And you were not introduced to him?"

"No."

From the beginning this was a conspiracy case, so the focus of Zaneth's interrogations was to establish that at least two people had discussed and agreed to a crime.

"Before you made your first trip to Chicago with Anne Newman," Zaneth asked Goldhart, "did you have a conversation with her in Hamilton?"

"I don't remember it."

"Try to remember whether you just picked her up without saying anything, or whether you had a conversation about where you were going, what you were going for and how much money you were to receive."

"I don't think we had no conversation."

". . . Did she not tell you you were going to Chicago?"

"She didn't say anything to me, just said we are going away."

"And you drove from Hamilton to Windsor?"

"That's right."

"The first trip you stopped to see Dave Armaly?"

"I guess that's his name."

"Did you ask Mrs. Newman on your way to Windsor what it was all about?"

"I knew what it was all about."

"How did you know?"

"I knew who they were."

"Who were they?"

"Anne Newman and Rocco Perri."

". . . You knew when you went to Windsor to see this man Dave Armaly that you were going to the United States to get a load of alcohol?"

"Yes."

"Did she tell you Dave Armaly had been a customs officer?"

"No she didn't."

"Did she tell you Dave Armaly was in a position to make connections at the tunnel and bridge?"

"She didn't mention anything, just said I would be able to come through."

Goldhart admitted to being paid by Anne Newman after every trip he made, and that occasionally he slept at Rocco's place during trips between Chicago and his home in Toronto, although he never saw Rocco, only the maid. After a few minutes Zaneth pressed on to the matter of the customs officers who allowed him over the border unchecked.

"How many officers did you pass during the time you were working for Newman?"

"There was a bunch of them there at the time, four or five, maybe more."

"Only one spoke to you?"

"That's all."

"Was that the same one all the time?"

"No."

"There were four or five that passed you through that you knew they had been fixed?"

"I never looked at them."

"Answer my question," said Zaneth. ". . . The mere fact your car was not examined you know this was the officer that had been fixed for you to come in?"

"I knew it was fixed, that's all."

"You never paid money to the officers yourself while you were working for Perri and Newman?"

"I handed them an envelope."

"To whom?"

"Armaly."

"Where?"

"In Detroit."

It was Anne Newman, Goldhart admitted, who gave him the envelope.

"Tell me this," Zaneth asked. "Did you, at any time when you were working for Rocco Perri, ever determine where he got his alcohol?"

"I never wanted to know."

"I didn't ask you whether you wanted to know, I asked you if you ever found out?"

"No."

Goldhart's interrogation filled fewer than half the pages Armaly's had, and Zaneth had to work tenaciously to get even that much. But by the end, he knew that Goldhart was going to be a vital witness for the Crown.

After more interviews and evidence gathering, with commissioners from both Canada Customs and the RCMP pestering him for news, Zaneth produced a preliminary case summary on July 26. He named eight customs officials "directly connected with this unfortunate state of affairs," and fifteen people, with more to be determined, who had benefited illegally from their actions. And he was able to recommend four possible charges under the following sections:

Section 573 of the Criminal Code, for conspiracy to commit indictable offences.

Section 444 of the Criminal Code, for conspiracy to defraud the government.

Section 160 of the Criminal Code, for breach of trust by a public officer.

And Section 250 of the Customs Act, for bribery.

Of these first two, Zaneth much preferred the first one. And he liked the last two even more. Now it was a matter of getting the higher-ups and the Crown's senior counsel, whoever it ended up being, to agree with him.

On Friday, July 28, RCMP and customs officials, including Commissioner Scully, gathered in the office of the RCMP's assistant commissioner to get it all from Zaneth personally. Astounded by what he heard, Scully wanted to suspend the port officers involved immediately. But the RCMP men told him to wait. Decisions needed to be made regarding their prosecution. In the meantime, there were two informants—Armaly and Goldhart—who were now officially government employees, being kept at a hotel in Toronto and paid four dollars per day each to sit and wait for a trial. Would the commissioner authorize the continued funding of this expense? Scully agreed.

In the tenth year of the Great Depression, every dollar counted, and that was true even when it came to deciding who would be appointed senior counsel. Bogart's name had dropped off the list, and now Zaneth was recommending William N. Tilley, who'd handled the government's case against Gooderham & Worts. For such an important case, it was vital to get the best legal talent available. The trouble was, Tilley charged five hundred dollars a day. Any decision was going to have to go through H. H. Ellis, the departmental solicitor for National Revenue.

By August 4, a decision had been made, and the pricey Tilley was out. Instead, the senior counsel for the Crown would be Toronto's Thomas N. Phelan. He was good—a lawyer with thirty-five years of experience, it was Phelan who had managed to put away Ned Italiano and Tony Brassi in the 1929 Toronto narcotics case—and as a bonus he charged only three hundred a day.

The conflict between Frank Zaneth and Thomas Phelan began almost instantly. Zaneth wanted the go-ahead to begin arresting suspects, but three days after his appointment, Phelan sent Zaneth a letter. "It seems to me," he began, "that further investigations might be directed . . ." and he proceeded to enumerate the evidence that he felt still needed to be gathered—licence numbers of automobiles passing through customs, bank accounts of the people involved, hotel registers in Detroit, Chicago and Toronto to prove the presence of the bootleggers on specific dates. "It seems to me," Phelan said again near the end of his long list, "that the customs books and records themselves ought to, if available, supply a good deal of helpful evidence."

As if Zaneth needed to be told that. Three days later, Zaneth sent a copy of Phelan's letter, along with his itemized responses, to the RCMP's O division commander in Toronto. Every one of Phelan's suggestions was being, or had already been, looked into. And Zaneth was continuing with his interrogations; he had new people to talk to and follow-up interviews to conduct. Everything was in hand.

On Monday, August 21, Zaneth met with Phelan to talk about the evidence he'd gathered. Apparently it was all Zaneth could do to contain his frustration, but he had allies on the force to whom he made it known. One of them, Inspector F. W. Schutz, followed up with an archly polite communiqué—attaching a copy of the RCMP *Gazette*, no. 26, dated August 2, 1939—to remind Phelan who the real expert was in these sorts of cases. "It will be noted," he wrote, "that this copy contains an article on "Conspiracy" by D/Insp. F.W. Zaneth, which, it is considered, may possibly be of some value to you in connection with the present case."

Inside the RCMP, concern was building over the possibility that Rocco Perri and Anne Newman would catch wind of what was coming and find a way to disappear. Zaneth, Schutz and others tried to impress upon Phelan that every delay in hopes of finding yet more proof just increased the risk.

But evidence wasn't the only issue. The lawyer and the detective couldn't even agree on the charges. In his own recommendations,

Zaneth had made clear that he thought a charge under Section 573—conspiracy to commit indictable offences—was easier to prove than a charge under Section 444—conspiracy to defraud the government (since some smuggled goods might simply be banned and not subject to duty). Phelan saw it exactly the other way around. Although he did allow that success in making a charge under 444 stick would depend on the strength of the evidence.

Zaneth immediately wrote to his divisional commander, who forwarded the note to Phelan, making his case again for a charge under Section 573. But Phelan, rather dismissively, stuck to his guns. "Dear Mr. Zaneth," he wrote, skipping over the protocol of rank. "The difference between Sec. 573 and 444 is that the former is directed to a conspiracy to commit a <u>specific</u> offence; the latter is directed to a conspiracy to commit a <u>general</u> offence; and as a general rule it is easier to prove the general than the specific."

Hearing this, Inspector Schutz told one of his men to get on the phone with Phelan and "place before him our opinion" that the charge should be under 573. If Phelan wanted, he could add secondary charges, one of which could be under 444 if it pleased him. Then he wrote to RCMP Commissioner Wood, pushing hard for Zaneth's position—"May I again stress that our position in this matter has not changed"—but pleading in any case for a resolution. The whole process was at a standstill. Phelan had been talking to H. H. Ellis, the departmental solicitor for National Revenue, expressing his doubts about the strength of the evidence, and now Ellis wanted to review everything with Commissioner Scully. And even if they decided something today, Phelan had left town and wouldn't be back until Monday, and since he was the senior counsel making the case in court, he had the last word.

Intensely frustrating, the whole thing. But it was unseemly to commit vexation to paper, so in his letter to Commissioner

Wood, Schutz could only hint at it. "As you are aware," he wrote, "we are fully seized with the great possibility that the two principle [*sic*] co-conspirators, herein, namely Rocco PERRI and Anne NEWMAN, may, at any time, go into hiding." Commissioner Wood thought it best to have his assistant commissioner send, by special messenger, a friendly note to Commissioner Scully. In it, R. R. Tait began by observing that there, ah, seemed to be a delay in coming to a decision, and he assured the commissioner of the force's great appreciation, were he to pick up the telephone soon. As for which charges to bring, Tait admitted that "it is only natural that we would be guided, to a considerable extent, by the advice of counsel, but, at the same time, it is felt that you will agree that Inspector Zaneth has had a good deal of experience in cases of this type during the past four years and has had a very real opportunity to form an opinion as to the charges which are most likely to succeed on the basis of the evidence which he has already compiled." Deep breath.

By Monday, with Hitler on Poland's doorstep and Europe poised for war, both the RCMP and the commissioner of customs agreed it was time to start arresting people. Thomas Phelan, having told everyone he didn't think the case was strong enough, officially shrugged and refused to take responsibility for what happened in court. Warrants were issued the next day for the arrest of bootleggers Rocco Perri, Anne Newman, Sam Miller, René Charron and Sam Motruk, and for Canada Customs examiners Carl Gough, Edward Mansell, Wilfred Fletcher, Norman LePain and two others, Harry Jarvis Smith and Harold Houston Smythe.

The focus was on capturing Perri and Newman, who were in Toronto—staying with Annie's sister, Leah Romberg, and her family at 14 Wells Hill Avenue—and expected to remain there for at least two more days. To do that, the RCMP needed to lure them into the open, so they enlisted an underworld agent to arrange a meeting with them. A little after five o'clock on Wednesday, August 30, as two RCMP officers—Sergeant F. E. Smith and Constable H. S. Bateman—kept their eye on the Wells Hill home, Rocco and Annie emerged. As they got in their car and drove off, Smith and Bateman made their move. They stopped the car just a couple of blocks away, at the corner of Bathurst and Nina streets, and at 5:15 they officially had Rocco and Annie under arrest.

Immediately Frank Zaneth sent a telegram to Commissioner Wood: "WARRANTS TO APPREHEND THE FOLLOWING ISSUED AND EXECUTED AGAINST ROCCO PERRI AND A NEWMAN STOP." Most of the other suspects were arrested the next day. Rocco and Annie were immediately taken to the Don Jail and fingerprinted. They slept at the Don overnight, and at three-thirty the following afternoon officers escorted them to the RCMP's Toronto office, where they were held under guard until 6:25 when it was time to head to Union Station and board the train to Windsor. As they were transferred to the train station, the press swarmed like bees.

For a change it was the *Evening Telegram* that made the most of its opportunity, splashing the front page with a story headlined "Mounties Launch Drive to Crush Gangland in Ontario." Rocco, so used to the attention, smiled broadly and stopped for pictures—cigarette in one hand, valise in the other—as he was escorted to the train. It was all new to Anne Newman, however, and she hated it, trying to hide her face with a newspaper and looking furtively over her shoulder at the press chasing her as a female RCMP officer whisked her along.

The *Telegram* reporter managed to get a few quotes out of Rocco as he walked between his uniformed escorts, and it was as if the coming trial couldn't have been further from his mind. "Let's talk about the war," he suggested. And when asked who his lawyers would be, he said, "There's a lot of time for that. In the meantime I'm getting a free ride to Windsor." A *Toronto Daily Star* reporter and his photographer raced ahead by car and managed to board the train at Chatham, then apparently got close enough to engage Rocco in conversation. Again it was Europe Rocco wanted to discuss, and like a seasoned marketing executive, he positioned himself in the coming conflict. He'd left Italy so long ago, he said, he hardly remembered it. "Canada is my country," he insisted. "Canada is part of the British Empire. I would fight for it." He brushed off questions about his recent encounters with bombs: "There aren't any left in Canada. They've taken them all across to Europe. They need them over there." As for his arrest, Rocco smiled: "The only thing I'm sorry about is that I had a date. A lotta fun, this life."

By nightfall on September 1, 1939, after finally putting handcuffs on Sam Motruk, the RCMP had arrested everyone it wanted to arrest with the exception of Montreal's René Charron, who couldn't be found. Returning from Windsor, satisfied at least that something had been accomplished, Zaneth became aware that Thomas Phelan was still fixed on a major charge of conspiracy under Section 444 of the Criminal Code. Yet again Zaneth made his arguments against it. He all but staked his reputation on the issue, saying Phelan was "in error." It was "obvious" to him that the main charge should be conspiracy to commit an indictable offence under Section 573, with its connection to Section 250 of the Customs Act (bribery). The whole RCMP command structure rallied around him and, in meetings and in memos, pressed Phelan and H. H. Ellis to agree.

Of course, equipped with only circumstantial physical evidence—notebook names, hotel and phone records, a few uncancelled tourist permits for cars that left Canada legally and re-entered loaded with booze—the Crown's case, Zaneth's case, rested almost entirely on the testimony of its three witnesses, David Armaly, Milton Goldhart and Victor Bernat. This worried Zaneth enough that he arranged to have Armaly and his wife moved to a furnished cottage near the Ottawa River in Woodroffe, Ontario. The Armalys had to supply their own cutlery and when they arrived there was no linen. But they liked the cottage, and the government covered the rent, food and three dollars per diem. Any mail they wanted to send had to be given to the RCMP so that it could be postmarked from Toronto. The other two witnesses were billeted out to the homes of RCMP officers, Bernat in Amherstburg and Goldhart in Lindsay, and paid smaller per diems.

Zaneth admitted the added expense and trouble were regrettable but absolutely necessary. The arrests had effectively shut down the activities of a number of American gangsters—caused a "violent furor" among them, according to Zaneth's boss—and now there was pressure to make the witnesses, "through intimidation or bribery," either disappear or change their stories. He couldn't allow that to happen.

AFTER all the effort to get Rocco Perri and Anne Newman behind bars, they were free the next day. To the amazement of the RCMP, whom no one had consulted, Windsor's magistrate released them on ten thousand dollars' bail each. "Arrangements for the racketeer and his companion, ashen-locked Anne Newman, went through in record time," announced the *Windsor Daily Star*. Rocco returned immediately to Hamilton by car while Annie continued to Toronto. Furious, the RCMP kept Rocco under watch, and took some comfort from his "self-confident" attitude, which suggested he was unlikely to skip the country before the trial.

On September 7, after talking again with solicitor H. H. Ellis and one of the customs department's own inspectors, Thomas Phelan finally relented and agreed to two main charges under Section 573 of the Criminal Code—conspiracy to commit an indictable offence, specifically the offence of bribing a customs official, or accepting a bribe to allow smuggling, under Section 250 of the Customs Act. And he included an additional charge, his favourite: conspiracy to defraud the government by evading customs duties, under Section 444 of the Criminal Code. It was everything Zaneth had been asking for, and no one could say Phelan was happy about it.

Leaving nothing to chance, Zaneth involved himself in the arrangements to have all three Crown witnesses driven to Windsor, properly housed and ready to appear before a special grand jury the following week. He instructed the transporting officers to keep their eyes open and make sure no one tried to interfere.

Everything went as well as he could have hoped. On the morning of Tuesday, September 12, Phelan presented his evidence and his witnesses at the Essex County Courthouse, just outside of Windsor. The grand jury returned "true bills" on all charges, and the trials—there would be three of them—were set for the following January.

Initially, Phelan was pleased with the way Armaly handled himself in the witness box: "I think the Court at the trial will be favourably impressed by him." But the more Phelan thought about it over the next few days, the more he studied what evidence he had and tried to work out how he was going to make the case to the jury, the less pleased he became. By Saturday, he'd become "very much disturbed."

He didn't have enough to get a conviction; he was sure of it. Besides the utter lack of solid physical evidence, there was another problem: Armaly. Not that he wasn't a good witness; it was possible he was *too* good. Phelan feared that the jury would look at Armaly as the instigator of the conspiracy and start to doubt his testimony. So the senior counsel called a meeting with the RCMP and made it clear: He wanted a detective detailed to study the evidence they had and try to get more. He wanted Armaly's statement corroborated "in every minute detail." Were there telegrams on file from Rocco Perri and Anne Newman? If there were he wanted them in his hand. He wanted to be able to prove they were the instigators, not Armaly. Phelan handed the RCMP his brief in which he had outlined twenty-two points of concern.

Immediately Zaneth travelled to Ottawa and reinterrogated Armaly and his wife to pull out additional useful details, or to see if he could shake what he'd already been given. Investigators were dispatched to hotels to look for occurrences of the aliases Armaly had used—"David Roy" or "Sam Ballis." As much as possible, the evidence was confirmed, and Zaneth promised to do more. On September 22, he handed in a six-page memorandum responding to every one of Thomas Phelan's questions.

Unfortunately, many of his answers were not what Phelan wanted to hear. There were no witnesses to Sam Miller paying money to Armaly. No exact dates noted for cars coming through customs. No records of Armaly banking his bribes (he was spending them all at the craps table). In sum, there would never be the weight of direct, tangible evidence Phelan hoped for.

Zaneth's memo did, however, include a helpful two-page lesson in conspiracy law, which boiled down to this: Where secret plots were concerned, circumstantial evidence was pretty much the norm, and a participant's testimony was usually proof enough. He listed all the legal precedents, too, which Phelan no doubt appreciated.

But all that simply underlined the fact that an important federal case still rested on the testimony of three criminal accomplices.

And with so much time to pass until the trials in January, and no practical or reasonable way to restrain their movements, those three men were at risk of taking what Assistant Commissioner Tait called "a prolonged holiday from Canada."

Already some of the accused were working hard to find out where the Crown witnesses were being kept, and the buzz in the underworld said that information was leaking from Windsor. Inspector Schutz in Toronto sent a stern note to the RCMP's Windsor detachment, telling them essentially to keep their mouths shut. Meanwhile, Armaly and his wife, stuck with only one of their children in a summer cottage in a rapidly cooling Ottawa region, were missing the rest of their kids and wondering when Rocco Perri was going to have David "bumped off." The deputy minister of justice summed it up neatly for the attorney general of Ontario: "The whole situation is very disquieting."

Deep into the fall, the Crown and the Mounties fretted and argued about their evidence. At one point Phelan was so fed up that he tried to assign some junior lawyers to deal with Zaneth, but Zaneth complained they were out of their depth. In the absence of hard evidence the Crown lined up extra witnesses—hotel clerks, telegraph and phone company employees—to vouch for what the star witnesses would say.

As the leaves turned, those star witnesses were becoming a problem. Milton Goldhart, rotting away in tiny Lindsay, said he wanted to enlist in the Royal Canadian Air Force. The Mounties couldn't stop him, and rationalized it this way: maybe it would keep him out of trouble until the trial. So they drove him into Toronto, where it seemed he would stay with his parents, and asked him to keep in touch. Then they crossed their fingers really hard—because, as a commanding Mountie said, a disappeared Goldhart "would seriously inconvenience us."

Meanwhile David Armaly, his wife and their youngest child were forced to find new accommodations in Ottawa (relatives were taking care of their other three children). The RCMP upped Armaly's per-diem money a little, but he was becoming increasingly agitated. And soon reports came in that Anne Newman was trying to reach him.

In the first week of December, five weeks before the trial, the work, the worry and the constant, relentless travelling finally got to Frank Zaneth. Just turned forty-nine, he suffered what RCMP internal memos called a "nervous breakdown."

In the medical parlance of the 1930s, a nervous breakdown meant something a little different from what it suggests today. The memos contained no specific details of what happened, but very likely Zaneth collapsed from exhaustion. A doctor who examined him noted: "no suggestion of hysteria but very tense and intent." He was hospitalized for several days, then sent on seven weeks' medical leave to recuperate. On December 30, as he was making his way to Miami Beach, Florida, he stopped at the Hotel Pennsylvania in New York City and sent a letter to a friend. "I am still very weak," he wrote. "I hope that a few days in a warmer climate will help me."

It was good for Zaneth that he got himself far away from Toronto, because back there the news was getting worse. At the Rex Hotel, on the corner of Queen and St. Patrick streets, the thing the RCMP dreaded actually happened: Rocco Perri met with Milton Goldhart to talk about how to get him out of the country. Rocco even gave him a wad of cash to make his trip a little more comfortable. The Mounties learned about the meeting because it was attended by a third man who happened to be an informant, and he let the force know they were now dealing with an emergency.

Multiple copies of Goldhart's picture were sent to bus terminals, border checkpoints and U.S. Immigration in Detroit. Thomas

Phelan arranged for a subpoena to be served on Goldhart at his parents' house the next day. An arrest warrant was issued too, but it could only be executed if Goldhart was stopped at the border. The RCMP had considered dispatching officers to arrest him immediately, but they were anxious not to turn him into a hostile witness. They hadn't quite grasped that he already was.

The next day, Goldhart was gone. RCMP constables headed to the border to meet buses and trains arriving from Toronto. Lookouts with binoculars took up positions on international bridges. The Mounties never saw him again. "It almost seems a pity that he was not arrested as soon as his probable intentions were known," wrote Customs solicitor H. H. Ellis to RCMP Commissioner Wood. Dryly, he suggested Wood consider taking steps to ensure that Anne Newman didn't disappear as well.

A SERIES of three trials, set to begin on January 15, 1940, at the Supreme Court of Ontario in Windsor, separated the defendants into three distinct conspiracy groups. The first trial would pit the Crown against Sam Miller and the four customs officers: Carl Gough, Edward Mansell, Wilfred Fletcher and Norman LePain. The second trial would prosecute Rocco Perri, Anne Newman and those same four officers. A third trial put Sam Motruk together with the two other accused customs examiners, Harry Jarvis Smith and Harold Houston Smythe. It gave the Crown three cracks at prosecuting official corruption, but only one shot at Rocco Perri.

The rumours of jury tampering began almost two weeks before the first trial, with at least one member of the jury, and possibly others, said to have received instructions from a prominent Windsor Liberal to vote Not Guilty. It was likely coincidental that the lawyer representing Anne Newman was Windsor Liberal MP

Paul Martin the future secretary of state and minister of national health and welfare (and father of future Prime Minister Paul Martin Jr.). Rocco would be defended by an expensive Toronto lawyer, Joseph M. Bullen, KC, who had just defended Stinson Aircraft Corporation in Canada's first-ever aviation accident suit.

Mere days before the trials were set to start, David Armaly seemed ready to bolt. Having learned its lesson, the RCMP assigned a Corporal Hunt, from the Ottawa office, to spend time with him every day—take him out driving in the patrol car if necessary. Apparently it worked. As the Crown began to present its case in Trial No. 1, its first and main witness took the stand. "Armaly did exceedingly well," said Staff Sergeant G. J. Archer, who reported to the commanders on each day's events. Archer gave Corporal Hunt a special pat on the back. "This witness has been far from easy to handle."

Unfortunately for the Crown, that was the high point. In cross-examination, the defence attacked Armaly's character, brought up his past as a gambler and card dealer, and used his wife's corroborating testimony—that she had handed bribe money to officials—against him. "You're also dragging your wife into this?" thundered one of the defence attorneys. "I thought there were some things you wouldn't do." Armaly's credibility took an even harder blow with the revelation that he had accepted per-diem money from the RCMP, even as he was receiving welfare payments. (One or the other was legal, but not both.) And that was before the defence picked apart the Crown's indictments against the accused officers, noting the lack of specifics in the times and places of the alleged crimes. According to Carl Gough's lawyer, Keith Laird, the whole thing was "the biggest frame-up in the history of Essex County."

After just two days, Archer's reports to his superiors turned grim: "It must be admitted at this time that the Crown case against the Customs officers is extremely weak." It looked that way to the judge too. Even before the trial's closing arguments, Mr. Justice McFarland called Thomas Phelan into his private chambers and asked whether, in the event of a Not Guilty verdict, he intended to go ahead with the next two cases. He did.

The trial was over on January 23, and Phelan had done what he could. "Should a dismissal result," Archer wrote to his superiors, "no criticism should be attached to him." A jury of Windsor citizens deliberated for five hours and found Sam Miller guilty of conspiracy to defraud and conspiracy to commit an indictable offence. But it returned Not Guilty verdicts on each of the customs officials—upstanding Windsor men, every one—whom the judge said could now "return to your families without stigma." Thomas Phelan steeled himself for what lay ahead.

Trial No. 2—the Rocco Perri and Anne Newman edition—began the next day.

Armaly was every bit as good the second time as he was the first. "The amazing David Armaly," wrote the *Windsor Daily Star*, "continued in his cool, unperturbed manner to disclose the story of alcohol smuggling that over a period of years has defrauded the Dominion Government of more than $250,000 according to testimony." But this time he was cross-examined even more effectively, revealed in all his glory to be, as Sergeant Archer put it, "a first-class scoundrel."

Forgery, welfare cheating, gambling, smuggling, bribing officials—these were the crimes to which Armaly admitted. "Is there much in the Criminal Code you haven't done?" asked J. M. Bullen. And as Paul Martin took his turn laying into Armaly, Archer was astonished to hear details of a private meeting he had conducted months before with Armaly and Goldhart, to clear up conflicts in their official statements. "I cannot understand in what manner Mr. Martin became possessed of his facts," Archer wrote. He'd forgotten about the reported meeting between Goldhart and Rocco at the Rex Hotel, before Goldhart disappeared.

The defence was now so confident of victory that it hardly even bothered to defend the accused customs officers. In fact, once Armaly was off the stand, perhaps the hardest work at defence came on the street outside the courtroom. Anne Newman was still mortified at having her picture taken by the press, and when a *Windsor Daily Star* photographer tried to snap off a shot, she screamed and lunged at him. Rocco, who'd been locking the door of their car, turned toward the commotion. Nothing upset him as much as a threat to the woman he loved. "I'll get you, you son of a bitch!" he yelled. As the photographer ran, Rocco picked up a rock and hurled it at him. "Come back and fight, you coward!" He was still seething later inside the courtroom.

As the second trial progressed, Frank Zaneth felt well enough to travel to Windsor, and he was sitting among the gallery spectators on January 30, as Thomas Phelan gave his closing argument. He saw a memorable, two-hour performance that received compliments from the judge. But, alas, it wasn't enough. On February 1, after a full day's deliberation, the jury returned Not Guilty verdicts on every defendant in the second trial. As Rocco, Anne Newman and the customs officials were discharged, Sam Miller's wife was so happy for Annie that she rushed over and kissed her.

In the end, only Sam Miller and Sammy Motruk did any time for the Windsor conspiracy. Miller got two years in Portsmouth Penitentiary; Motruk three years and a fine of four thousand dollars. Thomas Phelan, who grew increasingly "disgruntled" with the testimony of various customs employees, pushed for perjury charges against one of them and won a conviction. (Zaneth was engaged in this proceeding, which is an indication that his health had improved.) The only other key figure to do time was, ironically, David Armaly, who was found guilty of welfare fraud for having accepted government assistance while he was being paid by the RCMP. He spent three months in jail.

The lesson for the RCMP, wrote Staff Sergeant G. J. Archer—besides not using a welfare cheat as a witness in a trial where all the jurors were quite obviously poor—was that a conspiracy conviction required hard proof. The testimony of a co-conspirator can too easily be discredited, said Archer, and "the evidence of an accomplice cannot be corroborated by another accomplice."

It was the perfect illustration of Rocco Perri's genius. For all the credit that Bessie Perri and later Anne Newman received as the brains behind the Perri racket, they were always more exposed to prosecution. Rocco was smart enough to stay in the background, working the levers, always smiling.

27

PRIGIONIERO
Captive

THERE WAS NO LEGAL WAY TO GET AT ROCCO. HE WAS too protected and too disciplined. Years earlier, it had taken something extraordinary—a Royal Commission—to create the opportunity for authorities to put him away, and even then it was only for five months. To actually lock him up for a significant length of time, to finally put Rocco Perri out of business, would take something monumental.

It took a world war.

By the spring of 1940, the Allies were thoroughly bloodied. The Soviet Union had invaded Finland in March. By the middle of April, Germany had occupied Denmark, was hammering at Norway and would soon march into France. As the Nazis pushed their way into one territory after another with little resistance, Italy's strutting Fascist dictator, Benito Mussolini, began making noises that he would soon launch his country into war against France and Britain.

In Canada, the RCMP saw an opportunity.

Since well before the beginning of the conflict in Europe, in fact since 1936, the Mounties had been monitoring Fascists in Canada the way they had Communists two decades before, keeping an eye on what they considered a growing internal threat. With the start of the war in September 1939, the RCMP had been preparing to act.

They worked under the direction of a federal committee consisting of three people: J. F. MacNeill, KC, a lawyer with the Department of Justice; RCMP Superintendent E. W. Bavin, and a counsellor in External Affairs named Norman Robertson, who had been appointed chairman by Minister of Justice Ernest Lapointe. The committee's work consisted of building a list of names, all resident Italians who seemed prime targets for arrest in the event of war. Robertson was ambivalent about the job. He knew the list included not just members of the Fascio—a local political party sworn to execute the orders of *il Duce* in the cause of the Fascist Revolution—but also members of Italian community organizations like the Sons of Italy and an after-work club, the Dopolavoro, many of whom posed little if any threat. But Robertson was caught between the orders of his federal minister and the zeal of the RCMP, who saw a chance not only to defend Canada against Fascism but to deal with other irritants.

On May 2, 1940, RCMP Commissioner Stuart Wood issued a directive, referring to the "Italian question," that called on his division commanders to "submit any names of Italians whom you would consider a menace in case Italy enters the war on the side of Germany." And just to be clear that he was opening a door wide for them, he added, "Kindly submit the names of Italians who may prove dangerous or whose activities during the past would warrant internment."

As suggestions came in from divisions across the country, Wood sent a note to the minister of justice on May 17, proposing that

Crown counsels be appointed to examine the names. He listed six qualified lawyers, one of whom was Thomas Phelan, who had so recently failed in pressing his case against Rocco Perri. Wood suggested that the chosen lawyers be notified immediately so that they would be "ready to move into action with the police."

Like every other high-ranking member of the RCMP, Frank Zaneth was asked for his input. But Frank Zaneth, especially so. A man famous for dealing with conspirators, for seeing these men up close, and an Italian himself—his opinion regarding whose names should be on the list would have carried special weight. Zaneth gave his input a week after the Windsor perjury case he was engaged in reached a conclusion, and on May 29, Norman Robertson submitted to Minister Lapointe a secret memo on RCMP letterhead with his committee's report. He attached two appendices. "The persons whose names and addresses are listed in Appendices I and II to this report are all residents of Canada, of Italian birth, and members of the Fascio," he wrote. "The Committee feels that members of the Fascio of Italian nationality are clearly 'dangerous persons' who should not be left at large in time of war."

And there was Rocco's name.

All the RCMP needed now was a declaration of war. A few minutes after one o'clock on June 10, 1940, Mussolini did his part in Rome, stepping out onto the balcony of the Palazzo di Venezia to declare war on Britain and France. At about 2:30 p.m.—several hours before Canada's Parliament responded with an official declaration of war against Italy—Ottawa issued orders for its internment receiving centres to open, and for the RCMP to start bringing people in.

The arrests in Hamilton came without warning just before supper time. Police cars fanned out across the city, and officers simultaneously came through the doors of homes, restaurants, liquor dives and factories, taking some fifteen men into custody (a number that, in Hamilton, would eventually reach nearly eighty). In Toronto that night, seventy-seven men were detained and by the end, some weeks later, police across Canada—sometimes with the help of eager citizens—had arrested nearly six hundred men. Many of the arrests came in Montreal, where nearly a thousand police officers from six forces descended on Italian homes and businesses. Men were grabbed off buses. There were arrests in many of the Ontario towns where Italian settlements had made it easy for Rocco to extend his reach—Guelph, South Porcupine, North Bay, Welland, Niagara Falls. There were arrests across Canada, from Vancouver to Cape Breton. For those Italians who were left behind, violence and job losses followed. Store windows were smashed, and non-naturalized Italians were taken off the relief rolls. An editorial in the *Globe and Mail* decried the hysteria, the hooliganism, and the "foolish and feeble" federal policy that had led to them.

Despite his pre-emptive declaration that he had no interest in Italy and would fight for Canada (almost as if he'd known what was coming), Rocco was the first important mob figure outside of Montreal arrested that night. He was picked up at 243 Hughson Street North, where he may have been staying in an attempt to elude the police. If Annie wasn't there at the time, it's doubtful Rocco had a chance to let her know he was being taken. Along with the other Hamilton men grabbed without warning, he was taken first to the Barton Street jail. They were later processed at the Automotive Building on the CNE grounds in Toronto. Then he was put on a train to an internment camp in the forest near Petawawa, Ontario.

Before long he was joined by other Italian crime figures. Frank Ross was arrested on August 20. The order to pick up Charles Bordonaro was signed on September 5, and he was eventually jailed for failing to report as an Enemy Alien. Tony Papalia avoided capture for a while, but ultimately he arrived at Petawawa too. So did Michael Perri, Mike Romeo, Luigi Mascia, Domenico Longo, John Taglierino and the Sacco brothers from Niagara Falls. At first prospective detainees were routinely labelled "important members of the Fascio," but eventually that formality was abandoned. One of Rocco's men, Giovanni (John) Durso, brother-in-law of Frank Ross, was taken from his Hess Street North home on January 16, 1941, for the reason that "he is considered to be a dangerous man and should be placed in the same category as Rocco Perri and others of that kind who have been interned." Eventually anyone who seemed a possible sabotage suspect became fair game—that included men who were "weak-minded," or men who were "shiftless" or poor and might do anything for money.

It was such an easy way to incarcerate suspected gangsters that the RCMP could hardly contain itself. In his letter recommending the internment of Hamilton gangster Frank Corde, Commissioner Stuart Wood filled three pages with Corde's supposed transgressions and associations (including with Rocco Perri). Then he admitted that "although there is little proof to support our information," he was sure the Italian government would use the Mafia against Canada if it could. He was wrong, of course—Mussolini considered the Mafia a direct threat to Fascism—but for the RCMP it was a convenient misapprehension.

A few dozen Italian Canadians from western Canada wound up in a camp in Kananaskis, Alberta. For the rest, Petawawa was now home. The men were housed behind barbed wire in large sixty-man barracks heated by two or three stoves. Rocco, like the rest, handed over his belongings when he arrived. In return he received leather boots, gumboots, socks and underwear, and sets of summer and winter work clothes. The back of each denim shirt featured a large, circular red sniper target; a long red stripe marked each pant leg.

At night he slept on a narrow bunk bed surrounded by other non-Fascists. During the day he laboured in one of several work groups—some cut and planted trees, others worked in maintenance, or the kitchen—and received twenty-five cents a day.

For a while Rocco worked in the kitchen. Now and then in Hamilton he'd enjoyed cooking up huge pots of spaghetti sauce, so in Petawawa he worked alongside Joseph Constantini, a Union Station employee who was disgusted by the food when he arrived and thought he could do better. Very briefly they were joined by a fifty-two-year-old chef named Carlo Scarabelli who had worked in New York's Waldorf Astoria and for decades had cooked for diplomats and visiting royalty at Ottawa's Château Laurier Hotel. Scarabelli was released from the camp after about five weeks; Constantini after nine months. Rocco's internment lasted almost three and a half years.

Throughout that time, he behaved with the dignity and generosity that people who knew him had come to expect. "There was a goodness about him," one of Anne Newman's nephews, Harry Romberg, would remember later. "Something about him attracted people."

He played cards and *bocce*, watched concerts put on by his fellow internees, freely shared the contents of care packages from Annie, and traded chocolate for cigarettes. Guards and most fellow internees treated him with respect, and he used his influence quietly. A story emerged from the recollections of internees that one day a man from Rocco's barracks asked the guards for new shoes to replace the worn-out ones on his feet. No one paid him any heed. Rocco said he would look after it, and a while later he returned with a new pair of shoes.

It was a lonely and vastly diminished existence, but Rocco was still Rocco. He's said to have sent a letter to his mother in Platì, explaining that "I am shut up in a camp for prisoners of war, but I am well." And from appearances, he was. A picture of him among a group of eleven internees in 1942 shows him standing in the elevated back row. He is the only man in the picture expressing friendship, resting his hands comfortably on the shoulders of the two men in front of him. And his face, not surprisingly, shows the most genuine smile.

IIIIIIIIIIIIIIIIIIIIIIIIIIIIIIIIII

AS WAR RAGED OVERSEAS, FRANK ZANETH WAS CALLED west. The prairies had been hit by an epidemic of safe-blowing, and to put a stop to it the RCMP dispatched Zaneth to F division headquarters in Regina. He was to lead a three-province effort to train officers and direct investigations.

Given his previous luck, it was only natural that this move would cause Zaneth more monetary hardship. He had been instructed to live in the officer's mess at a cost of two dollars per day, and thanks to some kind of bureaucratic shuffle, he lost his hard-won four-dollar per diem for married officers. He hated living in the mess, and with taxes higher in Saskatchewan, he could hardly afford it. This was on top of the fact that his Rita-related expenses were now one hundred dollars per month. (A wartime ban against sending money to Italy meant Zaneth had to bank the money and send it to his father-in-law when the ban was lifted.)

In July 1940, Zaneth, struggling with his eyesight and new glasses that gave him unbearable headaches, asked to have his per diem restored, and in August it was. But it was as if he were cursed. A year later, having transferred to K division in Alberta, his four-dollar per diem was lost again in bureaucratic confusion. By October 1941, Zaneth was worried about going into debt. "I naturally feel that I should not be put to that inconvenience," he wrote, "even though 'F' Div. insists that it is up to 'K' to straighten things out."

On October 28, 1941, Zaneth received a letter from Assistant Commissioner W. F. W. Hancock, letting him know an adjustment was coming: "I am sorry that you are having so much difficulty with your vouchers, etc., and I think you will realize that it is no fault of mine."

A couple of weeks later, on November 11, Commissioner Wood wrote Zaneth to congratulate him on the success of his "Safe-Blowing Squads." More than that, he thanked Zaneth for his "conscientious and loyal work, which is a credit to the Force." Four days later, thanks to another expense-voucher mix-up, he directed that Zaneth's pay be docked thirty dollars per month.

28

TERMINE
Ending

ONE BY ONE, MANY OF ROCCO'S KNOWN ASSOCIATES—
including Mike Perri, Frank Corde, one of the Romeo brothers, Luigi Mascia, Giovanni (John) Durso, John Taglierino,
both Ross brothers—were set free. Some of these may have obtained
"bought releases." Others were just lucky. As time passed, RCMP
Commissioner Wood wrote letters in support of releasing any number of Italian internees. "The need for men in our industries is great at
this time," he would write below a list of names. "These men are not
considered to be a menace to the safety of the State." But Rocco—
internee P298—remained hidden away. In July 1942, he was one of
the remaining Italians shipped to an internment camp in Fredericton,
where newer barracks housed 160 men. It wasn't until September 28,
1943, that Rocco—having agreed to stay out of Hamilton and get a
real job—was finally allowed to walk free. He had been among the
first to arrive, and he was one of the last to leave.

He returned to a reality far different from the one he'd known.

For a start, Anne Newman wasn't there to welcome him home.
In Rocco's absence she'd sunk her energies into an international

gold high-grading racket. A gang of one woman and ten men, including a young Toronto optometrist, they turned miners into gold thieves and assayers into scam artists. Complicit miners would sneak fragments of gold out of mines, while assayers would give false weights on their measurements, reading twelve ounces of gold as ten and skimming off the two missing ounces for Newman's group. They melted down the gold into bars and "buttons," then smuggled it into the United States, in canvas vests, at a rate of at least ten thousand dollars a week. Annie, now living with her sister Leah Romberg and her family in Toronto, had bought the Metro Theatre on Bloor Street West as a front and worked out of an office there. Police were able to prove that over one particular stretch of time she had handled forty-four $1,000 bills, representing a tiny fraction of the fortune involved.

Unfortunately for Newman and the rest of the ring, on October 4, 1941, a U.S. customs officer noticed something suspicious about a Buffalo resident named Harry Julius, who was returning home from Canada. When he searched Julius, he found a vest laden with thousands of dollars in gold, and soon the whole ring was uncovered. In June 1942, after a complicated month-long trial, Newman was sent away for three years in Kingston's Prison for Women.

The power structure of the Ontario–New York underworld axis had also changed dramatically. In the vacuum created by the internments of Rocco and many from his gang, Buffalo's Stefano Magaddino had taken over. The fifty-four-year-old Magaddino wielded a far heavier hand than Rocco ever had, and the likes of Tony Papalia, Frank Ross and Charlie Bordonaro had quickly fallen in with him. By the time Rocco Perri was freed, in other words, "Rocco Perri" had ceased to exist. He had few friends, no organization and no power. It was everything the RCMP had wanted.

Even his home had changed—166 Bay Street South in

Hamilton, still legally owned by Anne Newman, had been turned into a boarding house by her sister. When Rocco first returned from Fredericton, he lived with the Rombergs at 14 Wells Hill Avenue in Toronto. For the purposes of government paperwork, he became a doorman and janitor for Annie's Metro Theatre. What he really did with his time, though, was nurse a newfound bitterness. He was fifty-five years old, and he had lost everything. The government had used a cheat to incarcerate him, his allies had abandoned him, and the law had put the woman he loved behind bars. He had not come to *l'America* for this.

His brooding lasted through the fall, but it's possible that by December he was already back in the game. Gangster Donald (Mickey) McDonald—who for a time was considered Canada's "Public Enemy No. 1"—cited Rocco in court as the mystery man behind a December 13, 1943, hijacking of a load of liquor from the Western Freight Line's warehouse. Whether or not that was true, there's no doubt that by the spring Rocco was taking action.

On Monday, April 17, 1944, he attended a funeral in Hamilton. There he saw his brother Mike, who'd found work as a John Street grocer, and perhaps a few of his old associates as well. On Thursday of that week, he returned to Hamilton to stay for a few days at the Murray Street East home of his cousin Joe Serge, who'd been one of the chief mourners at Bessie's funeral.

There were reports of a meeting in Serge's house that brought Rocco together with some of the old gang—possibly including Tony Ross and Giovanni Durso—where he may have talked about his plans. On the afternoon of Saturday, April 22, he went to Bay Street South to get a good look at what had become of his house, and made the decision then to ask Harry Romberg, Annie's brother-in-law, to clear out the tenants. He wanted to move back home.

The next day, Rocco apparently woke up with a headache. He

rubbed his eyes, came downstairs to the kitchen and washed down a couple of aspirin with coffee. Then he stood at the window looking out at a blustery, rainy day.

There are two versions of what happened next.

According to what Joe Serge later told police, sometime between ten-thirty and eleven o'clock, Rocco decided to go out for a walk in that lousy weather. Dressed in a blue pinstripe suit, with a pair of black Oxfords on his feet, he pulled on a beige spring overcoat and set a light brown fedora on his head. Then he headed out the door.

According to the story related years later to Italian-born Toronto-based author Antonio Nicaso by Rocco's nephew, Giuseppe Perri, the telephone rang for Rocco that morning. He was told there was something that needed attending to. "They instructed him to go to John Street where someone would meet him," said his nephew. If true, that might explain why he seemed to be dressed for business.

In either case, Rocco walked out the door and never came back.

He had left his car parked across the street, and it took Joe Serge two days of looking at that unmoving vehicle to call the Hamilton police and report Rocco missing. When Detective Ernest Barrett and an RCMP corporal showed up at his door, he told them Rocco hadn't seemed worried of late. In fact, he "was in good spirits all the time." Then he pointed out Rocco's car and gave Detective Barrett the keys so he could search it.

Barrett found not much—two unaddressed Easter cards in the glove compartment and a pair of black overshoes, size 7½, on the rear seat, and some old newspapers. But then, hidden among the newspapers, he found a handwritten note. It was a kind of angry love letter, a man lamenting that he had been fooled into thinking a woman had loved him, though she was afraid to show her face with him in public. It was unsigned, unaddressed and scribbled in an English too illiterate to have been Rocco's work. Joe Serge had seemed so eager for Detective Barrett to search Rocco's car that he may well have written and planted it himself. Amid the jumble of misspelled words, it contained a line that hinted at farewell—"I soon sacrificed my selfe and not jgive you any worry."

If the note added to the questions around Rocco's disappearance, Joe Serge certainly seemed unwilling to provide answers. While Rocco's car was still parked across the street, a reporter named Alfred McKee knocked on Serge's door. When it opened, McKee would later write, "A man pointed a gun at me and told me to get going." After that, no newspaper tried to pry further into the mystery of what happened to the little mob boss who had reigned so well, and so colourfully, for so long.

THERE are two theories for what became of Rocco: One, he was murdered by rival gangsters. According to this theory, when Rocco walked out of Joe Serge's house that April morning, he went to a meeting from which he was lured or muscled into a car, taken somewhere secluded and killed. Later that summer, a close Perri associate, Toronto bootlegger and drug trafficker Louis Wernick, told a friend that Rocco "is in a barrel of cement at the bottom of Hamilton Bay." Independently, police had heard the same thing. This is the story that grew into legend.

It is undoubtedly true that Stefano Magaddino would not have tolerated a resurgent Rocco Perri in territory he now controlled, and would have acted quickly if he perceived a challenge. By then he had plenty of Hamilton lieutenants willing to carry out his orders—the Ontario arm of the Magaddino family was known as the "Three Dons," headed up, it was said, by Tony Sylvestro (a.k.a. Tony Ross). Supporting this theory is the fact that, following Rocco's disappearance, Magaddino's hand could be seen in the murders of two other Perri associates.

On September 8, 1944, Rocco's man Giovanni Durso went missing. Three days later his car turned up on the banks of the Welland Canal but, as with Rocco, Durso's body was never found. Then on January 15, 1945, gunmen approached Louis Wernick as he was walking to a streetcar. They pulled him into a car and took him to a hidden location where they shot him five times in the head, throat and torso. Then they dumped him in a snowbank on Evans Avenue near Long Branch Racetrack. Police were certain the orders to kill Wernick had come from Buffalo.

The second theory about Rocco's disappearance holds that he fled to Mexico. Moses Mulholland, then chief inspector with the Toronto Police Service, spoke a couple of times about hearing that's where Rocco had gone. He may have heard it from the FBI, who allegedly received tips about Rocco smuggling in Mexico in 1945. Either way, Mulholland figured no one was likely to find him—"Mexico is a big country."

In this scenario, Rocco walked out of Serge's house in his pinstripe suit, but before he arrived at his destination someone, possibly Tony Ross, alerted him to Magaddino's plans and helped spirit him to safety. This version, from Antonio Nicaso, has Rocco travelling first to Massena, New York, and then farther south, with the help of none other than his old friend Sidney Gogo, who had managed to reclaim his confiscated boat, the *Hattie C*. To support that idea, Nicaso relates a story in which Joe Romeo spoke to a friend about Rocco in 1948, assuring him, "Don't worry, he's fine and is living in Mexico." Nicaso also claims to have seen a letter, written in Italian, that Rocco sent to Joe Serge in 1949, telling his cousin he was in excellent health.

There were at least three other men who believed, about a year after Rocco's disappearance, that he was still alive. Late on February 25, 1945, three masked gunmen invaded the Hamilton home of a man that the *Globe and Mail* reported as Alfred Calderone (Nicaso suggests this man was Joe Serge) and demanded, "Where's Rocco Perri?" Calderone said he didn't know, but the gunmen were certain he did. When they failed to get the answer they wanted, they tied up Calderone and his wife and daughter with neckties, then took a diamond ring, six hundred dollars in cash and a revolver from Calderone's safe.

Four years later, the final reverberations from Rocco's disappearance may have been felt in the MacNab Street North home of Frank Ross. On October 18, 1949, an argument between Frank and his brother Tony led to Frank shooting Tony at close range, then turning the gun on himself. Their elderly mother ran screaming from the house and Frank, dead, and Tony, critically wounded, were found with almost eight thousand dollars in their pockets. But whether Frank had shot his brother for helping Rocco escape, or whether he'd been suffering from a prolonged and worsening mental disturbance, as the police were told, remains a mystery.

But happy in Mexico or encased in cement, Rocco was beyond worrying about any of this. He was, now and forever, just a memory in the place he'd once been king.

||||||||||||||||||||||||||

I N March 1943, a judge of the Probate Court in Springfield, Massachusetts, granted Zaneth's request to have his marriage to Rita annulled, and he was finally released from his obligation. That freed him to take one last stab at love. At the age of fifty-three, stationed in Montreal, he met Edith Didsbury, a slender, petite secretary sixteen years younger than him. Edith seemed to adore Frank, and the two exchanged vows on September 23, 1944. He immediately asked for the four-dollar per diem allowed to married officers, and it was granted two days later.

His newly wedded status in no way kept Zaneth away from the action. During a conscription crisis in Drummondville, Quebec, in February 1945, he organized raids to ferret out draft dodgers, and then was caught in the middle of a riot that became known as the Battle of Heriot Hill. A mob that fluctuated between five hundred and fifteen hundred people advanced on the RCMP detachment, smashing windows and overturning police cars as Zaneth and a line of officers tried to hold them back. In the midst of the melee, Zaneth stopped one of his own men from beating up a prisoner. Thanks to dramatic coverage in the *Montreal Gazette*, the riot gained such notoriety that Zaneth, and particularly his heritage, came up for debate in the House of Commons. "What is the country of origin of Inspector Zaneth?" asked Joseph A. Choquette, a member of the Bloc Populaire. "What is his racial origin? When did he enter Canada? Has he been naturalized?" Choquette had ten such questions about Zaneth in all. But little more came of it after Commissioner Wood sent a friendly note to the minister of justice, suggesting that the Member for Stanstead may have had a hidden agenda: The previous November, Zaneth had been in charge at Montreal when Choquette was detained for smuggling in American cigarettes.

On October 1, 1945, the RCMP promoted Zaneth to super-intendent and increased his pay to $2,720 a year. In November, the *Gazette* profiled Zaneth and dubbed him "Ace of Undercover Men." By 1949 he had been in the RCMP for thirty-one years, and Commissioner Wood, who had long since become a great admirer, made him an assistant commissioner. With his salary nearly doubled to $4,421, Zaneth was appointed director of training.

From a poor, immigrant homesteader, he had fashioned himself into the model Mountie, mandated to turn every new recruit into a facsimile of himself. He worked at that task for two years, until 1951 when, at the age of sixty, he finally retired. By the time he left the force, he was regarded with awe. The men who knew him traded stories about his cool resolve—such as the time he'd been attacked by a vicious dog and, leaving his revolver in its holster, calmly wrestled the canine to submission. An RCMP deputy commissioner who'd worked with Zaneth in 1930s Montreal later said that colleagues referred to him as a "'BTO'—a big time operator."

After he left the force, Zaneth and Edith lived for a while in Toronto, then spent a couple of years in Miami Beach, before they returned to Quebec. In 1959—a year after the death of Grace Russell—they moved north of Montreal to New Glasgow, where they lived quietly and happily for more than a decade. Though Edith was small and increasingly frail, she devoted herself to taking care of Frank.

And then on the morning of April 15, 1971, with his health failing, eighty-year-old Frank Zaneth was handed one last heartbreak. In the sunroom of their home, with no warning at all, he found Edith on the couch, barely alive. Just sixty-five years old, she died in his arms. He lasted barely two weeks without her, and died on May 2. (He was survived by his daughter, Rena, who died in 1997 at the age of 87.)

A friend, going though his things later, found a notebook in which Zaneth had written a quote from George Washington: "I hope I shall always possess firmness and virtue, enough to maintain what I consider the most enviable of all titles, the character of an Honest Man."

⁕

GIVEN ROCCO PERRI'S TWENTY-YEAR HOLD ON THE public imagination, it's strange that his disappearance hardly rated a mention in the *Toronto Daily Star*, the paper that had revelled most in his notoriety. But attention is fleeting, and by that point Rocco had been out of the public eye for too long. With the war stretching into its fifth year, heroes were going missing every day. Who had time to wonder about the whereabouts of a forgotten gangster?

And there's another reason Rocco faded from view. Unlike New York City's Bonanno and Gambino families, or the Magaddinos in Buffalo, the Rizzutos in Montreal, or any of the other infamous mob families through the years, there were no Perri sons to carry on the family name. After Rocco's disappearance, Hamilton became even more infamous as a centre of mob power, led into the 1950s by Tony Papalia's son, Johnny (Pops) Papalia. Had he survived, Rocco's son, little Anterico, would have been twenty-six the year Rocco disappeared, old enough perhaps to build on what his father had created. Instead, Rocco's legacy ended the moment he vanished.

Perhaps that's fitting. Rocco Perri, the teenager from Platì who'd dreamed of prosperity in a new land and found it—the mob boss who was averse to guns, charming to the press, devoted to his

Jewish "wives," happy to work with any Italian, and always, always smiling—had never been a *mafioso* in the classic mould. He was an entrepreneur. He was one of a kind. Like Frank Zaneth, he was a pioneer.

ACKNOWLEDGEMENTS

Capturing and weaving together the full lives of Rocco Perri and Frank Zaneth was a daunting task, particularly since as a novelist and magazine journalist I'd never tackled anything like it before. Thankfully, a number of people aided my efforts.

Authors Charlotte Gray, Charles Foran, Jennifer Wells, Erik Larson and Ken McGoogan provided constructive advice, particularly in the early stages when my confidence needed a boost.

With research necessarily going on across a number of fronts at the same time, it was so helpful to have the assistance of researchers Darin Kinsey and Rob Martin in Ottawa, who knew the ins and outs of Library and Archives Canada. And I can't say enough about the great work done by Jessica Rose in Hamilton, who, using tools like Ancestry.com, managed to track down many of the vital bits of government documentation that cast new light on the lives of Rocco, Bessie, Frank, Grace and Olive. My contacts at the Archives of Ontario, chiefly Sarah Fontaine and Attilio DeBartolo, were exceedingly patient with me as I crawled through my archival research. Translator Antonio D'Alfonso provided welcome assistance at those times when I had to work with the Italian language. And Mary Symonds in Toronto and Marnie Burgess in Hamilton provided a great deal of valuable research help.

I was also thankful that when I put calls out to libraries in Sudbury and Moose Jaw for help in tracking down local newspaper stories from decades or even a hundred years ago, Margaret Sun in Reference Services (Sudbury) and Ken Dalgarno (Moose Jaw) didn't hesitate to dig around and send me whatever they could find. The same was true of Richard Vieira at the RCMP *Gazette*, and Chantal Renaud at the RCMP *Quarterly*, who were equally quick to respond. Meanwhile, Adam Montgomery at the University of Saskatchewan and Dr. Chelsea Maedler at Dalhousie University offered valuable insights into historical medical practices and attitudes relating to the breakdown of Frank Zaneth and the death of Anterico Perri.

The images in the book come from a variety of sources, and I'm thankful for the help of Tammie Danciu at the *Hamilton Spectator*, Jennifer Dell and Charity Blaine at the Hamilton Public Library, and the staff at the Toronto Public Library for their assistance. Thank you as well to the Rivers Family in Springfield for making it possible to include rare pictures of Frank Zaneth.

Finally, my acknowledgements would not be complete without expressing thanks to my editor at HarperCollins, Jennifer Lambert, for encouraging me to take on this all-consuming project, and to my agent at Westwood Creative Artists, Carolyn Forde, for her tireless efforts on my behalf.

A NOTE ON SOURCES

Rocco Perri and his associates weren't the sort of people to leave behind journals and memos for historians to find. So much of their day-to-day lives remains shrouded in darkness. But the newspapers of the period, particularly the *Toronto Daily Star*, worked very hard to observe and record the moments when Rocco, Bessie and others came into the light, usually because of brushes with the law. Those newspaper stories, whether brief items or long, well-reported articles, were invaluable to my research. There was hardly a day, during the months I spent compiling material for *The Whisky King*, when I wasn't grateful for the efforts of reporters and editors nearly a century ago.

In addition to press accounts, a significant amount of documentary evidence exists to illuminate the efforts of law enforcement in investigating the activities of Ontario's underworld over the course of four decades. This book owes an enormous debt to the trailblazing work of authors James Dubro and Robin Rowland who, thirty years ago, wrote the first biography of Rocco Perri, *King of the Mob*, and who identified a great many of the archival documents (chiefly the Ontario Provincial Police reports at the Archives of Ontario, as almost no Hamilton Police documents have survived) that proved crucial in writing this account. Dubro and Rowland also wrote the first book about Frank Zaneth, *Undercover*, which helped point the way to thousands of pages of relevant RCMP documents stored at Library and Archives Canada in Ottawa. One of my great pleasures in researching this book was examining the actual typed and handwritten reports from detectives in the thick of their investigations. Some documents, however, existed only as old microfilm copies, many of which appeared illegible. It took every computer enhancement trick I knew to be able to make out the words on those murky pages, a process of discovery akin to brushing clay from a fossil. But to compensate for the frustrations there were also delights, as I was able to uncover new documents that revealed important and heretofore unknown facts in the personal lives of Rocco Perri and Frank Zaneth.

It's important to note that this is a work of history, not fiction. In very rare instances, to bridge a small gap in a known sequence of events, I have offered a suggestion as to what probably occurred. Aside from those two or three occasions, which I've noted here, everything in the book has a written or documentary source. That includes every statement that appears between quotation marks; there is no imagined dialogue in this book. I have detailed my sources, with special emphasis on quoted lines and phrases, in an extensive list of citations that can be found on my website, www.trevorcole.com. What follows here is a broader outline of the most significant sources, and some background for a few of my new findings.

Chapter 1 *Tragico* – Tragedy

The events of this chapter are pieced together largely from detailed newspaper accounts of the arrests and the long inquest that followed the Gogo shooting. The paragraph that begins *"On the buyer's end"* constitutes my proposal for what Rocco and his men were doing just before they arrived at the foot of Leslie Street. Aside from that, I've built the narrative from the statements of witnesses and participants, adjusting as much as possible for what was sometimes contradictory and even deliberately misleading testimony.

CHAPTER 2 *PAESE – COUNTRY*

The main source for the facts of Rocco's early life in Platì (and later in Massena, New York) is *Rocco Perri: The Story of Canada's Most Notorious Bootlegger*, an English translation of the book *Il Piccolo Gatsby*, written in Italian by Antonio Nicaso. The date I give for Rocco's voyage to America differs from past accounts, which were based on Rocco's application for naturalization (in which he probably misremembered). The actual manifest of the SS *Republic* says "Rocco Perre" arrived in Boston from Naples as a sixteen-year-old in April of 1904, not 1903 as previously thought. Meanwhile, most of the information about Franco Zanetti's childhood comes from *Undercover*, by James Dubro and Robin Rowland. A conversation with the Rivers family, who were related to Frank through his now deceased nephew, Bill, offered additional insight, as did time spent researching the street and business directories of the era.

CHAPTER 3 *INIZIO – BEGINNING*

The truth of Franco Zanetti's first marriage has been misunderstood until now. Previously, it was thought that Zanetti worked in his brother's grocery store and married a woman named Rita Scevola-Ruscellotti in Hartford. Newly discovered documents, including the original marriage licence obtained from the courts in Hartford, establish both the facts of Frank Zanetti's marriage to Grace Russell and his true occupation at the time of the marriage.

(Frank did indeed marry a woman named Rita Scevola, but not until years later.) Also newly discovered are the facts about their daughter, Rena May Zanetti, which come from the 1910 Birth Registry for the City of Springfield.

My version of Rocco Perri's early life in Ontario, based on clues from Rocco's letter to Frank Griro and information I was able to gather about Cobalt, differs substantially from previous accounts, which were based on Rocco's own unreliable summary in his naturalization application (which placed him in Parry Sound, far from any criminality). The information about Griro comes from Archives of Ontario files (RG 22-3920-8947). The translation of Rocco's letter to Griro is an amalgamation of the original police translation from 1911 and a modern interpretation from translator Antonio D'Alfonso, done at my request.

Chapter 4 Persuasione – Persuasion
Some facts of Zanetti's life in Moose Jaw, particularly the information about his work on his homestead, come from *Undercover*, but much comes from original RCMP documents at Library and Archives Canada (RG 18, vol. 4839). As well, I was able to track down new documents related to Zanetti's land purchase and sale through Saskatchewan's Information Services Corporation. The story of Dr. Feltas comes from several reports in the Moose Jaw *Evening News* of 1914. Information about the end of Grace and Frank's marriage comes from reports in the *Springfield Union* in February 1915.

Both newspaper coverage and the medical health officer's 1911 report provided details of life in the Ward, while information from the Archives of Ontario and the Canada Census of 1911 helped place the Toben family (whose name also appeared as Tobin and Tobsen).

The story of Rocco's Elk Lake adventure comes from documents housed at the Archives of Ontario (RG 23-26-38, file 1.1, box B222931).

The slim details regarding the life of little Anterico Perri, who has never been written about before, come from a newly discovered record of the child's death in the Archives of Ontario, dated October 4, 1914. His approximate date of birth, May 1914, is extrapolated from his age, shown as five months on his death record. The scenario presented of his death is based on research into his condition and the treatment methods available in 1914.

CHAPTER 5 MERCE – COMMODITY

John C. Weaver's *Hamilton: An Illustrated History* was tremendously helpful in painting a picture of the early days of Hamilton. Information about the May 1906 riot comes from *Whisky and Ice* by C. W. Hunt. The facts around Zaneth's application to the RNWMP come from the main Zaneth files at Library and Archives Canada (RG18, vol. 4839).

Insight into Rocco's gambling activities comes from *King of the Mob*, *Whisky and Ice*, and various stories, including Ernest Hemingway's, in the *Toronto Daily Star* and *Star Weekly*. Quotes and facts from Bessie's first appearance in court come from the *Hamilton Spectator*, March 6, 1917.

CHAPTER 6 EBBREZZA – INTOXICATION

The early part of the chapter owes a great deal to information found in *Outlaws of the Lakes* by Edward Butts, along with *Whisky and Ice* and *Booze Boats and Billions*, both by C. W. Hunt, *The Bronfmans* by Nicholas Faith, and *Brewed in Canada* by Allen Winn Sneath. The rest comes largely from newspapers of the period, which were obsessed with the subject of drinking, temperance and prohibition.

CHAPTER 7 COMPLICAZIONE – COMPLICATION

The section on the Bronfman brothers is informed largely by Nicholas Faith's *The Bronfmans*. C.W. Hunt's excellent biography of J. B. Kerr, *Whisky and Ice*, provided the facts about Kerr and his early working relationship with Rocco. The paragraphs describing Celona's murder and related events are based on inquest testimony in the *Hamilton Herald*, April 18 and April 24, 1918, and trial testimony in the *Herald*, November 14 and 15, 1918, and the *Hamilton Spectator*, November 15, 1918.

Regarding Olive Rutledge: Previous books put Olive's age at thirty when she left home, but documents discovered during the research for this book, including the registration of her birth in Hastings County, show that she was born on July 6, 1896, which puts her at twenty-one or twenty-two when she met Rocco. No one knows exactly how that meeting occurred, but I've presented a reasonable possibility. Other information about Olive and her relationship with Rocco comes from subsequent reports in the *Hamilton Spectator* and the *Hamilton Herald* in February 1922. Details of Tony Martino's murder came from OPP files in the Archives of Ontario (RG 22-392-0-6792 and RG 22-392-0-6798) and from reports in the *Hamilton Herald*, January 1919.

CHAPTER 8 FIDUCIA – CONFIDENCE

The chief source for the initial overview of bootlegging and organized crime in southern Ontario is Dubro and Rowland's *King of the Mob*. The details come largely from Rocco's testimony during the Royal Commission on Customs and Excise, April 4, 1927 (LAC RG 33-88, vol. 12). Information regarding Verona/Sciarrone and the murder of Fortunato Tedesco comes from OPP files in the Archives of Ontario (RG 23-26-2, file 1.19, box B222906). The description of Zaneth's early investigations is taken again mostly from LAC's Zaneth files as well as from newspaper reports of the trials in Winnipeg.

My version of Olive's life with Rocco also differs somewhat from previous accounts, which seem to have been based on a February 1922 *Hamilton Spectator* story that presented information from Olive's father, George Rutledge, who in fact was largely in the dark about what had been going on with his daughter. During my research, the discovery of a St. Catharines listing for Olive, Rocco and their children in the 1921 Census (which jibed with the facts of Rocco's familiarity with St. Catharines) opened the door to a depiction that seems closer to the likely truth.

The story of Rocco's big win at the racetrack comes from Antonio Nicaso's *Rocco Perri*.

CHAPTER 9 DELIRIO – DELUSION

C. W. Hunt's books *Whisky and Ice* and *Booze Boats and Billions*, and C. H. Gervais's *The Rumrunner's Scrapbook*, were helpful sources on early Prohibition activity. An observation in an OPP report regarding the Domenic Paparone murder provided the information about Rocco's waterfront warehouse. Regarding Rocco and Bessie's new home, previous books have described 166 Bay Street South as a nineteen-room mansion, but this seems to have been wishful thinking. During her testimony before the Royal Commission in 1927, Bessie said the house had eight rooms, while the 1921 Census listed it originally as a nine-room house, corrected to seven. Historic City of Hamilton and fire insurance planning documents provided further details about the structure, supported by photos in various newspapers.

Again, the details of Zaneth's work and marriage come from LAC files. The facts about Grace Russell come from documents including the 1920 U.S. Census. (A curious side note regarding the marriage of Raymond Fountain and Zaneth's former wife, Grace Russell: Apparently it came so quickly—a mere month—after the death of Fountain's first wife, Noelia, that her relatives suspected she'd been poisoned. According to local newspaper accounts, they requested an exhumation of the body and an autopsy, but the woman's death was found to have resulted from other causes.)

The facts surrounding the subterfuge that facilitated bootlegging by Rocco, Bessie and others comes largely from testimony by the various participants during the Royal Commission on Customs and Excise (LAC RG 33-88, vol. 11). The details of Rocco's time with Olive's family come from articles published in the *Hamilton Spectator* and *Herald* in February 1922.

CHAPTER 10 *RISOLUZIONE* – RESOLUTION

I built the narrative of this chapter by weaving together the facts, quotes and descriptions from newspaper reports and inquest testimony published in the *Hamilton Herald* and the *Hamilton Spectator* from February 15 to 28, 1922. Regarding the name of Morison's stenographer, Hamilton newspapers were confused about her identity at the time, but the city directory listings for 1922 prove she was Miss Velma Williamson.

CHAPTER 11 *PERICOLO* – DANGER

The documents relating to Rocco's attempts to become naturalized seem to have mysteriously and fairly recently vanished from Library and Archives Canada—no amount of searching could locate them—so the information for this section necessarily comes from Dubro and Rowland's *King of the Mob* (which includes the story of Charles W. Bell's attempt to drum up political support) and Nicaso's *Rocco Perri*. RCMP files at LAC and *Undercover* provided the information about Zaneth's work in Quebec. The richly informative criminal investigation records at the Archives of Ontario (RG 23-26-2; for specifics, see www.trevorcole.com) provided details for the sections dealing with the spate of murders in 1922. Information about the Good Killers came from *Gangsters and Organized Crime in Buffalo* by Michael F. Rizzo, as well as *King of the Mob* and newspaper reports. It was Nicaso who first pointed out the similarities between the letter found on Loria and 'Ndrangheta writings.

CHAPTER 12 GUAIO – PROBLEM

Information about the murder of Constable Joseph Trueman and the subsequent investigation came from the extensive OPP files at the Archives of Ontario (RG 22-392-0-6292) and from reports in the *St. Catharines Standard*.

CHAPTER 13 PASSAPORTO – PASSPORT

As with the majority of the sections dealing with Frank Zaneth's life and career, this information came from the Zaneth files in Library and Archives Canada.

CHAPTER 14 COMPLICI – ACCOMPLICES

Information about the sale of Gooderham & Worts comes largely from C. W. Hunt's *Booze Boats and Billions* and from testimony at the Royal Commission on Customs and Excise (LAC RG 33-88). There were several sources for the information about the scandal involving Hamilton Police Chief Whatley, including J. C. S.'s reports in Archives of Ontario (RG 4-32, file 1828), and articles in the *Globe* and the *Hamilton Spectator* in March and April, 1924, and in the November 13, 1930, issue of *Hush*.

CHAPTER 15 CATTURA – CAPTURE

Details about the final phase of the Trueman murder investigation came largely from the Archives of Ontario (RG 22-392-0-6292 and Stringer's journals contained in the Dahn Higley collection, box B223090).

CHAPTER 16 PROPAGANDISTA – PROPAGANDA

Articles in the *Toronto Daily Star* (November 17, 18, 19 and December 11, 1924), the *Toronto Evening Telegram* (November 20, 1924), the *Hamilton Spectator* (November 20, 1924) and the *Hamilton Herald* (November 21, 30 and December 3, 10, 1924) provided most of the information for this chapter. Dubro and Rowland's *King of the Mob* offered additional insight.

CHAPTER 17 VELENO – POISON

C.W. Hunt's *Whisky and Ice* again provided fascinating details about J. B. Kerr, while newspaper reports informed the picture of Prohibition-era whisky and drinking. James H. Gray in *Booze* found Sam Bronfman's recipe for fake rum in his 1927 Royal Commission testimony. The RCMP files at Library and Archives Canada offered the information about Frank Zaneth.

The sources for the complex poison liquor scandal were many. Most of the information regarding the Jopp Drug Company and the Falls Tonic Manufacturing Company came from two June 1926 reports by Mark H. Crehan Jr., an agent of the Special Alcohol Division, 3rd District, New York, now preserved in the Archives of Ontario (RG 4-32, file 1765, box B740893). Meanwhile, inquests at the time offered up reams of information. The Toronto *Daily Star* reported on them extensively and some transcripts (along with J. C. S.'s reports) reside at the Archives of Ontario (RG 4-32, file 1765, box B740893). The facts about Joseph Henry Sottile come mostly from the Archives of Ontario (RG 23-26-93, file 1.9, box B247445 and RG 4-32, file 1828 (2), box B740894), with additional facts, including that of the bootlegging priest, from Dubro and Rowland. As focus turned to the involvement of Rocco's gang, the *Hamilton Spectator, Hamilton Herald* and *Toronto Daily Star* published a number of stories that proved helpful.

Chapter 18 *Indagine* – Investigation
Library and Archives Canada houses multiple volumes containing thousands of pages of testimony from the 1927 Royal Commission on Customs and Excise (RG 33-88), many of which were used in the writing of this chapter and others (for specifics, see www.trevorcole.com). Additional details came from reportage in the *Toronto Daily Star* and the *Globe*. Allan Levine's *King* provided a few details about William Lyon Mackenzie King's role.

Chapter 19 *Spergiuro* – Perjury
The *Toronto Daily Star*'s exhaustive coverage of the 1927 Gooderham & Worts trial, and Rocco and Bessie's role in it, provided the bulk of the material for this chapter. The *Hamilton Spectator* and the *Globe* offered additional information.

Chapter 20 *Soldi* – Money
Many of the documents contained in the RCMP files about Frank Zaneth's career (LAC RG 18, vol. 4839) have to do with quibbling about money, either by Zaneth or by his superiors. The subject of Zaneth's support for his wife in Italy comes up in several memos, including one from Commander F. J. Mead on January 5, 1936. In his two books on the bootlegging era—*Whisky and Ice* and *Booze Boats and Billions*—author C. W. Hunt uncovered many of the details about the U.S. Coast Guard's efforts against smuggling.

Articles about Bessie Perri published in the *Toronto Daily Star* in August 1930 provided the details of her fascination with dia-monds, her activities with her children and her early interest in narcotics. An article in an October 1930 issue of *Hush* offered some additional information on the narcotics trade. Files on the RCMP's investigation of Rocco and Bessie's involvement with drugs are found at LAC (see below).

CHAPTER 21 *STUPEFACENTI* – NARCOTICS
CHAPTER 22 *CONFIDENZA* – TRUST

The RCMP documents at Library and Archives Canada include a thick file on Frank Zaneth's investigation of Rocco and Bessie Perri (RG 18, vol. 3313A), which informed the Zaneth narrative in these chapters. A few additional details came from Dubro and Rowland's *Undercover*, which also gives a full account of the forgery case involving Frank Wise and Flavio Masi. Articles in the *Toronto Daily Star* from July and September of 1929 helped flesh out the picture.

CHAPTER 23 *AGGUATO* – AMBUSH
CHAPTER 24 *DOPO* – AFTERMATH

Dubro and Rowland offer a fuller version of Zaneth's pursuit of Tony Roma in *Undercover*. The LAC's RCMP files (RG 19, vol. 3313A) provided further details about the Perri gang's drug ship-ments and Bessie's run-in with her New York suppliers.

The details around Bessie's murder and funeral, and of her rela-tionships with the Perri gang and others, came largely from the *Toronto Daily Star*'s intense coverage (supplemented by the *Toronto Evening Telegram* and the *Hamilton Spectator*). Information about John Miller's investigation into her murder came from the Archives of Ontario's OPP files (RG 23-50-2, microfilm 40-189). Additional insights into her murder, including the probable involvement of

Frank Ross, came from a confidential letter to his bosses by *Daily Star* editor Milford Smith (Milford Smith Collection, Hamilton Public Library). In *King of the Mob*, Dubro and Rowland spend some time on the Joe Leo mystery.

CHAPTER 25 CAMBIAMENTO – UPHEAVAL
CHAPTER 26 COSPIRAZIONE – CONSPIRACY

Newspapers from Hamilton to Toronto to Sudbury reported dutifully on what Rocco was getting up to with Jessie Leo in the period after Bessie's death, and it was chiefly the *Toronto Daily Star*'s reporting that informed the section on Rocco's gambling expansion and its explosive results (with some quotes from the *Hamilton Spectator*). Information about Zaneth's conspiracy investigations, regarding the likes of Harry Davis and the Bronfmans, came from the Zaneth files at LAC as well as from Dubro and Rowland's *Undercover*. Nicholas Faith's *The Bronfmans* provided further insight into the business of Seagram, and *King of the Castle* by Peter C. Newman offered a few select details from the trial.

The majority of the information about Rocco Perri and Anne Newman's Windsor smuggling conspiracy with David Armaly and his crew came from the extensive files at LAC (RG 18, vols. 6087, 6089, 13), which give a fascinating glimpse into how the RCMP's legal efforts unfolded, and how their frustrations mounted. A few additional details came from Dubro and Rowland, including the revealing quotes from Milton Goldhart.

CHAPTER 27 PRIGIONIERO – CAPTIVE

Library and Archives Canada has a small but illuminating cache of documents related to the internment of Italians in 1940, including what appears to be a complete or nearly complete list of the hundreds of men detained, one of whom was Rocco Perri. (RG 18, vol. 3563;

RG 117, vol. 705). According to authors James Dubro and Robin Rowland, it was Zaneth who saw to it that Rocco Perri's name was at the top of the list of Italians to be interned. It's a reasonable conclusion, although I could not find the supporting evidence. Additional information about the internees, and life in the camps, came from the website Italian Canadians as Enemy Aliens: Memories of World War II (www.italiancanadianww2.ca), a project of the Columbus Centre, sponsored by Citizenship and Immigration Canada. The detail of the letter apparently sent by Rocco to his mother came from Nicaso's *Rocco Perri* (which is also where I found the somewhat suspect story about Rocco getting shoes, reported to Nicaso by Angelo Principe, whose name could not be found on any official list of internees).

The RCMP files of LAC (RG 18, vol. 4839) provided the information about Zaneth's ongoing money battles with his employer.

CHAPTER 28 TERMINE – ENDING

The *Toronto Daily Star* provided the information of Anne Newman's arrest for gold high-grading, while LAC files (RG 117, vol. 705) offered nuggets about Rocco's arrangements for his return to civilian life. The lay of the land, criminally speaking, including Stefano Magaddino's apparent takeover, came largely from *Their Town*, edited by Bill Freeman and Marsha Hewitt, and Nicaso's *Rocco Perri*. Dubro and Rowland's *King of the Mob* contained elements from Hamilton police reports regarding Rocco's disappearance, which, like his naturalization papers, seem to have gone missing in the years since. The Archives of Ontario (RG 23, series E-92) and reports in the *Toronto Daily Star* offered up the details of the Ross brothers' 1949 clash. The details of Frank Zaneth's last few years, and observations of the men who knew him, came from LAC files (RG 18, vol. 4839) and from *Undercover*, which offers a longer account of Frank's retirement with Edith.

A NOTE ON PROPER NAMES

The events of this book occurred during a time when officials and newspapers took an ad hoc approach to recording and reporting the names of immigrants. There was little care and no consistency, which meant, for example, a name like *Sciarrone* also appeared in various documents and accounts as *Sciaroni*, *Scaroni*, *Sciarone*, *Saranie*, *Schroni* and *Shoroni*. For the purposes of this book, in each case where research turned up multiple versions of a person's name (with the exception of aliases), judgment was used to settle on a single spelling.

SELECTED BIBLIOGRAPHY

Augimeri, Maria C. *Calabrese Folklore.* Ottawa: National Museum of Man, Mercury Series, 1985.

Bagnell, Kenneth. *Canadese: A Portrait of the Italian Canadians.* Toronto: Macmillan of Canada, 1989.

Butts, Edward. *Outlaws of the Lakes: Bootlegging & Smuggling from Colonial Times to Prohibition.* Toronto: Lynx Images, 2004.

Cawthorne, Nigel, and Colin Cawthorne, editors. *The Mammoth Book of The Mafia.* Philadelphia: Running Press, 2009.

Dickie, John. *Blood Brothers: A History of Italy's Three Mafias.* New York: PublicAffairs, Perseus Books Group, 2014.

Dubro, James, and Robin Rowland. *King of the Mob: Rocco Perri and the Women Who Ran His Rackets.* Toronto: Penguin, 1987.

Dubro, James, and Robin Rowland. *Undercover: Cases of the RCMP's Most Secret Operative.* Markham, ON: Octopus Publishing Group, 1991.

Faith, Nicholas. *The Bronfmans: The Rise and Fall of the House of Seagram.* New York: St. Martin's Press, 2006.

Freeman, Bill, and Marsha Hewitt, editors. *Their Town: The Mafia, the Media, and the Party Machine.* Toronto: James Lorimer & Company, 1979.

Gervais, C. H. *The Rumrunners: A Prohibition Scrapbook.* Thornhill, ON: Firefly Books, 1980.

Gray, Charlotte. *The Massey Murder: A Maid, Her Master, and the Trial That Shocked a Country.* Toronto: HarperCollins, 2013.

Gray, James. *Booze.* Toronto: Macmillan of Canada, 1972.

Higley, Dahn D. *O.P.P.: The History of the Ontario Provincial Police Force.* Toronto: The Queen's Printer, 1984.

Hunt, C. W. *Booze Boats and Billions: Smuggling Liquid Gold!* Toronto: McClelland & Stewart, 1988.

Hunt, C. W. *Whisky and Ice: The Saga of Ben Kerr, Canada's Most Daring Rumrunner.* Toronto: Dundurn Press, 1995.

Levine, Allan. *King: William Lyon Mackenzie King, a Life Guided by the Hand of Destiny.* Vancouver/Toronto: Douglas & McIntyre, 2011.

Mangione, Jerre. *America Is Also Italian.* New York: G. P. Putnam's Sons, 1969.

Mangione, Jerre, and Ben Morreale. *La Storia: Five Centuries of the Italian American Experience.* HarperCollins, 1992.

Montague, Art. *Canada's Rumrunners: Incredible Adventures and Exploits During Canada's Illicit Liquor Trade.* Canmore, AB: Altitude Publishing, 2004.

Moray, Alistair. *The Diary of a Rum-Runner: The Plain, Unvarnished, Day-By-Day Account of Eleven Months Off New York with a Crazy Ship, a Mutinous Crew, Lurking Hijackers and the Inquisitive Federal Authorities.* Mystic, CT: Flat Hammock Press, 1929.

Morton, James. *Gangland International.* London, UK: Little Brown and Company, 1998.

Newman, Peter C. *King of the Castle: The Making of a Dynasty–Seagram's and the Bronfman Empire.* New York: Atheneum, 1979.

Nicaso, Antonio. *Rocco Perri: The Story of Canada's Most Notorious Bootlegger.* Mississauga: John Wiley & Sons Canada, 2004.

Paoli, Letizia. *Mafia Brotherhoods: Organized Crime, Italian Style.* New York: Oxford University Press, 2003.

Rizzo, Michael F. *Gangsters and Organized Crime in Buffalo: History, Hits and Headquarters.* Charleston, SC, The History Press, 2012.

Sneath, Allen Winn. *Brewed in Canada: The Untold Story of Canada's 350-Year-Old Brewing Industry.* Toronto: Dundurn Press, 2001.

Steinke, Gord. *Crossing the Line: Mobsters & Rumrunners of Canada.* Edmonton: Folklore Publishing, 2003.

Weaver, John C. *Hamilton: An Illustrated History.* Toronto: James Lorimer & Company, 1982.

Williams, David Ricardo. *Call in Pinkerton's: American Detectives at Work for Canada.* Toronto: Dundurn Press, 1998.

Zucchi, John E. *Italians in Toronto: Development of a National Identity, 1875-1935.* Kingston and Montreal: McGill-Queen's University Press, 1988.

INDEX